History Has Made Us Friends

History Has Made Us Friends

Reassessing the Special Relationship between Canada and the United States

EDITED BY

Donald E. Abelson and Stephen Brooks

McGill-Queen's University Press
Montreal & Kingston • London • Chicago

ISBN 978-0-2280-2101-8 (cloth)
ISBN 978-0-2280-2102-5 (paper)
ISBN 978-0-2280-2154-4 (ePDF)
ISBN 978-0-2280-2155-1 (ePUB)

Legal deposit second quarter 2024
Bibliothèque nationale du Québec

Printed in Canada on acid-free paper that is 100% ancient forest free (100% post-consumer recycled), processed chlorine free

This book has been published with the help of a grant from the Canadian Federation for the Humanities and Social Sciences, through the Awards to Scholarly Publications Program, using funds provided by the Social Sciences and Humanities Research Council of Canada.

Funded by the Government of Canada | Financé par le gouvernement du Canada | Canada | Canada Council for the Arts | Conseil des arts du Canada

We acknowledge the support of the Canada Council for the Arts.

Nous remercions le Conseil des arts du Canada de son soutien.

McGill-Queen's University Press in Montreal is on land which long served as a site of meeting and exchange amongst Indigenous Peoples, including the Haudenosaunee and Anishinabeg nations. In Kingston it is situated on the territory of the Haudenosaunee and Anishinaabek. We acknowledge and thank the diverse Indigenous Peoples whose footsteps have marked these territories on which peoples of the world now gather.

Library and Archives Canada Cataloguing in Publication

Title: History has made us friends : reassessing the special relationship between Canada and the United States / edited by Donald E. Abelson and Stephen Brooks.

Names: Abelson, Donald E., editor. | Brooks, Stephen, 1956– editor.

Description: Includes bibliographical references and index.

Identifiers: Canadiana (print) 20240299329 | Canadiana (ebook) 20240299310 | ISBN 9780228021025 (paper) | ISBN 9780228021018 (cloth) | ISBN 9780228021551 (ePUB) | ISBN 9780228021544 (ePDF)

Subjects: LCSH: Canada – Relations – United States. | LCSH: United States – Relations – Canada.

Classification: LCC FC249 .H57 2024 | DDC 327.71073 – dc23

This book was designed and typeset by Peggy & Co. Design in 11/14 Minion Pro.

Contents

Tables and Figures

Tables

Figures

Acknowledgments

In the academic world in which Steve Brooks and I have been immersed for over three decades, we have been incredibly fortunate to collaborate with several talented colleagues and friends. This volume represents what can be achieved when scholars who share similar passions and interests are willing to contribute their time and energy to produce a thought-provoking collection of essays that explore one of the most important and enduring bilateral relationships between sovereign states on the globe. When Steve first approached me about the idea of writing a book that delved more deeply into the question of whether the Canada–US relationship should continue to be regarded as "special," I knew instinctively he was on to something. As Canadian policy-makers learned during four tumultuous years of the Trump presidency, when it comes to working with the US, they could ill afford to take anything for granted. I would like to express my profound gratitude to Steve for initiating this endeavour and for his willingness to embrace a study that raises several important, timely, and relevant questions about how Canada and the US, despite innumerable domestic and external pressures, have managed to nurture and navigate this complex relationship through periods of great uncertainty.

Of course, this study would not have been possible without the enormously valuable contributions of several of the most prolific and recognized scholars of Canada–US relations. We are forever indebted to them and to their scholarly gifts, which continue to pay handsome dividends.

We are also incredibly grateful to Dr Anna Zuschlag, the project/research manager at the Brian Mulroney Institute of Government, St Francis Xavier University, upon whom we rely for her keen attention to detail and masterful skill in helping prepare this and other manuscripts for publication. Finally, we would like to acknowledge the enthusiasm and professionalism with which we as editors, and the book we presented to McGill-Queen's University Press (MQUP), have been received. For years, Philip Cercone, executive director of MQUP, has welcomed the various projects, some fully formed, others still in the development stage, that Steve and I have proposed, but never has he tried to stifle our enthusiasm. We would like to thank Philip and his wonderful team at MQUP for once again providing a home for us and our colleagues to engage in the marketplace of ideas. This is a book of which we are deeply proud.

Donald E. Abelson
Stephen Brooks

History Has Made Us Friends

Introduction
A Special Relationship?

DONALD E. ABELSON AND STEPHEN BROOKS

On 15 September 2021, the creation of a new security alliance was announced. AUKUS, a security pact between Australia, the United Kingdom (UK), and the United States, has as its stated goal "to sustain peace and stability in the Indo-Pacific region" and to "protect a rules-based international order" (United Kingdom 2021). Its fundamental if not directly acknowledged aim is the containment of China's military influence and territorial ambitions in that region of the world. US president Joseph R. Biden Jr situated the agreement within the history of defence cooperation among the three countries. "For more than a century," he said, "we have stood together for the course of peace and freedom, motivated by the beliefs we share, sustained by the bonds of friendship we have forged, enabled by the sacrifice of those who have gone before us, and inspired by our shared hope for those who will follow us" (White House 2021b). A week later, President Biden stated that "the United States has no closer or more reliable ally than Australia" (Maddeux 2021). Australian prime minister Scott Morrison referred to the pact as "a forever partnership for a new time between the oldest and most trusted of friends" (Westcott 2021). In a speech in the House of Commons the day after the announcement of AUKUS, UK prime minister Boris Johnson referred to the ties of history and values among the three partners, adding that "one of the great prizes of this enterprise is that Australia, the UK and the US will become inseparable partners in a project that will last for decades" (Johnson 2021).

Meanwhile, the Canadian government was rather silent. But many in the Canadian media and some experts on Canada–US relations and Canadian foreign and defence policy were not so reticent. The fact that Canada was not a partner to the new security pact, despite being a Pacific nation and long-time security ally of the US, and that the Canadian government appeared neither to have been invited to the talks that preceded its creation nor to have requested to be part of these *pourparlers*, was interpreted by some commentators and policy analysts as the latest proof that the long-assumed special relationship between Canada and the US was over (Carvin and Juneau 2021; Heisler 2021). Prime Minister Justin Trudeau did little to dispel this impression. Asked about Canada's non-participation in this security alliance, his response was that the pact was primarily about Australia's desire to acquire nuclear submarines and that Canada did not support this ambition (Reuters 2021).

Only eight months earlier, the Canadian media had trumpeted the fact that the first phone call made by President Biden to another national leader after his inauguration had been to Justin Trudeau. "Who a US president chooses to call first sends a message," intoned CBC journalist Ian Hanomansing, "and Joe Biden called up Justin Trudeau" (CBC News 2021). A summary of the call released by the Prime Minister's Office stated that the two leaders agreed "to advance the important work of renewing the deep and enduring friendship between Canada and the United States" (Canada 2021a), a sentiment echoed in the White House press release regarding the call (White House 2021a). "It's definitely a big deal," said former US ambassador to Canada Bruce Heyman. "To get the first call is a recognition of the importance of the relationship" (Porter 2021).

The fact that this recognition came just two days after President Biden's cancellation of the Keystone XL Pipeline, a decision made on his first day in office and one that, officially at least, was lamented by the Canadian government (Canada 2021b), was not overlooked in all the bonhomie surrounding the call between the president and the prime minister. A week after the pipeline announcement, the president signed an executive order that put in motion the Buy American Act. The White House provided no assurances that Canadian suppliers would be exempted from that act, a fact that Canadian business leaders perceived as a worrying signal from the new administration. Nevertheless, although the term "special relationship" was not on all lips, there was a strong sense, at least on the Canadian side, of a return to some of the qualities associated with what former Liberal cabinet minister Allan Rock called a "mystical" relationship between the two countries (as quoted in Porter 2021).

One might ask what happened between the near elation prompted by that 22 January 2021 telephone call and the announcement almost eight months later that the US would be entering into a new security pact about which the Canadian government appeared to know little, except that it had not been invited. The answer is, "not much," or at least nothing that had not been evident in Canada–US relations for decades (Ljunggren 2021). A tendency to idealize and even fetishize the special relationship, attributing to it unrealistic qualities and a character that is not able to accommodate serious and persistent disagreements, has long existed. Even during the most trying moments in Canada–US relations under the Trump presidency, when the death of the special relationship was widely proclaimed, most of what arguably makes the Canada–US relationship special, unique, exceptional, distinctive – adjectives used to describe this quality have been numerous and the meanings ascribed to them various – remained in place. At the same time, however, this bilateral relationship is embedded in a world whose economic, geostrategic, and political contours are quite different from those that existed when Prime Minister Lester Pearson could confidently speak of Canadians' "friendly intimacy toward the Americans (and the admitted benefits of our special economic relations)" (Pearson 1975, 115).

Questions of whether, when, and why the special relationship went into decline or even ended presume, of course, that it once existed. During the 1950s and 1960s, however, when it was widely taken for granted by Canadians and their opinion leaders that a special quality distinguished their country's ties to the US from America's other bilateral relations, there was no consensus on the nature of the relationship or if indeed whether such an arrangement would be advantageous to Canada (Sigler and Goresky 1974). Since then, pronouncements on the state of Canada–US relations have ranged from healthy to dead, or somewhere between these extreme assessments. The one constant is that a concept that originated many decades ago, in circumstances very different from those that exist today, continues to have a serious hold on the Canadian imagination. It remains, at least implicitly, the yardstick against which the condition of the Canada–US relationship is measured.

This book offers a fresh and more nuanced perspective on the dynamics and nature of the special relationship between Canada and the US. It tackles an old and familiar concept that to many is rather slippery and politically contested and recasts it in ways that are more fluid and manageable. We begin by examining the origins and history of the idea of the special relationship, the various meanings attributed to it, and how it has been conceptualized. In the chapters that follow, the recent state and likely future trajectory of Canada–US relations will be assessed to determine whether the concept of the special relationship describes accurately both the features and the associated consequences of this "enduring" partnership.

Throughout this book, we argue that the special relationship has been understood too narrowly by those who, in recent decades, have dismissed it as a relic of times past or indeed as something that never truly existed except at the level of political rhetoric (Thompson and Randall 2008, 1). At the same time, it is undeniable that the special relationship that existed in the 1950s and 1960s is not identical to the one that exists today. The error lies in two common tendencies. One involves clinging to an outdated ideal of what is believed to have been a golden era in Canada–US relations, one that perhaps can be recaptured given the right chemistry at the top and perhaps with a bit more integration through policies and institutions. The other involves the outright refutation of the concept of the special relationship. It is dismissed as something based on a misreading of history and, in the eyes of some, as a dependency relationship that served US interests at the expense of Canadian sovereignty.

Origins and Evolution

The idea of the special relationship between Canada and the US predates the term. Indeed, it may be argued that it was first found in the Articles of Confederation and Perpetual Union, the first constitution of the United States, ratified in 1781. Article XI formalized overtures made to the northern colonies of British North America by the Continental Congress in the early years of the Revolutionary War: "Canada acceding to this confederation, and joining in the measures of the united states, shall be admitted into, and entitled to all the advantages of this union: but no other colony shall be admitted into the same, unless such admission be agreed to by nine states."[1] The invitation was, of course, never acted upon. Nevertheless, it reflected the belief of many Americans, and a significant segment of the population in the northern British North American colonies that eventually would become Canada, that the societies of what prior to the Revolutionary War had all been British colonies had much in common and that they should unite in independence from British rule (Hanc 2017).

The idea that special bonds connected the peoples of the US and the British North American colonies, and that political and economic integration was a logical and even inevitable consequence of these ties, was immediately countered by a narrative of difference. Military and clerical elites in the northern colonies, as well as much of the economic elite, rejected the idea of an alliance with the American revolutionaries. After the war, their voices were bolstered by the Loyalists who had rejected the Revolution and who, many of them, had fought in support of the British Crown. The contrasting narratives of similarity and difference have persisted to the present day and, moreover, have influenced Canadian politics throughout the country's history (Doran 1984, ch. 3; Thomas and Sands 2022; Thompson and Randall 2008).

This first glimmering of the idea of a special relationship would not be reignited in a serious manner until the early twentieth century. The occasion was the signing of the International Boundary Waters Treaty between Canada and the US in 1909 and the creation of the International Joint Commission (IJC),[2] heralded at the time as a model of international cooperation (Macfarlane and Clamen 2020). In more than a century since the treaty and the IJC were agreed to, they have been pointed to on countless occasions, if oftentimes a bit too effusively than may have been warranted, as an exemplary model of shared sovereignty and consensus decision-making, and as an early pillar of the special relationship. Indeed, Canadian prime minister William Lyon Mackenzie King, in a 1928 speech at the League of Nations, cited the consensus model of decision-making embodied in the IJC as proof of how Canada lived in "perfect harmony … with their neighbours to the south" (as quoted in Hillmer 2004, 94).

From the American side, the first high-level acknowledgment that a special relationship existed between Canada and the US was made in President Franklin Delano Roosevelt's (FDR) 1938 speech at Queen's University in Kingston, Ontario. He said, "I give to you assurance that the people of the United States will not stand idly by if domination of Canadian soil is threatened" (Roosevelt 1938). FDR did not use the words "special relationship," but the sentiment he expressed, based on the premise that the security interests of the two countries were one and that the countries were bound by a shared history, values, and interests, anticipated the relationship that would unfold in the years after the Second World War. His sentiments regarding the intimacy of the Canada–US relationship were also reflected in the Carnegie series of studies on Canada–US relations, published between 1936 and 1941 (Carnegie Endowment 1941).

The special relationship as shorthand for a bilateral relationship *sans pareil* would make its appearance in 1944 and 1945 in a pair of speeches given by Winston Churchill (see Reynolds 1988, 94–5). The 1945 speech included Canada in the notion of the special relationship. It was, however, in his 1946 speech at Westminster College in Fulton, Missouri, that Churchill amplified the UK–US special relationship to a fuller degree. The avoidance of another world war, Churchill told his American audience, would not be possible "without what I have called the fraternal association of the English-speaking peoples. This means a special relationship between the British Commonwealth and Empire and the United States" (Churchill 1946).

The term "special relationship" is rooted in the idea of an Atlantic alliance whose principal partners are the US and the UK. Since Churchill's speeches, the idea and history of the special relationship most often have been thought of as referring to the US–UK relationship. Moreover, and importantly, the term has had connotations of shared history, cultural affinity, and common security interests and world views (Bartlett 1992; Dimbleby and Reynolds 1989; Dumbrell 2001).

The notion of a special relationship between Canada and the US was fuelled by the post–Second World War decline of the British Empire and the multiplication and deepening of ties between Canada and its southern neighbour. As Morton (2003) writes, "in 1945 most Canadians looked across the Atlantic for their heritage but Britain, our counterweight to the US since 1784, was falling fast" (52). The global power equilibrium that emerged from the war was vastly different, dominated by the Cold War rivalry between the US and the Soviet Union. Britain was no longer a counterweight to US influence, although there was lingering denial of this in some quarters. This denial would surface in Prime Minister John Diefenbaker's atavistic notion of a British Empire free trade agreement and the proposed diversion of 15 per cent of Canada's trade to the UK, and in the Canadian flag debate's nostalgia for a British past whose relevance to modern Canada was quickly fading.

It is unclear precisely when Canadian opinion leaders began using the term "special relationship." In the 1960s, however, the Canadian government successfully lobbied for exemptions from some US trade laws. It appears to have been the surprise that Canada might be treated as just another country that caused government officials and opinion leaders to begin using the term with some frequency. This development was not merely a matter of adopting a new adjective. "Special," in this case, was generally intended to signify that Canada would receive favourable treatment that was not likely to be extended to the US's other economic partners.

Acceptance of the special relationship in Canada was far from universal. Indeed, the embrace of the special relationship generated considerable opposition that ranged from mild to virulent forms of a Canadian nationalism premised on the rejection of American influence in its various forms. At the milder end were proposals for limits on American investment in Canada and trade and tax rules favouring Canadian corporations, as embodied in the recommendations of the Royal Commission on Canada's Economic Prospects (1956), the ill-fated Liberal budget of 1963, and the Report of the Task Force on Foreign Ownership (1970). The virulent end of the spectrum was summed up in the provocative titles of two books published in 1970, *Close the 49th Parallel Etc.* (Lumsden 1970) and *Silent Surrender* (Levitt 1970). The deep anti-Americanism reflected in these works was also embraced by much of English-speaking Canada's cultural community (MacLennan 1960; Mowat 1958) and those on the left of the country's political spectrum.

In the US, the special relationship was much more likely to be thought of as the one with the UK, as remains true today. But if it was far more often found in the speeches of Canadian politicians and the writings of Canadian political journalists than in those of their American counterparts, the idea was, in large measure, reciprocated from the American side. In his 1961 address to the Canadian Parliament, President John F. Kennedy acknowledged the long and undefended border between the two countries and their common heritage, following this with his often-cited summary of the Canada–US relationship: "Geography has made us neighbors. History has made us friends. Economics has made us partners" (Kennedy 1961). The famously rocky personal relationship between Kennedy and Diefenbaker, and the well-known dressing down that Pearson received from President Lyndon Johnson after he gave a speech on the Vietnam War at Temple University in Philadelphia, have sometimes been interpreted as indications that the relationship was not so special after all. In fact, however, the ability of the relationship to weather such personal differences at the top was testimony to exactly those factors on which it rested, identified in Kennedy's 1961 speech.

It was surely in full awareness of how the special relationship had come to be associated in Canada with "exemptionalism" that President Richard Nixon pronounced it dead in his 1971 address to the Canadian Parliament. Nixon (1972) said:

> Our policy toward Canada reflects the new approach we are taking in all of our foreign relations – an approach which has been called the Nixon Doctrine. That doctrine rests on the premise that mature partners must have autonomous, independent policies: each nation must define the nature of its own interests; each nation must decide the requirements of its own security; each nation must determine the path of its own progress.

The president's attempt to soften the blow by couching it in terms of the sovereignty and self-interest of mature nations, and thus as something that Canadians should be eager to understand and embrace, did not prevent a deluge of hand-wringing in the Canadian media.

At the same time, however, it is likely that Prime Minister Pierre Trudeau was not particularly concerned with the prospect that the special exemptions the US had afforded Canada since the late 1940s (Doran 1984, 79) and that were highly publicized in the 1960s would be ending, and that the exceptional intimacy that had characterized Canada–US relations at the diplomatic and bureaucratic levels over the preceding couple of decades was drawing to a close. As will be explained in a later chapter, Trudeau's attitude toward the US appears to have ranged from indifference to mild dislike at the affective level, coupled with disagreement on most of the important global issues during his time as prime minister. He clearly supported greater distance between Canada and the US on the grounds that it was good for Canada politically, economically, and culturally.

The Trudeau years (1968–79, 1980–84) saw a good deal of attention paid to the idea of the special relationship by students of Canadian foreign policy and Canada–US relations, generated by what appeared to most to be mounting evidence of its decline. As Richard Leach wrote in 1977, "the special relationship may not be in danger of dissolving, but it is now under a great deal of stress" (Leech 1977, 145). At the same time, however, the trade and investment relationship between Canada and the US remained the largest and most extensive in the world.

The explanation for this apparent disconnect, Charles Doran argued in his 1984 book, *Forgotten Partnership*, lay in the fact that the special relationship operated on two rails, one structural and the other involving politics and policy. At the structural level, he observed, "the Canadian-American relationship continues to appear unique or special, because no other pair of countries can demonstrate the combination of close governmental interaction, institutional ties and buffers, pacific conflict resolution, and extensiveness of cross-border bureaucratic and private sector activity" (Doran 1984, 83). At the policy level, however, Doran observed a different picture. He noted that "the factors that have made the relationship special in the past – consultation, preferential economic treatment for Canada, and a secure, hospitable atmosphere for US investment – have all begun to erode" (83).

At least one of the factors that Doran pointed to as a cause of the decline – or at least transformation – of the special relationship since the 1950s has appeared to be irreversible. It involved what by all insider accounts was the extraordinarily dense and, by and large, mutually sympathetic network of contacts at the level of each country's diplomatic service and state bureaucracies. We would argue that this winding down of the supposed "golden age" of the special relationship does not by itself mean that it no longer exists. Nor do the highly visible and often protracted policy differences that have been quite common since the 1970s signify the end of those qualities that make the Canada–US relationship exceptional.

As it happened, fresh wind was blown into the sails of the special relationship with the election of the Conservative government under

Brian Mulroney in 1984. At the policy level, the repeal of the National Energy Program, the reform of the Foreign Investment Review Agency – renamed Investment Canada in 1985 and with a revised mandate to promote foreign investment (its slogan, "Canada Is Open for Business," was widely seen as welcoming American investment) – and the privatization of the Canada Development Corporation were among the high-profile changes that signalled a rejection of the economic nationalism agenda that had been pursued during the Trudeau years. The launching of free trade negotiations with the administration of President Ronald Reagan, initiated by the Mulroney government, eventually culminating in the Canada–US Free Trade Agreement of 1989, was a historic reversal of Canadian governments' traditional reluctance to push formal economic integration beyond sectoral agreements. All of this, as Donald E. Abelson shows in his chapter, was reinforced by the personal relationships between Prime Minister Mulroney and Presidents Reagan and George H.W. Bush. To the dismay of Canadian nationalists, the special relationship appeared to be back, even though there were several prominent issues, including acid rain, the Strategic Defense Initiative, disinvestment in the South Africa of the apartheid era, and even trade, where the Canadian and US governments were at loggerheads during these years.

Throughout this book we will argue that the special relationship has never depended on personal relationships at the top. Nevertheless, these relationships have made an important difference in Canada–US relations at various moments in our shared history. This was perhaps especially so during the Diefenbaker–Kennedy years, the premiership of Pierre Trudeau, and the Mulroney–Reagan/Bush years. But even when the impact has involved a de-emphasis or even rejection of the special relationship, the structural characteristics that undergird Canada–US relations have ensured its survival. Those relations have clearly been able to adapt, largely in response to changes in the broader international setting in which the bilateral relationship is embedded and that affect the relationship at the political and policy levels. As Donald Trump's presidency demonstrated, the relationship is able to survive not only neglect at the top but also outright abuse.

The resurgence of the idea of the special relationship during the Mulroney years has been followed by three decades of intermittent reflection on whether the relationship continues to warrant the label. An important constant has been the fact that the term continues to arise in conversations about Canada–US relations, particularly at what are believed to be high and low points. When American presidents visit Ottawa and heap praise on Canada, as Bill Clinton did in 1995 and Barack Obama in 2016, or when Canada is the first country to receive a phone call from an incoming president, Canada's media are rife with talk of the health of the special relationship. And when the relationship hits rocky patches, as it did when the Liberal government of Jean Chrétien refused to join the American-led invasion of Iraq, when presidents Obama and more recently Biden denied approval for the Keystone XL Pipeline, and during virtually all the Trump presidency, this leads to a flurry of questions about what happened to the special relationship. The term acts as a sort of benchmark – and, for some, a gold standard – when it comes to assessments of the state of this bilateral relationship. As former Liberal cabinet minister Allan Rock intoned after the first phone call between Prime Minister Trudeau and President Biden, "we've forged a bond that is beyond practical … It borders on mystical" (Porter 2021).

Rock is correct. There *is* a mystical quality to the idea of the special relationship, at least on the Canadian side of the border. But it never has been shared to a significant degree on the American side. The aura of mysticism that Rock refers to is created by our shared history and the disproportionate space that the US occupies in the Canadian imagination. Charles Doran goes so far as to argue that this psychological-cultural dimension of Canada–US relations is the most complex and perhaps also the most important determinant of these relations, beyond even their economic and geostrategic aspects (Doran 1984, 85).

To understand whether and in what ways Canada–US relations continue to be special, exceptional, unique, distinctive – or whatever other word one chooses to use to describe what is thought to be a bilateral relationship that possesses a character that is *pas comme les autres* – a hard examination of the concept of the special relationship is needed. As we will see, there is no agreement in the rather abundant literature on what this term signifies. Defining it, however, is a necessary step toward understanding its contemporary nature and relevance.

A Slippery and Contested Concept

Academics who have explored the special relationship in international affairs and foreign policy focus on relations between the US and the UK since the Second World War. It comes as little surprise, therefore, that much of the theorizing about the concept is based on the history and analysis of that relationship. The principal conclusions include the following.

THE ROLE OF INTERESTS AND SENTIMENTS

Most of what has been written about the US–UK special relationship acknowledges that, in terms of the factors giving rise to it and sustaining it over the years, both the interests of the respective parties and their sentiments toward each other have mattered (Butterfield 1987; Louis and Bull 1986; Pitts-Tucker 2020; Reynolds 1985).

The interests that have mattered in the case of the US–UK special relationship are those related to security and the international order. So it has been since the Second World War. Indeed, many of those who argue that a special relationship no longer exists in any meaningful way between the US and the UK argue that this has been due in large measure to Britain's declining relevance to American geopolitical interests (Conley 2010).

Sentiments – what some have called emotional ties and cultural affinities – are dismissed by some of being of distinctly secondary importance; others, though, argue that they are what keep the special relationship glued together and are why it has survived for so long. "History, tradition, affinity have been crucial to the alliance, rather than peripheral," write Dawson and Rosecrance (1966, 51). The British Council, in a 2018 analysis of the UK–US special relationship, concludes that it is as much a cultural as a political phenomenon, emphasizing what it finds to be the "underlying cultural affinity between the two countries," "underpinned by popular culture cross-over, mutual attraction, and shared values and concerns" (Donaldson 2018, 27).

PRIVILEGED AND CLOSE CONSULTATION

An exceptional degree of consultation between state officials, not found in the relations between the US and its other allies, is seen to have been a key attribute of the special relationship between the US and the UK. Kimball quotes Henry Kissinger, who acknowledged that there existed during his time as US Secretary of State "a pattern of consultation so matter-of-factly intimate that it became psychologically impossible to ignore British views" (Kimball 1998, 2). Reynolds (1985) argues that "the special relationship has been in part a deliberate British creation – a 'tradition' invented as a tool of diplomacy" (2). It was, he maintains, a relationship that was assiduously cultivated and nurtured by the British, the weaker party in the asymmetrical special relationship, in order to leverage its influence in international affairs.

Some commentators view the Biden administration's unilateral decision to withdraw from Afghanistan in the summer of 2021, criticized in the UK, as a recent example of that special relationship having fallen by the wayside (Landler 2021). Others maintain that a special relationship continues to exist in the form of security and intelligence relations between the two countries, the recently agreed AUKUS being a case in point (Chatham House 2020; Vinjamuri and Kundnani 2021).

PERSONAL CONTACTS AND FRIENDSHIPS

This factor is related to the previous one. The personal relationship between Churchill and FDR is often held up as the model for how such relationships have facilitated an exceptional degree of cooperation between the US and the UK. In more recent times, the relationship between George W. Bush and Tony Blair is often seen as having been crucial to the reawakening of the special relationship. But there also have been rather indifferent to downright chilly relationships at the top, President Trump's indifference toward prime ministers Theresa May and Boris Johnson being the most recent case.

According to this understanding of the special relationship, personal contacts and friendships reach well below the level of presidents and prime ministers. Facilitated by a shared language and a similarity of values, this network of personal relationships exists at the level of diplomats and military and intelligence officials of the two countries (Dumbrell 2001, 1). It has been characterized by some as a product of the "anglosphere," a community of shared values and world views across the Anglo-American democracies that has set them apart and made cooperation between them more fluid than with their other allies (Bennett 2004).

By the same token, some view demographic change, particularly on the American side, as contributing to the declining importance of personal contacts and friendships in the US–UK special relationship:

> The United States, with its growing and increasingly diverse population, will assume a greater share of the West's inhabitants, and thus greater political weight in the Atlantic Alliance, as the populations of most European countries age and decline. As the [European share of the population] shrinks in the United States, the percentage of Americans with a natural feel for Europe as a whole and for the "mother country" in particular can only diminish, progressively undermining the civilizational foundations of the special relationship and British influence in America. (Conley 2010)

ASYMMETRY BETWEEN THE PARTNERS

"Avoid public confrontation; seek private influence. Propitiate openly; manipulate secretly" (Reynolds 1985, 2). Thus does Reynolds describe the British strategy for maintaining a special relationship with the US. The tactics are clearly those of a weaker party, and indeed virtually all of what has been written about the US–UK special relationship acknowledges its asymmetry and how this has affected the behaviour of the respective parties.

But asymmetry does not mean that the special relationship provides security, economic, or other benefits solely to the weaker partner, or that in the event of a conflict of interests between the two countries the more dependent one will always or even usually lose. Most of the literature on the US–UK special relationship concludes that both sides have benefited from their unequal partnership. Some disagree. Toward the end of the Bush–Blair era, Wallace and Phillips (2009) wrote that "one of the greatest illusions in the contemporary British concept of the special relationship is that there remains across the Atlantic a special and sentimental attachment to Britain, beyond shared interests and welcoming rhetoric" (281). The benefits of the relationship, they conclude, are chiefly on the American side.

A SOCIALLY CONSTRUCTED NARRATIVE

From the moment Churchill described the US–UK relationship as special, the idea of this particular relationship being different in important ways from other bilateral partnerships – and certainly those that either country had with other countries – entered the conversation on international relations and foreign policy. Britain established a sort of proprietary claim to the term "special relationship," applying it in a monopolistic manner to the country's relationship with the US. This narrative might have seemed obvious and founded on the facts of the Atlanticism that emerged during and after the Second World War. But if it seemed to be simply a statement of fact at that time, it has not always been so. The relationship has long experienced ups and downs, and the special quality usually has been insisted upon more loudly and persistently from the British side of the ocean.[3]

Nevertheless, a narrative of specialness, forged in the cauldron of very different geopolitical times, has survived down to the present day. As Anna Pitts-Tucker (2020) writes, "Britain and America have been largely socialised into the assumption that their relationship is indeed 'special.'" This, she argues, has more than rhetorical significance. The narrative of the special relationship has influenced habits of thinking about foreign policy and the international order, particularly in the UK, but also on the American side. Its evocative power was evident at the time of the AUKUS agreement. "I'm someone who thinks that there has been, is and will always be a special relationship," said Charles Kupchan of the Council on Foreign Relations, who was a member of the National Security Council during the Clinton and Obama administrations. "Having spent some time in the White House, I came to the conclusion that if there's one country out there whose interests and perspectives line up most often with the United States, it's the United Kingdom. Is that historical, is it cultural, is it linguistic? I don't know, but I think it's a fact and so the question is how to make the most of that" (as quoted in Smith 2021).

BEYOND THE US–UK CASE

Theorizing about the special relationship has not been limited to the US–UK partnership. It is the case, however, that most references to a special bilateral relationship involve the US and some other country, such as Canada, Israel, Australia, or New Zealand. A 2009 book about America's special relationships includes those countries but also chapters on the Netherlands, Russia, and Iran (Dumbrell and Schäfer 2009). The term special relationship has also been used to describe many bilateral relationships that do not include the US. It is argued by some, for example, and not just by Russian politicians in recent years, that a special relationship rooted in history and culture has long existed between Russia and Ukraine (Calamur 2014). A special relationship between Russia and Belarus has also been identified (Belarus 2022). Australia and New Zealand form another pair of countries whose bilateral relationship has often been described as special or unique (MacDonald and O'Connor 2012).

Indeed, Harnisch (2017) has identified more than fifty international relationships, many of which do not involve the US, that have been described as special. He proposes that the designation "special" be limited to those bilateral relationships where countries' foreign policies toward each other – and, indeed, the decision-making processes by which they resolve bilateral differences – are distinctive from those that either country has with other partners. "Special relationships," Harnisch (2017) writes, "refer to durable and exclusive bilateral relationships between autonomous polities that are based on mutual expectations of preferential treatment by its members and outsiders and through the entanglement of their (external) governance functions."

MacDonald and O'Connor (2012) observe that any definition of a special relationship "comes down to identifying which of the many factors in a special relationship are potentially the most important, be they cultural, military, economic, racial, religious, or linguistic" (178). They argue that the economic dimension of a bilateral relationship, no matter how extensive and important to at least one of the partners, is not on its own sufficient to make the case for a special relationship. If it were otherwise, some countries that share little in terms of common security interests, political and legal systems, and cultural and historical affinities would have to be included. They point to the cases of Australia and New Zealand: both these countries are increasingly being drawn into the Asian orbit in terms of their economic relations, yet they have not developed either the rhetoric or the structures and practices of consultation with China and other Asian trading partners that are aspects of a special relationship. Their relationships with Asian partners remain primarily transactional, lacking the tissue of shared values, histories, and institutions that facilitate cooperation and mutual trust.

Canadian and American scholars have made significant contributions to theorizing on the special relationship, focusing on the bilateral relations between Canada and the US. The frequently used description "joined at the hip" is a sort of shorthand for the scope, density, and intimacy of Canada–US relations. Writing about these relations in 1979, Barry (1979) observed that "by any standard the Canada–US relationship is unique in the international system, unmatched in the range and intensity of its intimacy and complicated by huge asymmetry in the capabilities of the two countries" (114). Whereas the literature about the US–UK special relationship focuses on shared interests and world views regarding international order and security, the Canada–US literature is grounded largely in the vast network of economic, cultural, and geographic ties between the two countries that Barry alluded to (see, for example, Dawson and Speer 2016, 5–8). Shared security interests are also part of this network, of course, although the centrality of those ties to the special relationship has declined somewhat over the past several decades.

The theoretical question that has preoccupied many of the most interesting analyses of the Canada–US relationship has involved the consequences of the obvious asymmetry in the relationship (Anderson 2018; Bow 2007, 2009; Keohane and Nye 1977). Indeed, much of what has been written about the Canada–US special relationship argues that, historically, Canada has been quite successful in negotiating with the US on issues when the interests of the two governments have diverged. The reasons given are varied. Keohane and Nye (1977) use the Canada–US case to argue that "the political processes of complex interdependence, and more particularly the role of transnational and transgovernmental actors, lead to a more equal pattern of outcomes in intergovernmental bargaining than one would predict from the (highly asymmetrical) structure" (179). Bow argues that the successes Canada experienced on some highly contentious issues during the era of "quiet diplomacy" (1950s–1960s) were largely due to shared diplomatic norms and a mutual commitment among diplomats and bureaucrats on both sides of the border to a problem-solving approach to resolving differences (Bow 2007, 126–7; see also Gotlieb 2006; Ritchie 1983). Anderson argues that what might be seen as unexpected Canadian victories against steep odds, given the asymmetry in the Canada–US relationship, have not been due to a special relationship. Instead, he makes the case that the dynamic of bilateral negotiation and conflict resolution is context- and issue-specific, and that differences between Canada and the US in the emphasis each country has placed on issue categories – the hierarchy of issues for each government – have been a key factor explaining what might otherwise appear to be Canada's surprising successes (Anderson 2018).

Asymmetry is also the focus of another theoretical contribution to the study of the Canada–US relationship. This one has flowed from the dependency school of Canadian political science. Those who work in this tradition argue that the concept of a special relationship serves principally to mask a dependency relationship and the fundamental inequality in benefits that is at the heart of such a relationship. In the case of Canada, academics, politicians, and opinion leaders on the left have made this argument since the 1960s. One early debunker of the special relationship concept, the philosopher George Grant, was not on the left in any conventional sense; even so, his 1965 book *Lament for a Nation* shared many of the premises and conclusions of the political and academic left. Grant's lament for what he saw as the inevitable absorption of Canada into the American empire rejected both the idea that Canada benefited from its increasingly intimate ties with the US and the notion that the Canadian government could resist pressures from Washington on any issue that seriously mattered to the masters in the Canada–US relationship (Grant 1965). A generation of prominent left-leaning Canadians, including the philosopher Charles Taylor, political scientist Stephen Clarkson, nationalist publisher Mel Hurtig (one of the first co-chairpersons of the Committee for an Independent Canada), political activist and a founder of the Council of Canadians, Maude Barlow, and, more recently, Naomi Klein and Avi Lewis, have all amplified this theme. They share the belief that the function of the special relationship concept was primarily ideological, being to obfuscate the power of American capital in Canada and the cultural, economic, and political costs experienced by Canada as a result of this relationship.

A Forgotten Partnership?

Charles Doran is the foremost American scholar of Canada–US relations of his generation. In titling his 1984 book *Forgotten Partnership: US–Canada Relations Today*, Doran argued that a natural partnership existed between Canada and the US and that "in the annals of world statecraft it has few parallels in terms of scope or amity" (Doran 1984, 10). But despite its exceptional character, the relationship was under stress. "Some of the benefits of long-enjoyed partnership seem to have been forgotten. Likewise forgotten, perhaps, is the awareness of how difficult such an edifice as the US–Canada relationship is to build and how simple it is to undermine" (11).

These observations, made almost four decades ago, have an obvious and important resonance in our own times. The years of the Trump presidency were rocky ones for the Canada–US relationship. The tone and optics of the relationship have improved immeasurably since the 2020 election of President Joe Biden. All of this sweetness and light has not been matched, however, by harmony and cooperation in matters of trade and energy, as well as some aspects of foreign policy, that many (probably most) Canadians believed would follow upon Trump's departure (Abelson and Lajeunesse 2020). The partnership's exceptional character and the reasons for nurturing it appear to have been largely forgotten.

Of course, it could be a forgotten partnership because it has long ceased to be the "natural partnership" that Doran believed it to be. The world has moved on, and with it, perhaps, the Canada–US bilateral relationship. Just as there is no shortage of debunkers of the US–UK special relationship, perhaps whatever special relationship may once have existed between two neighbours who share what has long been described as the world's "longest undefended border" has receded into history.

This appears to be the view of those who argue that a continentalist partnership of the US, Canada, and Mexico is a preferable approach to managing relations between the US and its neighbours (Pastor 2011; Robertson 2011). Recent summits of the "Three Amigos" – the presidents of the US and Mexico and the prime minister of Canada – have generated considerable criticism from the Canadian side, based on worries that placing Canada's relationship with the US on a par with US–Mexican relations can only end by diminishing the importance and uniqueness of the Canada–US relationship. On the eve of the January 2023 meeting of the three national leaders, the Canadian–American Business Council's CEO, Maryscott Greenwood, said, "[Canada] wants to have its own unique relationship with the U.S., so we'll see if Canada is going to embrace or resist the 'North American idea.'" The trilateral continentalist vision that seems to be the preferred model among many American policy-makers tends to be seen by their Canadian counterparts as a perspective that diminishes the importance (certainly for Canada) and special quality of the bilateral relationship between the two northern neighbours (Manley and Giffin 2009).

If the matter were to be decided by the amount of attention paid by the American media and lawmakers to their country's northern and southern neighbours, respectively, one would be hard-pressed to conclude that there continues to be a special relationship between Canada and the US. But as the subsequent chapters will show, the relationship remains, by any reasonable standard, exceptional in many ways. Whether it should be described as "special," "unique," "distinctive," or "exceptional" is, we would argue, largely a matter of semantic quibbling. The bottom line is that Doran's 1984 observation that the relationship has few parallels in terms of "scope or amity" remains true and is likely to continue to be so for quite some time.

This book is inspired by Doran's magisterial analysis of the Canada–US relationship. His insistence that this relationship, to be properly understood, needs to be situated in a broader international context is taken seriously in all the chapters that follow. "At every point in history," Doran (1984) writes, "the international system has impinged on US–Canada relations and has shaped outcomes. Indeed, the historical equilibrium of global power has determined outcomes perhaps to a greater degree than any other factor" (29–30).

This argument has obvious relevance for any assessment of what so often has been described as the special relationship between these two neighbours. The highs and lows that have marked the course of that relationship have been influenced both by the currents of geopolitics and by the particularities of the Canada–US bilateral relationship. To say it is a special relationship does not and has never meant that it is free from serious stress. It is the special qualities of this relationship that have enabled it to survive and thrive, and to manage differences of interests, policies, and values that have sometimes seemed unbridgeable.

Chapters and Contributors

The book has three sections. The first focuses on key themes in the study of Canada–US relations, including the attitudes of Canadians toward the US, the challenges Canada faces in manoeuvring its way through the complex world of Washington policy-making, and how Canadian policy-makers attempt to position themselves strategically inside the Washington Beltway, particularly when the US is preoccupied with more pressing global issues. In the second section, we turn our attention to the so-called special relationship between Canada and the US by exploring the extent to which personal relations between leaders of the two countries may help or hinder the bilateral relationship and whether the friendships that are nurtured between prime ministers and presidents can act as a buffer against competing political pressures and prevailing cultures in their respective countries. In the concluding section, we focus on how Canada and the US have sought to navigate several important policy files on the bilateral agenda, including trade, Arctic sovereignty, the environment, defence cooperation, and border security.

PART ONE: UNDERSTANDING THE CANADA–US LANDSCAPE

The Canada–US relationship is widely recognized among scholars of comparative politics and international relations as one of the most important and enduring bilateral relationships on the globe. But what do Canadians generally think about their southern neighbour and the many social, economic, and security policies it pursues? In the section's first chapter, Michael Adams and Andrew Parkin, two experts in amassing and interpreting large data sets on, among other things, the attitudes of Canadians toward the US, do just that. Their analysis tracks, over several years during the free trade era, how Canadians perceive various policies advanced by the US. The authors then paint a fascinating picture of the myriad factors that both bring the two countries together and drive them apart.

In the following chapter, Roy Norton offers a sweeping analysis of the many steps Canada has taken over the past several decades to position itself more strategically inside the Washington Beltway. As only a former Canadian diplomat and an academic could, Norton draws on his years of experience working on the Canada–US file in Washington, DC, to assess the many challenges Canada has faced in making its presence felt. His many valuable insights, gleaned from observing and participating in countless discussions on Canada's behalf in the US, will resonate with those who have often questioned what more the Canadian government can do to ensure its voice is heard in key policy-making circles.

In the section's final chapter, Michael K. Hawes and Christopher J. Kirkey draw on a single case study – the dissolution of the Soviet Union – to reveal the many challenges Canada faces in making itself known in Washington, DC. As the remaining great power in a unipolar world, the US, according to the authors, rarely perceived Canada as a priority. Hawes and Kirkey acknowledge that their assessment of Canada–US relations in an international system characterized by unipolarity represents a moment in time; even so, that moment reveals important lessons about how to manage the Canada–US relationship.

PART TWO: WHAT IS SO SPECIAL ABOUT THE CANADA–US RELATIONSHIP?

Greg Anderson explores Donald Trump's protectionist leanings, which are deeply rooted in US trade policy. His observations offer a warning against interpreting recurring patterns of behaviour as revolutionary. In the next chapter, Asa McKercher and Susan Colbourn build on Norton's insights about how Canadian policy-makers operate in Washington by focusing more on the relations between several Canadian prime ministers and American presidents. They doubt that the friendships between leaders of the two countries necessarily determine whether progress on key policy files will be made; still, they recognize the value of close personal interactions. In the subsequent chapter, Donald E. Abelson is more convinced that friendship between prime ministers and presidents can at times be invaluable. He argues that friendships between leaders can play an important, if not decisive role, in both facilitating cooperation on multiple policy fronts and in managing dissent, particularly when competing national agendas could easily generate tensions and divisions in the bilateral relationship. Using the Mulroney–Reagan years as a backdrop, Abelson emphasizes the importance of friendship and how it can be used to advance the Canada–US file.

The two remaining chapters in this section explore how politics played out at the federal and provincial levels in Canada can shape

Canada–US relations. Stephen Brooks reminds us that the strength and vitality of the Canada–US relationship cannot be taken be for granted, particularly when we consider the many political, cultural, ideological, and economic pressures that at times have pulled the two countries apart. Brooks explores how Canadian nationalists, and the various forms of nationalism they have espoused, have posed an ongoing threat to those invested in maintaining the "special relationship" between Canada and the US. Rather than impugning Canadian nationalists for their attitudes toward the US, he brings to light why their ongoing concerns deserve to be addressed in any meaningful discussions about closer integration between Canada and the US.

Finally, Stéphane Paquin examines the relationship between the US and Quebec, especially under the leadership of former Premier Jean Charest. Paquin explains in considerable detail why the US has for decades figured so prominently on Quebec's list of international priorities and describes the lengths Charest was prepared to go to strengthen his province's ties the US, even when doing so created unrest with other Canadian provinces that were less than enthralled with the direction in which the US was moving. Paquin's study delves into why the US is so important to Quebec and how that province's relations with Washington can create turmoil in other parts of Canada.

PART THREE: COOPERATION AND CONFLICT ON THE CANADA–US BILATERAL AGENDA

The final section of this book examines the extent to which Canada has been able to make advances on four important policy fronts in Canada–US relations, including the environment (Debora L. VanNijnatten and Andrea Olive), Arctic sovereignty (Adam Lajeunesse), defence (David G. Haglund and Wesley Nicol), and border security (Sara K. McGuire). In each of these case studies, the authors go to great lengths to showcase how and why Canada has been able to make advances on key policy fronts and what steps still need to be taken for the country to achieve even more desirable policy outcomes. Negotiating as a junior partner in an asymmetrical power relationship will always remain a challenge for Canada in its dealings with the US. However, as these authors have shown, this reality has not prevented Canada from securing important gains. Negotiating skills, diplomacy, and personal and professional relationships, not to mention timing, must all be taken into account in reviewing these and other policy issues. These and other important lessons are revealed in the pages that follow.

Notes

1 For the Continental Congress's overtures, see https://www.amrevmuseum.org/canada-and-the-american-revolution.

2 In fact, the treaty was signed by the UK, which at the time had sole authority to sign international treaties on Canada's behalf. The first international treaty to be signed by Canada in its own right was the 1919 Treaty of Versailles.

3 Perhaps surprisingly, a 2021 survey found that Britons were about twice as likely as Americans to agree with the statement that the relationship between their countries is special (Walden 2021). Nevertheless, there is no doubt that the term has been and continues to be used far more often by political and opinion leaders on the British side of the ocean.

References

Abelson, Donald E., and Adam Lajeunesse, eds. 2020. "Canada–US Relations in the Age of Trump." *American Review of Canadian Studies* (special issue) 50, no. 1.

Anderson, Greg. 2018. "David and Goliath in Canada–US Relations: Who's Really Who?" *Canadian Foreign Policy Journal* 25, no. 2: 115–36. doi: 10.1080/11926422.2018.1542604.

Barry, Donald. 1979. "The Politics of 'Exceptionalism': Canada and the United States as a Distinctive International Relationship." *Dalhousie Review* 60: 114–37.

Bartlett, C.J. 1992. *'The Special Relationship': A Political History of Anglo-American Relations Since 1945*. London: Longman.

Belarus. 2022. "Belarus and Russia." Ministry of Foreign Affairs. https://mfa.gov.by/en/bilateral/russia.

Bennett, James C. 2004. *The Anglosphere Challenge: Why the English-Speaking Nations Will Lead the Way in the Twenty-First Century*. New York: Rowan and Littlefield.

Bow, Brian. 2007. "Out of Ideas? Models and Strategies for Canada–US Relations." *International Journal: Canada's Journal of Global Policy Analysis* 62, no. 1: 123–42.

– 2009. *The Politics of Linkage: Power, Interdependence, and Ideas in Canada–US Relations*. Vancouver: UBC Press.

Butterfield, Henry Ryan. 1987. *The Vision of Anglo-America: The US–UK Alliance and the Emerging Cold War, 1943–1946*. Cambridge: Cambridge University Press.

Calamur, Krishnadev. 2014. "Why Ukraine Is Such a Big Deal for Russia." *National Public Radio*, 21 February. https://www.npr.org/sections/parallels/2014/02/21/280684831/why-ukraine-is-such-a-big-deal-for-russia.

Canada. 2021a. Prime Minister Trudeau Speaks with the President of the United States of America Joe Biden. Prime Minister's Office, 22 January. https://pm.gc.ca/en/news/readouts/2021/01/22/prime-minister-justin-trudeau-speaks-president-united-states-america-joe.

– 2021b. Statement by the Prime Minister of Canada on the United States' Decision on the Keystone XL Project. Prime Minister's Office, 20 January. https://pm.gc.ca/en/news/statements/2021/01/20/statement-prime-minister-canada-united-states-decision-keystone-xl.

Carnegie Endowment for International Peace. 1941. *The Relations of Canada and the United States. A Series of Studies Prepared under the Direction of James T. Shotwell, Division of Economics and History*. New Haven: Yale University Press.

Carvin, Stephanie, and Thomas Juneau. 2021. "Canada's Exclusion from 'Three Eyes' Only Confirms What Was Already the Case." *Globe and Mail*, 17 September. https://www.theglobeandmail.com/opinion/article-canadas-exclusion-from-three-eyes-only-confirms-what-was-already-the/.

CBC News. 2021. "What President Biden's First Call with Trudeau Means for Canada–US Relations." *CBC News: The National*, 22 January. YouTube video, 1:50. https://www.youtube.com/watch?v=SBxMv64eTuY.

Chatham House. 2020. "100 Years of Special? The US–UK Relationship and the Future of Global Order." Research Event, July 7. London.

Churchill, Winston. 1946. "The Sinews of Peace ('Iron Curtain Speech')." Fulton, Missouri, 5 March. https://winstonchurchill.org/resources/speeches/1946-1963-elder-statesman/the-sinews-of-peace.

Conley, Heather. 2010. "A Washington Perspective: The Fraying Bonds of the Special Relationship." Center for Strategic and International Studies, 30 March. https://www.csis.org/analysis/washington-perspective-fraying-bonds-special-relationship.

Dawson, Laura, and Sean Speer. 2016. *Managing the Canada–US Relationship from the Honeymoon to the Long-Term*. Wilson Center. March. https://www.macdonaldlaurier.ca/files/pdf/MLISpeerDawsonCanadaUS-03-16-webready.pdf.

Dawson, Raymond, and Richard Rosecrance. 1966. "Theory and Reality in the Anglo-American Alliance." *World Politics* 19, no. 1: 21–51.

Dimbleby, David, and David Reynolds. 1989. *An Ocean Apart: The Relationship between Britain and America in the Twentieth Century.* New York: Vintage.

Donaldson, Alasdair. 2018. *A Special Relationship? Exploring the Future of UK–US Cultural Ties.* Manchester: British Council. https://www.britishcouncil.org/sites/default/files/j062_thought_leadership_a_special_relationship.pdf.

Doran, Charles. 1984. *Forgotten Partnership: US–Canada Relations Today.* Baltimore: Johns Hopkins University Press.

Dumbrell, John. 2001. *A Special Relationship: Anglo-American Relations in the Cold War and After.* London: Macmillan.

Dumbrell, John, and Axel R. Schäfer, eds. 2009. *America's "Special Relationships": Foreign and Domestic Aspects of the Politics of Alliance.* New York: Routledge.

Gotlieb, Allan. 2006. *The Washington Diaries, 1981–1989.* Toronto: McClelland and Stewart.

Grant, George Parkin. 1965. *Lament for a Nation: The Defeat of Canadian Nationalism.* Toronto: McClelland and Stewart.

Hanc, John. 2017. "When Nova Scotia Almost Joined the American Revolution." *Smithsonian Magazine*, 5 June. https://www.smithsonianmag.com/history/when-nova-scotia-almost-joined-american-revolution-180963564.

Harnisch, Sebastian. 2017. "Special Relationships in Foreign Policy." *Oxford Encyclopedia of Foreign Policy Analysis.* 27 July. doi: https://doi.org/10.1093/acrefore/9780190228637.013.486.

Heisler, Jay. 2021. "Snubbed by AUKUS, Canada, New Zealand Are Moving On." *VOA News*, 30 September. https://www.voanews.com/a/snubbed-by-aukus-canada-new-zealand-are-moving-on-/6252363.html.

Hillmer, Norman. 2004. "O.D. Skelton and the North American Mind." *International Journal* 60, no. 1: 93–110.

Johnson, Boris. 2021. "Aukus – in the House of Commons at 10:30 am on 16th September 2021." *TheyWorkForYou.* https://www.theyworkforyou.com/debates/?id=2021-09-16b.1119.0.

Kennedy, John F. 1961. Address before the Canadian Parliament in Ottawa. 17 May. *The American Presidency Project.* https://www.presidency.ucsb.edu/documents/address-before-the-canadian-parliament-ottawa.

Keohane, Robert, and Joseph Nye. 1977. *Power and Interdependence: World Politics in Transition.* Boston: Little, Brown.

Kimball, Warren F. 1998. "Fighting with Allies: The Hand-Care and Feeding of the Anglo-American Special Relationship." Harmon Memorial Lectures in Military History no. 41, United States Air Force Academy, Colorado.

Landler, Mike. 2021. "Biden Rattles UK with Afghanistan Policy." *New York Times*, 18 August. https://www.nytimes.com/2021/08/18/world/europe/britain-afghanistan-johnson-biden.html.

Leech, Richard. 1977. "Canada and the United States: A Special Relationship." *Current History* 72, no. 426: 145–9.

Levitt, Kari. 1970. *Silent Surrender: The Multinational Corporation in Canada*. Toronto: Macmillan.

Ljunggren, David. 2021. "What Special Relationship? Canada Grimaces amid Hail of US Trade Blows." *Reuters*, 22 January. https://www.reuters.com/business/what-special-relationship-canada-grimaces-amid-hail-us-trade-blows-2021-06-22.

Louis, William R., and Hedley Bull, eds. 1986. *The "Special Relationship": Anglo-American Relations since 1945*. Oxford: Clarendon Press.

Lumsden, Ian. 1970. *Close the 49th Parallel Etc.: The Americanization of Canada*. Toronto: University of Toronto Press.

MacDonald, David, and Brendon O'Connor. 2012. "Australia and New Zealand in the Anglo-American World." In *Anglo-America and Its Discontents: Civilizational Identities beyond West and East*, edited by Peter Katzenstein, 176–203. New York: Routledge.

Macfarlane, Daniel, and Murray Clamen, eds. 2020. *The First Century of the International Joint Commission*. Calgary: University of Calgary Press.

MacLennan, Hugh. 1960. "It's the US or Us." *Maclean's*, 5 November. https://archive.macleans.ca/article/160/11/5/its-the-us-or-us.

Maddeux, Sabrina. 2021. "Biden's Special Praise for Australia a Rebuke of Trudeau's Failed Foreign Policy." *National Post*, 22 September. https://nationalpost.com/opinion/sabrina-maddeaux-bidens-special-praise-for-australia-a-rebuke-of-trudeaus-failed-foreign-policy.

Manley, John, and Gordon Giffin. 2009. "A Table for Two, Not Three." *Globe and Mail*, 5 May, A13.

Morton, Desmond. 2003. "Uncle Louis and a Golden Age for Canada: A Time of Prosperity at Home and Influence Abroad." *Policy Options*. June–July. https://policyoptions.irpp.org/wp-content/uploads/sites/2/assets/po/the-best-pms-in-the-past-50-years/morton.pdf.

Mowat, Farley. 1958. "Get Tough." *Maclean's*, 7 June. https://archive.macleans.ca/article/1958/6/7/get-tough.

Nixon, Richard. 1972. Address to a Joint Meeting of the Canadian Parliament. *The American Presidency Project*. 14 April. https://www.presidency.ucsb.edu/documents/address-joint-meeting-the-canadian-parliament.

Pastor, Robert. 2011. *The North American Idea: A Vision of a Continental Future*. New York: Oxford University Press.

Pearson, Lester B. 1975. *Mike: The Memoirs of the Right Honourable Lester B. Pearson*, vol. 3. Toronto: University of Toronto Press.

Pitts-Tucker, Anna. 2020. "Analysing the 'Special Relationship' between the US and UK in a Transatlantic Context." *E-International Relations*, 2 August. https://www.e-ir.info/2020/08/02/analysing-the-special-relationship-between-the-us-and-uk-in-a-transatlantic-context.

Porter, Catherine. 2021. "Justin Trudeau Gets Call from Biden as Canada and US Mend Relations." *New York Times*, 22 January. https://www.nytimes.com/2021/01/22/world/canada/biden-canada.html.

Reuters. 2021. "Canada Left Out of Security Deal between U.S., Australia, and U.K. Trudeau Unconcerned." *National Post*, 16 September. https://nationalpost.com/news/world/china-fumes-over-australias-nuclear-sub-pact-with-u-s-britain-2.

Reynolds, David. 1985. "A 'Special Relationship'? America, Britain, and the International Order Since the Second World War." *International Affairs* 62, no. 1: 1–20.

– 1988. "Rethinking Anglo-American Relations." *International Affairs (Royal Institute of International Affairs 1944–)* 65, no. 1: 89–111. doi: https://doi.org/10.2307/2620984.

Ritchie, Charles. 1983. *Storm Signals: More Undiplomatic Diaries, 1962–1971*. Toronto: Macmillan.

Robertson, Colin. 2011. "Embracing the Americas, Starting with Mexico." *Policy Options*, 1 May. https://policyoptions.irpp.org/fr/magazines/provincial-deficits-and-debt/embracing-the-americas-starting-with-mexico.

Roosevelt, Franklin Delano. 1938. Address at Queen's University, Kingston, Ontario, Canada. 18 August. *The American Presidency Project*. https://www.presidency.ucsb.edu/documents/address-queens-university-kingston-ontario-canada.

Sigler, John, and Dennis Goresky. 1974. "Public Opinion on United States–Canada Relations." *International Organization* 28, no. 4: 637–68.

Smith, David. 2021. "US–UK 'Special Relationship' Faces New Challenges Despite Signs of Healing." *The Guardian*, 22 September. https://www.theguardian.com/world/2021/sep/22/us-uk-special-relationship-faces-new-challenges-despite-signs-of-healing.

Thomas, David, and Christopher Sands, eds. 2022. *Canada and the United States: Differences That Count*, 5th ed. Toronto: University of Toronto Press.

Thompson, John Herd, and Stephen J. Randall. 2008. *Canada and the United States: Ambivalent Allies*, 4th ed. Athens: University of Georgia Press.

United Kingdom. 2021. "UK, US, and Australia Launch New Security Partnership." 15 September. https://www.gov.uk/government/news/uk-us-and-australia-launch-new-security-partnership.

Vinjamuri, Leslie, and Hans Kundnani. 2021. "New UK–US Alignment Can Reshape Transatlantic Cooperation." Chatham House, 2 March. https://www.chathamhouse.org/2021/03/new-uk-us-alignment-can-reshape-transatlantic-cooperation.

Walden, Camilla. 2021. "Americans Are Twice as Likely as Britons to Believe the US and UK Share a 'Special Relationship.'" *YouGovAmerica*, 11 June. https://today.yougov.com/topics/politics/articles-reports/2021/06/11/americans-are-twice-likely-britons-believe-us-and-.

Wallace, William, and Christopher Phillips. 2009. "Reassessing the Special Relationship." *International Affairs* 85, no. 2: 263–84.

Westcott, Ben. 2021. "Australia's Decades-Long Balancing Act between the US and China Is Over. It Chose Washington." CNN, 17 September. https://www.cnn.com/2021/09/16/australia/australia-china-us-aukus-submarine-intl-hnk/index.html.

White House. 2021a. Readout of President Joe Biden with Prime Minister Trudeau of Canada. 22 January. https://www.whitehouse.gov/briefing-room/statements-releases/2021/01/22/readout-of-president-joe-biden-call-with-prime-minister-justin-trudeau-of-canada.

– 2021b. Remarks by President Biden, Prime Minister Morrison of Australia, and Prime Minister Johnson of the United Kingdom Announcing the Creation of AUKUS. 15 September. https://www.whitehouse.gov/briefing-room/speeches-remarks/2021/09/15/remarks-by-president-biden-prime-minister-morrison-of-australia-and-prime-minister-johnson-of-the-united-kingdom-announcing-the-creation-of-aukus.

PART ONE

Understanding the Canada–US Landscape

1

An Unexpected Shift

Canadians' Views of the United States in the Era of Free Trade

MICHAEL ADAMS AND ANDREW PARKIN

There are several "immovable objects" in Canadian politics: issues that every prime minister and government must grapple with regardless of the times. National unity is one. Immigration and the environment are others. And this list undoubtedly includes relations with the US. In good times and in bad, no government in Ottawa can pursue its own agenda without having to factor in the preferences of its counterpart in Washington. Relations between prime ministers and presidents can be friendly or strained, but they can never be ignored.

The permanence of Canada–US relations as a captivating political issue for two peaceful centuries creates the impression that nothing ever really changes. One way or another, successive Canadian governments must find ways to be supportive allies of the Americans without compromising their own independence. They have to respond to the policies not only of the president but also of the US Congress, which the president seldom controls. They have to counter the Americans' recurring shifts toward protectionism and ensure that the border stays open to trade and tourism. Presidents Richard Nixon, Ronald Reagan, and Donald Trump were all very different. Yet in each case, the Canadian government of the day was compelled to deploy similar defensive manoeuvres in Washington to ensure that Canada was not squashed under the steamroller of their respective presidencies and the "America First" sentiments of the US Congress and the US as a whole.

This continuity of the political agenda has obscured important changes at the level of public opinion. Four decades ago, Canadians had a favourable view of American society but were wary of being swallowed up by the giant US economy. The debate over the Canada–US free trade agreement centred on the question of whether closer economic ties between the two countries would inevitably erode Canada's distinctiveness and independence. Today, the commitment to free trade with the US is shared by all Canadian political parties. But as free trade has become more popular, views of our trading partner have soured. The closer economic alignment of the two countries has been accompanied by increased certainty among Canadians that they are a distinct society and by rising doubts about the direction in which American society is headed. These changes have emerged gradually over several decades and cannot be dismissed as a short-term aberration triggered by the advent of Trumpian populism in 2016.

This chapter tracks the profound and unexpected evolution in Canadian attitudes toward the US that has taken place over the past forty years. We will show that while the issues that Canadian governments confront in terms of Canada–US relations are long-standing, the sea change in Canadian public opinion is new. And this newer, more self-confident Canadian mindset should be taken into account by the country's political leaders as they navigate around the immovable object of Canada–US relations.

1984 to 1993: From Canada–US Free Trade to NAFTA

Our discussion begins with the election of Brian Mulroney as prime minister of Canada in 1984. At the time – the mid-1980s – several aspects of Canada–US relations were difficult to manage. A majority of Canadians, for instance, wanted more US government action to curtail acid rain and opposed the testing of American cruise missiles in Canada.[1] Yet Mulroney's counterpart – President Reagan – was not himself unpopular in Canada. Most Canadians had hoped that his Democratic opponent (Jimmy Carter) would win the 1980 presidential election; even so, by the mid-1980s, most of them (roughly 60 per cent in the mid-1980s) viewed Reagan favourably.

Most importantly, disagreements over environmental and defence policies notwithstanding, a strong majority of Canadians held favourable views of the US itself. America at the time was a military, economic, and cultural powerhouse – it was Canada's ally in the Cold War, and

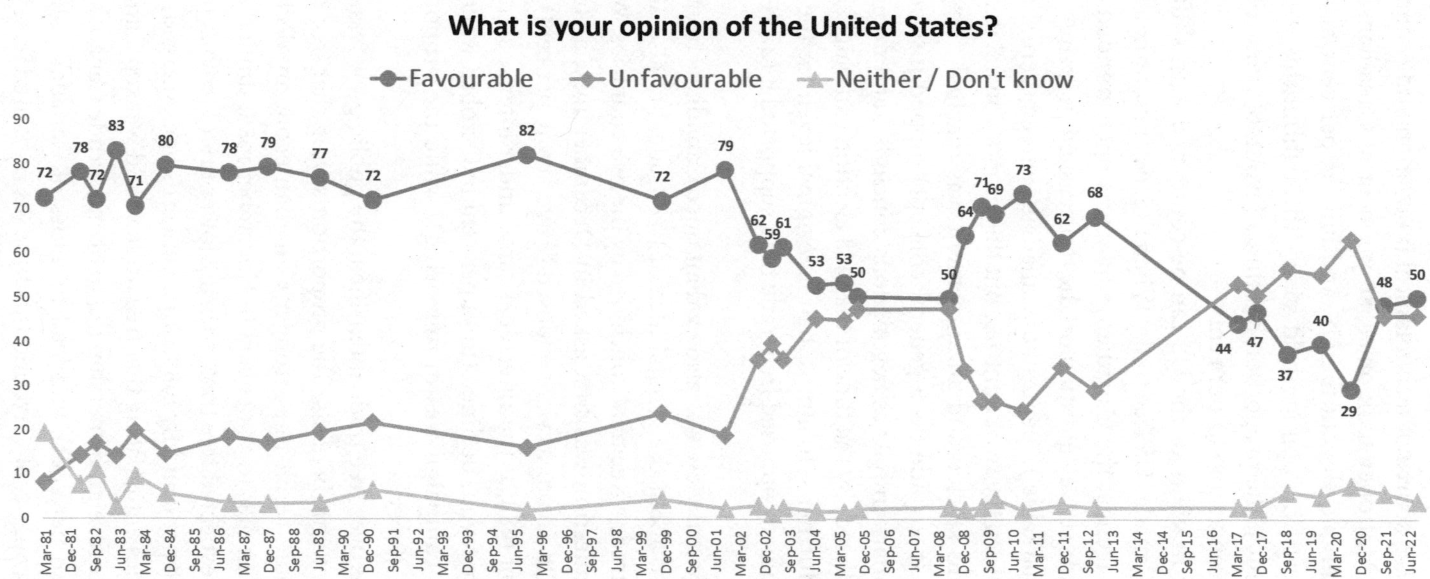

In general, what is your opinion of the US? Is it very favourable, somewhat favourable, somewhat unfavourable, or very unfavourable?

Figure 1.1 Canadians' opinions of the United States
Source: Environics Institute

it was admired as a source of technological innovation and economic opportunity. As Mulroney took office, 80 per cent of Canadians said they had a favourable view of the US, and only 15 per cent held an unfavourable view. This opinion held steady throughout this period: from 1981 until 1995, the proportion holding a favourable view of the US ranged between 72 and 82 per cent.

This stability in views of the US can be contrasted with shifts in opinions about Canada–US free trade. When the idea first re-emerged on the political agenda, the Canadian public was open-minded. The first Focus Canada survey question on the topic, asked in spring 1984, found that a remarkable 78 per cent of Canadians agreed there should be free trade between the two countries. But this proportion fell steadily once negotiations started and an agreement was reached. Support for Canada–US free trade (as a general concept) dipped just below the 50 per cent mark in 1987 as negotiations concluded and domestic opposition mobilized. By the time of the 1988 election campaign, support had fallen further – to almost half its original level; for the first time, more Canadians opposed free trade than supported it (44 versus 41 per cent).

This more divided view was also evident once Canadians began to be asked, not just about the general idea of free trade, but also about the specific free trade agreement concluded by the two countries. When this particular question was first asked in December 1987, as many Canadians were in favour as were opposed (41 versus 39 per cent). But over the course of 1988, as the agreement came under intense scrutiny, the proportion in favour declined (to 34 per cent in October, when the federal election campaign was in full swing), while the proportion opposed rose to 48 per cent.

As the debate over free trade intensified, the public grew less convinced of its economic benefits. The proportion saying that free trade with the US would result in a stronger Canadian economy declined from 53 per cent in 1985 to 36 per cent in November 1988; similarly, the proportion that expected free trade to bring lower prices to consumers fell from 60 to 49 per cent.[2] By 1988, other concerns had emerged, with sizeable minorities anticipating that free trade would weaken Canada's ability to regulate foreign ownership (44 per cent), erode Canada's cultural identity (40 per cent), and lead to a loss of Canada's political independence (37 per cent). Around this time (as measured in several

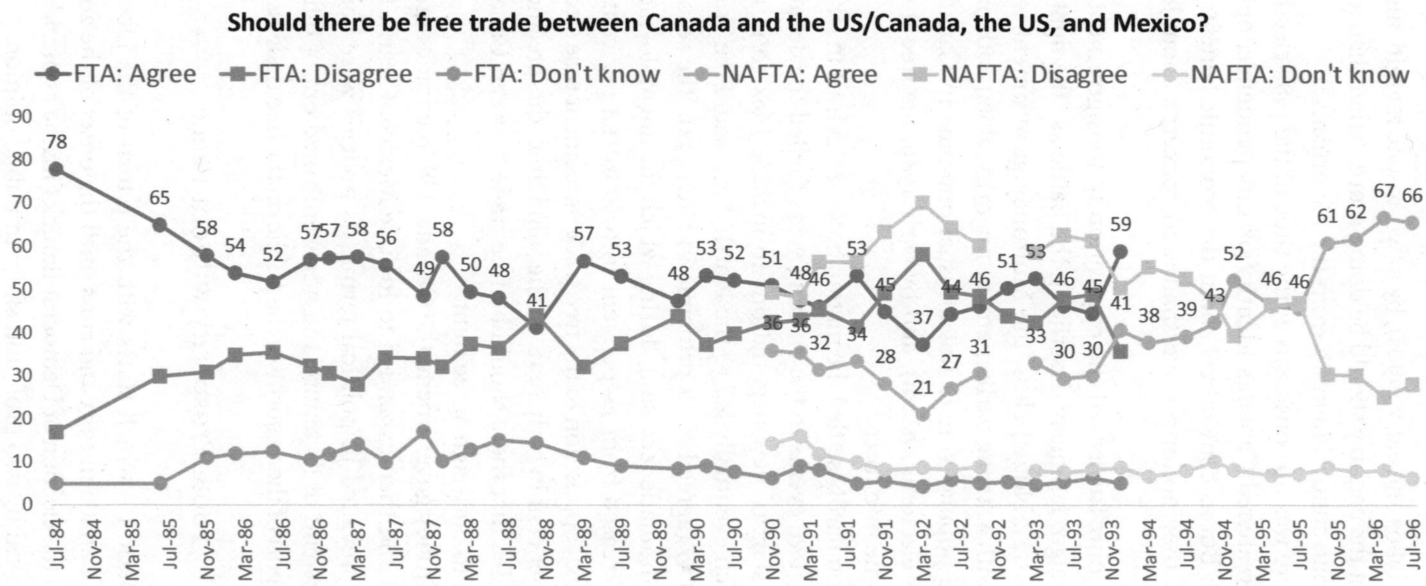

Please tell me whether you strongly agree, somewhat agree, somewhat disagree or strongly disagree that there should be free trade between Canada and the US?
Do you strongly agree, somewhat agree, somewhat disagree, or strongly disagree that there should be free trade between Canada, the US, and Mexico?

Figure 1.2 Opinions on free trade between Canada and the US / Canada, the US, and Mexico, 1984–96
Source: Environics, Focus Canada

surveys in the late 1980s and early 1990s), by a two-to-one margin, more Canadians thought the country should be doing more, rather than less, to develop a separate cultural identity from the Americans.

To be clear, there was no consensus at the time of the 1988 election that free trade threatened Canada's identity or independence; opinions were divided. But as convictions about the economic benefits of free trade eroded, they no longer overshadowed concerns about loss of sovereignty.

Liberal leader John Turner led the opposition to the agreement in the election campaign, famously describing the battle as "the fight of my life" (Litt 2011–12). Nonetheless, the Mulroney government won the 1988 election with a strong parliamentary majority, albeit with only 43 per cent of the popular vote (a not unusual outcome in Canada's first-past-the-post electoral system), and by early 1989, the free trade agreement had come into force.

The 1988 election hardly settled the matter, however, at least in terms of public opinion. Two events in the ensuing years fuelled the debate.[3] The first was the start of new negotiations to include Mexico in the arrangement, which eventually led to the North American Free Trade Agreement (NAFTA) (agreed to in principle in late 1992). The second was the onset of a dramatic recession, during which the unemployment rate in Canada increased from 7.5 per cent in 1989 to 11.4 per cent in 1993.[4] In this context, opposition to the free trade agreement rose steadily, peaking at 69 per cent in early 1992. At the same time, disagreement with the general idea that there should be free trade between Canada and the US began to outweigh agreement.

Under the Mulroney government, the Canada–US free trade agreement was enacted and then expanded to include Mexico. Clearly, the government had prevailed in political terms: its policies were being adopted. But at the end of its tenure, the PCs were voted out of office, having lost the support of the majority of the public on the free trade issue.

1994 to 2008: Prosperity without Peace

The subsequent period – which starts with the return of the Liberal Party to power in Canada in 1993 and runs until the onset of the 2008 financial crisis and the election of Democrat Barack Obama as president in 2008 – was marked by two profound shifts in public opinion.

The first of these shifts related to free trade (both in general and specifically with regard to NAFTA). Simply put, opposition to free trade began to melt away once the Progressive Conservative government that had championed it lost power (although that event in and of itself may not have been what caused the change). The first survey conducted after the 1993 election (in December 1993) found that 59 per cent agreed there should be free trade between Canada and the US – up 15 points from the previous survey four months earlier. Opinions on the free trade agreement specifically were more divided; even so, 46 per cent now favoured it, which was 11 points higher than in the previous survey. And this trend continued: the proportion in favour jumped a further 14 points over the next year, reaching 60 per cent in December 1994.

Opinions about NAFTA began to shift somewhat later than those for Canada–US free trade, but eventually the same trend took hold. Between 1994 and 1996, the percentage of Canadians agreeing that there should be free trade between Canada, the US, and Mexico jumped 20 points, from 46 to 66 per cent. By 2000, the proportion favouring free trade – now presented as trilateral and not just between Canada and the US – stood at 70 per cent. That same year, for the first time, Canadians were more likely to say that NAFTA had helped the Canadian economy than that it had hurt it.

In short, as the 1988 election and the recession of the early 1990s receded from memory, opinions on free trade in Canada became less divided. Initially, this change unfolded against a background of continuing positive feelings about the US itself. At the end of 1999, for instance, 72 per cent of Canadians said they had a positive opinion of the US – the same proportion as had held that view at the start of 1990s, and at the start of the 1980s. But shortly afterwards, the second profound shift in opinion that characterizes this period began to unfold.

The September 2001 terrorist attacks on the US had elicited feelings of empathy and solidarity from the Canadian public; in the aftermath of 9/11, in October 2001, the proportion of Canadians expressing a positive opinion of the US rose to 79 per cent. But one year later, it had fallen to 62 per cent – lower than at any previous time since the question was first asked in 1981 – and it continued to decline until it reached a low of 50 per cent in October 2005 (a remarkable 29-point drop in four years). Canadians with a favourable view of the US had

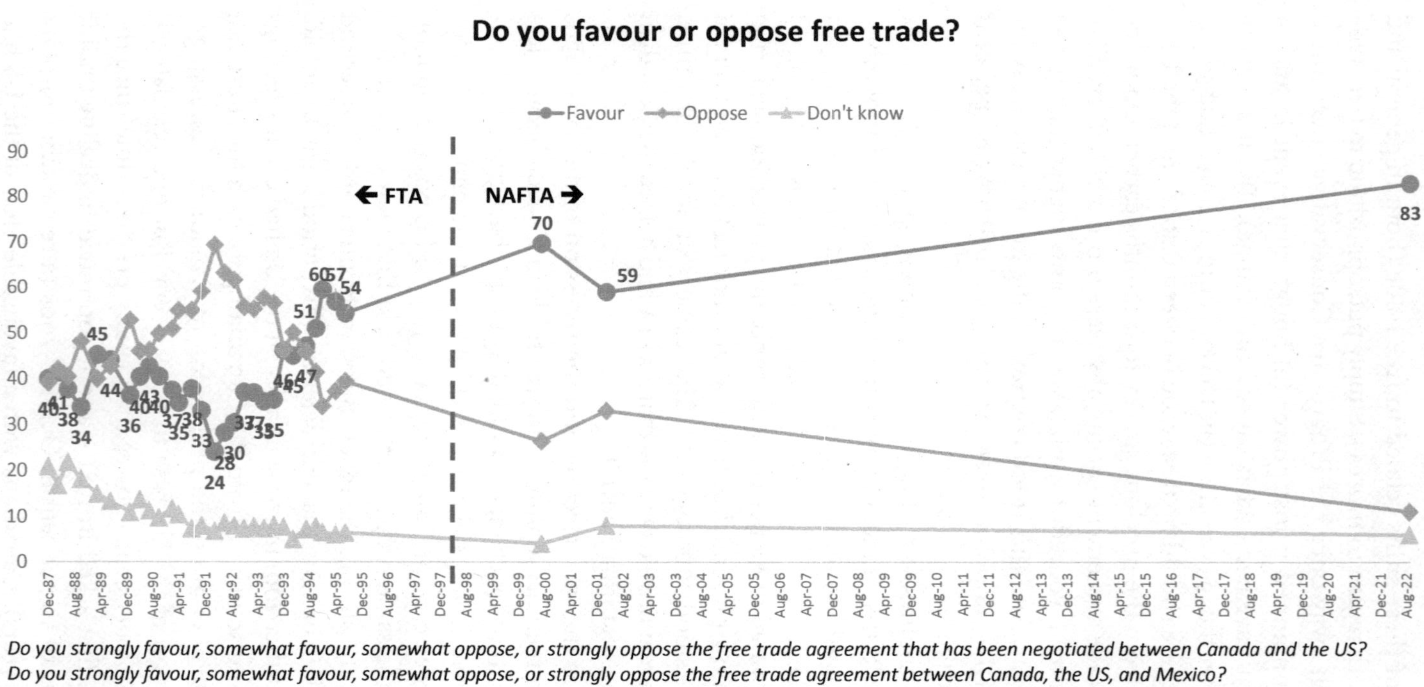

Figure 1.3 Support for the Canada–US free trade agreement and NAFTA, 1987–2022
Source: Environics, Focus Canada

previously outweighed those with an unfavourable view by a ratio of four to one; now the split was close to even.

Opinions of the US remained evenly divided for the rest of this period: just prior to the 2008 presidential election, 50 per cent viewed the US favourably, while 48 per cent had an unfavourable view.

What accounts for this shift? While the immediate reaction of Canadians to the 9/11 attacks was supportive, opinions shifted as the scope and scale of the US military response grew. In particular, Canadians grew increasingly opposed to US military intervention in Iraq (both hypothetically, as the Americans made the case for an invasion, and then once the invasion itself was launched). This is evident in answers to questions about Canada's potential involvement in such an intervention. Prior the invasion, disapproval of potential Canadian involvement grew from 52 per cent when the question was first asked in March 2002, to 65 per cent a year later in March 2003. A few months later, after the invasion was launched, 69 per cent of Canadians said the Liberal government led by Jean Chrétien had made the right decision by not participating. This proportion would grow to a striking 82 per cent by July 2004.

Not surprisingly, views of the US president also soured. In the summer of 2003, 62 per cent of Canadians expressed an unfavourable view of George W. Bush; two years later, this figure reached 79 per cent. This compares to only 24 per cent who had had an unfavourable opinion of George H.W. Bush when he was president twenty years earlier. Bush Jr's unfavourable rating among Canadians was also more than twice as high as the highest level reached by Ronald Reagan.[5]

A comparison of how Canadians viewed the 2000 and 2004 US presidential elections helps illustrate the extent of the shift in public opinion. The proportion of Canadians hoping that George W. Bush would win the election in 2004 was almost half what it had been in 2000 (15 per cent, compared to 28 per cent), while the proportion rooting for the Democratic Party candidate increased from 45 per cent (for Al Gore in 2000) to 70 per cent (for John Kerry in 2004). No less importantly, the proportion with no preference or opinion dropped from 27 per cent in 2000 to 13 per cent in 2004 (note that in the 1996 election year, 39 per cent of Canadians had expressed no preference or opinion about who they would prefer to win the US presidency, incumbent Democrat Bill Clinton or Republican challenger Bob Dole). The candidacy and then the

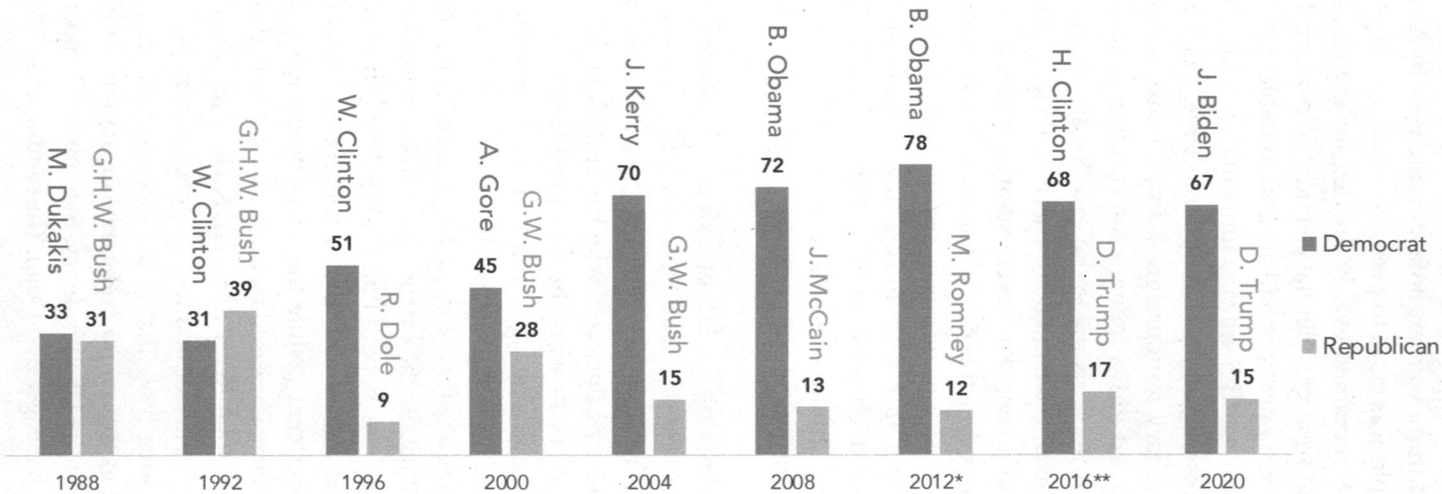

*2012 = Forum Research **2016 = Mainstreet Research

Figure 1.4 Canadians' preferred candidate for US president, 1988–2020
Source: Environics, Focus Canada, and the Environics Institute

presidency of George W. Bush, and the military actions his administration pursued, thus served to make Canadians not just more supportive of the Democratic Party candidate but also much less indifferent to US politics.

2009 to 2016: The Obama Interregnum

The sharp decline in favourable opinion of the US was immediately reversed following the election victory of Barack Obama in 2008. In January 2009, when Obama was inaugurated, 64 per cent of Canadians viewed the US favourably, up fourteen points from the previous summer. By October 2010, the favourable rating had reached 73 per cent – a level comparable to that which characterized the period prior to the Bush Jr presidency. Things were back to normal.

The end of the 2000s, however, were marked not only by a change in political leadership in the US but also the abrupt end of a period of sustained economic growth and the onset of a global financial crisis. The annual unemployment rate jumped from 6.2 per cent to 8.4 per cent between 2008 and 2009.[6] The proportion seeing either the economy or unemployment as the most important problem facing Canadians jumped from 17 per cent in the summer of 2008 to 61 per cent by the end of that year.

This is important to our story because of the way in which the previous recession, in the early 1990s, was linked to weakening support for free trade. Did the recession of 2008–09 have a similar impact on support for free trade?

Unfortunately, this is a question we cannot answer directly: after the period of growing support for free trade in general, and NAFTA specifically, in the early 2000s, key questions on the issue stopped being asked in the Focus Canada surveys. This includes the question about whether, in principle, there should be free trade between Canada, the US, and Mexico, and more specifically about whether one supported or opposed the NAFTA agreement. This, in itself, is a useful clue that the issue had become much less salient in political debates.[7] Surveys at the time did ask about trade but with a focus on the possibility of expanding Canada's international trade overall, not on NAFTA (in the autumn of 2008, as the economic situation began to worsen, 81 per cent of Canadians supported the proposal of a free trade deal with the European Union).

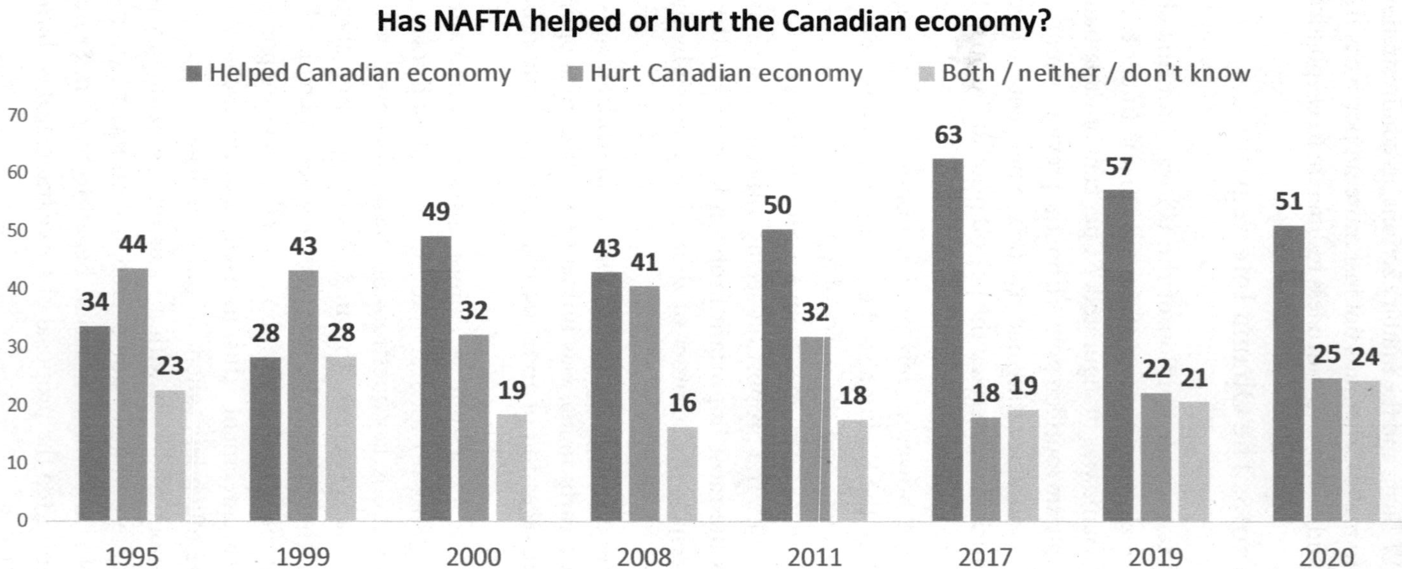

As you may know, Canada is part of NAFTA – a free trade agreement with the US and Mexico. On balance, do you think NAFTA has helped the Canadian economy or hurt the Canadian economy? [2020: As you may know, Canada is part of NAFTA – a free trade agreement with the US and Mexico that was recently renegotiated by all three countries...]

Figure 1.5 Has NAFTA helped or hurt the Canadian economy?
Source: Environics Institute

One question about NAFTA did continue to be asked during this period, however: whether, on balance, NAFTA has helped or hurt the Canadian economy. In mid-2008, views were evenly divided and slightly less positive than they had been in 2000. Nonetheless, the proportion saying the agreement had helped the Canadian economy was much higher than it had been in the 1990s, and by 2011 it had risen further, to 50 per cent (compared to 32 per cent who say the agreement had hurt the economy) – the highest positive assessment up to that point in time. This suggests that the economic downturn of the late 2000s was not accompanied by a souring of views on trade deals with the US in the way it had been fifteen or so years earlier.

2016 to the Present: America First!

On the morning of 9 November 2016, Canadians – like their American neighbours – woke up to an abruptly changed world. Donald Trump had won the US presidential election, defeating the Democratic Party candidate Hillary Rodham Clinton.

This development immediately affected not only how Canadians viewed the occupant of the White House but also how they viewed the US more generally. A few months after Trump's inauguration, only 44 per cent said that in general, they had a favourable view of the US – lower than the previous nadir reached during the presidency of George W. Bush. As the Trump presidency unfolded, the favourability rating continued to decline, reaching a stunning 29 per cent in September 2020 (a 44-point drop from the highest-ever rating under Obama reached twelve years earlier).

By that time, opinions in Canada were being shaped not only by Trump and his positions on familiar issues such free trade (he had insisted that NAFTA be renegotiated) but also by broader developments such as the COVID-19 pandemic and the conflicts over racism that followed the murder of George Floyd, a Black American, by white police officers in Minneapolis. "Trumpism" appeared increasingly as something that went beyond the political style of one leader, to describe a broader form of divisive politics in America that made it much more difficult to respond effectively to social crises, such as the pandemic and systemic racism.

In the wake of these events, it is notable that Canadians' opinions of the US did not rebound to the historical norm with the defeat of Trump at the end of 2020, the way they had with the defeat of George W. Bush. Opinion certainly did improve: in September 2021, with President Joe Biden now in office, 48 per cent of Canadians held a favourable view of the US, representing a gain of 19 points from the previous year's survey. But that survey – and the latest one, conducted in 2022 – nonetheless finds that Canadians are more or less evenly divided between those who view the US favourably and those who do not. This represents a dramatic shift from any previous period (since the early 1980s) when the US was led by a Democratic president. For some Canadians, views of the US may have been shaped by the Biden administration's decision in 2021 to cancel the Keystone XL Pipeline project, which would have transported Albertan oil to the US market (Environics Institute 2021). But the looming presence of Trump and his supporters in US politics, and the prospect that he will be the Republican candidate in the 2024 election, no doubt plays a part in explaining these results, as do other related developments such as the storming of the US Capitol on 6 January 2021 by angry Trump supporters and the more recent US Supreme Court decision opening the door to the recriminalization of abortion.

Strikingly, this "reset" in opinions about the US has had no impact whatsoever on views about free trade. In fact, while Canadian opinion about the US in general has become more divided, opinions about free trade (or NAFTA) have become less so. In the September 2022 survey, the question about support for NAFTA was asked again for the first time in twenty years. The results confirm that the pro-free-trade consensus has solidified, with 83 per cent of Canadians now favouring a free trade agreement between Canada, the US, and Mexico and only 11 per cent opposed. This is the strongest support ever registered in Canada for a free trade agreement since the Focus Canada surveys first began asking about the issue forty years ago.

The extent of these changes in opinion can be illustrated by looking directly at the relationship between the two questions – covering views on free trade and opinions on the US more generally – at two points in time when they were both asked in the same survey (1991 and 2022). In 1991, among those in favour of the free trade agreement, only 12 per cent had an unfavourable view of the US; in 2022, the figure was 44 per cent. Similarly, in 1991, among those with an unfavourable

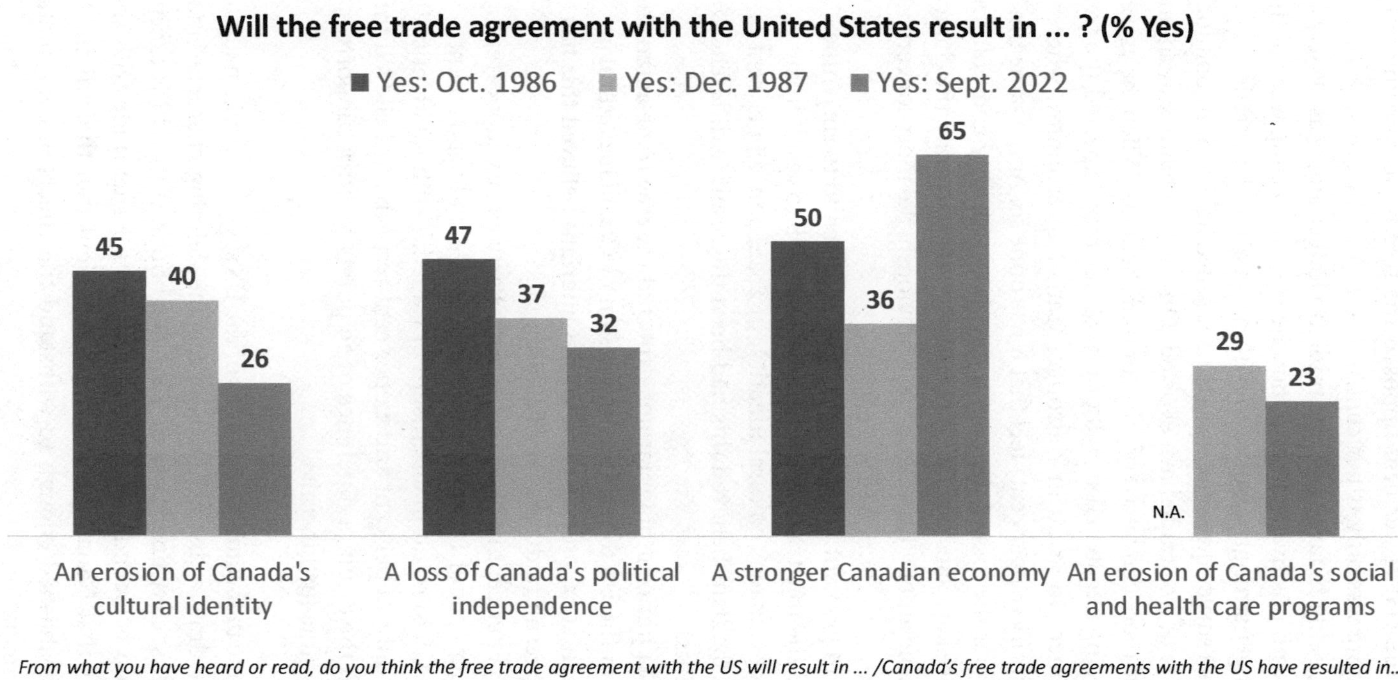

Figure 1.6 Impact of free trade on the economy and society
Source: Environics, Focus Canada, and the Environics Institute

opinion of the US, 71 per cent opposed the free trade agreement; in 2022, the figure was only 15 per cent.[8]

In short, being in favour of free trade no longer aligns as closely as it once did with positive feelings about the US; and feeling wary of the US is no longer strongly associated with angst about free trade.

Additional survey questions asked in 2022 shed light on how opinions on the merits of free trade have evolved. On the one hand, Canadians have become more convinced of the economic benefits. When the agreement was being negotiated in 1987, only 36 per cent expected the free trade agreement to result in a stronger Canadian economy, whereas today, a majority (62 per cent) feel that it has done so. At the same time, concerns about the loss of the country's cultural identity and political independence have subsided. With regard to cultural identity, the change is most notable among those who were previously the most concerned:

- In 1987, 46 per cent of Canadians aged eighteen to twenty-nine expected the free trade agreement with the US to result in an erosion of Canada's cultural identity; in 2022, only 28 per cent of young Canadians believed this had been the result (a difference of 18 points).
- In 1987, 44 per cent of Ontarians expected the free trade agreement with the US to result in an erosion of Canada's cultural identity; in 2022, only 26 per cent of Ontarians believed this has been the result (a difference of 18 points).
- In 1987, 53 per cent of New Democratic Party (NDP) supporters, and 46 per cent of Liberals, expected the free trade agreement with the US to result in an erosion of Canada's cultural identity; in 2022, only 24 per cent and 22 per cent respectively believed this had been the result (a difference of 29 points for NDP supporters, and 24 points for Liberals).

The decline in favourable opinions of the US suggests that Canadians increasingly draw a distinction between the defining characteristics of their own society and those of their neighbour. If the US is exceptional, so too is Canada. The rise in support for free trade with the US suggests that Canadians are more confident that their distinctiveness is established enough to withstand the effects of continental economic integration.

This sense of distinctiveness is no mere illusion. Our comparison of Canadian and American social values revealed that by the early 2000s, the two societies were on divergent rather than convergent paths (Adams 2003). This trend has continued uninterrupted over the first two decades of the twenty-first century (Adams 2023). Trump's presidency (and in particular Trump's frequently expressed racism and misogyny) may have epitomized some of the strongest value differences between Canadians and Americans (such as differences pertaining to attitudes toward authority or patriarchy) – but it is important again to properly position his period in office as only the most recent manifestation of, and not the beginning of, this divergence. Canada was moving in a different direction (toward less traditional and more post-material values) long before the outcome of the 2016 US presidential election became known. (This divergence, of course, does not mean that a small minority of Canadians might not be attracted to Trumpian discourse.)

A final update of public opinion data can bring some of these changes to light. On a range or social and public policy issues, the differences in attitudes between the two countries are stark. In 2022, a broad consensus exists within Canada on the question of abortion, with 82 per cent agreeing that "every woman who wants an abortion should be able to have one." In the US, while a majority (62 per cent) agrees, it is less one-sided – and 24 per cent strongly disagree (compared to only 9 per cent in Canada). Similarly, Canadians (62 per cent) are twice as likely as Americans (29 per cent) to agree that it should be illegal for civilians in their country to own handguns; Americans (52 per cent) are twice as likely as Canadians (25 per cent) to strongly disagree. Finally, Americans (29 per cent) are three times more likely than Canadians (9 per cent) to strongly disagree that "the government should reduce the income gap between the rich and the poor."

This is not to suggest that Canadians and Americans disagree on every issue, or that they do not share a wide range of values and preferences that reflect their common experiences of modern life in a developed, Western society. The point here is that, when Canadians express a sense of their distinctiveness, they do so with good reason and with the awareness that – contrary to expectations – this distinctiveness has not dissolved over time with the strengthening of trade links between the two counties.

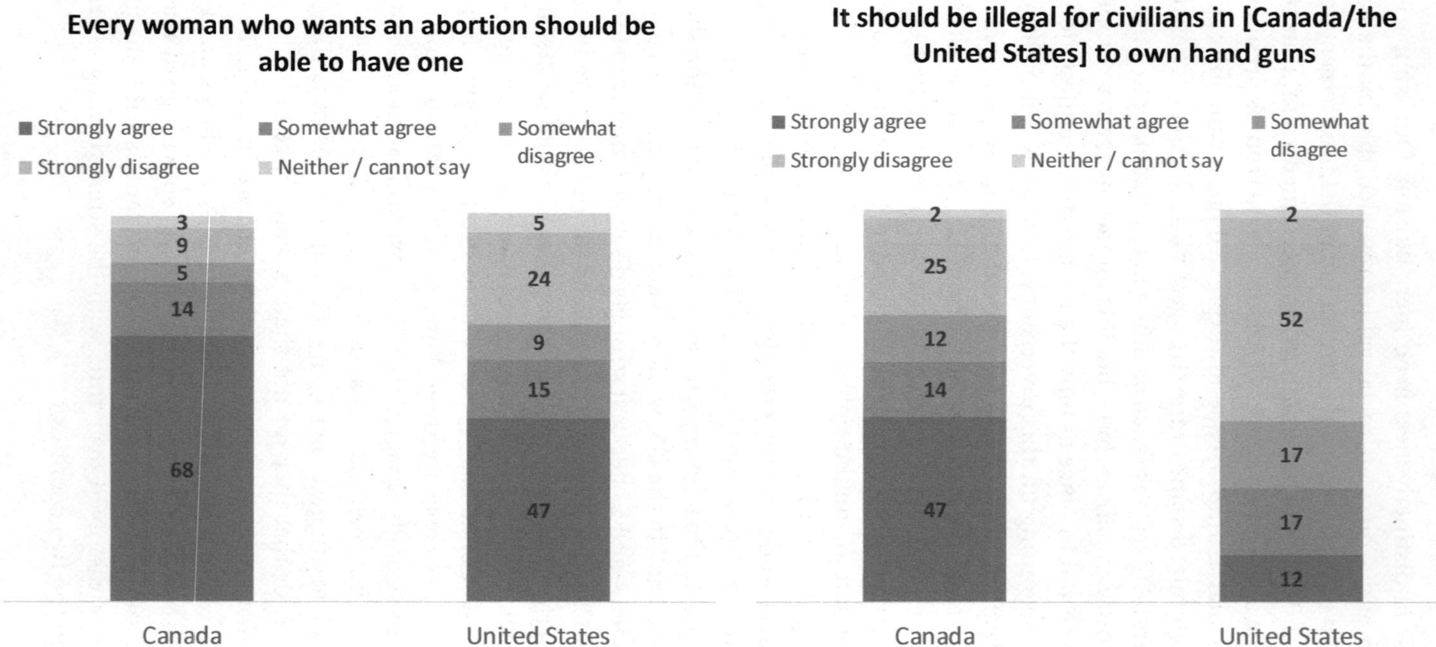

Figure 1.7 Canadian and American opinions on social issues (I)
Source: Environics Institute (2022)

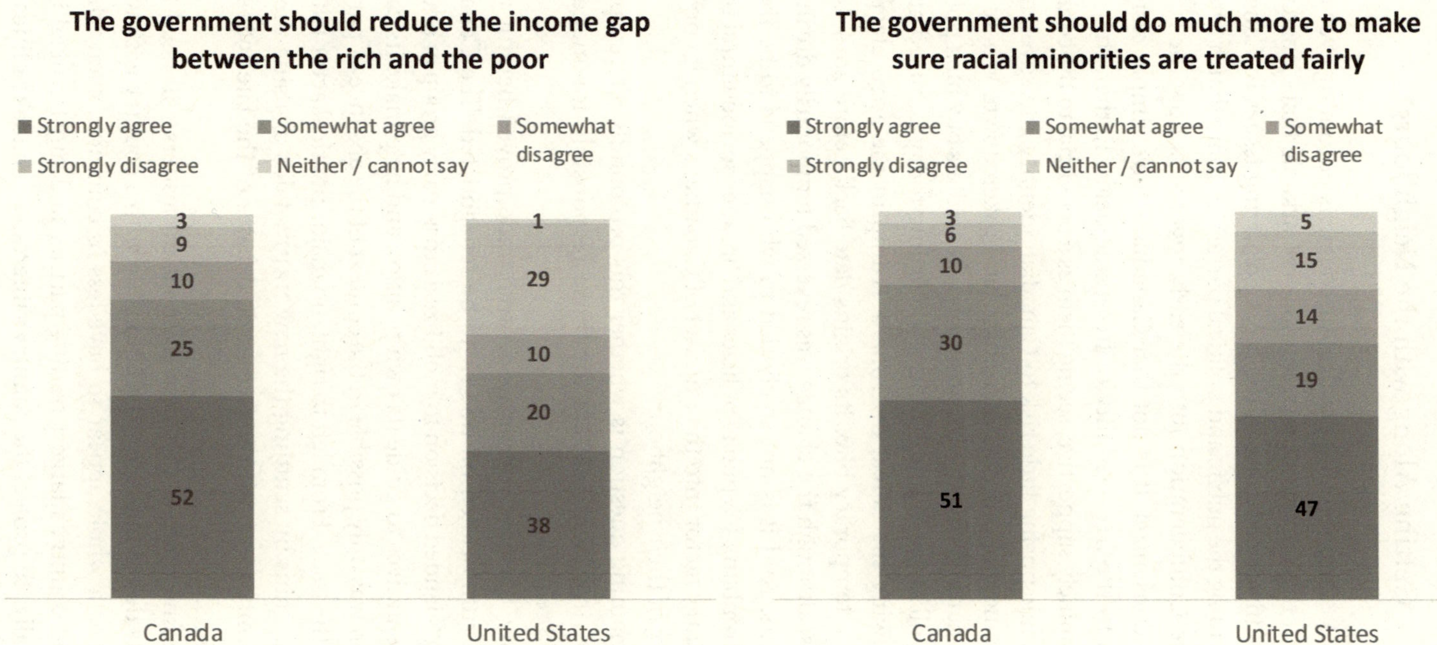

Figure 1.8 Canadian and American opinions on social issues (II)
Source: Environics Institute (2022)

Getting Along with the Neighbours

There is an assumption that political discourse is becoming ever more polarized. In this context, it is even more remarkable that Canada–US free trade – historically one of the most polarizing issues in Canadian politics, dividing the public and political parties for more than a century, from before Confederation into the early 1990s – is now the subject of a broad consensus. It is not that Canadians have simply resigned themselves to the irreversibility of free trade deals. Rather, they have become genuinely supportive, seeing them as a beneficial to the country's economy while posing little risk to Canadian identity and sovereignty.

At the same time, another consensus has broken down. Where once most Canadians viewed the US positively – regardless of which political party controlled the White House – the feeling today is mixed at best (even following the defeat of Donald Trump in the 2020 election). This is not a temporary blip. Its origins date back before 2016, to the early 2000s, although the change was reversed temporarily during the Obama years. And it is not solely tied to who happens to be the US president; troubling US public policies and broader sociocultural trends in that country factor into the mindset of Canadians when it comes to assessments of their neighbour.

The remaining question is whether this profoundly altered public opinion environment matters for those responsible for managing Canada–US relations.

Certainly, the new consensus on free trade proved helpful when President Trump called on NAFTA to be renegotiated. The Canadian government's lauded decision to mobilize a cross-party group of advisers and representatives to guide its own position and help make its case in Washington was only possible in the context of the absence of partisan divides on the issue. From left to right, no major political actor felt they could make gains by scuttling the new NAFTA talks or using them as an opportunity to revisit the free trade debates of the late 1980s and early 1990s.

At the same time, in this new era political leaders will need to be increasingly deft at managing a relationship with a country with whom Canadians as a whole appear to have less in common, even while it remains the country's largest trading partner and most crucial internationally ally. To protect the country's interests, Canada's political and business class must perpetually renew their efforts to maintain good relations with their US counterparts – to keep the border open and the trade flowing. But they must do so while American approaches to social issues (women's rights, the protection of racial minorities, immigration, gun control) diverge from their own. The trick will be to give offence to no one, neither to their American interlocutors nor to their supporters at home.

These changes no doubt shape what is meant by the "special" relationship. In pragmatic terms, the closeness of the two countries remains undeniable: geography and economics dictate that, from the Canadian perspective, there can be no substitute for the US as a trading partner, military ally, or travel destination. But as the two countries diverge culturally and politically, the specialness of the relationship starts to feel more transactional than fraternal.

For decades, the existential question facing Canadians in the context of Canada–US relations was this: what if the two countries end up with too much in common? Today, the question has become: what if they end up sharing too little?

Notes

1 All the public opinion data cited in this chapter are from the Environics Focus Canada surveys. Focus Canada was a syndicated survey conducted by Environics four or five times annually from 1976 to 2009. In 2010, the survey became an annual or semiannual study conducted on a not-for-profit basis by the Environics Institute for Survey Research. Due to space limitations, we cannot present details of all the results mentioned in the chapter. Details (including survey question wording, sample sizes, methodologies, and results) are available from the authors upon request.

2 In 1985, the survey question referred to "free trade with the United States and other countries"; in 1988, it referred specifically to the free trade agreement with the US.

3 These are not the only two events that may be relevant. This period was marked by a constitutional crisis and the introduction of a federal sales tax, both of which soured the public mood.

4 Unemployment rates obtained from Statistics Canada (2023).

5 The figure from Bush Sr is from early 1991; the highest unfavourable figure for Ronald Reagan was 38 per cent, registered in June 1988.

6 Unemployment rates obtained from Statistics Canada (2023).

7 It is also important to note that after 2009, the Focus Canada surveys became less frequent (annual or biannual rather than quarterly); after 2012, they also became shorter (focused on a smaller number of issues). These changes also affected how often certain questions were asked.

8 Recall that the 2022 survey question on the free trade agreement referred to NAFTA, whereas the 1991 question asked about the Canada–US free trade agreement.

References

Adams, Michael. 2003. *Fire and Ice: The United States, Canada, and the Myth of Converging Values*. Penguin Canada.

– 2023. "American Backlash, Canadian Compromise: 30 Years of Divergence." In *Canada and the United States: Differences That Count*, edited by David M. Thomas and Christopher Sands, 5th ed. Toronto: University of Toronto Press.

Environics Institute for Survey Research. 2018. *Canada's World Survey 2018: Final Report*. April. https://www.environicsinstitute.org/docs/default-source/project-documents/canada's-world-2018-survey/canada's-world-survey-2018---final-report.pdf?sfvrsn=17208306_2.

– 2021. *Attachment and Advantages: How Canadians View Their Country, Their Province and Their Neighbour.* https://www.environicsinstitute.org/projects/project-details/attachment-and-advantages-how-canadians-view-their-country-their-province-and-their-neighbour.

– 2022. "Public Opinion in Canada and the United States." *Focus Canada*. 9 December. https://www.environicsinstitute.org/projects/project-details/public-opinion-in-canada-and-the-united-states.

Litt, Paul. 2011–12. "The Fight of His Life: John Turner and the Free Trade Election." *Policy Options*, December–January, 70–7. https://policyoptions.irpp.org/wp-content/uploads/sites/2/assets/po/the-year-in-review/litt.pdf.

Statistics Canada. 2023. Table 14-10-0327-01 Labour Force Characteristics by Sex and Detailed Age Group, Annual. 6 January. doi: https://doi.org/10.25318/1410032701-eng.

2

Navigating the Canada–US Relationship

ROY NORTON

Canada began to "professionalize" its advocacy efforts in the US during the 1980s. Allan Gotlieb, Canadian ambassador to the US from 1981 to 1989, served during Prime Minister Pierre Trudeau's final term, when relations were at a "nadir" (Bromke and Nossal 1983/84, 346), as well as during Prime Minister Brian Mulroney's first term, when "the foundation of friendship that had been created and nurtured between Mulroney and [President Ronald] Reagan would pave the way for bilateral cooperation on multiple fronts" (Abelson 2022). Gotlieb's tenure marked the beginning of a transition from advocacy directed almost solely at the administration to targeting Congress and "influencers" across the country as well (Norton 2020). "Navigating the relationship" became a more sophisticated operation from that point forward.

Almost certainly, Canada has a wider range of issues ongoing with the US than any other country does (Allen 2022), necessitating that Canadian advocacy "be in a continuous campaign mode" (Robertson 2011, 140–1). On its face, Canada's capability to pursue its interests likely exceeds that of any other country advocating in the US. In addition to its prominently located embassy in Washington, DC, Canada maintains twelve consulates general and three trade offices across the US. The outreach efforts of the hundreds of staff employed at these facilities are supplemented, as of 2022, by fourteen honorary consuls (generally in states without a "permanent" Canadian operation): "In many places, we're the only foreign country present – or one of a very few. That does buy us good will" (Crosbie 2022). Only Mexico has more offices in the US, but many of them concentrate on consular matters, not advocacy.

Which is not to say that Canadian advocacy assets are always well coordinated. Or that that there's always consensus on priorities or on the degree to which each of our multiple interests should be pursued at any given moment. Or, for that matter, that we've figured out how best to maximize the odds of success.

This chapter will explore the extent to which a "special relationship" exists in the *advocacy context*. Key questions guiding that examination (to which the chapter will return in the concluding section) are the following:

- Do "practitioners" perceive the existence of a "special relationship"? If one exists, how does it – or how *would* it – affect our advocacy efforts?
- Do we stand a better chance of succeeding when relations between principals are warm? What happens when they're chilly?
- Does the "temperature" of the relationship affect access – in Washington, or beyond?
- How can we best equip ourselves to navigate US systems?

Previous works discussing the existence, nature, or extent of a Canada–US "special relationship" generally have not conducted their analysis through the prism of the implications for "advocacy." This chapter will do so, relying heavily on the perspectives of practitioners – those who, from the 1980s through the 2010s, were largely responsible for organizing or conducting Canada's advocacy operations in the US. The author was himself a practitioner (the second head of the embassy's Advocacy Secretariat and subsequently consul general in Detroit and Chicago). Twenty-one interviews were undertaken in preparation for writing this chapter: three with Canadian ambassadors (1989–93, 2000–5, 2016–19); six with former Canadian consuls general to US regions (Boston, New York, Atlanta, Miami, Los Angeles, and Seattle); four with assistant deputy ministers (ADMs) overseeing relations with the US (collectively covering the period from 2004 to 2013); the first and third heads of the Advocacy Secretariat at the Canadian embassy in Washington, DC; Alberta's senior representative in the US from 2007 to 2011 and Quebec's director general in the US from 2009 to 2012; the Canadian co-chair of the Canada–US Inter-Parliamentary Group (IPG) since 2014; the president of the Canadian Chamber of Commerce since 2007; the CEO of the Canadian American Business Council (CABC) since 2001; and the co-executive director of the Canadian Coalition on Acid Rain (CCAR) during the 1980s. Their observations will heavily guide this analysis.

What Is Advocacy? Who Does It?

A definition of advocacy commonly used at Global Affairs Canada (GAC) during Barack Obama's presidency was "the systematic exercise of influence on decision-makers and influencers to promote and defend Canada's interests" (GAC n.d., 1). "Public diplomacy," a less targeted activity, was understood as "promoting greater appreciation and understanding of not only our positions on specific issues, but our culture, society, values and institutions" (GAC n.d., 1).

Full-time advocacy is expensive. It's labour-intensive. It cannot easily be ramped up. In any event, GAC's mandate is global, while its resources are finite. The Canadian government periodically engages private sector legal expertise, but unlike many other countries, it rarely supplements its efforts in the US by hiring professional lobbyists (some interviewees feel that Canada loses out by not doing so). Several provinces (in 2022, Quebec, Alberta, and Ontario) maintain a US presence, principally to advocate for their own economic interests. For the most part, they collaborate closely with Government of Canada employees in the US (in fact, all of Alberta's and Ontario's US representatives co-locate in Canadian offices).

In addition to those paid by governments to advance national or provincial interests in the US on a *full-time* basis, there are hundreds – more likely thousands – of officials in federal or provincial bureaucracies *based in Canada* who periodically engage with their US federal or state counterparts to promote their government's objectives. A study by the Canadian School of Public Service cast light on the breadth and depth of cross-border official contacts (Heynen and Higginbotham 2004). These communication channels are part of the "hidden wiring" of Canada–US relations (Robertson 2021). This is not a recent phenomenon: both Charles Ritchie (ambassador from 1962 to 1966) and Allan Gotlieb described the pervasiveness of "functional contact" in their respective memoirs (Gotlieb 1991, 118; Ritchie 1983, 71). Michael Kergin, ambassador from 2000 to 2005, notes that "perhaps the one 'special' aspect of our relationship (as opposed to other countries, except Mexico) is how multilayered it is" (Kergin 2022).

Then there are the higher-profile contacts between *elected* officials at all levels of government in both countries. Add to these the contacts fostered and sustained by business communities and labour unions, and those developed by non-governmental organizations (NGOs) (e.g., representing farmers or environmentalists – in fact, all parts of civil society in both countries). Canadian and US academics and think tanks maintain extensive contacts. Hypothetically, a coordinated advocacy effort can energize broad swaths of decision-makers and influencers from the two countries' respective polities – all, in best-case scenarios, in pursuit of "win/win" solutions to shared challenges.

That, of course, is the ideal. Prior to Gotlieb's tour in Washington an all-out advocacy effort wouldn't have been contemplated. Instead, Canada relied on persuading US administrations that its "asks" should be accommodated. Hale (2011) describes five types of treatment from which Canada sometimes benefited; these included "exceptionalism" (special, often unique exceptions to US policies for Canada) and "exemptionalism" (exemptions to US policy accorded to Canada, usually on a reciprocal basis) (273–4). Traditional diplomacy, with its focus on the administration, periodically yielded desired exceptions and exemptions, although the "Nixon Shock" (15 August 1971) upended "the Canadian assumption that the US would always accord their country consideration when calculating the American interest" (Muirhead 2004, 439).

In the Olden Days …

Before the 1980s, formal advocacy by the ambassador and embassy staff overwhelmingly consisted of representations to the US Department of State, and sometimes to the White House directly. Gotlieb (1991) writes that he "was trained to deal with power that is readily identifiable, defined, and focused … to conduct diplomacy directly behind closed doors, where visibility, and the limelight were to be avoided, where confidentiality was the norm … where hierarchy and order prevailed in making rulings and decisions" (10).

A "special relationship," if it existed, was no guarantee of *access*, which has been described as "the adrenalin of diplomacy" (Burney 2005, 133). Ambassador Ritchie assumed his duties in 1962 when relations between President John F. Kennedy and Prime Minister John Diefenbaker were fraught. He observed that "for an embassy to be in disfavor with the White House at a time when the office of the President was at the height of its power and influence was a disconcerting experience. The word had swiftly percolated down into every department of the US Administration" (Ritchie 1983, 2). Gotlieb (1991) reported comparable difficulties: "When I arrived in Washington, access to the White House was very difficult for me to achieve because relations between the Reagan Administration and the [Trudeau] government … were not warm" (38). In a paradigm in which advocacy is focused on the US administration, "chilly" relations "at the top" can vaporize hopes of successfully advancing Canadian objectives in Washington, DC.

Transition to "New Diplomacy"

Never one to accept marginalization, Gotlieb (1991) conceived a "new diplomacy," one that required "different skills, techniques and attitudes" (vii). Christopher Sands (2020), director of the Canada Institute at Washington's Woodrow Wilson Center, credits him with transforming Canada's advocacy approach: "Allan Gotlieb redefined the role of Canada's ambassador in Washington, breaking new ground for a foreign representative by engaging directly with the US Congress and expanding Canadian outreach far beyond the White House and State Department to build relationships with executive branch departments, academic and think tank policy experts, and powerhouse lobbyists on K Street." Gotlieb concluded early on that Canada had to overcome its reluctance to lobby Congress directly (Gotlieb 1991, 22, 27–8). His thinking further evolved; by his 1989 departure, he was recommending a "multiplicity of instruments doctrine," in which Canadian businesspeople, provincial premiers, legislators, and others would become "active participants in the efforts to defend Canadian interests in the US" (117–18, 126–7).

This was precisely the direction Canada took as it fleshed out its "new diplomacy." In 2004 it established the embassy's Advocacy Secretariat. This initiative, like Gotlieb's pivot to Congress at a time when relations between Trudeau and Reagan were strained, coincided with another downward shift in relations "at the top." Frank McKenna, the former New Brunswick premier named by Prime Minister Paul Martin to become ambassador in 2005, said that the Canada–US relationship was as bad as it had been "for a long, long time … Something was broken, so there was a feeling that we had to try to fix it" (Sawler 2009, 77).

The "fix" took several forms. The Canadian government set aside its opposition to provinces establishing their own presence in Washington, DC (where, inevitably, they would advocate on bilateral irritants affecting their own economies). Alberta had been pressing Canada to house a provincial nominee at the embassy (a demand coincident with a US embargo on imports of Alberta beef due to an outbreak of bovine spongiform encephalopathy). With the "prohibition" on co-location lifted, Alberta quickly named as its "senior representative" a former member of the provincial cabinet. The fiction that Quebec's office in Washington, DC, existed purely to promote tourism was abandoned. Having already co-located representatives in consulates in New York and Los Angeles, and after taking considerable time to mull pluses and minuses, Ontario followed the lead of Alberta, placing a former cabinet minister in the embassy. Alberta then followed Ontario's lead and began placing representatives in select consulates.

One of the secretariat's mandates was to serve *all* provinces and territories, whether or not they had placed officials in the US. That extended to organizing visits by premiers and ministers to DC (consulates supported such visits in their own regions). Premiers – often several at once – took to attending (and sometimes presenting at) the annual February meetings of the National Governors Association (NGA) in Washington, DC. Valuable contacts were made, and these deepened over time, including at the annual summer meetings of the NGA (which rotate among the states), as well as at annual meetings of the various regional groupings of governors. A former consul general in Atlanta astutely observed that "governors are the farm teams," meaning that they frequently "ascended" to federal cabinet portfolios or won US Senate seats (Blais 2022).

The secretariat also supported dialogue between Canadian parliamentarians and their US counterparts (Norton 2009). While the IPG had existed since 1959, the frequency of visits to the US now accelerated. Today, parliamentary delegations travel between the two capitals and Canadian MPs and senators routinely attend national and regional meetings of the Council of State Governments (CSG) and the National Conference of State Legislatures (NCSL). Underscoring the distinct status of Canadian provinces in the US, most are dues-paying members of one – or more – of the NCSL, the CSG, and the regional CSG groupings that include border states. The Canadian co-chair of the

IPG since 2014 noted that US legislators work constructively with their Canadian counterparts "to find pragmatic solutions to challenges facing our two countries. They don't care about the state of relations 'at the top'" (MacDonald 2022).

The secretariat began generating state- and even district-level fact sheets and maps, which allowed Canadian advocates to illustrate to senators and representatives (and governors, state legislators, and influencers) the extent to which economic activities in their jurisdictions were linked to (perhaps even significantly depended upon) trade with Canada or employment-creating investment originating in Canada. Over time, these materials became increasingly sophisticated – for example, by including details of purchases made by Canadian-owned firms and the employment those firms generated. These materials soon became available online, enabling Canadian advocates to reveal, on iPads, our "Trade and Security Partnership Map," which included details about the number of Canadian visitors each year to their state or district, principal exports from their jurisdiction to Canada, border crossings, and other relevant "factoids." All of this was often buttressed by "success stories" provided by local business or agricultural leaders.

The data in those materials became more and more precise. This approach originated in a highly successful advocacy effort waged in the 1980s by the Canadian Coalition on Acid Rain. The CCAR developed "micro data" showing the amounts of acid-rain-causing emissions being generated in the districts of the representatives they were lobbying: "Gotlieb recommended this practice to Embassy staff. Enlightened self-interest was key; CCAR provided Members of Congress and staff data specifically relevant to them" (Hurley 2022). Learning is slow, however; it took two decades for Canada to equip itself, routinely, to present volumes of relevant data to US officeholders in their most compelling (and usable) forms.

Canada developed a high-profile campaign, CanadianAlly.com, to highlight its contributions to the War on Terror. It centred on Canada's (uncharacteristically) large military contribution and leadership role in Afghanistan. This focus helped overcome lingering perceptions among some US decision-makers that Canada had not taken seriously US concerns about security vulnerabilities post-9/11. It had the (desired) effect of eliding US irritation at Canada's decision *not* to join the Iraq "Coalition of the Willing" or to embrace the Ballistic Missile Defense

Program. The way those policies were announced by successive prime ministers was as damaging to the relationship as the decisions' substance, leading ADM Jon Allen to conclude: "Our PM should be wary about standing up in the House of Commons to announce a decision that won't be well-received in Washington without first informing the President" (Allen 2022).

Highlighting defence cooperation generally earns positive feedback from US lawmakers. Indeed, our militaries are highly integrated (something that distinguishes Canada from most US partners), "although this isn't something US elected officials are inherently aware of" (Crosbie 2022). CanadianAlly.com eventually ran its course, but the practice continues of Canadian diplomats being accompanied in their Hill calls by uniformed members of the Canadian military (dozens of whom are posted to the embassy).

Connect2Canada (C2C) – an online database/messaging vehicle for members of the Canadian diaspora in the US – was launched in 2005 on Canada Day. It endures, with approximately 65,000 "members" in 2022. That figure may sound high, but it represents only a small fraction of the (estimated) more than one million Canadians residing permanently in the US. There are myriad reasons why efforts to galvanize and mobilize expat Canadians in the US have fallen short of what other countries have achieved (see Horton and Norton 2020). Embassy outreach to C2C members can sometimes be counterproductive: "a singular obsession on one issue can result in recipients paying less attention on other issues that are also important to Canada" (Horton 2022). In this regard, Horton pointed to messaging related to the Keystone XL Pipeline (KXL) "dictated by Ottawa." Our consul general in Los Angeles at that time concurred: "KXL reminded our interlocutors poorly of Canada" (Fransen 2022). Bear in mind that California is home to the largest single concentration of Canadians in the US. Messaging aside, however, consuls general to Florida, Arizona, and Nevada emphasize the advocacy "advantage" associated with the very large numbers of Canadians visiting those states annually (more than three million to Florida [Leger 2022] and around 48 per cent of all foreign visitors to Las Vegas [Fransen 2022]). Governors and legislators understand that Canadians make a large contribution to their economies (Fransen 2022; Leger 2022).

During Michael Wilson's 2006–9 ambassadorship, the embassy began an annual blitz of senators and representatives in their Capitol Hill offices, conducted by the ambassador, senior embassy staff, and all Canadian consuls general in the US (who came to DC for the purpose). One of Wilson's innovations was to include in the visits Canadian business leaders whose firms had made considerable investments (with significant payrolls) in the legislators' districts and/or the US-based leaders of Canadian-owned facilities (usually Americans, who had instant "standing" with members of Congress) (Wilson 2022, 245). The ADM at GAC responsible for managing the Canada–US relationship at the time recalls how positively US interlocutors responded, during those meetings, to details about Canada's participation in Afghanistan (Feldman 2022). This "all hands on deck" outreach to Congress became a fixture of Canadian advocacy. The most recent iteration (at the time of writing) was the early December 2021 "diplomatic blitz" of Congress intended to make clear Canada's opposition to "Buy American" protectionism regarding electric vehicles (Norton 2022).

Structural Changes to Accommodate "New Diplomacy"

Coincident with the Advocacy Secretariat's creation, several "strategic networks" were formed to achieve greater advocacy coordination between consulates and the embassy. Their focus ranged from Great Lakes–related issues to border concerns, energy integration, the environment, innovation and, perhaps most creatively, the US Spanish-speaking population. This last "reflect[ed] an awareness that we were a 'black hole' among US Latinos" (Crosbie 2022). "HispaNet," it was hoped, would cause consulates to figure out together how best to connect with this increasingly powerful "community." The networks endured for several years before being disbanded as part of a government-wide budget-cutting exercise launched in 2012. In taking that decision, GAC satisfied (persuaded?) itself that patterns of advocacy coordination had become entrenched.

The Enhanced Representation Initiative (later renamed the North American Platform Program [NAPP]) was created in 2003 as a cost-controlling measure. GAC is mandated to advocate abroad on behalf of all departments – for example, Transport (see Norton 2012 and Savage

2015 regarding the treatment of one consulate's advocacy in support of "Canada's #1 national infrastructure priority"). Several departments/agencies – including Finance, Agriculture, Public Safety, and Export Development – post their own officers to the embassy and/or consulates. NAPP complemented GAC's activities, with departments like Agriculture and Innovation, Science and Economic Development, and several regional development agencies, providing significant ongoing funding. Others, like Environment and Natural Resources, slipped away after initially participating. The program has been judged a success at fostering advocacy coordination among its participants.

GAC and the embassy both "lead" in mandating advocacy efforts and in devising messaging and materials to be delivered. As the concept of "continuous campaigns" took firmer root, efforts to anticipate and "systematize" advocacy priorities and efforts were spawned (planning is a natural bureaucratic exercise). A perennial challenge, though, is that a great of advocacy is in response to US administration (or congressional) initiatives and cannot be anticipated. For example, during Obama's second term, it was logical for consulates (whose capabilities are limited) to "plan" for advocacy seeking a presidential permit for the KXL pipeline. And because a World Trade Organization (WTO) decision on Canada's challenge to the US's country of origin labelling (COOL) program was pending, consulates prepared a full-throated advocacy effort should the US reject (or refuse to implement) a decision favourable to Canada. But no consulate could have known during planning in 2011 that the Harper government, initially uninterested in joining the Trans-Pacific Partnership negotiations, would reverse itself, requiring that a lukewarm Obama administration be "persuaded" of the merits of having Canada at the table. Or, during the 2012 planning cycle, that a "no-holds-barred" national advocacy effort would be required after Washington Senators Maria Cantwell and Patty Murray, in 2013, introduced the Maritime Goods Movement Act (essentially a tax on ports competing with Seattle) – which would have devastated the Port of Vancouver (and ultimately died because it also would have hurt the ports of Los Angeles and Long Beach, who became key allies in Canada's efforts). The bottom line: due to capacity constraints, "best laid plans" for advancing Canadian interests sometimes must be abandoned (in favour of new priorities) or diluted (because there's an expectation at home – especially among political masters – that we must "do it all").

Doing it all, of course, comes at a cost; given resource limitations, odds are that on *no* issue will the Canadian effort be quite as thorough as imagined.

"Upping the Ante"

Gotlieb anticipated that Canada's case, whatever the issue, could be derailed if the country appeared to be "interfering in US domestic affairs" (Gotlieb 1991, 14, 37). In a sense, Prime Minister Stephen Harper proved his point (twice!) regarding the KXL pipeline. In a 2013 New York speech to the CABC, the Harper government "warned Canada would not 'take no for an answer'" (Bratt 2022, 175). Two years later, he said, "we have created overwhelming support for this project in the United States. Its adoption is inevitable" (Macdonald 2015). Beyond Harper himself, "the government sent Ministers to the US to chastise Americans and work the partisan divide. That got under the Administration's skin" (Robertson 2022).

Republicans controlled the House of Representatives in 2013 and both chambers in 2015. Overwhelmingly, they were "pro-KXL." However, the (required) presidential permit was an executive decision over which Congress had no authority. President Obama was under pressure from environmentalists (a key component of the Democratic coalition) to say "no." "Big Labor" is another important part of the Democratic coalition. But, as Canada's consul general in New York from 2011 to 2016 observed, "we don't come close to leveraging Canadian membership in cross-border unions" (from 2001 to 2019, the United Steelworkers Union was led by a Canadian, Leo Gerard) (Prato 2022). Ambassador Kergin (2022) is nuanced: "we must retain and develop relations with the party out of the White House while trying to avoid publicly challenging the Administration on politically sensitive policy issues."

Dissonance with US administrations wasn't invented by Harper. Diefenbaker, Lester Pearson, Pierre Trudeau, and Jean Chrétien all publicly criticized policies of contemporaneous presidents. And this did not end with Harper. Foreign Minister Chrystia Freeland spoke in Washington just days after the 2018 G7 summit in Canada ended in broadsides against Prime Minister Justin Trudeau by President Donald J. Trump and his senior staff. Her speech was interpreted as criticism of the Trump administration's approach to multilateralism. At a Washington conference in February 2022, Freeland's former cabinet colleague, Finance Minister Bill Morneau, described her remarks as having been "unhelpful." The constant seems to be that while such interventions may please select Canadian audiences, they often work against Canada's US agenda.

Of course, with the possible exception of Richard Nixon, no president before Trump so persistently and publicly disparaged his Canadian counterpart. And, as registered by pollsters, no president has ever been more unpopular among Canadians than Trump. Those two realities made it difficult for Trudeau to "turn the other cheek" in the face of Trump's provocations. Effectively, they also made it impossible for Canada to offer Trump a state visit. Which meant that one of the "tools" historically used by Canadian prime ministers to cement relations with the US (and advance Canadian objectives along the way) was off the table during Trump's presidency.

Which was especially unfortunate, given the "existential threat" Trump created for Canada (and Mexico) in April 2017 when he proposed withdrawing the US from the North American Free Trade Agreement (NAFTA). Efforts by Canada to salvage at least a "draw" from the ensuing negotiations took many forms, including "cultivation" by the Prime Minister's Office of Trump's son-in-law, Jared Kushner (Anderson 2020, 41; Panetta 2022). John Geddes observed a more concerted campaign at the "highest levels" than was the "norm": "Trudeau flooded the US zone with endless visits by top cabinet ministers, supportive provincial premiers, and squads of diplomats – all designed to cultivate a network of US business and political support for NAFTA that might pressure Trump." Geddes also noted the effort's bipartisanship, citing early 2018 remarks in DC by then Opposition Leader Andrew Scheer: "We're here to support our government's efforts in maintaining and protecting what we have in NAFTA. I believe it is important to send that signal to interests here in Washington" (Geddes 2018). The prime minister himself travelled extensively in the US during this period (including to New York City, Chicago, Texas, and California). In July 2017, just months after Trump's threat to "rip up" NAFTA, Trudeau attended the NGA summer meeting in Rhode Island (Stone and Morrow 2017). Former New Brunswick Premier David Alward, who served as consul general to New England (based in Boston) from 2015 to 2020, calls it his "proudest day" (as consul general): "The PM's speech connected the dots for Governors." Trudeau met individually with eight governors that day (Alward 2022).

In tandem with White House visits, Trudeau would call on congressional leaders. And in November 2019, he received House Ways and Means Committee Chair Richard Neal (D-MA) in Ottawa. This courting of well-placed Democratic legislators involved some risk: "[United States Trade Representative Robert] Lighthizer got cross with us; the Trump Administration made the point that we were interfering in their domestic affairs by playing with Democrats on labour and the environment" (Robertson 2022). David MacNaughton, Canada's ambassador at the time, acknowledged that "it's risky to cultivate enemies [of the administration]. [But] it's a calculation we had to make. On several of the major [US–Mexico–Canada Agreement/Canada–US–Mexico Agreement] issues where we made no progress, we were confident that Democrats [by virtue of their control of the US House] would hang tough. It's possible we would have gotten what we wanted through negotiations, but we would have had to give up a lot" (MacNaughton 2022).

Retaliation – or threats thereof – became "a thing" under the Harper and Trudeau governments. Harper–Obama relations were initially good: Obama made his first presidential visit abroad to Ottawa in February 2009; in response to the 2008 financial crisis and recession, the US, Canada, and Ontario were the three contributors to a multibillion-dollar fund to prevent General Motors and Chrysler from going under. The responsible ADM at the time noted, though, that "there were no discernible corollary benefits" (i.e., on other advocacy priorities) from Canadian/Ontario participation to save the auto firms (Feldman 2022). Proving her point, the massive stimulus package Obama presented to Congress included Buy American provisions prohibiting sourcing from Canada. The Canadian government had introduced its own stimulus package – which did *not* discriminate against procurement from the US. As part of the advocacy effort to change US legislation, Canada threatened to exclude US providers. The embassy and consulates mounted a pan-US campaign to have the restrictions repealed (Choquette-Levy and James 2011, 40–6). Eventually, after most of the Obama stimulus had been spent, a compromise was reached. One of its important features was that Canadian provinces, traditionally reluctant to accede to the WTO's Agreement on Government Procurement (which prohibited discrimination against other signatories to the agreement), were "cajoled" by the Canadian government into doing so (Hale 2011, 289), even though not all US states had bound themselves by signing the WTO agreement. This is another example – among several – of Canada equipping itself with "clean hands" (i.e., neutralizing US opposition) in pursuit of a major advocacy objective.

Country of origin labelling (COOL) is a recurring bilateral irritant (Hale 2011, 287). It resurfaced during Obama's second term, when Canada–US relations were viewed as at "the low ebb of the cycle" (Ibbitson 2014). Notwithstanding a WTO decision favouring Canada, the US administration determined to overtly discriminate against meat imports from Canada. The Harper government reacted by detailing $1 billion of the retaliatory tariffs it would impose on selected US exports to Canada. The extent to which these tariffs were targeted against "politically sensitive" sectors was path-breaking. Canadian representatives in the US were equipped with data that allowed them to call on individual legislators, as well as firms and business organizations in their districts, and quantify for them the local employment losses that could result from retaliatory tariffs. Support for Canada's position came from US meat processors, retailers, restaurateurs, and even the US Cattlemen's Association. Our consul general in Atlanta at the time notes that "some Members thanked me for coming and giving them a 'heads up.' Others were irate. But all were sensitized. We were threatening to target chicken exports with our tariffs. Generally, they don't raise beef – so COOL wasn't naturally 'their issue.' But we made it their issue – because they raise and export chicken. Many spoke up against the Administration's plans to proceed" (Blais 2022). The Obama administration backed down; Canada abandoned its threat to retaliate.

In June 2018, the Trump administration invoked section 232 of the Trade Expansion Act, imposing tariffs of 25 per cent on imports of Canadian steel and 10 per cent on imports of Canadian aluminum. Underscoring that even "when relations [with the Administration] are chilly, there are ways for us to get our point across," Ambassador MacNaughton notes that "we engaged actively on [section] 232 tariffs with the US military and intelligence communities, impressing on them how psychologically impactful it was on Canadians, effectively, to be declared a national security threat" (MacNaughton 2022). Having "practised" on COOL, Canada's government launched a consultative process to identify US imports that, if sanctioned, would cause greatest grief (including to members of Congress). This time, threats were insufficient, so Canada retaliated proportionately. In August 2019, after extensive negotiations (impacted by private sector and legislator pressures on both governments), the two countries repealed their tariffs and countermeasures and ended WTO litigation. "Peace" prevailed for only a year, however; in August 2020, the US reimposed a 10 per cent tariff on certain Canadian aluminum exports (again under section 232). Canada protested loudly, musing about retaliation. After one month, the US tariffs were withdrawn.

Then, in December 2021, with the "more friendly" Biden administration in office, Deputy Prime Minister Freeland and Trade Minister Mary Ng, responding to Buy American strictures in the Build Back Better Act that could have destroyed Canada's automotive industry, wrote to congressional leaders outlining actions Canada would take, including the possibility of retaliatory tariffs (Freeland and Ng 2021; Norton 2022). The bill appeared to die shortly thereafter, obviating need for retaliation. Rather remarkably, it resurfaced (and passed) in the summer of 2022 – but without the provisions Canada had found offensive.

Based on these four experiences over twelve years, initiated by Conservative and Liberal governments against Democratic and Republican administrations, one could conclude that retaliation (or threats thereof) against egregious US behaviour might be the most effective way for Canada to secure preferred policy outcomes. Scotty Greenwood, long-time CABC CEO, feels that in response to Trump's section 232 tariffs "it was important for Canada to mean it and do it." She feels that "an impression was made; it moved the needle" (Greenwood 2022).

This may have worked better in practice than "theory" projected. Ambassador Derek Burney (2005) wrote that "retaliation was always tempting but can be short-sighted" (152). Ambassador MacNaughton (2022) opines: "Retaliatory measures are a fine line to walk. We can't win a full trade war. The US is much more important to us than we are to them. We shouldn't threaten unless we're prepared to follow through. But it's potent when we invoke it. We must pick our targets well; not necessarily the highest value, but the most politically impactful."

Denis Stevens (2022), who served as consul general in Seattle, then as the embassy's deputy head of mission from 2013 to 2017, posits that "a true 'special relationship' would transcend raw interests." Its existence, conceivably, would make advocacy almost unnecessary. He went on to say, however, that "there's certainly no thumb on the scale because Canada is asking." Which may mean that from an advocacy perspective that there isn't a "special relationship." Or that there are different kinds – but each of such limited potency that tactics like retaliation have become essential elements in Canada's advocacy "toolbox."

Do "Practitioners" Perceive the Existence of a "Special Relationship" (or Relationships)?

The short answer: there's a divide. Colin Robertson (2022) insists that we have one "but it's not privileged." He adds, importantly, "we're generally seeking something from them." Denis Stevens (2022) echoes that thought: "Historically, I'm not sure Canada saw the 'special relationship' as a two-way street, one that conferred obligations as well as entitlements." John Prato, whose consulate in New York City houses Canadian security officials, a senior representative of Canada's Finance Department (liaising with Wall Street and US regulatory officials), and an officer of the Ontario government, and interacts extensively with Quebec's senior representative in the US (based in the city), perceives "different levels of special relationships" (Prato 2022). Alberta's senior representative contends that "the relationship is special – economically" (Mar 2022). A former embassy minister responsible for advocacy asserts "there is, but not because it's described as such by the Americans. It's a 'stealth' special relationship: people-to-people, all levels of government, especially important on the regulatory side" (Horton 2022). Quebec believes it has several "special relationships": "with New York, with New England Governors, with the Council of State Governments – Eastern Region, with Great Lakes/St. Lawrence Governors" (Parisella 2022).

Perhaps more relevant to this chapter's analysis is this question: If one exists, how does it – or how would it – affect our advocacy efforts? The views of Consul General Alward and Ambassador MacNaughton are representative: "It's counterproductive for us to fixate on a 'special relationship.' Doing so is an excuse not to invest resources to the extent we should, out of a belief that we don't have to" (Alward 2022). MacNaughton (2022) adds: "The sense that relations are special can induce complacency. This pertained under both Obama and Biden." Practitioners argue that Canada should conduct its advocacy with absolutely no assumption of special treatment.

If "specialness" is illusory (or transitory, or particularistic), what about "temperature"? Which leads to the following question:

Do We Stand a Better Chance of Succeeding When Relations between Principals Are Warm? What Happens When Relations Are Chilly?

The Mulroney era represents the "gold standard" for what is achievable when there's an exceptional personal relationship between heads of government. Burney (2005) writes that "Ronald Reagan did not know a lot about Canada, but his affection for Brian Mulroney provided channels to others in the administration who had both knowledge and interest in Canadian affairs" (105). The US icebreaker *Polar Sea*'s 1985 voyage through Canada's Northwest Passage (which Canada contended was a violation of its sovereignty) offers an example. A diplomatic solution was, improbably, reached in 1987; it endures (but was disparaged by the Trump administration). Gotlieb (1991) contends that "[President] Reagan had no ideological position on the matter. He [mandated his administration to negotiate an "understanding"] because the Canadian PM convinced him that he should do something to help him" (113–14). Robertson (2022) believes that "we wouldn't have gotten the 1988 Free Trade Agreement if Reagan hadn't had such high regard for Mulroney." Horton highlights the 1991 Air Quality Agreement (to significantly reduce levels of acid rain): "it would not have gone ahead [absent] the warm personal relationship between PM Mulroney and President G.H.W. Bush" (Horton 2022).

Burney reminds us that Canada also pursues geostrategic and multilateral agendas in Washington (i.e., that our interests extend beyond "bilateral" issues). He believes that the "special access" Canada enjoyed by virtue of Mulroney's relationships with Reagan and Bush "allowed us to play an outsized role – for example, on matters ranging from German reunification to the US agreeing to seek UN approval for the coalition effort to evict Iraq from Kuwait." He acknowledges, however, that "it was a unique time. There's less scope today for a middle power [to have such influence]" (Burney 2022).

There have been other occasions when warm relations seemed instrumental in yielding outcomes sought by Canada. President Bill Clinton's 1995 speech to Parliament that effectively opposed Quebec separation was deeply appreciated by Prime Minister Chrétien. It's hard to imagine that, had relations been "chilly," the president would have obliged our prime minister by "intervening" in what the US had always considered a

Canadian domestic debate (Jehl 1995). Indeed, ADM Allen believes that, notwithstanding the exceptional Mulroney–Bush relationship, "Bush would not have given a speech on the Quebec Referendum" (Allen 2022). It's worth underscoring, though, that while Clinton's speech involved a departure from US practice, it did not involve a "choice" in favour of Canada over a US domestic interest.

Long-time diplomat (now senator) Peter Boehm recalls the 2005 Summit of the Americas in Argentina, where "the US was having difficulties with [Venezuelan president Hugo] Chavez." Prime Minister Martin intervened, and "Bush clearly appreciated the help" (Boehm 2022). Senior trade negotiator Elaine Feldman, who succeeded Boehm as ADM, notes that Martin repeatedly pressed Bush for a resolution to the enduring bilateral softwood lumber dispute. It's her understanding that while US officials continued to cling to their long-held positions, "President Bush told those responsible within his administration to 'get it done' – indicating a disposition to oblige PM Martin" (Feldman 2022). The 2006 deal, which remained in effect until 2015, involved sacrifice on both sides; the administration sold it to US interests as ensuring market stability and predictability.

Warm personal relations *below* the level of prime minister–president can also be vitally important. For various reasons, the relationship between Jean Chrétien and George W. Bush was sometimes "chilly." That could have devastated Canadian interests after 9/11, given initial (and ongoing) impulses, including in Congress, to severely "tighten" access at border crossings with Canada. A major US response to 9/11 was the creation of the Department of Homeland Security. In January 2003, Bush named Pennsylvania's governor Tom Ridge to be its first director. Ridge came from Erie, Pennsylvania (on Lake Erie); he knew Canada very well. In January 2002, Canadian Foreign Minister John Manley had become deputy prime minister, with special responsibility for security (in response to 9/11). He was Ridge's Canadian interlocutor. As ADM Boehm put it, "the Ridge–Manley relationship was absolutely critical to our navigating the aftermath of 9/11" (Boehm 2022).

We learned from Ambassadors Ritchie and Gotlieb how a chilly relationship between principals can frustrate Canada's agenda with the US administration. Adele Hurley, co-leader of the NGO advancing Canada's acid rain abatement objectives during the 1980s, insists that the poor relations between the two federal governments during the Trudeau–Reagan years "did not have an impact on our advocacy *because our focus was on Congress*, and we heeded the words of Democratic Speaker Tip O'Neill: *all politics is local* [italics in original]" (Hurley 2022).

Several interviewees for this chapter noted that members of Congress are often "aware" of the state of relations "at the top." But all insisted that "awareness" does not necessarily shape a prevailing attitude toward Canada. One consideration during Hurley's time in DC was that for the entire 1981–93 period that Republicans controlled the Executive Branch, Democrats dominated the House. The "new diplomacy" developed by Gotlieb means that the administration is no longer the exclusive focus of Canadian attention, and this has increased possibilities of "overcoming" poor relations "at the top" by directing some outreach efforts elsewhere. As Ambassador Kergin (2022) put it, "when relations PM-to-President aren't the warmest, we need to double down on getting into Congress and out in the regions." Consul General Alward (2022) amplifies this point: "when things are chilly at the top, we compensate at lower levels" – referring to governors, state legislators, business leaders, and other "influencers" beyond Washington.

Does the "Temperature" of the Relationship Affect Access – in Washington, or Beyond?

Jon Allen, director general for North America (2001–4), and later minister (political) at the embassy from 2004 to 2006 (before becoming ADM in 2010), contends that "our decision on Iraq did implicate our 'Five Eyes' relationship: we were essentially shut out of relations at State and especially at the Pentagon." He believes that while "Senators and Representatives know whether relations at the top are warm, that won't necessarily change their opinion. Generally, we'll still get in the door." He adds that "depth of knowledge of the issues and the players is generally more important than the temperature of the relationship" (Allen 2022).

Ritchie, Gotlieb, and Burney have told us how access is vital to the conduct of diplomacy. Trump's presidency (2017–21) offers an interesting case study of the impacts on access of "chilliness at the top." Ambassador MacNaughton (2022) insists there "never were any problems with access, even during the 'blow ups.'"

Consul General Louise Blais doesn't disagree but emphasizes that Canada had to play catch-up after Trump's presidential victory: "The Embassy had zero interest in engaging with Trump in the lead-up to the November election. They were convinced Clinton would win; they had a lot of ins with the Clinton team" (Blais 2022). From her Atlanta base, Blais was able to facilitate some timely introductions to Trump's New York inner circle after his win. Consul General Prato (2022) reinforces the point: "we didn't send anyone to the Trump nomination convention" (a departure from the norm).

As senior officials were nominated and confirmed, an unusual dynamic evolved. Denis Stevens, embassy deputy head at the outset of Trump's presidency, sheds interesting light:

> They [the Trump team] would ask us for meetings. They wouldn't wait for advice from their own experts [a function of their distrust of career bureaucrats, which played to our advantage]. They treated us nicely even when Trump sent adversarial signals. Someone like [Defense Secretary James] Mattis was charming, but firm: "you've got to progress to two percent" [of GDP on defence spending, committed to by Canada at the 2014 NATO Summit]. We got time and kindness because we weren't threatening. Only the UK was regarded more positively; they were thought to be more serious; they better resourced their military, intelligence, foreign policy, and development policy. (Stevens 2022)

Away from Washington, Canada has enjoyed exceptional access to decision-makers and influencers, no matter who is in charge in Washington or, it would seem, the temperature of relations at the top. ADM Boehm (2022) captures the sentiment: "Outside DC, the focus is on getting things done. If we wanted to get messages to Senators or Representatives, it often was much easier to do that via the Consul General in their home city; those contacts are less transactional and are more about relations over time." Gary Mar (2022), Alberta's senior representative to the US (2007–11), adds: "I can't think of an example where people outside of DC are all that concerned about the relationship at the top. Governors don't take their marching orders from the President. He's important – but not essential. Governors are concerned about local issues."

Conclusion: How Best to Equip Ourselves to Successfully Navigate US Systems?

Snippets of responses to this question permeate this chapter. This concluding section will highlight some of those,– and illuminate others not yet addressed.

As Horton (2022) puts it, it should be abundantly clear "no longer is it sufficient for Canada to say: 'this is what we want.' At minimum, the overture must be cast as 'working together on this could yield outcomes beneficial to both of us.'"

Interviewees consistently emphasized that in developing and executing strategies, Canada must, as Alberta's Gary Mar (2022) put it, "frame our advocacy in terms emphasizing US interests." Ambassador MacNaughton (2022) adds that "at the end of the day, they will pursue what's in their interests – and they're better than we are at determining those interests." Consul General David Fransen (2022) underscores that "the moment you get into 'transactional conversation,' no matter the issue, it becomes a matter of self-interest. US national interest – not some other country's interest." ADM Allen (2022) highlights a dilemma, however: "On the 'values' versus 'interests' continuum, interests come out on top 99 per cent of the time. However, we tend to talk about the relationship largely in terms of values."

At the onset of the year of Trudeau–Obama "bromance," Dawson and Speer (2016) wrote that "warm personal relationships are not a sufficient condition for effective bilateral engagement" (2). Gotlieb (1991) assessed that while "the goodwill of the President is an asset of immense value to a foreign power," the answer to the question of whether there is a benefit to Canada in standing high in the White House "has many qualifications and nuances" (96–9). The bottom line: "warmth at the top" is good to have, but rarely (less and less, in fact) is it sufficient for Canada to achieve its objectives.

The CABC's Greenwood posits that Canada can "'have' one issue per cycle for priority resolution. If you want more, you've got to enhance your standing." She casts this in terms of "what are you doing for us"? In the current context, she references the overarching US priority on access to critical minerals (Greenwood 2022). For the Trump administration, that might have been significant increases in defence spending. Key for

Canada is to understand its responsibilities and how it might – if it so chooses – improve the inclination of US decision-makers to constructively address Canadian priorities.

There are historical antecedents. The Canada–US Auto Pact (fundamental to developing a viable central Canadian auto industry) was signed in January 1965. Robertson contends that "we wouldn't have gotten the Auto Pact had we not gone into Cyprus" (Canada dispatched peacekeepers there in 1964) (Robertson 2022). Charles Doran (1984) wrote of an "implicit bargain" underpinning the "special relationship": the US extended "certain trade and finance concessions, plus strategic security, in return for a relatively open investment and trading situation" (22). With the Foreign Investment Review Act (FIRA) and the National Energy Program (NEP), the Pierre Trudeau government breached that "bargain." Had those policies been sustained, the Mulroney "ask" – that the US enter into free trade agreement negotiations – likely would have been spurned. But, as Niskanen (1987) observed, "the Mulroney Government substantially reduced US' concerns about restrictions on US investment in Canada, by easing the discriminatory provisions of the FIRA and the NEP" (8). In other words, Canada's successes under Mulroney didn't derive just from a "warm personal relationship." Through actions to ameliorate concerns about certain Canadian policies, political capital was created in Washington that could be cashiered in pursuit of Canadian objectives.

Mulroney did the same on acid rain. He recalls, "We wouldn't let go of it. We got in the Americans' face about it at every bilateral meeting until they realized we were serious" (Mulroney 2012). But, as Hurley notes, "key to our credibility was open acknowledgement that we – Canada – were 50% of the problem, but due to prevailing winds, we were downward of the inbound 50% of the pollutants from the US" (Hurley 2022). A major opponent of US action was John Dingell (D-Michigan), the powerful chair of the House Committee on Energy and Commerce. Dingell characterized the INCO smokestack, in Sudbury, Ontario, as "the largest point source of SO2 in the Milky Way" (Hurley 2022). Americans had made clear that Canada needed to clean up its own backyard first (Gunn, Yan, and Smol 2021). Mulroney equipped himself to neutralize US opposition, telling Congress that "he had negotiated a 50% reduction in sulpher dioxide emissions with the seven provinces east of Saskatchewan," adding that "we ask nothing more than this from you" (Troy and MacDonald 2011). Underscoring the transitory nature of relationships, Ambassador Kergin (2022) notes that Dingell "was one of our best friends on border issues."

Many Canadians herald the Chrétien government for not joining the 2003 US-led Coalition of the Willing in Iraq. As several interviewees noted, however, Canada paid a political price in Washington for that refusal. Stein and Lang (2008) quote Sheila Copps (who served as Chrétien's deputy prime minister for almost four years) saying, "We made a deliberate decision to go to Afghanistan because we knew that very shortly down the road we would be asked to participate in a US-led invasion of Iraq which we did not want to do – and this was a neat way of squaring the problem of Canada–US relations" (67). Bratt points out that Harper twice secured House of Commons resolutions extending Canada's leadership role in Afghanistan. He asserts that "the main reason why Canada, under three Prime Ministers went to – and stayed in – Afghanistan was a desire to support our American Allies post-9/11" (Bratt 2022, 169).

"Clean hands" (e.g., Cyprus, FIRA/NEP, acid rain, provinces signing the WTO Procurement Agreement) and assisting the US (e.g., in the 1990–91 Gulf War, in Afghanistan, and at the 2005 Summit of the Americas; in addition to Canadian leadership of the now dormant Lima Group, founded in 2017, to galvanize hemispheric countries to bring a peaceful end to Venezuela's crisis), are predicates to successful Canadian advocacy in the US – if we wish to be taken seriously.

Gotlieb (1991) argued that every advocacy objective required "a specifically tailored micro-strategy" (53). For Burney (2005), it's about more than that: "In Washington, serious problems get serious attention; it's much harder to attract time and effort toward solutions for lesser problems, even if tangible US interests are at stake" (180). He laments that Canada "has largely dealt itself out of the substance necessary to have substantive conversations" (Burney 2022).

The CABC's Greenwood argues that "to be 'special,' the relationship needs to be backed up by something – and continuously reinforced. The question for Canadians always should be: 'what do we bring to the table?'" However, "there tends to be a focus on the narrative, not on solving problems" (Greenwood 2022).

Canadian Chamber of Commerce President Perrin Beatty served in senior capacities in Mulroney's cabinet (including as defence minister).

He's seen what a government's single-minded focus on securing Canada's objectives in the US looks like – and can achieve. He regrets that the "relationship has gone from strategic to transactional." Beatty firmly believes that "the role of supplicant won't work when the other side doesn't see how helping you is in its self-interest." He calls for Canada to "position (itself) as providing solutions to some of the major issues [global security, Chinese competition, energy pricing, critical minerals, etc.], as opposed to repeatedly begging for special treatment. Far more important than warm personal relationships, is the existence of a plan. Canada needs to position itself to Americans as a strategic partner" (Beatty 2022).

Ambassador MacNaughton (2022) believes that "Trump woke us up." If so, good – because Consul General Prato contends that "we have not managed this well for a long time; difficulties were growing before Trump." He adds that "it shouldn't matter to Canada whether we get three Trumps in a row. We have to adapt; we haven't looked at this strategically enough" (Prato 2022).

When Consul General Blais (2022) says "we're totally in reactive mode," she captures a sentiment expressed by many interviewees for this chapter. The word "episodic" came up periodically (to describe Canadian governments' willingness to invest in navigating US systems). Consul General Alward (2022) observes that "we need an existential threat to get our act together." Which underscores a challenge identified by ADM Feldman (2022): "if there was no particular crisis, it was tough sledding to keep attention in Ottawa on the relationship."

What's intriguing is that during the Mulroney/Gotlieb/Burney time, Canada wasn't in reactive mode, per se. Instead, there was a "strategic" agenda to advance interests (e.g., free trade, Arctic sovereignty, acid rain abatement) while retaining full scope to pursue an independent foreign policy where we disagreed with the US (e.g., on South Africa and Central America). To be sure, the US was a different place then compared to now. Except that we were beginning to target Congress, our array of advocacy tools and tactics didn't exist. They have since been put in place so that, with further buttressing, a serious agenda can be promoted in the US. Interviewees for this chapter generally agree that scope for successful navigation of US systems is *maximized* when a well-conceived, medium-term strategy guides robust and sophisticated outreach efforts.

References

Abelson, Donald E. 2022. "Brian Mulroney, Ronald Reagan, and the Politics of Friendship." *Mulroney Papers in Public Policy and Governance* no. 8 (May). https://www.mulroneyinstitute.ca/sites/mulroney/files/2022-05/MPPG%20No%208%20Abelson_web.pdf.

Allen, Jon. 2022. Interview by Roy Norton. 29 May.

Alward, David. 2022. Interview by Roy Norton. 5 July.

Anderson, Greg. 2020. "Trump's 'American System' and Canada." *American Review of Canadian Studies* 50, no. 1: 32–47.

Beatty, Perrin. 2022. Interview by Roy Norton. 2 June.

Blais, Louise. 2022. Interview by Roy Norton. 5 July.

Boehm, Peter. 2022. Interview by Roy Norton. 5 July.

Bratt, Duane. 2022. "Stephen Harper and the Politics of Canada–US Relations." In *Harper's World: The Politicization of Canadian Foreign Policy, 2006–2013*, edited by Peter McKenna, 165–88. Toronto: University of Toronto Press.

Bromke, Adam, and Kim Richard Nossal. 1983/84. "Tensions in Canada's Foreign Policy." *Foreign Affairs* 62, no. 2: 335–53.

Burney, Derek. 2005. *Getting It Done: A Memoir*. Montreal and Kingston: McGill-Queen's University Press.

– 2022. Interview by Roy Norton. 26 June 2022.

Choquette-Levy, Nicolas, and Patrick James. 2011. "Structural Realism and Transaction Costs in the US–Canadian Partnership." In *Forgotten Partnership Redux: Canada–US Relations in the 21st Century*, edited by Greg Anderson and Christopher Sands, 31–55. Amherst: Cambria Press.

Crosbie, Bill. 2022. Interview by Roy Norton. 18 June.

Dawson, Laura, and Sean Speer. 2016. *Commentary: Managing the Canada–US Relationship from the Honeymoon to the Long-Term*. From a Mandate for Change to A Plan to Govern Series no. 12 (March). Ottawa and Washington: Macdonald Laurier Institute and Wilson Center. https://www.macdonaldlaurier.ca/files/pdf/MLISpeerDawsonCanadaUS-03-16-webready.pdf.

Doran, Charles. 1984. *Forgotten Partnership: US–Canada Relations Today*. Baltimore: Johns Hopkins University Press.

Feldman, Elaine. 2022. Interview by Roy Norton. 22 June.

Fransen, David. 2022. Interview by Roy Norton. 13 June.

Freeland, Chrystia, and Mary Ng. 2021. Letter to US Congressional Leaders on the Build Back Better Act. 10 December. https://www.international.gc.ca/transparency-transparence/briefing-documents-information/

parliamentary-committee-comite-parlementaire/2022-02-07-ciit.aspx?lang=eng#a4_1.

GAC (Global Affairs Canada). n.d. "Advocacy and Public Diplomacy in the United States: Considerations." GAC internal working document.

Geddes, John. 2018. "How NAFTA Was Saved: The Bitter Fight and the Final Breakthrough." *Maclean's*, 1 October. https://www.macleans.ca/news/canada/how-nafta-was-saved-the-bitter-fight-and-last-minute-recovery.

Gotlieb, Allan. 1991. *I'll Be with You in a Minute Mr Ambassador: The Education of a Canadian Diplomat in Washington*. Toronto: University of Toronto Press.

Greenwood, Mary-Scott "Scotty." 2022. Interview by Roy Norton. 28 June.

Gunn, John, Norman Yan, and John Smol. 2021. "Lessons Learned from the Acid Rain Battles: Big Environmental Problems Can Be Solved." *Globe and Mail*, 18 March. https://www.theglobeandmail.com/canada/article-lessons-learned-from-the-acid-rain-battles-big-environmental-problems.

Hale, Geoffrey. 2011. "Nobody's Partner: Canada and Congress." In *Forgotten Partnership Redux: Canada–US Relations in the 21st Century*, edited by Greg Anderson and Christopher Sands, 269–301. Amherst: Cambria Press.

Heynen, Jeff, and John Higginbotham. 2004. *Advancing Canadian Interests in the United States: A Practical Guide for Canadian Public Officials*. Ottawa: Canada School of Public Service.

Horton, Deanna. 2022. Interview by Roy Norton. 6 June.

Horton, Deanna, and Roy Norton. 2020. "Canada's Eleventh Province; America's Eleventh City? Planet Canada and a Call to Action." 19 November. Washington, DC: Canada Institute, Wilson Center. https://www.wilsoncenter.org/article/canadas-eleventh-province-americas-eleventh-city-planet-canada-and-call-action.

Hurley, Adele. 2022. Interview by Roy Norton. 26 June.

Ibbitson, John. 2014. "A Deep Freeze in Canada–US Relations." Centre for International Governance Innovation. 21 November. https://www.cigionline.org/articles/deep-freeze-canada-us-relations.

Jehl, Douglas. 1995. "Clinton, in Talk to Canadians, Opposes Quebec Separation." *New York Times*, 24 February. https://www.nytimes.com/1995/02/24/world/clinton-in-talk-to-canadians-opposes-quebec-separation.html.

Kergin, Michael. 2022. Interview by Roy Norton. 7 June.

Leger, Louise. 2022. Interview by Roy Norton. 29 June.

MacDonald, Michael. 2022. Interview by Roy Norton. 30 June.

Macdonald, Neil. 2015. "The Myth of Canada's 'Special Relationship' with the US." *CBC News*, 29 September. https://www.cbc.ca/news/politics/canada-election-2015-neil-macdonald-munk-debate-1.3247934.

MacNaughton, David. 2022. Interview by Roy Norton. 21 June.

Mar, Gary. 2022. Interview by Roy Norton. 31 May.

Muirhead, Bruce. 2004. "From Special Relationship to Third Option: Canada, the US, and the Nixon Shock." *American Review of Canadian Studies* 34, no. 3: 439–62.

Mulroney, Brian. 2012. "Acid Rain: A Case Study in Canada–US Relations." *Policy Options,* 1 April. https://policyoptions.irpp.org/magazines/harpers-foreign-policy/acid-rain-a-case-study-in-canada-us-relations.

Niskanen, William. 1987. "Stumbling toward a US–Canada FTA." *CATO Institute Policy Analysis* no. 88 (June). https://www.cato.org/sites/cato.org/files/pubs/pdf/pa088.pdf.

Norton, Roy. 2009. "Canadian Advocacy in DC." *Canadian Parliamentary Review* (Autumn): 23–6. http://www.revparl.ca/32/3/32n3_09e_Norton.pdf.

– 2012. "'Get the Bridge': Real Life Diplomacy in Detroit." *bout de papier Magazine* 26, no. 3: 9–11.

– 2020. "Advancing Canada's Interests in the USA: A Practitioner's Take on How Allan Gotlieb Changed Advocacy Forever." 27 May. Washington, DC: Canada Institute, Wilson Center. https://www.wilsoncenter.org/article/advancing-canadas-interests-usa-practitioners-take-how-allan-gotlieb-changed-advocacy.

– 2022. "Canada Rolls the Dice and Engages Congress on Subsidies for Zero-Emission Vehicles." *The Hill Times,* 4 January. https://www.hilltimes.com/2022/01/04/canada-rolls-the-dice-and-engages-congress-on-subsidies-for-zero-emission-vehicles/336360.

Panetta, Alexander. 2022. "Jared Kushner Memoir Chronicles Frustrations of Negotiating Trade Deal with Canada." *CBC News,* 20 August. https://www.cbc.ca/news/world/kushner-book-usmca-cusma-1.6556647.

Parisella, John. 2022. Interview by Roy Norton. 23 June.

Prato, John. 2022. Interview by Roy Norton. 20 June.

Ritchie, Charles. 1983. *Storm Signals: More Undiplomatic Diaries, 1962–1971.* Toronto: Macmillan of Canada.

Robertson, Colin. 2011. "Partnership Lost or Partnership Gained?" In *Forgotten Partnership Redux: Canada–US Relations in the 21st Century,* edited by Greg Anderson and Christopher Sands, 127–47. Amherst: Cambria Press.

– 2021. "The Hidden Wiring of the Canada–US Relationship." *Policy Options,* 27 August. https://www.policymagazine.ca/the-hidden-wiring-of-the-canada-us-relationship.

– 2022. Interview by Roy Norton. 8 June.

Sands, Christopher. 2020. "The Canada Institute Mourns the Loss of Allan Gotlieb." Press release, 24 April. Washington, DC: The Wilson Center. https://www.wilsoncenter.org/article/press-release-canada-institute-mourns-loss-allan-gotlieb.

Savage, Luiza Ch. 2015. "Land of the Freeloaders: The Battle for a New Cross-Border Bridge: Inside Canada's Protracted Struggle to Build a Critical Cross-Border Bridge and How America Got Away without Paying a Penny." *Maclean's*, 21 May. https://www.macleans.ca/news/canada/land-of-the-freeloaders-the-battle-for-a-new-cross-border-bridge.

Sawler, Harvey. 2009. *Beyond Politics: Frank McKenna*. Vancouver: Douglas and McIntyre.

Stein, Janice Gross, and Eugene Lang. 2008. *The Unexpected War: Canada in Kandahar*. Toronto: Penguin Canada.

Stevens, Denis. 2022. Interview by Roy Norton. 29 June.

Stone, Laura, and Adrian Morrow. 2017. "NAFTA Negotiations Teeter as Trump Threatens to Rip Up Pact." *Globe and Mail*, 11 October. https://www.theglobeandmail.com/news/national/nafta-negotiations-teeter-as-trump-threatens-to-rip-up-pact/article36541968.

Troy, Gil, and L. Ian MacDonald. 2011. "US Presidents and Canadian Prime Ministers: Good Vibes, or Not." *Policy Options*, 1 March. https://policyoptions.irpp.org/fr/magazines/canada-us-conversations-and-relations/us-presidents-and-canadian-prime-ministers-good-vibes-or-not.

Wilson, Michael. 2022. *Something within Me: A Personal and Political Memoir*. Toronto: University of Toronto Press.

3

Polarity and the International Political System

Canada, the United States, and the Special Relationship

MICHAEL K. HAWES AND CHRISTOPHER J. KIRKEY

A persistent feature of scholarly inquiries dedicated to exploring the emergence and persistence of the so-called Canada–US special relationship is the identification of causal factors and hallmark features linked to and indeed anchored in a place-based North American framework. Historical, social, political, economic, security, environmental, and cultural explanations specific to North America have dominated the discourse explaining why Canada and the US developed such close ties. Colonial expansion; the critical role of migration; the intermingling of peoples; a shared commitment to liberal democratic values, ideas, institutions, and practices; the tremendous growth in cross-border economic and commercial engagement (signified most notably by the Auto Pact, the Canada–US Free Trade Agreement, the North American Free Trade Agreement [NAFTA], and the United States–Mexico–Canada Agreement [USMCA]); the protection of the continent against threats to its security (most visibly through the establishment, operationalization, and mission expansion of the North American Aerospace Defense Command); federal and subnational agreements and treaties to advance environmental protections; the pervasive presence and role of American culture; joint participation in amateur and professional sporting associations; the impact of integrated transportation networks; and the relationships between prime ministers and presidents have all been cited as crucial ingredients in facilitating a special relationship – a relationship long characterized by exceptionalism and exemptionalism. There is no question that these factors have all contributed to the vibrancy and long-term health of relations between Ottawa and Washington.

For all the emphasis placed on domestic factors as the overriding or exclusive variables underpinning the relationship, one element that has largely been absent in our understanding of Canada–US engagement is the prevailing distribution of power in the international political system. We argue here that the number of great powers and who they are is arguably the most crucial element in shaping and influencing the direction of relations between the two nations. Most observers date the emergence of the special relationship to the post-1945 period. There are clear reasons for this, reasons that are grounded in the power distribution of the international system. In the pre-1945 multipolar world, Canada – while remaining linked to the imperial parent of Great Britain – was beginning to slowly divest itself of its colonial ties. The US was a growing point of focus for Canada during this period but would not, until the conclusion of the Second World War, emerge as Canada's principal centre of international engagement. More than anything else, the emergence of a bipolar world and the prevailing conditions that characterized the global distribution of power and influence (with only two great powers) are what incentivized Canada and the US to seek a sustainable and highly collaborative partnership.

The international system underwent a profound structural shift in 1991. Specifically, the post–Second World War international political system that featured two great powers (which lasted from 1945 to 1991) changed to a system that, at least for now, can be considered unipolar (with the US currently recognized as the sole great power). This shift has significant implications for the direction of the Canada–US relationship.

Bipolarity and the Special Relationship

What did the emergence of a bipolar international structure, which persisted until the political dissolution of the Soviet Union in December 1991, involve? A bipolar world contains these features: only two preponderant powers are present in the international political system (in recent history, of course, the US and the Soviet Union); the competition between the great powers – military, territorial, economic, ideological, and so on – is truly global in scope and zero-sum in nature and fosters calculated timely foreign policy initiatives and responses; and clarity of threat for the great powers exists – each great power realizes that the other poses by far the single greatest threat to its survival, and the need to balance power against only one rival weakens the possibilities of miscalculation, "misperception, confusion and unpredictable interaction" in the formulation and exercise of foreign policy (Gaddis 1993, 35).[1] Each great power, in the absence of others, recognizes and subscribes to the need, first and foremost, to create and maintain defensive and deterrent capabilities to balance power. In short, each great power is self-reliant for its continued survival, as was the case during the Cold War era for the Soviet Union and the US. Alliances, such as the North Atlantic Treaty Organization (NATO) and the Warsaw Pact, "merely formalize a built-in polarity" and, given the significant differences in material resources among states, are helpful but add "relatively little" (Liska 1962, 161–7).[2] The structural realities of bipolarity provide the necessary condition for the great powers to effectively, as Gilpin put it, "control and regulate interactions within and between their respective spheres [East and West] of influence" – thus, allies in a bipolar configuration have minimal opportunity (i.e., they enjoy little bargaining leverage) to impact the foreign policy decisions of the great powers except on issues of tremendous need and in the absence of attractive alternative options (Gilpin 1981, 29). Under conditions of bipolarity, the defection of allies has no notable impact on the overall health of the prevailing balance of power. "Third parties," Waltz reminds us, "are not able to tilt the balance of power by withdrawing from one alliance and by joining the other" (Waltz 1979, 169). However, a bipolar distribution of capabilities is vulnerable to two potential critical developments: the inability or failure of one of the two great powers to maintain the balance, or the emergence of a new great power (Gilpin 1981, 90–1).

As the decidedly smaller, weaker, non-great power in the Canada–US relationship, the former was especially motivated to engage Washington across issues cooperatively. Canada recognized that the international political system was bipolar, and its overriding consideration was that the US played a key leadership role. As an ally of the US in a clearly defined and highly structured environment, Canada's manoeuvrability was circumscribed and constrained. Its bargaining power and influence (both with the US and on the management and direction of salient issues in international politics) was, at best, muted. Canada depended on the US for its continued existence in the nuclear age. It was, by many accounts, overwhelmingly a "consumer of security" (Waltz 1979, 70). Restraints on independent foreign policy initiatives that might challenge the core direction of US security and economic policies were both real and tangible. And in that environment, security trumped trade. Canada would have had considerably less influence and fewer opportunities – and the constraints would have been even more significant – had one of the two great powers not been the US. In short, Canada's long-standing positive relationship with the US, described by Wolfers as the "extreme of amity," directly served to prevent the country from being subjected to the full range of structural effects that smaller, less powerful states commonly experience in a bipolar environment (Wolfers 1962, 25–35). The height of Canada's leverage with the US came in the late 1940s and continued through the early 1960s. During this time, the principal means available for the Soviet Union to launch a devastating nuclear attack against the US was by long-range bomber aircraft, and such an attack would have had to overfly Canadian territory en route to the US (Jockel 1987). The US's need to access Canadian airspace and territory to counter this threat (there were no attractive military and geographic alternatives available to Washington) benefited Canada. However, it was necessary for Canada to demonstrate that it was able to contribute effectively to the defence of the West, if only selectively and on a small military/economic/human scale.

Unipolarity and the Special Relationship

The collapse of the Soviet Union ushered in an era of unipolarity, with the US being the sole great power in the international political system. The principal characteristics of a unipolar system include a global environment marked by the following central operating features: the presence of a discernible disproportionate imbalance of power and influence in the world, vested in a single state (in our current case, the US); the absence of imminent hostile state-level or national threats to the survival of the great power; an increase of influence for the sole great power and considerably less restraint on its international behaviour as the structural reality of the non–zero-sum unipolar environment is decidedly more permissive;[3] and an increase, given the absence of a counterweight with equal capabilities, in the scope and range of its involvement throughout the international political system.[4] Furthermore, the internal dynamics inherent in a unipolar structure facilitate a relaxed, permissive environment for all states – an environment that, for states with sufficient capabilities, contains the necessary framework (especially given the lessening of constraints and the increase in meaningful opportunities for external behaviour). As well, the great power can be expected to no longer favour or choose to follow the norms, rules, and conditions central to international institutions and multilateral arrangements, favouring instead what Walt (2009) calls "ad hoc coalitions of the willing," assembled "less for [the] capabilities they produce than for the appearance of legitimacy they convey" (117). The great power will opt to undertake balancing against potential national security threats principally through the independent development and deployment of internal capabilities (Brown 1994, 72). The purpose, roles, and scope of alliances all change in a unipolar world. One might predict the end of partnerships (given the removal of an external threat). Partnerships are prone to expand in terms of the number of participants and territorial reach, subject to ongoing efforts by the great power to redefine burden-sharing arrangements among its members. Operational commitments and financial responsibilities that serve political ends for the great power are more dispensable in a unipolar world than in a bipolar world. A key result is that states allied with the great power will see a marked decrease in bargaining power, and "leverage opportunities" will "dramatically decline" (Walt 2009, 220). A unipolar system prompts other states, independently or through vehicles such as alliances, to attempt to balance against the great power (96–7). Given the fluid distribution of capabilities over time in the international political system (principally driven by the uneven growth of states), unipolarity is unlikely to be a permanent condition. In Layne's (1993) words, it is a temporary "geopolitical interlude" (246).

What has the emergence of a unipolar world meant for the US–Canada special relationship? In general terms, the operational characteristics endemic to unipolarity have sharply lessened the incentives for both nations to deepen (let alone sustain) their existing collaborative partnership. First, let's consider what the disappearance of the Soviet Union and the advent of the unipolar structure of the international political system led by its principal ally, the US, has meant for Canada. How has it impacted Canada's approach toward navigating the special relationship?

First, and of critical importance to Canada, is the fact that the sole remaining great power is indeed the US. A unipolar system dominated by Russia – a Russia that continued to be viewed as a genuine threat – would have promoted very different policies and actions by Canada since 1991. As important as that is, the dynamics of the current system have further eroded Canada's ability to influence the US (which was not meaningful in the prior bipolar context), except on issues of the tremendous need for the former and in the absence of attractive alternatives. A critical constraint that is largely overlooked and little understood is Canada's ability in a unipolar world to convince the sole great power – a long-standing friend and ally – to make a meaningful commitment to pressing issues in the international political system. While specific issues that suggest or perhaps demand international action may be compelling to Canada, there is no guarantee of interest in Washington, let alone a commitment to US engagement. Indeed, the incentive system is such that the sole great power is likely to be less involved than it was during the bipolar era. In a bipolar environment, issues are examined and decisions are taken based on a competitive, zero-sum calculus; that dynamic, which is intimately responsible for shaping a wide range of foreign policy behaviours, no longer prevails in a unipolar world.

Under these circumstances, Canada is less likely to defer or unquestionably conform to the policies, interests, and rules advanced by the US. In a unipolar world, active participation in multilateral forums and international institutions is more important for Canada and much less critical for the US. In an environment in which consistently securing the involvement of the great power proves to be a challenge, Ottawa's foreign policy behaviour should be marked by increased efforts to ensure the regularized cooperation of other states in the international political system. Many states will similarly require coordinated, collaborative international action to achieve their foreign policy objectives. The structural logic of such a system suggests that Canada will continue participating in previously established international institutions and rules-based multilateral arrangements for two key reasons. First, it helps offset the external behaviour of the great power by modifying or constraining the use of unilateral US power (or trying to do so). And, second, it provides forums through which Canada can enhance its foreign policy autonomy and international standing.

Any review of Canada's engagement with the international community since 1991 can largely be ascribed to the permissive and flexible characteristics of the current unipolar distribution of capabilities in the system, even in the face of divergent foreign policy pursuits. Liberal governments led by Prime Ministers Jean Chrétien (1993–2013) and Paul Martin (2003–6) championed normative pursuits of distributive justice. This was characterized as following a human security agenda reliant on "soft power," with the Mine Ban Treaty (1997) and the International Criminal Court (1998), while rejecting participation in the security-oriented US-led coalition that instigated war against Iraq in 2003, as well as Washington's plans for ballistic missile defence. Conservative minority and majority governments under Prime Minister Stephen Harper (2006–15), by contrast, emphasized defence and security and participated in combat activities in Afghanistan and Libya. Harper offered unquestioning support to the Israeli state despite its indiscriminate bombing of Gaza, accelerated expansion of West Bank settlements, and air strikes on Lebanon that killed seven Canadians. He also strongly supported Ukraine after Russian incursions into Ukrainian territory. Prime Minister Justin Trudeau, elected in 2015, immediately identified his commitment to pursuing a foreign policy based on constructive engagement. In the fall of 2015, he went on a summit binge. The most dramatic divergence was at the climate change conference in December 2015, where Trudeau enthusiastically endorsed the Paris Accord. Later, in April 2018, he and Emmanuel Macron signed an agreement under which the two governments would work hand in hand to combat climate change – all of this at a time when the US administration was dialling back any commitments relating to climate change.

American foreign policy behaviour toward the international community, specifically Canada, directly reflects and is intensely shaped by our current unipolar condition. The change from a world populated by two great powers to only one means that every president since Bill Clinton has had considerable flexibility in defining and choosing which levers of national power to exercise to advance and secure America's principal interests selectively. It should therefore come as no surprise that an American president – openly determined to question and, at times, to refute the core guiding principles of US foreign policy, to challenge the multilateral institutions that have come to define the international system, to be skeptical of the international treaties that have underpinned Washington's international engagement since 1945, and for our purposes, be openly and repeatedly critical of the Canada–US special relationship – was elected in 2016. It was inevitable, from our perspective, that a post–Cold War president would, sooner rather than later, openly challenge this framework and call into question the need to continue the prevailing Canada–US partnership.

Simply put, the need for collaborative engagement and cooperation with Canada (and the world) is nowhere as acute for Washington. This has arguably been most visible during the recent presidency of Donald Trump. Trump's engagement with the international community – described as "a doctrine of disentanglement, retrenchment, and realignment" by Ross Douthat in the *New York Times* – sought to fundamentally redefine and reimagine what America's national interests were and how it engaged with the world (Douthat 2019). At its core, Trump's doctrine was driven by a political calculus grounded in the unwavering belief that American participation in the world was too expansive and expensive. Perhaps more to the point, the burden of leadership was not equitably shared. American commitments, most especially existing institutionalized multilateral trade and security arrangements (the UN, the WTO, the G7, NATO, and so on), were, as constituted, perceived as serving the needs of others and not the US. The costs associated with these operations were being disproportionately (i.e., unfairly) underwritten by the US, a practice that had to stop. US foreign policy under Trump was, above all else, characterized by an apparent effort to "correct" these imbalances. Regardless of the issue, the actor, or the institution, Trump pursued an unrelenting campaign of orchestrating significant change in America's foreign relations. International agreements that were viewed as counterproductive to US national interests, such as the Trans-Pacific Partnership (TPP), the Paris Climate Agreement, the Joint Comprehensive Plan of Action on Iran's nuclear activities, and the Intermediate-Range Nuclear Forces (INF) Treaty, were all dismissed, criticized, and then abandoned. The nations with which Trump attempted to reconfigure Washington's relationship are especially noteworthy; they include Russia, China, North Korea, Iran, Afghanistan, Pakistan, Cuba, Israel, Syria, Egypt, Yemen, Turkey, Britain, France, Germany, Mexico, and, interestingly, Canada.

Consistent with the fundamental realities of a unipolar world, the US, under Trump's leadership, sought to redefine America's relationship with Canada, heretofore its closest ally and nearest neighbour. Washington was now pursuing an America First strategy. In the post–Cold War world, this meant that exemptionalism and exceptionalism were clearly off the table, to a new level. Early in the Trump administration, there were pointed demands from the White House to revisit and "fix" unsatisfactory bilateral and multilateral trade and security arrangements, punctuated by unpredictable on again–off again negotiations. The principal targets of the disagreements were NAFTA and NATO.

NAFTA

A key element in Trump's platform had been his America First promise. He had pledged to restore greatness to America. He blamed, among other things, unfair trade practices, cheap foreign labour, and foreign-friendly trade agreements as the principal culprits in America's economic decline. He specifically targeted the nascent TPP and NAFTA. NAFTA was a frequent target of his during campaign rallies. During the Republican Party's presidential primaries, as the Republican presidential candidate, and ultimately as US president, he hammered home the message that NAFTA was the most flawed international agreement ever crafted between nations. "NAFTA," Trump declared during the first presidential debate on 26 September 2016, was the "single worst trade deal ever approved in this country" (BBC News 2016). Since coming into force in 1994, its terms and conditions had systematically worked to directly disadvantage and harm the US while enriching Canada and Mexico. The latter, owing to comparatively lower labour rates and less stringent environmental standards and enforcement, was disproportionately responsible for injuring the US manufacturing sector. Tens of thousands of working-class plant employees' jobs were being terminated as companies relocated their factories to Mexico. By benefiting from preferential access to the world's most significant single national market, Canada had developed healthy annual trade surpluses through its engagement with the US. In addition, Trump argued that Canadians embraced a protectionist approach in specific sectors – notably, dairy products – that effectively made American products too expensive in Canada or that blocked them completely. As president, Trump repeatedly demanded during press conferences, speeches, and Twitter statements that NAFTA be immediately renegotiated or scrapped.

Negotiations to revise NAFTA unfolded in 2017 and continued – punctuated by acrimonious exchanges between President Trump and Prime Minister Trudeau and senior officials in Washington and Ottawa – through September 2018. Significant progress was realized in late August 2018, when the US and Mexico announced that they had agreed to revise key elements of NAFTA. Apart from the specific points of agreement, the accord's most notable feature was Canada's absence. The Trump administration wanted to have outgoing Mexican president Enrique Peña Nieto sign the accord before his 1 December departure and then use the bilateral agreement as leverage against Canada – that is, it intended to compel Ottawa to be more flexible in the negotiations and agree to a trilateral arrangement. The question was now, "How would Canada respond?" The White House wasted no time in declaring that the US was willing to move on without Canada. "Ideally, we'll have the Canadians involved," indicated Robert Lighthizer, US trade representative and principal American negotiator. "If we don't … we will notify [Congress] that we have a bilateral deal that Canada [at a later date] is free to join" (Swanson, Rogers, and Rappeport 2018). President Trump was decidedly less equivocal in his remarks, taking to Twitter on 1 September to declare that "there is no political necessity to keep Canada in the new NAFTA deal. Canada will be out if we don't make a fair deal for the U.S. after decades of abuse" (Bowden 2018).

Periodic negotiating sessions between the US and Canada – led by principal negotiator Steve Verheul, Global Affairs Minister Chrystia Freeland, and Canadian ambassador to the US David MacNaughton – took place throughout September (Chase 2018). Seemingly little progress was made. With a negotiating deadline of 30 September looming, President Trump exerted stronger pressure on Canadian authorities to reach an accord quickly. On 26 September, the president noted that he had refused to meet with Prime Minister Trudeau during the UN General Assembly sessions in New York, as Canada was treating the US "very badly" (Rappeport and Tankersley 2018). Trump then unveiled a direct threat: if Canada were unprepared to move forward and conclude a new trilateral trade agreement expeditiously, the US would impose a new 25 per cent tax on any car exported into the US from Canada – a move that, if carried out, would cause severe economic hardship to the province of Ontario, "putting an estimated 250,000 people out of work" and negatively impacting the Canadian economy (Porter 2018).

"Frankly, we're thinking about taxing cars coming in from Canada," Trump stated during a news conference. "That's the mother lode. That's the big one. We're very unhappy with Canada's negotiations and negotiating style" (Porter 2018). Reaffirming his intense dislike of NAFTA and underscoring how the trilateral arrangement had worked to the disadvantage of the US, the president stated, "I don't like Nafta. I've never liked it. It's been terrible for the United States. It's been great for Canada and Mexico. We're very well along with Mexico. The relationship is very good. We'll see what happens with Canada. They're charging us 300 per cent tariffs on dairy. We can't allow that to happen" (Porter 2018). As for Canada, Prime Minister Trudeau reaffirmed Ottawa's continued interest in reaching a new trade accord: "we will keep working as long as it takes to get the deal right for Canada" (Porter 2018).

Seasoned observers were commenting by late September that President Trump's demands were having an increasingly corrosive effect on the ability of negotiators to reach a mutually satisfactory trade arrangement as well as on the overall US–Canada relationship. "Mr. Trump's apparent disdain for Canada and threats of economic warfare, seeming to relish in the prospect like some kind of neighbourhood bully has taken the bilateral relationship into a state of political disrepair" (Herman 2019). Canadian officials, recognizing that 75 per cent of the nation's trade was with the US, were concerned about the prospect of a 25 per cent tax on automobile exports. Moreover, believing that a revised NAFTA agreement was undoubtedly better than no continental free trade agreement, Ottawa worked feverishly worked to forge one. As John Ibbitson, opinion writer for the *Globe and Mail*, succinctly put it: "This country must have a trade agreement with the United States, even if it means making substantial concessions" (Ibbitson 2018a).

Following a weekend of intense videolink negotiations between Washington and Ottawa, the two parties agreed on revisions to NAFTA. The new agreement, the USMCA, was finalized on 30 September 2018. Among other provisions, the accord satisfied US concerns about access to the Canadian dairy market by allowing the US to sell a greater range and volume of products to Canada, and provided for a significant increase in pharmaceutical patents by Canada to ten years. It also revamped the rules governing auto manufacturing to generate automotive production jobs in the US. For Canada, the USMCA meant, above all else, that the threat had been averted "of a disastrous North American trade war" and that preferential access to the US marketplace would continue for an extended period (Clark 2018). Significantly, the revised trade deal included an updated Chapter 19, a protocol for resolving disputes among the three partner nations that engaged an independent body with the authority to issue binding decisions. The US had sought to remove that chapter; the Canadian negotiators had insisted that it be kept. Thus, Canada would still be able to challenge perceived punitive US tariffs without having to engage with the US judicial system. This satisfied "Mr. Trudeau's long-standing red line in the negotiations" (Fife and Morrow 2018). Canada also secured a commitment from the Trump administration to forgo imposing tariffs on Canadian automobile exports. Canada was, however, unable to convince the US to reverse course and rescind the steel and aluminum tariffs placed on Canada in June 2018 (Fife and Morrow 2018; Rappeport 2018).

Lighthizer and Freeland declared that the new trade arrangement "will give our workers, farmers, and businesses a high-standard trade agreement that will result in freer markets, fairer trade and robust economic growth in our region" (Rappeport 2018). The USMCA is a "great deal for all three countries," insisted President Trump on his Twitter account (Rappeport 2018). Speaking at a news conference in the White House Rose Garden, Trump underscored that "we had powerful tensions … it was just an unfair deal, whether it was Mexico or Canada, and now it's a fair deal for everybody. It's a much different deal. It's a brand-new deal. It's not NAFTA redone. Throughout the campaign, I promised to renegotiate NAFTA; today, we have kept that promise" (Landler and Rappeport 2018; Weiner 2018). "Like any important negotiation, we had to make compromises," Prime Minister Trudeau stated at the close of negotiations. "Today is a good day for Canada … We preserved the most important parts of NAFTA" (Rappeport 2018).

The USMCA was signed by President Trump, Prime Minister Trudeau, and President Peña Nieto at an international summit meeting in Buenos Aires on 30 November 2018. Meeting face-to-face for the first time since the negotiations concluded, Trump observed: "We worked hard on this agreement … It's been long and hard. We've taken a lot of barbs and a little abuse, and we got there. It's great for all of our countries" (Baker 2018).

NATO

From President Trump's perspective, Canada's engagement in and contributions to NATO were insufficient. Seeking to exert greater American power and influence, the US under Trump consistently advanced the position that Canada must "do more." From Washington's perspective, Ottawa needed to commit additional financial and material assets to the alliance. Canada, and indeed, many other members of NATO, have for more than fifty years been repeatedly prodded by Washington to increase their funding and material commitments to the alliance (note the efforts made during the presidency of George H.W. Bush). At no time, however, were those calls marked by the level of presidential vitriol displayed during the Trump presidency. The existing burden-sharing arrangement, in which the US carried a disproportionate share of the responsibilities and costs of operating NATO while other countries (including Canada) made less equitable contributions, was an ongoing source of frustration to the president. "We're the schmucks that are paying for the whole thing," Trump declared at a campaign rally. "Many countries owe us a tremendous amount of money for many years back, where they're delinquent, as far as I'm concerned, because the United States has had to pay for them" (Tasker 2018). "The president wants a strong NATO," insisted John Bolton, national security adviser to the president, in late June 2018 (Davis 2018). "When people talk about undermining the NATO alliance," Bolton noted, "you should look at those carrying out steps that make NATO less effective militarily" (Davis 2018).

Trump's public criticisms and the demands he levelled at Canada reached their peak in June and July 2018. As a calculated pre-emptive measure in advance of the July 2018 NATO summit in Brussels, he dispatched letters to the political leaders of several member countries, including Canada's Prime Minister Justin Trudeau, urging fellow alliance partners to do more for NATO. Noting the "growing frustration" in the US with the alliance's current commitments, Trump bluntly stated that the US expected "to see a strong recommitment by Canada to meet the goals to which we have all agreed in the defence investment pledge" (Davis 2018; Wright 2018). That pledge, agreed to at the 2014 Wales summit, committed all NATO signatories to spend 2 per cent of their GDP on national defence by 2024.[5] Canada's military spending was well known to NATO and President Trump going into the 2018 summit. Ottawa was clearly in the bottom third of NATO member spending (1.36 per cent of GDP in 2017, 1.23 per cent in 2018), only surpassing Belgium, the Czech Republic, Hungary, Italy, Luxembourg, Slovenia, and Spain (Berthiaume 2016, 2018; Tasker 2018). Trump's letter to Trudeau, while acknowledging the security commitments made by Canada, as part of NATO, in Afghanistan, Iraq, and Syria, nonetheless bluntly pointed out that those contributions "do not excuse any of us from our commitments to ensure that NATO has the resources it needs … Canada's continued defence spending of less than two per-cent undermines the alliance's security. It provides validation for other allies that are also not meeting their defence spending commitments" (Wright 2018).

Ottawa's immediate reaction was to underscore Canada's unwavering commitment to NATO, noting that the nation had a "long-standing role as an active contributor to global peace and security. Canada is proud to have contributed to every NATO operation since the alliance's founding more than six decades ago" (Wright 2018). Trump's call to action came only weeks after an acrimonious and generally unproductive G7 meeting held in Charlevoix, Quebec, after which Trump publicly labelled Prime Minister Trudeau as "dishonest and weak" (Austen 2018).

To more tangibly counter American calls for increased defence spending on NATO, Canada, "signalling that what countries do for NATO is what counts," took two related steps to enhance its operational commitment to the alliance. First, Canada – punctuated by a visit from Prime Minister Trudeau on the eve of the Brussels summit – renewed (for an additional four years, through 2023) and expanded its commitment (from 455 to 540 members of the Canadian forces) to lead NATO's multinational Enhanced Forward Presence (AFP) battlegroup in Latvia. At the summit, Ottawa committed to "assuming command of NATO's new, multinational non-combat training and capacity-building mission in Iraq in its first year of operation" (Leuprecht, Sokolsky, and Derow 2019, 168). This new operation engages some 250 Canadian Forces members and four Griffon helicopters.

The final communiqué to emerge from the Brussels Summit reaffirmed the NATO signatories' "commitment to all aspects of the Defence Investment Pledge … and to submit credible national plans on its implementation" (Pinkerton 2018). Sensitive to the criticisms levelled at Canada by President Trump, Prime Minister Trudeau, on leaving Brussels, underscored that ultimately, the more important metrics are always: "Are countries stepping up consistently with the capacities that NATO needs? Are we leading in different opportunities? Are we contributing the resources and demonstrating the commitment to the alliance that always needs to be there?" (Pinkerton 2018).

For Trump, the conclusion of the multilateral alliance meetings focused on two related points: his demand that NATO members move to meet the agreed 2 per cent defence spending threshold without delay and that the target be increased to 4 per cent (Austen 2018).

Conclusion: Recognizing the Impacts of Polarity on Foreign Policy Behaviour

This chapter has argued that any meaningful scholarly examination of the Canada–US relationship, whether it is unique or not, must recognize and incorporate the influence of the distribution of power in the international political system as a crucial variable. We are not suggesting that systemic forces are exclusively determinative or that we need only to employ a systems-level approach if we are to fully understand the foreign policies of states and hence the contours of the Canada–US relationship. It is essential to acknowledge and understand that explanations based on North American place-based forces – especially domestic politics, societal forces, and governmental processes (whether national or subnational) – are inevitably incomplete. Our chapter maintains that it is vital to factor in both the constraints and the opportunities imposed by the structural realities of the international system if we are to fully appreciate those forces responsible for shaping Canada–US relations. Waltz reminds us that structure in and of itself "does not by any means explain everything" (Waltz 1979, 174). It does, however, provide the necessary foundation to analyze the conduct of the special relationship.

The former bipolar world and the current unipolar one have discouraged Canada and the US from pursuing a closer, more collaborative relationship. While clear benchmarks of the special relationship that emerged in the post-1945 period today persist, the current international distribution of power no longer generates (nor does it facilitate) the same degree of substantial foreign policy incentives to induce significant collaborative engagement between Ottawa and Washington. Our examination of Washington's recent efforts to advance American influence vis-à-vis Canada suggests that the US has successfully redefined the Canada–US relationship by securing modest yet meaningful gains from Canada. These include concessions in the provisions of the USMCA and an enhanced operational commitment to the NATO alliance. These developments are consistent with the workings of the current unipolar international system, where the US can be expected to exert disproportionate power and influence. At the same time, states, including close allies such as Canada, must engage and positively respond to issues of significance to the great power.[6] The prevailing unipolar international system will continue to have a marked influence on the trajectory of the relationship between the US and Canada.

Notes

Portions of this chapter appeared in the introduction and first chapter of Michael K. Hawes and Christopher J. Kirkey (eds.), *Canadian Foreign Policy in a Unipolar World* (Toronto: Oxford University Press, 2017) and in our essay (chapter 10) in Timothy M. Gill (ed.), *The Future of U.S. Empire in the Americas: The Trump Administration and Beyond* (New York: Routledge, 2020).

1 Kenneth Waltz (1979) called this "the clarity of dangers" and "the uncertainty about who has to face them" (172).

2 As such, these multi-state alliances were not "indispensable" to the great powers of the USSR and the US (Liska 1962, 171). As Jervis (1997) puts it, "under bipolarity, superpowers do not need allies because they have sufficient resources" (112).

3 What Finnemore (2009) calls "minimal restraint."

4 It is referenced as "excessive expansion" by Jervis (2009, 197).

5 Regarding Canada's 2 per cent pledge and Canadian military procurement, see Charron and Fergusson (2022, 1–6).

6 With the election of Joe Biden as US president in 2020, both the US and Canada moved to re-establish a positive, decidedly less confrontational working relationship. See the joint statement issued on 23 February 2021, titled "A Roadmap for a Renewed US–Canada Partnership" (White House 2021).

References

Austen, Ian. 2018. "When It Comes to NATO, Do Actions Count More Than Budgets? The Canada Letter." *New York Times*, 13 July. http://www.nytimes.com/2018/07/13/when-it-comes-to-nato-do/actions-count/more.html.

Baker, Peter. 2018. "Trumps Signs New Trade Deal with Neighbours after Acrimonious Negotiations." *New York Times*, 30 November. http://www.nytimes.com/2018/11/30/world/americas/trump-Trudeau-Canada-mexico.html.

BBC News. 2016. "Nafta: Single Worst Deal Ever Approved." 27 September. http://www.bbc.com/news/av/world-us-Canada-37479586/nafta-single-worst-deal-ever-approved.

Berthiaume, Lee. 2016. "Canada among the Bottom Third of Allies in Defence Spending, NATO Says." *Ottawa Citizen*, 3 February. https://ottawacitizen.com/news/politics/canada-among-bottom-third-of-allies-in-defence-spending-nato-says.

– 2018. "Canada Expected to Spend Less on Defence in 2018 Than Last Year; NATO Report Says." *Global News*, 10 July. https://globalnews.ca/4324547/canada-spending-less-defence-nato-report.

Bowden, John. 2018. "Trump: No 'Political Necessity' to Keep Canada in NAFTA Deal." *The Hill*, 1 September. https://thehill.com/policy/finance/404696-trump-no-political-necessity-to-keep-canada-in-nafta-deal.

Brown, Seyom. 1994. *The Causes and Prevention of War.* New York: St Martin's Press.

Charron, Andrea, and Jim Fergusson. 2022. "2% or Else …?" *Quick Impact*, North American Arctic Defence and Security Network.

Chase, Steven. 2018. "Canada, US Take Time Out on Deadlocked NAFTA Talks." *Globe and Mail*, 12 September. https://www.theglobeandmail.com/business/international-business/article-freeland-touts-canada-us-relationship-as-nafta-talks-resume/.

Clark, Campbell. 2018. "Canada Made Concessions on NAFTA, But New Deal Avoids Major Damage to the Economy." *Globe and Mail*, 1 October. https://www.theglobeandmail.com/politics/article-Canada-made-concessions-on-NAFTA-but.html.

Davis, Julie Hirschfeld. 2018. "Trump Warns NATO Allies to Spend More on Defence, or Else." *New York Times*, 2 July. http://www.nytimes.com/2018/07/02/world/europe/trump-nato.html.

Douthat, Ross. 2019. "The Trump Doctrine." *New York Times*, 29 January. http://www.nytimes.com/2019/01/29/opinion/trump-doctrine-Venezuela-afghanistan.html.

Fife, Robert, and Adrian Morrow. 2018. "Canada, US Reach Tentative NAFTA Deal; Trump Approves Pact." *Globe and Mail*, 1 October. http://www.theglobeandmail.com/politics/article-Canada-us-reach-outline-of-NAFTA-deal.html.

Finnemore, Martha. 2009. "Legitimacy, Hypocrisy, and the Social Structure of Unipolarity: Why Being a Unipole Isn't All It's Cracked Up to Be." *World Politics* 61, no. 1: 58–85.

Gaddis, John Lewis. 1993. "The Long Peace: Elements of Stability in the Postwar International System." In *The Cold War and After: Prospects for Peace*, edited by Sean M. Lynn-Jones and Steven E. Miller, 1–44. Cambridge, MA: MIT Press.

Gilpin, Robert. 1981. *War and Change in World Politics*. Cambridge: Cambridge University Press.

Herman, Lawrence L. 2019. "Canada–US Relations Descend to New Lows." *Globe and Mail*, 28 September, B4.

Ibbitson, John. 2018a. "NAFTA Nightmare Is Quickly Becoming a Reality." *Globe and Mail*, 28 September, A5.

– 2018b. "Trudeau's New NAFTA Fight Isn't Over Yet." *Globe and Mail*, 3 December. https://www.theglobeandmail.com/politics/article-trudeaus-new-nafta-fight-isnt-over-yet.

Jervis, Robert. 1997. *System Effects: Complexity in Political and Social Life*. Princeton: Princeton University Press.

– 2009. "Unipolarity: A Structural Perspective." *World Politics* 61, no. 1: 188–213.

Jockel, Joseph T. 1987. *No Boundaries Upstairs: Canada, the United States, and the Origins of North American Air Defence, 1945–1958*. Vancouver: UBC Press.

Landler, Mark, and Alan Rappeport. 2018. "Trump Hails Revised NAFTA Trade Deal and Sets Up a Showdown with China." *New York Times*, 1 October. http://www.nytimes.com/2018/10/01/us/politics/nafta-deal-trump-Canada-mexico.html.

Layne, Christopher. 1993. "The Unipolar Illusion: Why New Great Powers Will Arise." In *The Cold War and After: Prospects for Peace*, edited by Sean M. Lynn-Jones and Steven E. Miller, 244–90. Cambridge, MA: MIT Press.

Liska, George. 1962. *Nations in Alliance: The Limits of Interdependence*. Baltimore: Johns Hopkins University Press.

Leuprecht, Christian, Joel Sokolsky, and Jayson Derow. 2019. "Paying It Forward: Canada's Renewed Commitment to NATO's Enhanced Forward Presence." *International Journal* 74, no. 1: 162–71.

Pinkerton, Charlie. 2018. "Canada Part of NATO Communique Affirming Defence Spending Target Despite PM's Remarks." *Politics*, 11 July. https://politics.ca/2018/07/11/canada-part-of-nato-communique-affirming-defence-spending-target-despite-pms-remarks.

Porter, Catherine. 2018. "For Canada, a Sigh of Relief More Than a Celebration in New NAFTA Deal." *New York Times*, 1 October. http://www.nytimes.com/2018/10/01/world/canada/trudeau-NAFTA-canada.html.

Rappeport, Alan. 2018. "US and Canada Reach Trade Deal to Salvage NAFTA." *New York Times*, 30 September. http://www.nytimes.com/2018/09/30/us/politics/us-Canada-NAFTA-deal-deadline.html.

Rappeport, Alan, and Jim Tankersley. 2018. "Trump Berates Canada and Threatens Car Tariffs as NAFTA Talks Falter." *New York Times*, 26 September. http://www.nytimes.com/2018/09/26/us/politics/trump-Canada-NAFTA-tariffs.html.

Swanson, Ana, Katie Rogers, and Alan Rappeport. 2018. "Trump Reaches Revised Trade Deal with Mexico, Threatening to Leave Out Canada." *New York Times*, 27 August. http://www.nytimes.com/2018/08/27/us/politics/us-Mexico-NAFTA-deal.html.

Tasker, John Paul. 2018. "Trump Says NATO Allies Like Canada Are 'Delinquent' on Military Spending. Is He Wrong?" *CBC*, 11 July. http://www.cbc.ca/news/politics/trump-nato-allies-delinquent-military-spending-1.4742588.

Waltz, Kenneth N. 1979. *Theory of International Politics.* Reading: Addison-Wesley.

White House. 2021. "A Roadmap for a Renewed US–Canada Partnership." 23 February. https://www.whitehouse.gov/briefing-room/statements-releases/2021/02/23/roadmap-for-a-renewed-u-s-canada-partnership.

Wolfers, Arnold. 1962. *Discord and Collaboration: Essays on International Politics.* Baltimore: Johns Hopkins University Press.

Wright, Theresa. 2018. "Trump Letter to Trudeau Expresses 'Growing Frustration' over Canada's Failure to Meet NATO Spending Commitments." *National Post*, 22 June. https://nationalpost.com/news/politics/trump-sends-letter-to-trudeau-calling-for-increase-in-nato-defence-spending.

PART TWO

What Is So Special about the Canada–US Relationship?

4

Trump's "American System" and Beyond

The Sources of Continuity in Contemporary Canada–US Trade Relations

GREG ANDERSON

Donald Trump's ascendancy to the White House generated a remarkable amount of commentary aimed at deciphering what would turn out to be one of the most chaotic and disruptive presidencies in American history. Commentaries and analyses published in advance of every new US administration ask important questions; stakeholders, both domestic and foreign, try to anticipate the scope of change in US policy and calibrate their responses. What world view will the new president bring to the Oval Office? What will be the specific preferences of the new president? How strongly will he maintain those preferences? Who will be the president's closest advisers? What are *their* world views? How likely will they be to influence presidential decision-making?

Answers to these questions were hard to come by where Donald Trump was concerned. His 2016 campaign for president was anything but "normal," and this stymied conventional analyses and answers to the above questions. Interestingly, Trump's political and policy inexperience made learning about who would surround him in the Oval Office even more important. The unwillingness of so many Republican "Never Trumpers" to associate themselves with the new president meant that a host of less familiar figures came to occupy – and quickly leave – key positions in the administration (Tenpas 2019).

That so few of these figures had any previous links to Mr Trump would result in an additional fluidity to policy-making as relationships with the president formed, hardened, or fell apart. As the Trump administration unfolded, uncertainty and instability became hallmarks of policy-making, all of this exacerbated by the president's inexperience with policy, his disinterest in details, and his evident preference for sowing confusion over creating coherence.

One important exception to all the chaos, incoherence, and frequent incompetence was the Trump administration's policy-making in international trade. A long list of critiques can be levelled at the Trump administration's trade policy, particularly if one is opposed to exploding the post-war status quo rather than addressing its weaknesses. Yet none of Trump's actions were particularly out of step with other periods in the history of US tariff policy, including vis-à-vis Canada. Moreover, although President Trump's policy instincts on most issues might not have had a long history, his instincts on trade (for good or for ill) were deep within his DNA.

In April 2017, Trump followed through on his belief that the North American Free Trade Agreement (NAFTA) was the "worst trade agreement ever negotiated" by the US and threatened to formally withdraw from it. Desperate diplomatic efforts in Ottawa and Mexico City transformed the threat into a hastily organized renegotiation, which consumed much of the next eighteen months. Then, in the middle of those negotiations (June 2018), the US expanded its tariffs on steel (25 per cent) and aluminum (10 per cent) so that they applied to a number of new countries, including Canada, Mexico, and the European Union (EU).

For many, Trump's actions were heart-stopping. However, the purpose of this chapter is to ask whether the trade policy actions of an extraordinary presidency toward Canada were in fact all that extraordinary. That the question is posed at all suggests that what we witnessed was not so extraordinary. Indeed, my argument is that Trump's actions were a departure from the status quo but not from historical norms in American trade politics.

Prosperous Interregna

Donald Trump's threat to formally withdraw from NAFTA early in his administration brought the US within a whisker of blowing up an agreement that had been a political football for nearly all its existence. Indeed, twenty-five years after its signing, NAFTA, rightly or wrongly, had come to symbolize nearly every ill associated with the spread of globalization. Two categories of politicians evolved during the period: those who pandered to voters by exaggerating the shortcomings of free trade, and those who did not want to talk about it at all. A prime example in the latter category was President Bill Clinton, who, after spending much of his early political capital in 1993 ensuring NAFTA's passage in the US Congress, seldom mentioned the agreement again during his two terms in office. Plenty of other politicians on the campaign trail pointed to NAFTA as a signature failure of US trade policy; then senator Barack Obama declared to distressed workers during the 2008 Ohio Democratic primary campaign that he had been "opposed to NAFTA from the start." Like many other presidents before him, Obama quickly changed his tune on trade because of the strategic utility that trade negotiations offer in America's overall post-war foreign policy (Destler 1997; Pastor 1982).

Trump, however, actually followed through on his campaign rhetoric on trade, which sent economic shock waves through capitals around the world, none stronger than in Ottawa and Mexico City, where market access to the US has been a matter of existential importance for decades. Tables 4.1 and 4.2 depict a number of stark realities confronting Canada and Mexico regarding their relative dependence on trade with the US.

RECIPROCITY REVISITED

Canada has long had a temperamental economic history with the US: at times it has been drawn to the American Colossus, at times it has feared its lure. A common reading of Canadian economic history highlights the struggle to knit together economically and politically a small population across a vast geography (Norrie, Owram, and Emery 2002). The Colossus as an obvious source of financing for that effort has loomed large.

President Trump's threat to withdraw from NAFTA in 2017 reminded historically minded Canadians of the day in 1866 when the US Congress cancelled the Reciprocity Treaty. After eight years of negotiations between the US and the British North American colonies, the Elgin–Marcy Reciprocity Treaty of 1854 had brought a period of free trade covering all natural resources and agricultural products. Popular history about Reciprocity is that it brought significant economic benefits to pre-Confederation Canada, particularly after the Civil War disrupted supplies

Table 4.1 NAFTA asymmetries

	1975	1987	1994	2000	2012	2015	2016	2017	2018	2019	2020
Canada GDP (in US$ billions)	$170	$420	$560	$770	$1,780	$1,550	$1,528	$1,649	$1,722	$1,741.5	$1,643
% of North American GDP	9	7.9	7.0	6.5	9.3	7.5	7.15	7.4	7.3	7.1	6.9
Exports + imports as % GDP	47	53	67	85	63	65.4	52.5	52.4	53.5	52.3	48.9
Mexico GDP (in US$ billions)	$88	$140	$420	$581	$1,178	$1,144	$1,078	$1,159	$1,222	$1,269	$1,076
% of North American GDP	4.7	2.6	5.9	5.2	6.1.	5.5	5.05	5.2	5.2	5.2	4.5
Exports + imports as % GDP	17	33	38	64	66	72.9	71.6	72.6	75.85	73.1	75.35
United States GDP (in US$ billions)	$1,600	$4,700	$7,017	$9,764	$16,240	$17,946	$18,745	$19,543	$20,612	$21,433	$20,937
% of North American GDP	86	89.3	87.7	88.2	84.5	86.9	87.8	87.4	87.5	87.7	88.5
Exports + imports as % GDP	16	19	22	26	29	28.1	19.7	20.2	20.75	19.6	18.3

Source: World Bank (n.d.)

Table 4.2 NAFTA export partners 2020 (rank order and percentage of total)

	Canada	Mexico	United States
Exports to	United States (73.25) China (4.86) UK (3.83)	United States (79.24) Canada (2.67) China (1.87)	Canada (17.83) Mexico (14.87) China (8.72) Japan (4.48)
Imports from	United States (48.84) China (14.09) Mexico (5.52)	United States (43.92) China (19.19) S. Korea (3.84) Japan (3.63)	China (19.01) Mexico (13.01) Canada (11.48) Japan (5.09) Germany (4.88)

Source: World Bank, World Integrated Trade Solution

from the US South (Haynes 1892; Masters 1963, 1969; Saunders 1936). Scholars have subsequently challenged that view (Officer and Smith 1968), but the impression that Reciprocity was a boon to Canada has lingered.

The mid-nineteenth-century diplomatic language transmitting the Americans' intent to withdraw from Reciprocity could not have been more different from Donald Trump's brand of bombast. Indeed, in communicating the joint resolution withdrawing from the 1854 treaty, Charles Francis Adams, US envoy to Great Britain at the time, said, "I have the honor further to inform you that I am directed to notify Her Majesty's Government that, as it is consistent no longer for the interests of the United States to continue this Treaty in force, it will terminate and be of no further effect, as provided by the terms of the instrument, at the expiration of twelve months from the date of reception by your Lordship of this notice"[1] (Great Britain Foreign Office 1866a). The sentiment in the US Congress was that Reciprocity had become one-sided and was not in America's interests; Great Britain protested with evidence that the agreement was working for both parties (Great Britain Foreign Office 1866b).[2] No one quite said it was the "worst agreement ever negotiated," but Reciprocity was done.

LONGING FOR RECIPROCITY

Canadians' frustration over the cancellation of the Reciprocity Treaty would linger for decades. Indeed, over the next 120 years, Canadian politicians regularly flirted with concluding new preferences arrangements with the American Colossus. In 1891, Canada's Liberal government, led by Wilfrid Laurier, had as part of its election platform the pursuit of free trade with the US. That year's federal election pitted Laurier's promotion of free trade against the continuation of incumbent Prime Minister John A. Macdonald's "National Policy" program of protection and high tariffs (Dales 1979; Forster 1979; Phillips 1979). The Liberals were soundly defeated that year but did not shelve the idea of free trade. Laurier's Liberals did form the government in 1896, winning three more mandates in 1900, 1904, and 1908. However, by December 1908, the Laurier government had entered the final stages of quiet negotiations with the Americans over a new free trade deal. As frustrated as many Canadians had become with the effects of National Policy measures, Parliament was stunned to learn of the completed reciprocity deal when it was announced by Finance Minister William Fielding in January 1911 (Granatstein and Stuart 1997).

The secrecy of the deal fuelled anti-American sentiment, which helped scuttle both the deal and Laurier's bid for a fifth consecutive term in the 1911 federal election. Canada once again flirted with some form of reciprocity in 1947 at a time of balance-of-payments challenges created by post-war economic disruptions. Negotiations once again reached an advanced stage before the Canadians withdrew for fear of nationalist political ramifications at home (Hart 1989). In 1965, Canadian proponents of reciprocity finally got a partial victory with the conclusion of the Auto Pact, which freed virtually all trade in autos and auto parts and significantly simulated the cross-border integration of that sector (Anastakis 2000, 2001).

However, any good feelings around reciprocity in auto manufacturing took a significant blow with the so-called Nixon Shocks of August 1971, when President Nixon imposed wage and price controls, initiated the demise of the post-war system of fixed exchange rates, and imposed an import surcharge of 10 per cent, all in an effort to stave off the deterioration of the US balance of payments (Gray 2007; Irwin 2013). Despite Ottawa's best efforts, the "special relationship" the two countries had developed in the post-war period was not enough to win Canada's exemption from the surcharge. Moreover, the Nixon Shocks pushed Canadian officials to think more seriously about moving the country away from such heavy dependence on the US market (Muirhead 2004).

In the 150 years between Reciprocity and NAFTA, the US lurched toward periods of economic nationalism that on occasion sideswiped Canada. In response, Canada routinely sought arrangements with the

US that would shield the Canadian economy from as many of the vagaries of US economic nationalism as possible.

In the late 1980s, Canadian efforts seemed to be rewarded in the form of a comprehensive free trade agreement with Washington complete with several dispute settlement mechanisms designed to rein in the arbitrary power of the Colossus. In 1990, Mexico City's proposal for free trade of its own with Washington soon morphed into a trilateral free-trade zone binding all three countries to dispute settlement (i.e., the NAFTA agreement); this promised the long-term market-access security the two smaller North American powers had long sought. Indeed, except for festering disputes like softwood lumber and the transformative effects on borders brought about by the 9/11 terrorist attacks, bilateral trade relations since the 1980s have been undeniably smooth (Anderson 2006; Macrory 2002).

Free trade became a political hot potato, especially in the US, where NAFTA provided fodder for scoring populist political points and inspired threats to renegotiate the agreement's terms. Still, NAFTA withstood twenty-five years of bluster from politicians about the evils of trade liberalization. That is, until Donald Trump came along.

Contending Over Commerce

Donald Trump's instincts on US trade policy were deeply rooted in a history of contending over trade that dates back to the very first ancient seafaring traders. As Irwin's masterful history of the intellectual origins of free trade so vividly depicts, foreigners arriving on domestic shores with exotic goods have always elicited suspicion from local populations (Irwin 1996, 1–25). Moreover, the default toward suspicion has made it easy for various local stakeholders to argue against the admission of foreign goods, regardless of their quality or price or the ease of acquiring them. At times, the threat posed by exotic foreign goods has been to "public morals," that is, the new products might somehow lead to the erosion of civic life, undercut local customs, and become the thin end of the wedge driving toward the eventual destruction of the community. More typical, however, has been the shamelessly commercial argument that local politicians so often make for preventing the onshoring of foreign goods: those goods would crowd out and destroy local industry.

Of course, the xenophobia embedded in this line of reasoning around protection can all too readily descend into forms of ethnocentrism and racism. For evidence of Trump's fealty to these time-honoured trade policy tropes, one need only revisit his June 2015 announcement that he was running for president, an announcement that assigned blame for a host of America's economic challenges to a conflation of poorly negotiated and enforced immigration and trade policies (*Time* 2015). However, Trump's instincts on economic policy were hardly novel. And Trump was remarkably consistent in his views on America's financial dealings with foreigners, right down to the rhetoric he used. In a 1987 interview with Larry King on CNN, Trump was already tapping into the rhetoric he would revisit when running for president in 2016:

> Well, it was very easy. I was tired, and I think a lot of people are tired, of *watching other countries ripping off the United States*. This is a great country. *They laugh at us behind our backs; they laugh at us because of our own stupidity and the leaders*. I mean, what we have, we have a Persian Gulf situation. You saw what happened today. Billions and billions of dollars are being spent on getting oil for Japan, and they're not paying anything for it … Larry, the country is losing 200 billion dollars a year. Two hundred billion. This country cannot continue to lose 200 billion dollars. Japan is one of the wealthiest machines ever created. Saudi Arabia – and it's not – hey, lemme tell ya, I'm a big beneficiary of Japan. They buy my apartments in spades. They're fine people. But they must be – they're laughing to themselves as to what's happening over here. We're not kidding ourselves. They're laughing to themselves, Larry, as to what's happening with this country [emphasis added]. (*Larry King Live* 1987)

Trump is hardly the only recent candidate for US president to have adopted a strongly anti-trade persona. Indeed, the 2008 Democratic primary campaign turned into a bitterly fought contest between Barack Obama and Hillary Clinton over who would enact the toughest measures on trade policy. As a candidate, Obama claimed during the Ohio Democratic primary fight that he had been "against the NAFTA from the start," only to turn around as president and embrace trade liberalization as a useful pillar of US foreign policy. Indeed, such was the anxiety around candidate Obama's anti-NAFTA rhetoric that it prompted Canadian officials to reach out to his campaign staff for clarity on his intentions for NAFTA. In what for a short time was known as "NAFTA-gate," those officials were allegedly told that Obama's rhetoric around a possible renegotiation of NAFTA was largely just that – rhetorical (CBC 2008). In late 2015, Democratic presidential primary candidate Hillary Clinton formally withdrew her political support for the recently completed Trans-Pacific Partnership (TPP), an agreement she had helped negotiate while serving in the Obama administration as secretary of state (*PBS News Hour* 2015).

Transformations in politicians' positions on trade as they shift from the campaign trail to the White House are a common, if hypocritical, feature of post-war presidential politics. Congressional authority over tariff policy was delegated to the Executive Branch through the Reciprocal Trade Agreements Act in 1934, later modified in the 1970s as Fast-Track Authority (Anderson 2012; Destler 1997; Pastor 1982, 1983; Zeiler 1992). Donald Trump was different in two important ways. First, while anti-trade rhetoric has become a standard feature on the campaign trail, Trump unquestionably supercharged that rhetoric's xenophobia and scapegoating. Second, and more importantly, Trump took advantage of more than eighty years of precedent around delegated congressional authority over tariff policy to follow through with his promises to upend US trade policy, impose steel and aluminum tariffs, launch a tariff war with China, and cancel NAFTA, although in the end, he instead renegotiated the latter.

Henry Clay's American System

An important historical parallel for thinking about the Trump administration's tariff policy comes from the mid-nineteenth century, a time when parts of the US were rapidly industrializing. At the time, Congress was more fully in control of its constitutional prerogatives over tariff policy – a source of income frequently responsible for more than 80 per cent of federal revenue through the middle of the nineteenth century (Bown and Irwin 2019).

The mid-nineteenth century also saw a shift in US tariff policy wherein the structure of tariffs would be deployed with industrial development squarely in mind. Between 1818 and 1828, the US

Congress put in place a number of initiatives that came to be known as the "American System." Those initiatives included tariff protections, the establishment of a national bank, and an infrastructure program backed by heavy federal subsidies. The American System was quickly associated with one of its strongest advocates, Henry Clay of Kentucky, Speaker of the House of Representatives (1811–25), so much so that textbooks and journal articles often refer to Henry Clay's American System (Baxter 2004; Coulter 1926; Campbell 1967; Van Atta 2001).

In March 1824, as speaker of the House, Henry Clay spoke over two days in support of further implementing elements of the American System. After painting a bleak picture of a present and future American economy dependent on an unstable, war-ravaged European market, Clay argued that the United States should focus its efforts at home:

> We have seen that an exclusive dependence on the foreign market must lead to still severer distress, to impoverishment, to ruin. We must then change somewhat our course. We must give a new direction to some portion of our industry. We must speedily adopt a genuine American policy. Still cherishing a foreign market, let us create also a home market, to give further scope to the consumption of the produce of American industry. Let us counteract the policy of foreigners, and withdraw the support which we now give their industry, and stimulate that of our own country …
>
> It is most desirable that there should be both a home and a foreign market. But with respect to their relative superiority, I cannot entertain a doubt. The home market is first in order, and paramount in importance. The object of the bill under consideration is to create this home market and lay the foundations of a genuine American policy. It is opposed, and it is incumbent upon the partisans of the foreign policy (terms which I shall use without any invidious intent) to demonstrate that the foreign market is an adequate vent for the surplus produce of our labor. (Clay as quoted in Irwin 2017, 141–2)

Because he was from Kentucky, Henry Clay was a relatively popular figure in the South. However, his American System tariff proposals were deeply unpopular there. Indeed, the conflicting economic interests of the newly industrializing, capital-rich North and the agricultural, labour-intensive (slave-holding) South with regard to the tariff were a simmering source of "sectional" tensions in the 1820s and 1830s. Clay argued that incentivizing further industrialization – even if it was in the North – would benefit southern consumers as they diverted their consumption from European production to northern US production in exchange for agricultural products. Many southerners, however, would have none of this. Indeed, many of them viewed the American System as imposing a tax on southerners' capacity to import from abroad, forcing them to substitute consumption with inferior and more expensive northern manufacturers. So contentious did the American System become that it fuelled the "Nullification Theory" and the Nullification Crisis of 1832, wherein Southern states argued they could simply disregard federal legislation they did not like (Irwin 2017, 154–65, 176–82).

The election of 1828 saw Andrew Jackson, a southerner, elected president. Jackson brought a brand of nationalism to the White House that some see paralleling the nationalism of Donald Trump in the early twenty-first century (Mead 2017). There are, in fact, numerous differences between Trump and Old Hickory (Lomazoff 2017), among them Jackson's apprehensions about the domestic effects of Clay's American System (Irwin 2017, 148–53,176–82).[3] Indeed, the Nullification Crisis, brought to a head by the American System, was a major source of concern for Jackson. Whereas Donald Trump was perfectly willing to weaponize tariffs against US trading partners with little regard for the negative spillover effects at home (Gu and Daily 2019), earning himself the moniker "tariff man," Andrew Jackson was acutely aware of the domestic divisions being exacerbated by the American System, and he sought to diffuse them to preserve national unity (Irwin 2017, 176–82).

In 1831, Henry Clay was re-elected to the US Senate. He used his first opportunity to speak on the Senate floor to mount a vigorous defence of his American System:

> I have now to perform the more pleasing task of exhibiting an imperfect sketch of the existing state of the unparalleled prosperity of the country. On a general survey, we behold cultivation extended, the arts flourishing, the face of the country improved, our people fully and profitably employed, and the public countenance exhibiting tranquility, contentment, and happiness …

> If the term of seven years were to be selected of the greatest prosperity which this people have enjoyed since the establishment of their present Constitution, it would be exactly that period of seven years which immediately followed the passage of the tariff of 1824. This transformation of the condition of the country from gloom and distress to brightness and prosperity, has been mainly the work of American legislation, fostering American industry, instead of allowing it to be controlled by foreign legislation, cherishing foreign industry. (Clay as quoted in Wolff 1994, 83–4)

Another important difference between mid-nineteenth-century and early twenty-first-century US trade policy is that the overt goal of Clay's American System was to stimulate nascent industrialization, whereas the ostensible goal of Trump's twenty-first-century American System – tariffs and withdrawing from agreements – was to reindustrialize (Tankersley 2019; Van den Bossche et al. 2018). Evidence of "reshoring" over the past decade or so has been limited. During the Trump presidency, it did not appear to be accelerating. Any evidence that it did is anecdotal (Oldenski 2015; Tankersley 2019; Van den Bossche et al. 2018).

The "Make America Great Again" System?

Donald Trump demonstrated repeatedly throughout his four years in office that "special relationships," old norms, and existing institutional arrangements were all up for reconsideration (and/or attack). The administration's withdrawal from the TPP – on Trump's third day in office –was not a great surprise to many. Indeed, while the Obama administration had worked diligently to complete the agreement, it faced a steep climb to approval on Capitol Hill and had been rejected as inadequate by the 2016 Democratic presidential nominee, Hillary Clinton, even though she had supported its completion during her time as secretary of state. However, it was the announcement of Trump's intent to use tariffs on solar panels, washing machines, and steel and aluminum to defend US manufacturing that sent tremors through US trading partners. The subsequent implementation of those tariffs in 2018, with no consideration for allies like Canada, turned those tremors into shock waves.

Trump's threat to formally withdraw from NAFTA in April 2017 dropped a policy bomb on the Canadian and Mexican capitals. Only an alleged intervention by Trump's son-in-law Jared Kushner after the pleadings of Prime Minister Justin Trudeau and President Enrique Peña Nieto convinced the US president of the merits of "renegotiating" NAFTA rather than simply withdrawing from it. The ensuing renegotiation, which continued until October 2018, was, to put it charitably, a haphazard, chaotic affair. The new agreement, the US–Canada–Mexico Agreement (USMCA), could be considered a "win" for what it preserved, but it was hardly the "modernization" of NAFTA that many – both critics and supporters – had been calling for in the two and a half decades since it was implemented.

The NAFTA negotiations had been a massive undertaking for all three countries in the early 1990s. Bureaucracies were reorganized, war rooms established, public consultations initiated, and positions hammered out and advanced in the nearly four years between June 1990 and December 1993. When the NAFTA renegotiation commenced in August 2017, none of the three governments had done much to lay the foundations for a complex renegotiation. Each country had a set of predictable positions that experts could readily foresee, but stakeholder consultations were hastily thrown together, and trade policy experts fresh from agreeing over the terms of the TPP were suddenly pitted against one another, with US negotiators confusingly taking positions in the NAFTA renegotiations they had not taken in the TPP negotiations just a year before.

Canada and Mexico made public showings of their solidarity vis-à-vis Washington throughout 2017 and early 2018. Their aim, they said, was to preserve NAFTA's essential trilateralism while both fixing and building upon its best qualities. However, by the late spring of 2018, Canada and Mexico were on different tracks in the renegotiation talks. Each of the bilateral dyads in the NAFTA area deals with unique issues, for example, immigration, defence, and intelligence cooperation. However, by the summer of 2018, Canada had gone home to await the outcome of bilateral talks between Washington and Mexico City, disingenuously claiming that they were in regular communication with their Mexican counterparts and were simply waiting for those talks to be completed. Once a US–Mexico deal was reached in August 2018, and President Trump indicated his willingness to advance ratification bilaterally, pressure mounted for Canada to come to terms as well.

On 1 October 2018, a renegotiated NAFTA text was announced. In many respects, the USMCA was a significantly updated NAFTA. Indeed, much of the language, including the topics of negotiation, amounted to significant updates, cribbed, ironically, from the text of the TPP (see table 4.3). In 1994, for example, e-commerce did not exist and was not a topic of negotiation under NAFTA. In the 2018 USMCA, e-commerce had morphed into "digital trade," labour and the environment are part of the main text, and issues such as state-owned enterprises, competition policy, and corruption merited treatment as stand-alone topics.

Two of the most important "upgrades" of NAFTA in the new USMCA were with respect to labour and the environment. The NAFTA debate permanently embedded these topics as part of the global trade agenda, but it dealt with them only outside the main text, in the form of two side agreements. Moreover, of the two, only the environmental side agreement survived. Meanwhile, the multilateral system was accumulating more experience with the environment (Esty 1994), and both labour and the environment were increasingly being incorporated into the main text of regional trade agreements. While scholars noted these changes, they also pointed to the weakness or absence of enforcement mechanisms to support them (Craik 2013; DiMento and Doughman 1997; Hufbauer and Schott 2005). In the year after the initial USMCA text was released, House Democrats in the US Congress pushed the Trump administration to strengthen enforcement even further. As announced in December 2019, the revised USMCA text significantly strengthened commitments and enforcement in both areas. Specifically, Mexico committed to significant reforms to its labour laws, agreed to new minimum wage requirements for goods to qualify under rules of origin, and agreed to new enforcement teeth involving "rapid response investigation" powers (Annex 31-A). Significantly, and somewhat surprisingly given the Trump administration's orientation toward environmental rules, the USMCA environment chapter directly incorporates NAFTA's institutional legacy on the environment and augments it with new enforcement powers. Perhaps most importantly, in both instances the burden of evidentiary proof has been shifted to the accused party (rather than the accusing party) to demonstrate factual adherence to the rule of law.

NAFTA actually has several dispute settlement mechanisms. In 1994, the state-to-state mechanisms of Chapter 20 were thought to be among the most important; these mechanisms were supposed to facilitate

Table 4.3 NAFTA and its descendants

NAFTA (January 1994)	TPP-12 (February 2016)	USMCA (October 2018)
Preamble	Preamble	Preamble
1. Objectives	1. Initial Provisions and General Definitions	1. Initial Provisions and General Definitions
2. General Definitions	2. National Treatment and Market Access	2. National Treatment and Market Access for Goods
3. National Treatment and Market Access	3. Rules of Origin	3. Agriculture
4. Rules of Origin	4. Textiles and Apparel	4. Rules of Origin
5. Customs Procedures	5. Customs Administration	5. Origin Procedures
6. Energy and Basic Petrochemicals	6. Trade Remedies (AD/CVD)	6. Textiles and Apparel
7. Agriculture and Sanitary and Phytosanitary Measures	7. Sanitary and Phytosanitary Measures	7. Customs Administration and Trade Facilitation
8. Emergency Action	8. Technical Barriers to Trade	8. Recognition of Mexican Ownership of Hydrocarbons
9. Standards-Related Measures (Technical Barriers)	9. Investment	9. Sanitary and Phytosanitary Measures
10. Government Procurement	10. Cross-Border Trade in Services	10. Trade Remedies
11. Investment	11. Financial Services	11. Technical Barriers to Trade
12. Cross-Border Trade in Services	12. Temporary Entry for Business Persons	12. Sectoral Annexes
13. Telecommunications	13. Telecommunications	13. Government Procurement
14. Financial Services	14. Electronic Commerce	14. Investment
15. Competition Policy, Monopolies and State Enterprises	15. Government Procurement	15. Cross-Border Trade in Services
16. Temporary Entry for Business Persons	16. Competition	16. Temporary Entry
17. Intellectual Property	17. State-Owned Enterprises	17. Financial Services
18. Publication, Notification, and Administration of Laws	18. Intellectual Property	18. Telecommunications
19. Review and Dispute Settlement in Antidumping/ Countervailing Duty Matters	19. Labor	19. Digital Trade
20. Institutional Arrangements and Dispute Settlement Procedures	20. Environment	20. Intellectual Property
21. Exceptions	21. Cooperation and Capacity Building	21. Competition Policy
22. Final Provisions	22. Competitiveness and Business Facilitation	22. State-Owned Enterprises
	23. Development	23. Labor
	24. Small and Medium-Sized Enterprises	24. Environment
	25. Regulatory Coherence	25. Small and Medium-Sized Enterprises
	26. Transparency and Anti-corruption	26. Competitiveness
	27. Administrative and Institutional Provisions	27. Anti-corruption
	28. Dispute Settlement	28. Good Regulatory Practices
	29. Exceptions	29. Publication and Administration
	30. Final Provisions	30. Administrative and Institutional Provisions
		31. Dispute Settlement
		32. Exceptions and General Provisions
		33. Macroeconomic Policies and Exchange Rate Matters
		34. Final Provisions

the resolution of the most high-profile, sensitive disputes, including interpretation and review of the agreement itself. In practice, Chapter 20 was ineffective, running up against sovereignty issues as parties routinely blocked the formation of panels. The USMCA's dispute settlement chapter (Chapter 31) borrows a "fix" of this problem (embedded in the TPP) by eliminating the ability of parties to indefinitely block panel formation.

Another pleasant surprise in the renegotiation was that NAFTA's provisions regarding temporary entry of professionals survived unscathed. The US created an entirely new category of visa, the TN visa, as part of its NAFTA implementation in 1993–94. It was a unique addition to the US visa system that has never been repeated in the context of US trade policy. Given the Trump administration's general hostility toward immigration, and particularly its obsession with visa policies that allegedly admitted too many foreign workers to the US, NAFTA's provisions should surely have been on the chopping block. Instead, the USMCA actually improved upon NAFTA's temporary entry provisions by simplifying the standard, and also by steering it away from specific job categories toward more generalized educational criteria.

Unfortunately, the news was not all good. Indeed, the USMCA arguably also represents a significant setback for trilateralism. First and foremost, it now contains a "sunset" clause (Article 34.7) that automatically terminates the agreement after sixteen years unless the parties extend its life after formal reviews every six years.

Many observers expected changes to the investment provisions of NAFTA (Chapter 11) when renegotiations began. There has been a worldwide move toward eliminating investor/state dispute settlement covering investment. Hence, the elimination of those mechanisms within the USMCA would not have been a big surprise, particularly given the Trump administration's view that investment protections incentivized the outsourcing of US jobs. Unfortunately, the USMCA has eliminated investment protections in the Canada–US context, although it leaves NAFTA's legacy Chapter 11 mechanism in place for a narrow set of sectors in the US–Mexico context. In other words, the USMCA has created a patchwork of governance mechanisms.

The initial October 2018 USMCA text appeared to have done something similar regarding the governance of trade remedy laws. Any disciplining of trade remedy laws was thought to be a major target for elimination by the Trump administration, particularly because of controversy surrounding the legality of those mechanisms under the US Constitution. During the NAFTA negotiations, Canada and Mexico fought to enshrine Chapter 19 in the text – a red-line issue for Canada, in particular, since the late 1980s. Strangely, the initial USMCA text dropped access to those mechanisms for Mexico, although that access was reinstated by the time the revised December 2019 text was released.

Perhaps the most significant blow to trilateralism is contained in the dispute settlement provisions around labour described earlier. The strengthened enforcement mechanisms are to be applauded. Unfortunately, there are, in fact, two "rapid response investigation" mechanisms: one (Annex 31-A) applicable to the US–Mexico dyad, and the other (Annex 31-B) to the Canada–Mexico dyad. There is nothing enforcing labour rights in the Canada–US context.

On the whole, the USMCA represented a smaller break from NAFTA's structure than many feared. Yet in important ways, the USMCA also represents an erosion of NAFTA's already weak standard for institutionalization in the service of the concept of trilateralism in North America.

"Tariff Man" and Canada

The foregoing has attempted to situate the Trump administration's approach to trade in a historical context to sort out how divergent this presidency was from previous administrations. On trade policy, there was less light to shine between the Trump presidency and the preceding ones than in nearly every other area of policy. While Donald Trump's views on trade frequently clashed with economic orthodoxy, they were easily the president's most consistent and longest held. Moreover, Trump's views and actions as president were in keeping with many age-old arguments against openness to the global economy. The economic logic of protectionism may be flawed, but protectionism has historically made for very good politics.

That Canada was drawn into Trump's chaotic trade policy vortex presented challenges for policy-makers trying to ensure that post-war trade rules continued to work in Canadian interests. However, the Trump administration's actions were merely another in a long string of periodic US market access restrictions that are part of the delicate dance Canada has always done in its relationship with the Colossus.

Biden's American System and Canada

Shortly after Joe Biden's 2020 election victory, the popular press was giddy with anticipation about the "grown-ups" being back in control. The 27 November *Financial Times* (2020) editorial noted that "for US allies the Biden slate marks a return to more traditional US engagement." The *Financial Times* was exactly right but also completely wrong. The adults were back but the return to tradition has not been the one they imagined.

In January 2021, President Biden and "the adults" assumed office and quickly became worthy heirs to the tradition of Henry Clay's American System described earlier in this chapter. For Canada, the arrival of the adults has proven to be a double-edged sword; those adults have embraced the Biden administration's shift in tone while also fighting to put out fires like the ones started by Trump. One way Canada has fought those fires historically has been by playing on the "special-ness" of Canada–US relations to encourage exceptional treatment from Washington. Put differently, Canada has often sought to foster an "exemptionalist" culture in bilateral relations in which Washington "exempts" Ottawa from sweeping policy measures (Anderson 2019). Scholars have periodically sought explanations for Canada's periodic ability to win concessions from Washington in the vaguely posited "special relationship" between the two countries, forged, in part, from the shared cultural experiences of two world wars and the construction of the post-war order. Even those who rightly note that any "exemptionalist" culture between the two countries exists in the context of stark asymmetries of power have nevertheless attributed collaborative solutions to aspects of some unique diplomatic engagement between the two; if Ottawa can just point out how integrated the two countries are, Washington will see the error in its ways. This was the strategy employed by Ottawa to win exemption from Trump's 2018 steel and aluminum tariffs, which succeeded the following year.

Yet now and again the "exemptionalist" approach seems to fail, notably after 9/11, when Canadian diplomacy impressed upon American policy-makers the need to keep the border porous to legitimate human and commercial traffic but, with very few exceptions, failed to arrest its thickening as a focal point of interdiction and delay (Anderson 2019). Another notable case of failure was the cancellation of the 1854

Reciprocity Treaty by the US Congress in 1866 (discussed earlier). Protests went unheeded, and Canadian efforts to ensnare America in a lucrative economic arrangement (1911 and 1947) were unsuccessful until 1988.

As of mid-2023, the pursuit of an "exemptionalist" culture has become a necessary part of Canadian diplomacy as the "adults" in the White House pursue a host of inward-looking, America-first economic policies reminiscent of Henry Clay's nineteenth-century American System. The Bush administration had recognized the need to keep the border porous after 9/11; the Biden administration certainly recognized much the same when the 2022 Trucker Convoy paralyzed Ottawa and blockaded two border crossings, including the Ambassador Bridge.

Yet that recognition has been offset by explicit efforts by Washington to incentivize new investment into the US and reshore productive capacities. Specifically, in 2021 and 2022, America invested heavily in infrastructure spending, climate change mitigation, and high-tech semiconductor production through major pieces of legislation that committed well over $2 trillion in spending, subsidies, and tax incentives to that end. The scale of the spending has left allies reeling and under pressure to put forward competitive programs of similar scale.

However, it is the Buy America provisions of US legislation that give allies like Canada the most cause for concern. Those concerns were heightened in the 2023 State of the Union Address in which Biden criticized previous administrations for finding workarounds and exceptions, stating explicitly "not any more." A case in point is the new $7,500 tax rebate for Americans who buy electric vehicles. In the original version of the Inflation Reduction Act, only vehicles meeting thresholds for US content in battery components and final assembly would qualify. Interventions by Senator Joe Manchin (D, West Virginia) and the recognition that the US cannot currently supply all such components led lawmakers to expand sourcing to its free trade partners; French, German, and Japanese electric vehicle makers were left in the cold.

Yet managing "Buy America" in the context of enormous infrastructure and climate change expenditures is only part of the problem for US allies. The US no longer seems committed to underwriting the open, post-war trading architecture it was so instrumental in establishing. The twin problematics of China's rise and contemporary anti-trade populism have accentuated that unwillingness. As a case in point, the Biden administration has not rejoined the TPP agreement negotiated while he was vice-president but cancelled by President Trump – an easy and obvious initiative for strategic positioning vis-à-vis China. Moreover, the Biden administration appears content with the renegotiated NAFTA, now a less trilateral and more protectionist arrangement. Moreover, at the recent North American Leaders' Summit in Mexico City, the three leaders chose not to address a series of disputes and looming problems with the USMCA's implementation (Hufbauer and Schott 2023). Multilaterally, the US has precipitated a crisis with the World Trade Organization's (WTO) Appellate Body that the Biden administration has yet to signal it wants to resolve. The heart of the problem is a long-standing difference of opinion between the US and EU over the interpretation of the legal texts themselves and whether Appellate Body rulings ought to establish precedent (Payosova et. al. 2018; Steger 2017). The philosophical differences date to the Bush administration, but as a result of the Obama administration's failure to reappoint appellate body jurists and the Trump administration's refusal to nominate new ones, the Appellate Body ceased being functional in late 2019. In 2020, a group of twenty-three members negotiated a stop-gap measure to advance adjudication of some WTO disputes, but doubts remain as to America's willingness to negotiate a lasting fix (Lester 2020; Starishinova 2021).

Conclusion

In 2020, the adults came back. But rather than returning to traditions in post-war trade policy anchored in underwriting an open, multilateral trading system, those adults chose to carry on with and advance an older nineteenth-century tradition of tariffs, subsidies, and nationalist preferences. Biden's American System may have less bombast than its predecessors, and certainly much less than Trump's rhetoric of American First. But the bumpy road ahead for Canada in navigating it will remain the same.

Notes

A version of this chapter appeared as "Trump's 'American System' and Canada" in the "Canada–US Relations in the Age of Donald Trump" special issue of the *American Review of Canadian Studies* 50 (2020): 32–47.

1 Charles Francis Adams was addressing Earl Russell.

2 Earl Russell was addressing Sir F. Bruce.

3 Jackson was not a fan of Clay generally, mostly due to Clay's role in the so-called Corrupt Bargain, which saw John Quincy Adams become president after the 1824 election was decided by the House of Representatives and saw Clay (one of four presidential candidates that year) throw his support behind Adams over Jackson.

References

Anastakis, Dimitry. 2000. "The Advent of an International Trade Agreement: The Auto Pact at GATT, 1964–65." *International Journal* 55, no. 4: 583–602.

– 2001. "Requiem for a Trade Agreement: The Auto Pact at the WTO, 1999–2000." *Canadian Business Law Journal* 34: 313.

Anderson, Greg. 2006. "Can Someone Please Settle This Dispute? Canadian Softwood Lumber and the Dispute Settlement Mechanisms of the NAFTA and the WTO." *Word Economy* 29, no. 5: 585–610.

– 2012. "Did Canada Kill Fast Track?" *Diplomatic History* 36, no. 3: 583–624.

– 2019. "David and Goliath in Canada–US Relations: Who's Really Who?" *Canadian Foreign Policy Journal* 25, no. 2: 115–36.

Baxter, M.G. 2004. *Henry Clay and the American System*. Lexington: University Press of Kentucky.

Bown, Chad, and Douglas A. Irwin. 2019. "Monkey Cage: Is Trump Right When He Tweets That Tariffs Bring in Government Revenue? Here Are 5 Things You Need to Know." *Washington Post*, 16 July. https://www.washingtonpost.com/politics/2019/07/16/tariff-revenue-trump-tweets-things-you-need-know.

Campbell, Randolph B. 1967. "The Spanish American Aspect of Henry Clay's American System." *The Americas* 24, no. 1: 3–17.

CBC. 2008. "Harper Aide Accused of Sparking NAFTA-Gate." 5 March. https://www.cbc.ca/news/canada/harper-aide-accused-of-sparking-nafta-gate-1.719090.

Central Intelligence Agency (CIA). n.d. *World Factbook*. https://www.cia.gov/library/publications/the-world-factbook.

Coulter, Ellis Merton. 1926. "The Genesis of Henry Clay's American System." *South Atlantic Quarterly* 25, no. 1: 45–54.

Craik, Neil A. 2013. "Regional Climate Policy Facilitation: The Role of the North American Commission on Environmental Cooperation." In *Climate Change Policy in North America: Designing Integration in a Regional System*, edited by A. Neil Craik, Isabel Studer, and Debora Van Nijnatten, 213–45. Toronto: University of Toronto Press.

Dales, John H. 1979. "'National Policy' Myths, Past and Present." *Journal of Canadian Studies* 14, no. 3: 92–4.

Destler, I.M. 1997. *Renewing Fast-Track Legislation*. No. 50, Policy Analyses in International Economics. Washington, DC: Peterson Institute for International Economics.

DiMento, Joseph F., and Pamela M. Doughman. 1997. "Soft Teeth in the Back of the Mouth: The NAFTA Environmental Side Agreement Implemented." *Georgetown International Environmental Law Review* 10: 651–752.

Esty, Daniel. 1994. *Greening the GATT*. Washington, DC. Institute for International Economics.

Financial Times. 2020. "The Grown-Ups Are Back in Charge in Washington." 27 November. https://www.ft.com/content/1b751d3e-e410-4e81-af75-775312cfeb62.

Forster, Ben. 1979. "The Coming of the National Policy: Business, Government, and the Tariff, 1876–79." *Journal of Canadian Studies* 14, no. 3: 39–49.

Granatstein, J.L., and Reginald C. Stuart. 1997. "Yankee Go Home? Canadians and Anti-Americanism." *American Review of Canadian Studies* 27, no. 2: 54–66.

Gray, William Glenn. 2007. "Floating the System: Germany, the United States, and the Breakdown of Bretton Woods, 1969–73." *Diplomatic History* 31, no. 2: 295–323.

Great Britain Foreign Office. 1866a. Correspondence Respecting the Termination of the Reciprocity Treaty of June 5, 1854, Between the United States and Great Britain, Presented to both Houses of Parliament by Command of Her Majesty. No. 1. 17 March 1865. Mr Adams to Earl Russell. London: s.n.

– 1866b. Correspondence Respecting the Termination of the Reciprocity Treaty of June 5, 1854, Between the United States and Great Britain, Presented to both Houses of Parliament by Command of Her Majesty. No. 2. 17 March 1865. Earl Russell to Sir F. Bruce. London: s.n.

Gu, Hallie, and Tom Daly. 2019. "US Farmers Suffer 'Body Blow' as China Slams Door on Farm Purchases." *Reuters*, 5 August. https://www.reuters.

com/article/us-usa-trade-china-agriculture/u-s-farmers-suffer-body-blow-as-china-slams-door-on-farm-purchases-idUSKCN1UV0XJ.

Hart, Michael. 1989. "Almost But Not Quite: The 1947–48 Bilateral Canada–US Negotiations." *American Review of Canadian Studies* 19, no. 1: 25–58.

Haynes, Frederick Emory. 1892. *The Reciprocity Treaty with Canada of 1854*, vol. 7, no. 6. Baltimore: American Economic Association.

Hufbauer, Gary, and Jeffrey Schott. 2005. *NAFTA Revisited: Acheivements and Challenges*. Washington, DC: Institute for International Economics.

– 2023. "North American Leaders Make Little Progress on the Hard Issues" [blog]. Washington, DC: Petersen Institute for International Economics. https://www.piie.com/blogs/realtime-economics/north-american-leaders-make-little-progress-hard-issues.

Irwin, Douglas A. 1996. *Against the Tide: An Intellectual History of Free Trade*. Princeton: Princeton University Press.

– 2013. "The Nixon Shock after Forty Years: The Import Surcharge Revisited." *World Trade Review* 12, no. 1: 29–56.

– 2017. *Clashing over Commerce: A History of US Trade Policy*. Chicago: University of Chicago Press.

Larry King Live. 1987. Interview With Donald Trump. CNN, 2 September. https://www.cnn.com/videos/tv/2016/05/09/donald-trump-1987-interview-larry-king-live.cnn.

Lester, Simon. 2020. "Can Interim Appeal Arbitration Preserve the WTO Dispute System?" *Cato Institute, Free Trade Bulletin* no. 77.

Lomazoff, Eric. 2017. "Why Donald Trump Is Not Andrew Jackson (and Why That Matters for American Constitutional Democracy)." *Maryland Law Review* 77, no. 1: 280–90.

Macrory, Patrick. 2002. *NAFTA Chapter 19: A Successful Experiment in International Trade Dispute Resolution*. Toronto: C.D. Howe Institute.

Masters, Donald C. 1963. *The Reciprocity Treaty of 1854: Its History, Its Relation to British Colonial and Foreign Policy and to the Development of Canadian Fiscal Autonomy*, vol. 9. Montreal and Kingston: McGill-Queen's University Press.

– 1969. *Reciprocity, 1846–1911*. Ottawa: Canadian Historical Association.

Mead, Walter Russell. 2017. "The Jacksonian Revolt: American Populism and the Liberal Order." *Foreign Affairs* 96, no. 2: 2–7.

Muirhead, Bruce. 2004. "From Special Relationship to Third Option: Canada, the US, and the Nixon Shock." *American Review of Canadian Studies* 34, no. 3: 439–62.

Norrie, Kenneth, Douglas Owram, and J.C. Herbert Emery. 2002. *A History of the Canadian Economy*, 3rd ed. Toronto: Harcourt Brace.

Officer, Lawrence H., and Lawrence B. Smith. 1968. "The Canadian–American Reciprocity Treaty of 1855 to 1866." *Journal of Economic History* 28, no. 4: 598–623.

Oldenski, Lindsay. 2015. "Reshoring by US Firms: What Do the Data Say?" Policy Brief PB15-14. Washington, DC: Peterson Institute for International Economics.

Pastor, Robert A. 1982. *Congress and the Politics of US Foreign Economic Policy, 1929–76*, vol. 5. Berkeley: University of California Press.

– 1983. "The Cry-and-Sign Syndrome: Congress and Trade Policy." In *Making Economic Policy in Congress*, edited by Allen Schick, 158–95. Washington, DC: American Enterprise Institute for Public Policy Research.

Payosova, Tetyana, Gary Clyde Hufbauer, and Jeffrey J. Schott. 2018. *The Dispute Settlement Crisis in the World Trade Organization: Causes and Cures*. No. PB18-5.

PBS News Hour. 2015. "Hillary Clinton Says She Does Not Support Trans-Pacific Partnership." 7 October. https://www.pbs.org/newshour/politics/hillary-clinton-says-she-does-not-support-trans-pacific-partnership.

Phillips, Paul. 1979. "The National Policy Revisited." *Journal of Canadian Studies* 14, no. 3: 3–13.

Saunders, S.A. 1936. "The Reciprocity Treaty of 1854: A Regional Study." *Canadian Journal of Economics and Political Science / Revue Canadienne de economiques et science politique* 2, no. 1: 41–53.

Starshinova, Olga. 2021. "Is the MPIA a Solution to the WTO Appellate Body Crisis?" *Journal of World Trade* 55, no. 5.

Steger, Debra P. 2017. "The Founding of the Appellate Body." *Ottawa Faculty of Law Working Paper* 2017–33.

Tankersley, Jim. 2019. "Trump's Push to Bring Back Jobs to US Shows Limited Results." *New York Times*, 13 August. https://www.nytimes.com/2019/08/13/business/economy/donald-trump-jobs-created.html.

Tenpas, Kathryn Dunn. 2019. "Tracking Turnover in the Trump Administration." Brookings Institution, Governance Studies. September. https://www.brookings.edu/research/tracking-turnover-in-the-trump-administration.

Time. 2015. "Here's Donald Trump's Presidential Announcement Speech." *Time*, 16 June. https://time.com/3923128/donald-trump-announcement-speech.

World Bank. n.d. DataBank. https://databank.worldbank.org/home.

Van Atta, J.R. 2001. "Western Lands and the Political Economy of Henry Clay's American System, 1819–32." *Journal of the Early Republic* 21, no. 4: 633–65.

Van den Bossche, Patrick, Brooks Levering, Johan Gott, and Yurl Castaño. 2018. "US Trade Policy and Reshoring: The Real Impact of America's New Trade Policies." Research Report. A.T. Kearney.

Wolff, Wendy, ed. 1994. *The Senate, 1789–1898, Classic Speeches 1830–1993*. Washington, DC: US Government Printing Office.

Zeiler, Thomas W. 1992. *American Trade and Power in the 1960s*. New York: Columbia University Press.

5

What's Love Got to Do with It?

Presidents, Prime Ministers, and the Making of the Special Relationship

ASA MCKERCHER AND SUSAN COLBOURN

What makes the special relationship between Canada and the United States special? Does the personal relationship between the sitting president and the prime minister of the day actually matter?

The answer is yes – and no. "The special relationship," as this volume's editors note in the introduction, "has never depended on personal relationships at the top." We agree. The special relationship between Canada and the US – if such a thing exists – is a product of a whole host of interactions between everyday Canadians and Americans and, to a lesser extent, their governments (Bothwell 2015).

Yet so much of the focus on Canada–US relations in the press and in the popular discourse continues to revolve around – to borrow the title of a 1983 bestseller – *The Presidents and the Prime Ministers* (Martin 1983). Relations at the very top can set an important tone, and their ebbs and flows can come to serve as useful proxies for broader currents in North American society. They can also help smooth over fractures that exist. At the same time, the Canada–US special relationship exists in spite of the sometimes poor relations between prime minister and president, the result of clashing personalities or ideological or policy differences. Moreover, specialness exists even as Canadian leaders often seek – for domestic purposes – to keep a distance between themselves and the occupant of the White House. At the same time, prime ministers are expected to maintain working ties with the president lest they risk upsetting the economy or harming military or security links. Maintaining this balance can be tough. For American presidents, meanwhile, good ties with the Canadian prime minister seldom factor into domestic politics, a sign of the power disparity between the two countries.

Like the much-lauded Anglo-American special relationship, the notion of a special relationship between Canada and the US owes something to the exigencies of the Second World War. Just as Winston Churchill's wartime relationship with Franklin Delano Roosevelt (FDR) provided the foundations for an enduring partnership – and fodder for countless state dinner toasts – so, too, did Roosevelt's unique friendship with William Lyon Mackenzie King. FDR and King set a precedent for personal relations that has loomed over the wider bilateral relationship ever since.

A Special Relationship in the Making

The King–Roosevelt relationship began just two weeks after the Liberals' election victory in 1935. The president invited the new prime minister to the White House to review a proposed free trade pact. King was greatly impressed, doubly so because as the meeting concluded, Roosevelt encouraged him to maintain an open line of communication, stating, "I will always be glad to hear from you" (King, 8 November 1935). The president was true to his word, and a week later they met again to ink the trade deal. King was enthusiastic. The agreement, he wrote, was "the greatest achievement of my life, and one of the greatest on this continent in a century or more" (King, 11 November 1935).

Reversing some of the protectionism of the era, the trade pact was an important development, but King's self-adulation was a bit much. Yet it reflected the sense that Canada–US relations were special. Meeting Roosevelt in July 1936 amid the outbreak of the Spanish Civil War, King contrasted the "fear & hate there & the confidence and good will here" in North America (King, 31 July 1936). With revisionist powers on the march in Europe and Asia, the constructive relationship between Canada and the US – a small power and a great power – did appear *sui generis*. Roosevelt expressed this view publicly in his famous speech in Kingston, Ontario, in 1938: "We as good neighbors are true friends because we maintain our own rights to frankness, because we refuse to accept the twists of secret diplomacy, because we settle our disputes by consultation, and because we discuss our common problems in the spirit of the common good" (Roosevelt 1941a, 105).

As to whether the countries' leaders played a role in this apparent special relationship, we can see the notion rooted partly in King's own belief in himself. A meeting with Roosevelt in March 1937 left the prime minister convinced that he and FDR were "fulfilling … the mission of Unseen powers" (King, 14 March 1937). Partly, too, there was Roosevelt's friendly treatment of King, from the use of first names to the annual visits, often in intimate settings, including picnics at FDR's Hyde Park estate and chats in the White House's presidential bedroom or around the swimming pool at the "Little White House" in Warm Springs, Georgia. These discussions were marked by the president's "brotherly" manner, which, the prime minister reflected, made it "much easier to be myself … and talk naturally" (King, 17 November 1938).

Yet however much he valued his access to the president and cooperative ties with the US, King was also concerned about aligning too much with the Americans. FDR was genial enough, but as he recognized, a "change of leaders there [in Washington] might lead to vassalage so far as our Dominion was concerned" (King, 27 January 1939; Perras 2010). Hence, the apparent importance of the British counterweight within the so-called North Atlantic Triangle. When war broke out in 1939 and FDR announced only that his country deplored Germany's invasion of Poland, King was saddened that the president had responded with "mere words" (King, 3 September 1939).

This disappointment was temporary. On 5 September 1939, two days after Britain had declared war, Roosevelt called to clarify Canada's belligerent status, a move King saw as a "friendly gesture to indicate sympathy and readiness to co-operate in so far as might be possible" (King, 5 September 1939). Roosevelt's sympathies were clear, as he supported the Allies as much as US neutrality laws would permit. In this light, we have the August 1940 Ogdensburg Agreement setting up the Permanent Joint Board on Defence (PJBD) to coordinate continental defence efforts. It was followed by the April 1941 Hyde Park Declaration, which harmonized the production of war material, allowed Canadian-made supplies to be purchased by Britain via the Lend-Lease program, and increased US purchases in Canada to offset a trade imbalance. Both agreements were drawn up informally by president and prime minister, and there was no need for legislative approval, since neither was a treaty. As the president had scrawled atop the Hyde Park agreement while dining with his Canadian guest: "Done by Mackenzie and FDR at Hyde Park on a grand Sunday,

April 20 1941" (King, 20 April 1941). The informality attested to the strength of the leaders' personal relationship – evidence, perhaps, of a broader specialness.

While Canadian nationalists saw in these developments an effort by King to bring Canada into the American orbit – to coat the country in "cancerous slime," as one writer put it (Morton 1964, 321) – the prime minister was mindful of maintaining a distance. There was a need, he wrote soon after the fateful Hyde Park meeting, to ensure "two peoples and two governments on this continent" (King, 23 April 1941). Such a view was reinforced that August, when FDR and Churchill met in secret at Argentia, Newfoundland. Angry at being excluded, King ranted that it was vital for Canada to be "a nation wholly on her own" (King, 7 August 1941). King's pique was noted. Subsequently, throughout the war, whenever the American president and his British counterpart met in North America, Canada's prime minister was invited along. Even so, there was no chance of the Canadians playing a larger role in the war's direction. When Churchill suggested bringing the Canadians into high-level talks in 1943, Roosevelt opposed the move on the grounds that it would mean a "deterioration" of the senior Anglo-American war council "into a debating society" (Roosevelt 1943). King was hardly perturbed, for he himself had no inclination to see Canada take on more responsibilities. Regarding the wartime conferences between Roosevelt and Churchill held at Quebec City in 1943 and 1944, King likened his role to "that of the General Manager of the Chateau Frontenac," the hotel where the summit was held (Moran 1966, 117).

The demands of the war meant that the two leaders met less frequently, although their relationship remained warm. "Isn't it fine that we can all talk so freely, concealing nothing?," FDR asked King after a late-night chat at the 1943 Quebec conference (King, 24 July 1943). The easy rapport seemed a reflection of the deepening wartime ties between the two governments. A 1942 report by Canada's Department of External Affairs (DEA) characterized the "personal friendship" at the top as "one of the really significant factors in Canadian–American affairs." While Ogdensburg, Hyde Park, and other agreements represented what was "probably an historically inevitable development," DEA officials contended that the personal tie meant that "they were all effected more quickly, with less of a bargaining or of a bullying spirit involved in the negotiations, and with greater and more mutual satisfaction in the results" (American and Far Eastern Division 1942).

King and Roosevelt's relationship was recognized as important but not vital to the functioning of bilateral relations. It also set a high bar for future presidents and prime ministers. King was the last foreign visitor to meet with FDR. He had spent a night at the White House just weeks before the president's death, and he was the only foreign head of government at Roosevelt's funeral. Indeed, their relationship continued into the afterlife, with FDR reaching out from the beyond grave to advise King to carry on in politics (Stacey 1976, 209–11).

King's idiosyncrasies were an important element of his perceived special relationship with Roosevelt. Conversely, he felt little connection with Harry Truman, FDR's successor. He rejected characterizations of Truman as a "crook" but was worried about his lack of experience, given that he had only been vice-president for a few months (King, 12 April 1945). After they met in October 1946, King judged the new president akin to a "business executive," which seems not to have been a compliment. The president was at pains to emphasize "his friendship for Canada," and he invited King to talk with him "at any time," a Rooseveltian suggestion that pleased the prime minister (King, 28 October 1946). However, the Truman–King relationship was nowhere near as close as the one between King and FDR and had little of the productive informality. Moreover, the prime minister remained leery of having too close a relationship with the Americans, who were seeking "to get Canada under their aegis" (King, 30 March 1948).

King's concerns aside, bilateral interdependence continued apace, whether in terms of trade and investment or intergovernmental cooperation on military, economic, and security issues. The Hyde Park and Ogdensburg agreements carried on into the post-war years, with US officials recognizing that they constituted "the two big symbols of our extraordinarily close relationship" with Canada (Foster 1948). Indeed, the sense that relations were growing too close led King to scotch a proposed customs union in 1948, one of his last official acts.

A Relationship in Transition

The year 1948 also saw Truman elected to his own term as president, as well as a passing of the guard in Canada, as King retired and Louis St Laurent became prime minister. As secretary of state for external affairs (SSEA) from 1946 to 1948, St Laurent had already done much to promote cooperative ties between Ottawa and Washington, and he continued to take this approach. At his first meeting with Truman in February 1949, the new prime minister raised several outstanding issues, including the emerging North Atlantic Treaty Organization (NATO), a US base in Newfoundland, and the St Lawrence Seaway project. In the view of a notetaker, the effect of the presidential–prime ministerial discussion was to establish a rapport that "certainly should make easier the conduct of relations" (Wrong 1949a). So easy was the discussion that Canadian diplomats were "disturbed" that St Laurent might "expect too concrete results" from the meeting. As SSEA Lester B. Pearson warned the prime minister, "Mr. Truman's amiable offers of assistance and cooperation may be somewhat difficult to implement" (Wrong 1949b; Pearson 1949). In practice, informal arrangements of the sort concluded between King and FDR were unlikely. For instance, Truman was sympathetic to the Canadians regarding the St Lawrence Seaway, a decades-long sore spot. As the president recognized, Ottawa had been "very patient and cooperative." Nonetheless, congressional opposition remained a roadblock to a bilateral agreement (Department of State 1952).

Sympathies aside, Truman had little time for Canada. Within his administration, it was only Dean Acheson, secretary of state from 1949 to 1953 and a Canadian by ancestry, who "took a special interest" in his country's northern neighbour (Bothwell 1992, 38). Much of Acheson's ardour waned as the Korean War sparked notable differences between the two allies. In March 1951, with the war effort bogged down and the fighting threatening to expand into a general conflict, Pearson gave a landmark speech in which he contended that the "relatively easy and automatic relations with our neighbour are, I think, over" (Pearson 1951). If there was a special relationship, it showed signs of strain.

So when Dwight Eisenhower became president in 1953, Canada was an agenda item. An early meeting between St Laurent and Eisenhower was arranged so that the president could "establish personal contact" with the prime minister "in keeping with past practice and our special relationships with Canada" (Dulles 1953). The *tête-à-tête* was a jovial one, as was a visit by Eisenhower to Ottawa later that year. The bonhomie between president and prime minister was such that one senior diplomat complained of reluctance on the Canadian side "to take issue with a celebrated guest or to raise embarrassing questions" about pressing matters, leaving it to officials "to say the unpleasant things" (Heeney 1972, 123).

Whatever unpleasantness existed, the Eisenhower–St Laurent era saw considerable bilateral cooperation, from the formation of a joint cabinet committee to manage booming trade and investment to a plethora of continental defence arrangements as well as completion of the St Lawrence Seaway. The relationship between president and prime minister seems to not have been overly friendly – they met in 1953 and then not again until 1956 – but nor was it marked by acrimony. Indeed, Eisenhower went out of his way to arrange some informal meetings with St Laurent, inviting him on a golf vacation at Augusta, Georgia, in December 1956. They had golfed earlier that year, too, in White Sulphur Springs, West Virginia, along with the Mexican president – despite Canadian complaints that inclusion of the latter would devalue the "special relationship with the United States" (Department of State 1956). Recalling these informal get-togethers with St Laurent, Eisenhower enthused that there had been "no agenda beforehand and no agreements arrived at," making them "the most enjoyable" conferences he had ever attended and a showcase of "good and easy relations" (Washington Embassy 1957). The ease of the Canada–US relationship seemed set to be tested when, in 1957, the St Laurent government was voted out, ending two decades of Liberal rule.

A Special Relationship under Strain

John Diefenbaker, the new Progressive Conservative (PC) prime minister, was an unknown quantity, and US officials worried that his nationalist rhetoric might translate into policy. Diefenbaker, though, soon assured Eisenhower of his friendly intentions (Diefenbaker 1957). The following year, after a snap election transformed the Tory minority government into a majority, the president invited his Canadian counterpart to Washington for a three-day visit meant to establish "the same mutual confidence and close working relationship" with the PC government as had existed with its Liberal predecessor (Dulles 1958). From this standpoint, the trip succeeded, and shortly thereafter the two leaders – to the astonishment of the president's staff – agreed to call each other "Ike" and "John" (Whitman, 15 July 1958).

There was ample cooperation between Ike's administration and John's government, including the conclusion of agreements setting up the North American Air Defense Command and a joint cabinet committee on defence, mirroring the one dealing with economic matters. However, these developments at the bureaucratic level seemed to occur in spite of the prime minister, who, the Americans quickly learned, had a penchant for delay and obfuscation. "When he sees him," Eisenhower remarked of the Canadian prime minister, "they agree but when Mr. Diefenbaker speaks in public he blames America for all Canada's troubles" (Macmillan 1959). The president "was distressed," he confided to aides, "that a Liberal government in Canada seems more desirable … than a Conservative government" (Goodpaster 1960). In an effort to smooth over a choppy relationship, Eisenhower opted to give Diefenbaker "a little more of the red carpet treatment," inviting him to the White House in June 1960 (Herter 1960). The meeting was a success insofar as the two leaders got on well together, affirming a belief that bilateral relations between their governments "had been unequalled in the past" (Bryce 1960).

There were outstanding issues, but in the waning months of his administration, Eisenhower was unwilling to press Diefenbaker hard over a delay in acquiring nuclear weapons or Canada's continuing to trade with revolutionary Cuba. On one of his last days in office, the president hosted the Canadian prime minister for the signing of the Columbia River Treaty; this was followed by a banquet featuring "most of the brass from Cabinet, Congress etc." Diefenbaker was "delighted with his treatment," and the visit, an aide observed, was "all the more nostalgic" because of the prime minister's lack of a relationship with the incoming president, John F. Kennedy (JFK). As Canadian diplomats recognized, there was little doubt that this absence of personal ties between president-elect and prime minister was "going to introduce an incalculable factor into relations with the United States" (Heeney 1961a; Robinson 1961).

The Kennedy–Diefenbaker relationship was famously strained. As the president would later put it of a meeting that included himself, Diefenbaker, and British Prime Minister Harold Macmillan, "there we sat, like three whores at a christening" (Robinson 1963). The acrimony between them came later. When Kennedy took office, Diefenbaker raced Macmillan to be the first foreign leader to meet the president in February 1961 and then ensured that the new US leader's first foreign visit was to Canada that May. The meetings were friendly enough. After their May summit, Diefenbaker confided to his brother that he and Kennedy "got along very well together. The opinion I formed of him when I first met him – a brilliant intellect and a wide knowledge of world events – was not only borne out but intensified as a result of our discussions in the last two days" (Diefenbaker 1961a).

Strains were soon apparent. Throughout the summer of 1961, the president and prime minister corresponded over Canadian acceptance of nuclear warheads, a long-standing issue. Diefenbaker seemed on the point of accepting the weaponry until a White House press leak prompted him to break off contact with the president and halt negotiations. Through an aide, Kennedy soon contacted the Canadian embassy in Washington to inform them that he was "disturbed" that his "close personal contact with Mr. Diefenbaker was allowed to slip" (Diefenbaker 1961b; Heeney 1961b). There was no recovery.

In the spring of 1962, the personal relationship shattered. The issue at hand was not nuclear weapons but Britain's decision to join the European Economic Community, a move Kennedy strongly supported. Since Britain's turn to Europe would threaten Canadian exports, thereby lightening the British counterweight to the US, a paranoid Diefenbaker saw Washington's support as a US "attempt to determine Canada's destiny" (Department of External Affairs 1962). The acrimony became personal when Liberal opposition leader Lester Pearson attended a White House gala for Nobel laureates and was photographed with the president. Although the arrangements for the soirée had been made well in advance, Diefenbaker had just called a federal election, which made it appear as if the gala was an attempt by Kennedy to undermine him. The prime minister summoned US Ambassador Livingston Merchant and launched into a vicious "tirade." Infamously, Diefenbaker threatened to blackmail the Americans with a document – the Rostow Memorandum, an innocuous list of talking points – that Kennedy had dropped during the president's 1961 visit to Ottawa. As Merchant reported back to Ottawa, the Canadian leader "was excited to a degree disturbing in a leader of an important country, and closer to hysteria than I have seen him, except on one other possible occasion." Likewise, Kennedy was incensed by the threat and vowed that he had "no intention of seeking a meeting with Diefenbaker in the near future" (Bundy 1962; Merchant 1962).

JFK was true to his word, even refusing to speak with Diefenbaker at the height of the Cuban Missile Crisis (years later, the prime minister would fabricate a phone call between himself and the president) (McKercher 2013, 110–11). After the Rostow Memorandum debacle, Kennedy had little reason to trust Diefenbaker, although in the interest of alliance solidarity, he might have done a better job of appeasing the prickly prime minister. In any event, throughout the nuclear standoff, Canadian officials and Canada's military assisted the Americans, a testament to the close cooperation between the two allied governments (McKercher 2011). But bilateral relations were in disrepair, only worsening as revived talks over Canada acquiring nuclear warheads collapsed. Diefenbaker's prevarications and public deceptions on the issue led senior American officials to issue a State Department press release calling the prime minister a liar. Kept in the dark, Kennedy was only mildly upset by his subordinates' action, urging them to avoid further public statements lest it provide further incitement for Diefenbaker to call an election and run "against us" (Ball 1963; for a different view of these events, see Stevenson 2014). An election did follow, one marked by Tory allegations of American interference to benefit Pearson's Liberals. At the end of it, Lester B. Pearson was prime minister.

The overlap between JFK and Pearson was short, but it helped quiet some of the acrimony of the preceding few years. The president held the new prime minister in high regard, and a meeting between them was organized at the Kennedys' Massachusetts compound. Short on substance but long on goodwill, the Hyannis Port gathering saw Pearson affirm Canada's nuclear commitment and the two leaders joke about Diefenbaker. As one participant recorded, the visit "was tinged with euphoria. The atmosphere was that of clearing skies after a storm – the clouds of suspicion covering Canada-U.S. relations had parted, the sunshine of friendship shone" (Ritchie 1983, 48). The storm clouds soon returned, as Canadian concerns over economic independence came to the fore. Kennedy's efforts to address the economic squabbling were cut short by his assassination. In a handwritten note to JFK's successor, Lyndon B. Johnson (LBJ), Pearson reminded the new president that he was the leader not just of the US but of "all the free democracies" (Pearson 1963).

Pearson's early outreach to Johnson paid dividends with a leader who put great stock in personal relationships. A month after LBJ took office, Pearson called to address a dispute over lumber. Johnson promised action, asserting his desire to "be a good neighbor" (Johnson 1963). The president expected help in return. As he explained to aides in early 1964, because he had helped Canada's prime minister, he had "felt free to telephone Pearson and ask him to reciprocate" by dispatching Canadian peacekeepers to Cyprus (NSC 1964). The Canadian prime minister earned credit with Johnson by agreeing to this request.

The two leaders shared a neighbourly desire for constructive relations even if they were personally mismatched. Used to the formality of diplomacy, Pearson found Johnson "an amazing combination of vitality and vulgarity" (Reid 1964). Visiting LBJ's Texas ranch in January 1965, the prime minister arrived in a three-piece suit and homburg, while the president greeted him in cowboy attire. Johnson made a gaffe, telling the press that he was delighted to welcome "Mr. Wilson" – the British prime minister. Pearson laughed off the incident, and throughout the visit, he referred to Johnson as "Senator Goldwater," the recently defeated Republican presidential candidate. Still, the trip was marked by a certain intimacy. Over morning coffee, Pearson and SSEA Paul Martin were invited to read through overnight telegrams and reports with LBJ, Secretary of State Dean Rusk, and McGeorge Bundy, the national security adviser. "I wondered," Pearson later wrote, "whether any other government leaders had that kind of free and easy relationship" (Pearson 1973, 127).

In early 1965, presidential–prime ministerial relations became less free and easy. Convinced that the US course of direct military intervention in Vietnam was "disastrous," Pearson used a public award ceremony at Temple University in Philadelphia to urge a pause in the American bombing of North Vietnam (Reid 1965). Summoning Pearson to Camp David, Johnson harangued him: "You don't come here and piss on my rug" (English 1992, 364). Pearson had delivered his advice on US soil, and it no doubt compounded LBJ's anger that he had written the prime minister a note of congratulations on receiving the award from Temple (Johnson 1965a).

A consummate politician, Johnson took the prime minister's comment in stride. As he complained to a Democratic senator, Pearson was friendly to the US but had to placate domestic critics of close Canada–US relations who had him "dodging and ducking" (Johnson 1965b). It helped that the prime minister sent several messages to the president expressing contrition for his comments at Temple and support for overall US goals in Vietnam (Pearson 1965). "I like Mr Pearson," LBJ reassured Canada's ambassador, and had "close relations" with him. He added, though, that he "did not like speeches … 'in his own yard' telling him what to do" (Washington Embassy 1966). Despite some tense moments, in the 1960s Canada and the US remained "tolerant allies" (Donaghy 2002).

A Special Relationship No More?

Tolerance seemed in increasingly short supply as the 1970s dawned amid the ongoing Vietnam War and increasing economic nationalism on both sides of the border. When Richard Nixon dispatched a new ambassador to Ottawa in 1969, he warned that Canada posed a "challenge," as did the country's new prime minister, Pierre Elliott Trudeau, who "was at times erratic with many of the characteristics so frequently associated with intellectuals" (Department of State 1969). Personally and politically, Nixon and Trudeau were an odd match. "It cannot be said that Nixon and Trudeau were ideally suited for each other," observed Henry Kissinger, adding that the prime minister "treated Nixon without any hint of condescension" while the president "accorded Trudeau both respect and attention" (Kissinger 1979, 383). In his memoirs, Trudeau put the matter plainly: "I can't say there was any warmth of feeling on either side. We did business together" (Trudeau 1993, 216).

There was much business to manage, even if Nixon made headlines by expressing the mistaken view that it was Japan, not Canada, that was his country's largest trading partner. There was a huge growth of intergovernmental contacts not only at the federal level but also among provincial and state governments. "I don't run an embassy here," Marcel Cadieux, Canada's ambassador in Washington, complained of the constant flow of officials. "I run a pissoir and a hot dog stand and no one comes near me unless they want to use one or the other" (Andrew 1993, 122). At a meeting of officials on the sidelines of Nixon's 1972 visit to Ottawa, attendees concluded that working relations were "harmonious" and that recent divisions over trade were "related more to details than to fundamentals." When the president and prime minister joined the session, Nixon agreed with this assessment, adding that there was "hardly an iota of disagreement between the two countries" (Department of External Affairs 1972).

This increasingly close cooperation contrasted with the bitterness between Nixon and Trudeau, which seems largely to have emanated from the White House. What seems to have set the president off was a comment that Trudeau – "that asshole" (Department of State 1971) – had made while visiting the Soviet Union in 1971, during which he decried the "overwhelming" US presence in Canada. "That Trudeau is a son of a bitch," Nixon told aides in July 1971, vowing, "I'll never go to that country while he's there" (Nixon 1971). The lack of warmth was noted in Canada, where the press speculated about the impact of the dearth of contact between the two leaders. In late 1971, the Canadians pressed for a meeting between president and prime minister so that Trudeau could show that he was on good terms with Nixon. As Ivan Head, Trudeau's foreign policy adviser, put it to Henry Kissinger: "What sense does it make for us to go off to Peking and to Moscow if we can't talk regularly and frequently with our closest friends?" (Head 1971). Grudgingly, the president hosted the prime minister in Washington. The meeting did little to improve Trudeau's standing in the White House. Rather, Nixon dismissed his Canadian counterpart as a "pompous egghead" (CBC News 2008). Nor did things improve when the president came to Ottawa in 1972, a development Nixon saw as a favour to that "that lousy son of a bitch." "That trip," he added, "we needed like a hole in the head" (Gill 2002). Famously commenting on Nixon's view of him – made public via the Watergate tapes – Trudeau quipped that he had "been called worse things by better people" (Trudeau 1993, 218). Still, in 1973, the prime minister went out of his way to call Nixon to express his "great confidence and respect" for the president as he faced intense criticism and scrutiny over "the Watergate thing" (CBC News 2013).

The personal acrimony subsided after Nixon resigned in August 1974, replaced by Gerald Ford. Although his time in office was short – the unelected incumbent lost his 1976 bid for the presidency to a Democratic upstart, Jimmy Carter – Ford's support proved crucial in securing Canadian membership in the nascent Group of Seven (G7) industrialized nations over French opposition (Bothwell 2007, 349).

The long list of irritants that had plagued Canada–US relations faded as the 1970s stretched on. "It is fair to say that several years ago there was some concern on both sides over the way the relationship was going," one anonymous US official stated before Trudeau visited Washington in February 1977. "But now attitudes have changed and there is a more favorable feeling" (Lavoie 1977). Jimmy Carter, a former governor, nuclear engineer, and peanut farmer, struck up friendly relationships with both Pierre Trudeau and Joe Clark. But dramatic moments did more to bolster any sense of a "special relationship" than personal ties. With the threat of Quebec separatism, Carter arranged for Trudeau to pay a high-profile visit to Washington, capped by a joint address to Congress. The Clark government, meanwhile, earned plaudits by helping six American hostages escape Iran; they were spirited out of the country with a carefully crafted cover story and Canadian passports.

The personal returned to politics with a vengeance in the 1980s. Pierre Trudeau, whose Liberals defeated Clark and the PCs at the polls in February 1980, prepared for a new counterpart in Washington, Ronald Reagan. Insiders assumed there might be difficulties. "The philosophies of government in the two countries appear in certain important respects to be diverging," one Cabinet paper on Canada–US relations concluded in late 1980 (Privy Council Office 1980). Sure enough, when Reagan took office in January 1981, large swathes of Canadians protested the presumed ideology of Reagan's Washington.

Reagan's relations with Trudeau were rocky. After their first meeting in Ottawa in March 1981, Reagan seemed pleasantly surprised. "Discovered I liked him," the president jotted down in his diary (Reagan 2009, 24). The widely circulated weekly magazine *Time* summed up this first meeting as "two men determined to like each other who find to their surprise that they actually do." Trudeau and Reagan reportedly shared a love of Robert Service poems, exchanging lines of poetry from memory (Isaacson 1981).

But the issues piled up – economic policy, relations with the Soviet Union, the prosecution of the Cold War – as did the differences between the two. Trudeau's style frustrated Reagan and, for that matter, many of the president's conservative advisers. One official dismissed the prime minister as an "erratic leftist" and decried his "pot-induced behavior" (Kaufman 1983). And after a NATO summit in the summer of 1982, a string of administration officials indicated that Trudeau's off-the-cuff remarks about the scripted nature of summits left Reagan offended. "That's not right – I spoke out at the summits," Reagan reportedly told advisers. "I was spontaneous" (Gotlieb 2006, 70).

Yet, despite the ideological and personal differences, Trudeau couldn't help but like the affable president. "I even got along quite well with Ronald Reagan," the long-time prime minister admitted in his later memoirs, "even though we were about as far apart in outlook and personality as two people could be" (Trudeau 1993, 220).

The Special Relationship Revived?

When Trudeau finally retired from politics in early 1984, observers south of the border assumed that Liberal rule would remain. Sure, the PCs had enjoyed huge favourability margins in recent months, but those advantages had evaporated. By May 1984, the PCs lagged six points behind the Liberals in the polls, plagued by "internal strife." The Central Intelligence Agency (CIA) predicted that even if the charismatic Brian Mulroney and his struggling party managed to pull off the impossible and win the 1984 election, virtually nothing would change in bilateral relations. "We do not believe that a Tory Ottawa could survive politically if it came to be seen adhering too closely to foreign policy made in Washington," one agency assessment noted (CIA 1984). On the first count, the CIA guessed wrong. Trudeau's successor, John Turner, lasted a short summer before losing to Mulroney and the PCs.

It did not take long after Mulroney's election for his government to come under fire for being too close with the Yanks. His rapport with Reagan was unmistakable. Perhaps nothing encapsulated the prime minister's friendship with Washington better than the so-called Shamrock Summit of March 1985. It was chock-full of symbolism: Held in Quebec City, Mulroney and Reagan met in the same room at the Château Frontenac where Mackenzie King had played host to Churchill and FDR during the wartime summits. Mulroney's meeting with Reagan was slated for St Patrick's Day, dovetailing neatly with their shared Irish heritage. The two famously embraced that theme. Flanked by their wives, Nancy and Mila, they undertook a rendition of "When Irish Eyes Are Smiling."

For some, the appearance illustrated nearly everything irksome about Mulroney's foreign policy. Canadians cringed at the sight of the prime minister crooning alongside the president. The historian Jack Granatstein later went one step further, speculating that the incident might rank as "the single most demeaning moment in the entire political history of Canada's relations with the United States" (Granatstein 1996, 251).

Seen from Washington, the summit heralded nothing short of "a revolution" in relations. Reagan aides acknowledged that Mulroney had no interest in "being seen as a lackey of Washington," but he would not undertake the kind of freewheeling initiatives that diverged from

US interests that Trudeau had (CBC News 1999). Allan Gotlieb, who had served as Canada's ambassador in Washington since the Trudeau years, marvelled at how much his stock – and his access – had risen, a telling admission given his earlier hopes for a Turner win in the 1984 election. "I sense I'm at the height of my powers and effectiveness," he concluded in early 1985 (Gotlieb 2006, 282). For Mulroney, the benefits seemed obvious. "To tweak the American Eagle just for the sake of doing so – to earn nothing but easy and cheap applause from Canada's anti-American lobby – is an abdication of leadership and a dereliction of Canada's duty as a trusted friend and ally," he later wrote in his memoirs. But to act as a friend, which occasionally meant "offering up the unvarnished truth," could earn respect and honesty in return (Mulroney 2007, 353–4).

Nor was this sense of a close relationship one-sided. Commenting on the Shamrock Summit, in his diary, Reagan wrote: "I have to believe U.S.–Canadian relations have never been better & certainly not at the leader level. Brian M. & I have really established a warm personal friendship" (Reagan 2009, 309). The friendly relationship did not rule out disputes, but it helped to either resolve them or keep them in perspective. And it paid dividends. As Colin Powell revealed, he and other US officials feared phone calls from Mulroney and Britain's Margaret Thatcher because they "could get the president to do anything they wanted" (Burney 2005, 100). As Donald E. Abelson stresses in his chapter in this volume, the Mulroney–Reagan relationship helped both to facilitate bilateral cooperation and to overcome internal dissent over closer ties. From this vantage point, the relationship did seem particularly special.

Mulroney's approach remained the same with Reagan's successor, fellow Republican George H.W. Bush. When the two met in Ottawa in February 1989, just days after Bush's inauguration, Mulroney seized the opportunity to affirm his government's continued support for the US. He freely admitted that the relationship had its ups and downs, including a strain of anti-American sentiment in Canada, but his government would deal with Washington "honestly and above board." "When the United States needed help," Mulroney vowed, "Canada would be there" (White House 1989).

The personal connection remained. Bush and Mulroney spoke often, touching base at regular meetings and in even more frequent telephone calls. Their conversations were friendly and relaxed, and the transcripts – preserved at Bush's presidential library – are peppered with supportive remarks and warm personal comments. "Barbara is here and sending her love," Bush told Mulroney, wrapping up one call in February 1991. The prime minister responded: "Please give her my love, too" (White House 1991).

Mulroney's relations with Reagan and Bush transcended friendly working ties. Brian and Mila Mulroney made regular trips to the Bush compound at Walker's Point, Maine, and George and Barbara Bush attended the wedding of the Mulroney's daughter, Caroline, in September 2000. After Reagan's death in 2004, Mulroney became the first foreign leader to give a eulogy at a presidential state funeral. He reprised the role at Nancy Reagan's funeral in 2016 and at George H.W. Bush's in 2018. On more than one occasion, personal bonds paid political dividends. Breakthroughs on acid rain and free trade came, at least in part, because Reagan insisted that his administration "do something for Brian" (Mulroney 2012).

After a decade marked by close ties under the Conservatives, Liberal leader Jean Chrétien campaigned on a different promise in 1993. If elected, his government would maintain a greater distance from the US. Chrétien vowed never to fish with the American president – an obvious dig at Mulroney – lest he end up on the hook like the fish. In practice, Chrétien traded fishing for golf. He and Bill Clinton regularly hit the links. After a knee injury in 1997, Clinton remarked that the latest summit between the two had unfolded according to plan, "except we didn't get to play golf" (Roberts and Blumenfeld 1997). Their easy rapport paralleled increasing economic and cultural integration between their two countries amid a period of continental and global integration.

Chrétien did not end up with the same kind of connection with Clinton's Republican successor, George W. Bush. On the campaign trail in 2000, the well-known Canadian comedian Rick Mercer pulled an easy stunt on the then candidate, informing Bush that he had received the endorsement of Prime Minister "Jean Poutine." Bush fell for it, graciously accepting the endorsement as a sign that Mr Poutine understood the candidate's commitment to a strong relationship with the US's northern neighbour (CBC News 2000). After Bush arrived in the Oval Office, relations fared little better. Initially, the two leaders seemed poised to get along. "It was love at first sight," the Canadian ambassador in Washington, Michael Kergin, later reflected of their first meeting in early 2001 (Azzi and Hillmer 2016, 727). But ties frayed as the two governments diverged, primarily over the war in Iraq. Journalists speculated that part of the problem stemmed from the Bush family's close ties to Mulroney, who, according to one report, viewed Chrétien "as an intellectual weakling" (McIlroy 2002). Close Chrétien aide Françoise Ducros's high-profile reference to Bush as "a moron" in conversations with reporters did nothing to help matters (CBC News 2002).

Bush took it in stride. "We didn't always agree," he remarked of his relations with Chrétien and with the next Liberal prime minister, Paul Martin, in a 2006 interview with CTV, "but I can understand people not agreeing with some of the decisions I made." Much of the speculation about the poor state of Canada–US relations, Bush concluded, came from name-calling. He dismissed this as "just part of politics." "If I was bothered about name-calling from Canada," he quipped, "I'd certainly be bothered about name-calling from the United States as well" (Bush 2008, 594–6). However sanguine Bush was, relations deteriorated enough, despite Martin's efforts to the contrary, that the Conservatives made better relations with the US a key plank of their party platform in the 2006 election.

Once in office, Stephen Harper made good on that promise. What followed was not a revival of the old friendships and chummy shared hobbies of the 1980s and 1990s but a solid, albeit low-key working relationship. Harper's approach, one observer noted, reflected the basic Mulroney dictum: "we can disagree without being disagreeable" (Robertson 2012). Another reason for a low-key approach was Bush's unpopularity among Canadians and polling that showed that the Harper government would face a "political risk" (Brodie 2018, 34) if it got too close to the president. Indeed, Bush made headlines in Canada by referring to Harper as "Steve" (CBC News 2006).

With Bush and his Democratic successor, Barack Obama, Harper worked to keep relations on an even keel (Anderson 2016, 139). Yet that proved difficult amid increasingly strained relations with the Obama administration, which drew out approval of the Keystone XL Pipeline. The issue poisoned relations, creating an "icy chill" (Heyman and Heyman 2019, 110.). Political columnist John Ibbitson concluded that the dispute was part of a larger cycle in which grievances piled up and relations bottomed out every decade or so. Only a new leader would be able to clean the slate. "This rhythm of irritation, freeze and renewal is cyclical," Ibbitson wrote in November 2014. "We happen to be at the low ebb of the cycle" (Ibbitson 2014).

Prime Minister Justin Trudeau seemed to prove the Ibbitson thesis. He quickly forged a friendly bond with Obama, visible in their public appearances together. At the Asia-Pacific Economic Cooperation (APEC) Summit in Manila, their first meeting in November 2015, Obama poked fun at the prime minister's newfound status as the so-called "APEC hottie" (Cullen 2015; McGraw 2015). Lighthearted exchanges became fixtures of their joint appearances. The two leaders traded friendly barbs about which country was better at hockey after Obama's hometown Blackhawks won the Stanley Cup and whether Justin Trudeau was the most famous Justin from Canada (Justin Bieber, the pop star hailing from Stratford, Ontario, being the other contender) (Gass 2016; Stars 2016). During a March 2016 state visit to Washington, Trudeau – no stranger to growing up with a parent in power – lauded Obama's daughters, Sasha and Malia, for their "extraordinary strength" and "grace" (Heil 2016).

This easy rapport provided regular fodder to journalists; a phenomenon driven in part by Trudeau's good looks. In the US, where reporting on Canada is rarely top-of-the-fold material, outlets carried breezy reports of their encounters. After Trudeau's 2016 state visit, the popular website Buzzfeed published an overview under the not-so-subtle headline "Obama and Canada's Hot Prime Minister Both Made Jokes About Justin Bieber" (Mack 2016). What impact these ties might have had on policy will remain a matter of speculation until the archival records open and we see the deliberations and debates that played out behind the scenes. But the chumminess was apparent. Bruce Heyman, Obama's ambassador in Ottawa, called this period a "Camelot moment: eighteen months during which two leaders were actually learning from each other, and two countries were learning from each other, too" (Heyman and Heyman 2019, 190).

Trumping the Special Relationship

The 2016 presidential election brought a dramatic shift. Trudeau found himself in a fraught and tense relationship with Obama's Republican successor, the former failing real estate tycoon and reality TV star,

Donald Trump. Before their first meeting in February 2017, Trudeau's preparations fixated on every possible detail to strike the right tone with the volatile new president. Eager to avoid an encounter akin to the painfully long handshake to which the president had subjected Japan's Shinzo Abe a few days earlier, Trudeau allegedly went so far as to practise shaking hands with senior aides on the short flight down to Washington before settling on a handshake with corresponding shoulder grip. The gesture, Canadian political reporter Alexander Panetta noted, seemed to sum up Trudeau's approach to Trump: "to seek contrast, not confrontation, and to be viewed as standing his ground, politely, with a dominant alpha male American leader" (Panetta 2019).

Nearly everything about Trump's diplomacy defied the normal standards of the office. He retained bizarre habits from his days in business, tearing stories out of magazines that bothered him, scrawling his reactions on top with a Sharpie, and sending them to the party he deemed responsible for this latest slight. In May 2017, when *Businessweek* carried a story on Trudeau under the title "The Anti-Trump," the president reportedly mailed a copy to the prime minister with a handwritten note in silver Sharpie: "Looking good! Hope it's not true!" The correspondence was so unusual that, according to reports, the Canadian ambassador thought it a prank and called the White House to confirm that the marked-up cover was, in fact, genuine diplomatic mail (Swan 2019).

Faced with a difficult situation, Trudeau turned to Brian Mulroney. The former prime minister had a personal relationship with Trump, and with Secretary of Commerce Wilbur Ross, not to mention familiarity with one of the major issues causing problems in the relationship since Trump's election: the North American Free Trade Agreement (NAFTA). Mulroney became the government's "unofficial Trump-whisperer" (Harper 2017). Some observers cringed. "It's kind of Brian Mulroney to re-embarrass himself every generation or so," one *Toronto Star* commentator quipped after it came out that the ex-PM had sung "When Irish Eyes Are Smiling" for a Mar-a-Lago audience, including President Trump (Salutin 2017).

Trudeau needed whatever help he could get. Trump's obsession with renegotiating trade arrangements relied on specious arguments and outright falsities that fed into the president's nativist and protectionist world view. Trade dominated relations, and, to mitigate Trump's hostile views, Trudeau and his team launched a "charm offensive" to reach US officials at every level of government, including the president's daughter. According to documents released in response to an Access to Information request, Canadian representatives held more than 1,300 such meetings with their US counterparts between 20 January 2017 – the date of Trump's inauguration – and 31 August 2018 (Taylor-Vaisey 2019).

Trump's outbursts made the task more difficult. After the G7 met in Charlevoix, Quebec, in the summer of 2018, Trump sent a parting shot on his Twitter account, accusing the prime minister of being "very dishonest and weak" and of lying about Canada's trade relations with the US. Trump aides piled on. Economic adviser Larry Kudlow insisted that Trudeau had "stabbed us in the back," undercutting the president before a scheduled summit with North Korean leader Kim Jong-un. Trump's top adviser on trade matters and future booster of the failed 2021 Capitol insurrection Peter Navarro went one step further, telling Fox News that "there's a special place in hell" for the prime minister. Chrystia Freeland, then foreign minister, dismissed the noise. Claims that Canada posed a national security threat to the US – the ostensible pretext for Trump's decision to introduce tariffs on Canadian steel and aluminum – were "absurd and frankly insulting." As for the Trump team's tough language, Freeland pushed back against the *ad hominem* attacks as not "a particularly appropriate or useful way" to conduct relations between close allies (Bilefsky and Porter 2018).

With Trump in the White House, popular outlets churned out retrospectives fondly looking back at the "ultimate bromance" between Obama and Trudeau. "See why we love to love these two together," the fashion magazine *Harper's Bazaar* exhorted readers (Algoo 2017; Hansler 2016). Obama's own actions spurred this kind of talk: prior to the 2019 election, he joined Trudeau for beers in Ottawa and endorsed the prime minister's re-election, taking to Twitter to call Trudeau a "hard-working, effective leader" (Obama 2019). In 2021, with another Canadian election campaign in full swing, the former president repeated his endorsement. "Justin has been an effective leader and strong voice for democratic values, and I'm proud of the work we did together," he tweeted days before voters across Canada headed to the polls (Obama 2021). Never before had a former president intervened in a Canadian election, a testament to the Obama–Trudeau bromance.

Perhaps because of Obama's embrace of Trudeau, increasingly Trump seemed to relish opportunities to lash out at the prime minister and disparage his policies, injecting a healthy dose of chaos into the relationship. In late 2019, after Canada's public broadcaster cut Trump's cameo from its airing of the 1992 film *Home Alone 2* to make room for advertising, the president tweeted "I guess Justin T doesn't much like my making him pay up on NATO or Trade!" (Trump 2019). These habits continued even after Trump grudgingly left office in January 2021. In February 2022, when the self-styled Freedom Convoy descended on Ottawa, the former president threw his weight behind their protests against what he wildly dubbed "the harsh policies of far left lunatic Justin Trudeau" (Morrow 2022).

To manage the highs and lows, Trudeau charted a careful course designed to keep the relationship as steady as possible. The prime minister regularly deflected questions on Trump's policies and leadership style. At critical moments, he hewed closely to the belief that saying nothing would be better in the long run, most notably in his drawn-out pause after being asked to comment on Trump's calls for military action against Black Lives Matter protests in the summer of 2020 (Gilmore 2020). The COVID-19 pandemic spared the two leaders any awkward in-person encounters during the president's tumultuous final year in office.

Trudeau's efforts to tread carefully did not always work out according to plan. At NATO's 2019 summit in London, cameras picked up the prime minister on a hot mic gossiping about the president with British prime minister Boris Johnson, French president Emmanuel Macron, Dutch prime minister Mark Rutte, and Princess Anne. Trump lashed out after seeing the video, calling Trudeau "two-faced" (Blatchford and Gardner 2019). In the wake of the dust-up, opposition politicians charged that Trudeau's comments might jeopardize the new North American trade agreement – itself a testament to just how much the personal shaped the political during the Trump years.

Canadians tended to chafe at Trump's style. His four years in office saw popular impressions of the US plummet to their lowest point in four decades. In one 2020 poll, just 29 per cent of respondents held a somewhat or very favourable view of the US, a sharp drop-off from 73 per cent in 2010 (Chase 2020). Attitudes rebounded after the 2020 election, when US voters opted to send Obama's former vice-president and long-time Democratic senator, Joe Biden, to the White House. By the summer of 2021, 61 per cent of Canadians held a favourable view of the US, according to one survey (McCarten 2021).

Biden's arrival on the scene brought an end to the theatrics of years past but not a sudden rejuvenation of Canada–US relations. In February 2021, as part of their virtual summit (a format reflecting the COVID-19 pandemic still raging), Biden and Trudeau released a forty-point road map to renew relations between the two countries (Prime Minister's Office 2021). But progress on the specifics remained sluggish. Months after the promised breakthroughs, veteran Canadian political correspondent Paul Wells likened it to an "arid news desert" (Wells 2021). Other commentators assumed that the way Canadians often viewed the relationship with the US was now outmoded. "In pursuing American interests," Aaron Shull and Michael Den Tandt argued, "the United States now looks to the Pacific, to Australia principally, as a bulwark against a rising China; it looks to Europe and sees a gathering Russian military threat. In this context, is it any wonder administration officials have little time to spare for Canadian entreaties about free trade in electric vehicles?" (Shull and Den Tandt 2021).

Trudeau's policies hardly helped matters. The Biden administration came to office focused on the security landscape emerging in the Indo-Pacific and the threat posed by the rising power of the People's Republic of China; Trudeau's government had no meaningful policy for the region. Reports in August 2022, some two years after the Canadians first undertook a review to develop an Indo-Pacific strategy, indicated that the working draft made no mention of China (Fife and Chase 2022). In the rapidly changing international context of the 2020s, Canada's unwillingness to play a more serious role in the world has made it less special to the US.

Conclusion

People make the "special relationship," but what sets relations between the US and Canada apart are not the bonds between leaders. Rather, it is the vast web of ties that criss-cross the border, most of them personal. "The relationship between Canada and the United States," as George W. Bush put it, "is really a relationship not necessarily by government only but by the peoples, by this interchange, by the exchanges we have, by the relatives on both sides of the border. And that's what really makes the relationship unique and very strong" (Bush 2006, 594–6).

As with other special relationships, the personal connections between leaders feature prominently in the mythology. Close ties, whether between King and Roosevelt or Mulroney and Reagan, have had an impact on policy. The reverse was also true. Personal acrimony can spill over into the political, as happened with Diefenbaker and Kennedy or Trudeau and Trump. But then there was Richard Nixon's loathing of Pierre Trudeau, which seemed to have little bearing on a growing intergovernmental interdependence. Important, too, has been the perception – at least for Canadian leaders – that personal relations with the president (either too close or not close enough) can come at a political cost, a consideration for Jean Chrétien and Stephen Harper.

In a wartime letter to King, when commenting on the importance or lack thereof of personal relations, FDR mused "that it is a grand and glorious thing for Canada and United States to have the team of Mackenzie and Roosevelt at the helm for times like these." Although "probably both nations could get along without us," the president wrote, "our association has brought some proven benefits to both nations" (Roosevelt 1941b). Or, to paraphrase King, good relations between president and prime minister are important when necessary but not necessarily important.

References

Algoo, Jennifer. 2017. "The Ultimate Bromance: Barack Obama and Justin Trudeau." *Harper's Bazaar*, 7 June. https://www.harpersbazaar.com/culture/features/g8638/justin-trudeau-barack-obama-photos.

American and Far Eastern Division. 1942. Report on Canadian Representation with the United States of America, 31 March. LAC, RG 25, vol. 6786, file 1415–40.

Anderson, Greg. 2016. "Canada and the United States in the Harper Years: Still 'Special,' But Not Especially Important." In *The Harper Era in Canadian Foreign Policy: Parliament, Politics, and Canada's Global Posture*, edited by Adam Chapnick and Christopher John Kukucha, 135–50. Vancouver: UBC Press.

Andrew, Arthur. 1993. *The Rise and Fall of a Middle Power*. Toronto: James Lorimer.

Azzi, Stephen, and Norman Hillmer. 2016. "Intolerant Allies: Canada and the George W. Bush Administration." *Diplomacy and Statecraft* 27, no. 4: 726–45.

Ball, George. 1963. Teleconference with the President, 31 January, 9:00 p.m. Princeton University, Seeley Mudd Manuscript Library, MC 031, box 103, folder 2.

Bilefsky, Dan, and Catherine Porter. 2018. "Trump's 'Bully' Attack on Trudeau Outrages Canadians." *New York Times*, 10 June. https://www.nytimes.com/2018/06/10/world/canada/g-7-justin-trudeau-trump.html.

Blatchford, Andy, and Laura Gardner2019. "Trudeau's Delicate Trump Strategy Takes a Hit." *Politico*, 4 December. https://www.politico.com/news/2019/12/04/trudeau-trump-two-faced-nato-075338.

Bothwell, Robert. 1992. *Canada and the United States: The Politics of Partnership*. New York: Twayne.

– 2007. *Alliance and Illusion: Canada and the World, 1945–1984*. Vancouver: UBC Press.

– 2015. *Your Country, My Country: A Unified History of the United States and Canada*. New York: Oxford University Press.

Brodie, Ian. 2018. *At the Centre of Government: The Prime Minister and the Limits on Political Power*. Montreal and Kingston: McGill-Queen's University Press.

Bryce, R.B. 1960. Notes on the Discussion in President Eisenhower's Office, June 3rd, 1960, 17 June. LAC, MG 31 E83, vol. 3, file 8.

Bundy, McGeorge. 1962. Note to George Ball, 8 May. John F. Kennedy Presidential Library, National Security Files, box 18, folder Canada, General, Rostow Memorandum and Related Materials 5/61–5/63.

Burney, Derek. 2005. *Getting It Done: A Memoir*. Montreal and Kingston: McGill-Queen's University Press.

Bush, George W. 2008. "Interview with CTV." 28 March. In *Public Papers of the Presidents of the United States: George W. Bush 2006*, bk. I. Washington, DC: US Government Printing Office.

CBC News. 1999. "Shamrock Summit Seen as 'Turning Point' for US–Canada Relations." 18 August. https://www.cbc.ca/news/world/shamrock-summit-seen-as-turning-point-for-u-s-canada-relations-1.171924.

– 2000. "22 Minutes Star Pulls Prank on George W. Bush." 22 March. https://www.cbc.ca/news/canada/22-minutes-star-pulls-prank-on-george-w-bush-1.212339.

– 2002. "Canadian Official Called Bush 'a Moron.'" 26 November. https://www.cbc.ca/news/world/canadian-official-called-bush-a-moron-1.321445.

– 2006. "Bush Can Call Me 'Steve': Harper."12 July. https://www.cbc.ca/news/canada/bush-can-call-me-steve-harper-1.612381.

– 2008. "Just-Released 1971 Recording Captures Talks between Nixon, 'Pompous' Trudeau." 8 December. https://www.cbc.ca/news/canada/just-released-1971-recording-captures-talks-between-nixon-pompous-trudeau-1.755465.

– 2013. "Pierre Trudeau Offered Nixon Support over 'Watergate Thing.'" 21 August. https://www.cbc.ca/news/politics/pierre-trudeau-offered-nixon-support-over-watergate-thing-1.1395894.

Central Intelligence Agency (CIA). 1984. Directorate of Intelligence Assessment. "Canada: Can the Progressive Conservatives Win?" CIA Records Search Tool, CIA-RDP85S00316R000100100007-3.

Chase, Stephen. 2020. "Canadian Opinions of the US at Lowest in Nearly 40 Years, Polling Program Shows." *Globe and Mail*, 15 October. https://www.theglobeandmail.com/politics/article-canadian-opinions-of-the-us-at-lowest-in-nearly-40-years-polling.

Cullen, Catherine. 2015. "Justin Trudeau, #APEChottie, Swarmed by Shrieking Admirers." 19 November. https://www.cbc.ca/news/politics/trudeau-apec-admirers-apechottie-shrieks-1.3325845.

Department of External Affairs. 1962. Meeting between Prime Minister Macmillan and Prime Minister Diefenbaker in the Privy Council Chamber, 30 April. LAC, RG 25, vol. 6151, file 50412-40-pt. 4.

– 1972. Record of Canada–United States Conversations, 14 April. LAC, RG 25, file 20-USA-9-Nixon.

Department of State. 1952. Memorandum of Conversation, 7 April. *Foreign Relations with the United States*, 1952–1953, vol. 6, Part 2, doc. 938.

– 1956. Memorandum of Conversation, 3 February. Dwight D. Eisenhower Presidential Library, John Foster Dulles Papers, General Correspondence and Memos Series, Memos of Conversation – General E Through I.

– 1969. Memorandum of Conversation, 20 August. *Foreign Relations with the United States*, 1969–76, vol. 41, doc. 98.

– 1971. Conversation among Nixon, Laird, and Kissinger. 19 May. *Foreign Relations with the United States*, 1969–76, vol. 39, doc. 51.

Diefenbaker, John. 1957. Letter to Dwight Eisenhower, 22 June. Dwight D. Eisenhower Presidential Library, Ann Whitman File, International Series, box 6, folder Canada (7).

– 1961a. Letter to Elmer Diefenbaker, 18 May. In *Personal Letters of a Public Man: The Family Letters of John G. Diefenbaker*, edited by Thad McIlroy. Toronto: Doubleday, 1985.

– 1961b. Note to Arnold Heeney, 9 November. LAC, MG 30 E144, vol. 1, file 16.

Donaghy, Greg. 2002. *Tolerant Allies: Canada and the United States, 1963–1968*. Montreal and Kingston: McGill-Queen's University Press.

Dulles, John Foster. 1953. Memorandum to Eisenhower, 6 May. US National Archives and Records Administration, RG 59, Central Files, 742.13/5–453.

– 1958. Memorandum to Dwight Eisenhower, 3 July. Dwight D. Eisenhower Presidential Library, Ann Whitman File, International Series, box 6, folder Canada (7).

English, John. 1992. *The Worldly Years: The Life of Lester Pearson, 1949–1972*. Toronto: A.A. Knopf.

Fife, Robert, and Steven Chase. 2022. "Canada Must Put China 'Front and Centre' in Indo-Pacific Strategy or It Risks Irrelevance, Experts Say." *Globe and Mail,* 3 August. https://www.theglobeandmail.com/politics/article-ottawa-indo-pacific-strategy-china.

Foster. 1948. Letter to Hickerson. 2 January. NARA, RG 59, 842.20 Defense/1–248.

Gass, Nick. 2016. "Obama Taunts Trudeau on Canada's Stanley Cup Drought." *Politico*, 10 March. https://www.politico.com/story/2016/03/obama-justin-trudeau-stanley-cup-220564.

Gill, Alexandra. 2002. "Nixon's 'Bushy-Haired Bastard' Bites Back." *Globe and Mail*, 22 March.

Gilmore, Rachel. 2020. "Trudeau's Long Silence: PM Pauses, Avoids Trump's Name in Reaction to Protests." *CTV News*, 2 June. https://www.ctvnews.ca/politics/trudeau-s-long-silence-pm-pauses-avoids-trump-s-name-in-reaction-to-protests-1.4965372.

Goodpaster, Andrew. 1960. Memorandum of Conference with the President, 3 June. Dwight D. Eisenhower Presidential Library, White House Office, Office of the Staff Secretary, State Department Subseries, box 4, folder June–July 1960.

Gotlieb, Allan. 2006. *The Washington Diaries, 1981–1989*. Toronto: McClelland and Stewart.

Granatstein, J.L. 1996. *Yankee Go Home? Canadians and Anti-Americanism*. Toronto: HarperCollins.

Hansler, Jennifer. 2016. "Obama and Trudeau: 5 Bromantic Moments." *ABC News*, 29 June. https://abcnews.go.com/Politics/obama-trudeau-bromantic-moments/story?id=40206461.

Harper, Tim. 2017. "Who Serves as Trump-Whisperer to Justin Trudeau? Brian Mulroney, Of Course!" *Toronto Star*, 20 June. https://www.thestar.com/news/canada/2017/06/20/who-serves-as-trump-whisperer-to-justin-trudeau-brian-mulroney-of-course.html.

Head, Ivan. 1971. Note to file, 29 November. LAC, RG 25, vol. 18493, file 20-1-2-USA-pt. 23.

Heeney, A.D.P. 1961a. Diary Entry, 22 January. Library and Archives Canada. MG 30 E144, vol. 2, file "Memoirs, 1961, Chapter 15, Diary #3.

– 1961b. Note to John Diefenbaker, 3 November. LAC, MG 30 E144, vol. 1, file 16.

– 1972. *The Things That Are Caesar's*. Toronto: University of Toronto Press.

Heil, Emily. 2016. "Trudeau Tells Obama Girls, at Their First State Dinner, He Understands What They're Going Through." *Toronto Star*, 11 March.

https://www.thestar.com/news/world/2016/03/11/trudeau-tells-obama-girls-at-their-first-state-dinner-he-understands-what-theyre-going-through.html.

Herter, Christian. 1960. Telephone Conversation with the President, 8 April. Dwight D. Eisenhower Presidential Library, Christian Herter Papers, box 10, folder Presidential Phone Calls 1–6/60 (2).

Heyman, Bruce, and Vicki Heyman. 2019. *The Art of Diplomacy: Strengthening the Canada–US Relationship in Times of Uncertainty*. Toronto: Simon and Schuster.

Ibbitson, John. 2014. "Obama, Harper Don't Like Each Other, and Only a New Leader Can Thaw Relations." *Globe and Mail*, 21 November. https://www.theglobeandmail.com/news/politics/obama-harper-dont-like-each-other-and-only-a-new-leader-can-thaw-relations/article21691812.

Isaacson, Walter. 1981. "Taking His Act on the Road." *Time*, 23 March.

Johnson, Lyndon B. 1963. Phone Conversation with Lester B. Pearson, 27 December. Lyndon B. Johnson Presidential Library, Recordings and Transcripts of Telephone Conversations and Meetings, White House Series, Presidential recording K6312.19.

– 1965a. Letter to Lester B. Pearson, 30 March. Lyndon B. Johnson Presidential Library, White House Central Files, Subject Files, box 19, folder CO43.

– 1965b. Telephone Conversation with Birch Bayh, 15 June, 1:20 p.m. Lyndon Baines Johnson Presidential Library, Recordings and Transcripts of Telephone Conversations and Meetings, White House Series, June 1965, box 7.

Kaufman, Michael. 1983. "Top US Official Quoted as Ridiculing Trudeau." *New York Times*, 23 December.

King, William Lyon Mackenzie. LAC, Diary, https://library-archives.canada.ca/eng/collection/research-help/politics-government-law/pages/diaries-william-lyon-mackenzie-king.aspx

Kissinger, Henry. 1979. *The White House Years*. Boston: Little, Brown.

Lavoie, Michael. 1977. "Carter to Meet with Trudeau in Wide-Ranging Talk." *Washington Post*, 20 February.

Mack, David. 2016. "Obama and Canada's Hot Prime Minister Both Made Jokes About Justin Bieber." *BuzzFeed News*, 11 March. https://www.buzzfeednews.com/article/davidmack/obama-and-canadas-hot-prime-minister-both-made-jokes-about-j.

Macmillan, Harold. 1959. Note, 22 March. National Archives of the United Kingdom, FO 371/1052/4.

Martin, Lawrence. 1983. *The Presidents and the Prime Ministers*. Toronto: Doubleday.

McCarten, James. 2021. "Canada's Opinions of US Markedly Higher With Biden in White House, Polls Suggest." *CTV News*, 10 June. https://www.ctvnews.ca/canada/canada-s-opinions-of-u-s-markedly-higher-with-biden-in-white-house-poll-suggests-1.5464347.

McGraw, Meredith. 2015. "President Obama Offers the 'APEC Hottie' Words of Wisdom." *ABC News*, 19 November. https://abcnews.go.com/Politics/president-obama-offers-apec-hottie-words-wisdom/story?id=35313010.

McIlroy, Anne. 2002. "Uneasy Neighbours." *The Guardian*, 2 December. https://www.theguardian.com/world/2002/dec/02/worlddispatch.usa.

McKercher, Asa. 2011. "A 'Half-hearted Response'? Canada and the Cuban Missile Crisis, 1962." *International History Review* 33, no. 2: 335–52.

– 2013. "Diefenbaker's World: *One Canada* and the History of Canadian–American Relations, 1961–63." *The Historian* 75, no. 1: 94–120.

Merchant, Livingston. 1962. Memorandum to George Ball, 5 May. John F. Kennedy Presidential Library, National Security Files, box 18, folder Canada, General, Rostow Memorandum and Related Materials 5/61-5/63.

Lord Moran. 1966. *Churchill: Taken from the Diaries of Lord Moran*. Boston: Houghton Mifflin.

Morrow, Adrian. 2022. Twitter post, 4 February, 1:05 pm. https://twitter.com/AdrianMorrow/status/1489661479561437186?s=20&t=p2E2jVoH_FR-TiL321E_Yw.

Morton, W.L. 1964. Review of *William Lyon Mackenzie King*, vol. 2: *The Lonely Heights, 1924–1932*." *Canadian Historical Review* 45, no. 4.

Mulroney, Brian. 2007. *Memoirs, 1939–1993*. Toronto: McClelland and Stewart.

– 2012. "Acid Rain: A Case Study in Canada–US Relations." *Policy Options*. April.

National Security Council (NSC). 1964. Summary Record of NSC Meeting 526, 3 April. Lyndon B. Johnson Presidential Library, National Security Files, NSC Meetings, box 1, folder NSC Meetings.

Nixon, Richard M. 1971. Recording, 6 July. Richard Nixon Presidential Library. Presidential Recordings, Rmn e5341.

Obama, Barack. 2019. Twitter post, 16 October, 1:58 pm. https://twitter.com/BarackObama/status/1184528998669389824?s=20&t=LQDPCLCoE149gfTBT_OdEA.

– 2021. Twitter post, 16 September, 12:31 pm. https://twitter.com/BarackObama/status/1438541175607242766?s=20&t=d8zI_NIR9Nj9223MiKU9dQ.

Panetta, Alexander. 2019. "Trudeau's Reelection Bid Faces the Trump Test." *Politico*, 2 May. https://www.politico.com/amp/story/2019/05/02/trump-justin-trudeau-canada-handshake-1400635.

Pearson, Lester B. 1949. Memorandum to St Laurent, 24 February. LAC, MG 26 L, vol. 235.

– 1951. Department of External Affairs. *Statements and Speeches* 51/14, 10 April.

– 1963. Letter to Lyndon B. Johnson, 3 December. Lyndon B. Johnson Presidential Library, National Security Files, Head of State Correspondence, box 1, folder Canada.

– 1965. Letter to Lyndon B. Johnson, 5 August. Lyndon B. Johnson Presidential Library, National Security Files, Head of State Correspondence, box 1, folder Canada.

– 1973. *Mike: The Memoirs of the Rt. Hon. Lester B. Pearson,* vol. 3, edited by John Munro and Alex Inglis. Toronto: University of Toronto Press.

Perras, Galen Roger. 2010. "The Myth of Obsequious Rex: Mackenzie King, Franklin D. Roosevelt, and Canada–US Security, 1935–1940." In *Transnationalism: Canada–United States History into the Twenty-first Century*, edited by Michael Behiels and Reginald Stuart. Montreal and Kingston: McGill-Queen's University Press.

Prime Minister's Office. 2021. "Roadmap for a Renewed US–Canada Partnership." 23 February. https://pm.gc.ca/en/news/statements/2021/02/23/roadmap-renewed-us-canada-partnership.

Privy Council Office. 1980. Memorandum, "Canada–United States Relations," 10 December. LAC, RG 25, vol. 28698, file 20-1-2-USA-pt. 61.

Reagan, Ronald. 2009. *The Reagan Diaries*, vol. 1: *January 1981–October 1985*, edited by Douglas Brinkley. New York: Harper.

Reid, Escott. 1964. Note, "L.B. Pearson." 27 August. LAC, MG 31, E46, vol. 35, file Pearson, Lester.

– 1965. Note, "L.B. Pearson." 27 March. LAC, MG 31, E46, vol. 35, file Pearson, Lester.

Ritchie, Charles. 1981. *Storm Signals: More Undiplomatic Diaries, 1962–1971*. Toronto: Macmillan.

Roberts, Roxanne, and Laura Blumenfeld. 1997. "Bridging the Golf between Nations." *Washington Post*, 9 April.

Robertson, Colin. 2012. "Stephen Harper's Management of Canada–US Relations." *Policy Options*. April.

Robinson, H. Basil. 1961. Note to Arnold Heeney, 18 January. LAC, MG 30 E144, vol. 1, file 16.

– 1963. Note to file, "General Colour of Hyannis Port Meeting." 15 May. LAC, MG 31 E83, vol. 12, file 1.

Roosevelt, Franklin Delano. 1941a. "Address at Queen's University." *Public Papers of the Presidents of the United States, 1938*. New York: Random House.

– 1941b. Letter to William Lyon Mackenzie King, 15 November. FDR Presidential Library, Roosevelt PSF, file PSF 1 Diplo correspondence – Canada.

– 1943. Letter to Winston Churchill, 24 July. In *Churchill and Roosevelt: The Complete Correspondence*, vol. 2, edited by Warren F. Kimball. Princeton: Princeton University Press.

Salutin, Rick. 2017. "Brian Mulroney, the Man with No Shame." *Toronto Star*, 22 February. https://www.thestar.com/opinion/commentary/2017/02/22/brian-mulroney-the-man-with-no-shame-salutin.html?rf.

Shull Aaron, and Michael Den Tandt. 2021. "Is US President Joe Biden Good or Bad for Canada?" Centre for International Governance Innovation, 13 December. https://www.cigionline.org/articles/is-us-president-joe-biden-good-or-bad-for-canada.

Stacey, C.P. 1976. *A Very Double Life: The Private World of Mackenzie King*. Toronto: Macmillan.

Stars, Jenny. 2016. "Obama and Trudeau Poke Fun at Cruz, Bieber, and Obama's Gray Hairs." *Washington Post*, 11 March. https://www.washingtonpost.com/news/morning-mix/wp/2016/03/11/obama-and-trudeau-poke-fun-at-cruz-bieber-and-obamas-gray-hairs.

Stevenson, Michael D. 2014. "'Tossing a Match into Dry Hay': Nuclear Weapons and the Crisis in US–Canadian Relations, 1962–63." *Journal of Cold War Studies* 16: 5–34.

Swan, Jonathan. 2019. "Inside Trump's Strange Pen-pal Diplomacy with Justin Trudeau." *Axios*, 11 August. https://www.axios.com/2019/08/11/donald-trump-justin-trudeau-sharpie-letters.

Taylor-Vaisey, Nick. 2019. "Canada's Next NAFTA 'Charm Offensive' Won't Look Like the Last One." *Maclean's*, 7 February. https://www.macleans.ca/politics/canadas-next-nafta-charm-offensive-wont-look-like-the-last-one.

Trudeau, Pierre Elliott. 1993. *Memoirs*. Toronto: McClelland and Stewart.

Trump, Donald. 2019. Twitter post, 26 December, 7:03 pm. https://www.thetrumparchive.com.

Washington Embassy. 1957. Telegram to Ottawa, no. 1174, 17 May. LAC, MG 26 N1, vol. 65.

– 1966. Telegram to Ottawa, no. 2163, 23 July. LAC, MG 31 E44, vol. 9, file Presentation of Credentials to President L.B. Johnson.

Wells, Paul. 2021. "The Biden–Trudeau Talk: Build Back Whatever." *Maclean's*, 3 August. https://www.macleans.ca/politics/ottawa/the-biden-trudeau-talk-build-back-whatever.

White House. 1989. Memorandum of Conversation, "President's Meeting with Prime Minister Mulroney," 10 February. George H.W. Bush Presidential Library, Memoranda of Conversations and Telephone Conversations.

– 1991. Telcon with Brian Mulroney, Prime Minister of Canada, 27 February. George H.W. Bush Presidential Library, Memoranda of Conversations and Telephone Conversations.

Whitman, Ann. 1958. Note, 15 July. Dwight D. Eisenhower Presidential Library, Ann Whitman File, Dulles–Herter Series, box 10.

Wrong, Hume. 1949a. Memorandum, 12 February. LAC, MG 26 L, vol. 235.

– 1949b. Memorandum, 18 February. LAC, MG 26 L, vol. 235.

6

Brian Mulroney, Ronald Reagan, and the Politics of Friendship

DONALD E. ABELSON

On 21 June 1984, President Ronald Reagan welcomed Brian Mulroney, then Official Leader of the Opposition in the Canadian Parliament, to the White House. It was the first time the leaders met, and over the course of a forty-five-minute discussion in the Oval Office, they exchanged ideas on a range of important bilateral issues. Although it was not unprecedented for an American president to extend an invitation to the leader of the opposition, it signalled to even the most casual observer of Canada–US relations that Reagan was prepared, indeed, anxious, to do business with Mulroney (see Bothwell 2015; Hale 2013; Stewart 2017). The optics of the meeting, and the media attention it generated, could not have gone over well with John Turner, who, nine days later, would be sworn in as Canada's seventeenth prime minister (see Litt 2011). Clearly, Reagan had little confidence that Prime Minister Pierre Trudeau's successor would hold on to the country's highest office after the Canadian federal election in the fall of 1984 (Mulroney 2007, 29–1).

It did not take long for Mulroney's charm and charisma to make an impression on Reagan, who five months later would go on to win one of the greatest landslides in American history, securing all but thirteen electoral votes. In a recent interview with L. Ian MacDonald, editor of *Policy Magazine*, a leading Canadian outlet on public policy, Mulroney recalled that, following the meeting, Reagan pulled him aside in the Rose Garden before their joint news conference and said, "Well, it certainly wouldn't hurt to have another Irishman, with the two of us running North America" (MacDonald 2021, 2). In his diary recalling the initial meeting with Mulroney, Reagan noted, "He's an Irishman thru & thru" (Brinkley 2007, 249).

In the federal election on 4 September 1984, Mulroney defied the prognostications of countless pundits by leading the Progressive Conservative Party to the largest electoral landslide in Canadian history, grabbing 211 seats in the House of Commons, an increase of 111 seats. The Liberals were left with only 40 seats, a dramatic fall from the 135 they held prior to the election. As the boy from Baie-Comeau, a small eastern Quebec town on the north shore of the St Lawrence River, celebrated this momentous victory (see MacDonald 1984; Murphy, Auf der Maur, and Chodos 1984; Sawatsky 1991), Reagan wasted little time extending his congratulations. "He's just won a tremendous victory," Reagan observed. "He's a super fellow. We got along fine & will continue to do so" (Brinkley 2007, 269). After three years of trying to navigate the Canadian–American file with Prime Minister Pierre Trudeau, whom Reagan "liked" (Brinkley 2007, 7) but at times considered rude, obnoxious, and arrogant (Brinkley 2007, 156), having Mulroney lead Canada as its eighteenth prime minister would have left a smile on the face of the fortieth president of the US.

For Reagan, Mulroney represented not only an ideological ally (although the two leaders would come to disagree on many policy files in the ensuing years) but also a kindred spirit who understood that the bilateral relationship with the US had to be treated as a priority, one that required careful and prudent management. In Mulroney, Reagan also saw a leader who appreciated the burden of responsibility the US had to bear on the world stage, as well as a friend to whom he could turn for advice and support when he found himself embroiled in political battles both at home and abroad. Although Mulroney was a political neophyte when he became prime minister, he did not need to be reminded of how important a close relationship with the US was for Canada and for the country's efforts to establish a stronger voice internationally. He also understood that by building stronger and closer ties with the US, he would inevitably contribute to heightened anti-American sentiments in Canada, but it was a price he was willing to pay. For Mulroney, Reagan represented a bold and visionary leader who would not capitulate to those intent on diminishing his authority. He was someone Mulroney could work with – a person he admired and a friend he would come to value (Larkin 2004). It did not take long for them to strike up a personal and political friendship, one that would lay the foundation for one of the most important periods in the history of bilateral relations between Canada and the US. Indeed, according to a panel of experts assembled by *Policy Magazine* (*Policy Magazine* 2021), the relationships forged by Brian Mulroney with President Reagan and President George H.W. Bush explain why Mulroney is widely regarded as Canada's greatest prime minister in overseeing the country's long and enduring partnership with the US.

The friendship between Canada's eighteenth prime minister and the fortieth US president, which grew over hundreds of hours during the nearly five years they worked together (LAC, MG 26, P18-4, vol. 19#45), would pave the way for bilateral cooperation on multiple fronts, most importantly, the passage of the 1988 Canada–US Free Trade Agreement. But the special relationship between them manifested itself in other ways not often discussed by scholars. For example, Reagan's fondness and respect for Mulroney helps explain why, when Mulroney was trailing in the polls in the lead-up to the 1988 federal election, the president worked closely with his advisers to figure out what they could do to boost the prime minister's popularity at home. As will be discussed, this was not the first time that Reagan would intervene to generate support for Mulroney and for Canada. And in many tangible ways, Mulroney would go to bat for Reagan. However, while the special ties between the two leaders facilitated cooperation and policy coordination on several issues affecting trade, defence cooperation, investment, and border security, their mutual respect also afforded them an opportunity to manage differences over many pressing concerns. These included, but were not limited to, the Strategic Defense Initiative (SDI), known as "Star Wars," and other policies with implications for the global arms race; Canada's insistence on the negotiation of an agreement to combat acid rain; and strategies for how best to navigate relations with Soviet leader Mikhail Gorbachev.

With few exceptions, the academic literature on international diplomacy devotes only modest attention to the important role that friendships between world leaders can play both in advancing shared policy goals and in finding ways to express and contain disagreement, often publicly, when the costs of a political fallout may be profound. While scholars have written dozens of books and hundreds of articles detailing how policy advisers and others toiling in the inner circles of presidents and prime ministers have helped influence their thinking on key policy matters (Ginsberg 2021), far less consideration has been given to how leaders representing the sovereign interests of their respective states work with one another even when they find themselves at odds over the direction of various policy initiatives.

The purpose of this chapter is not to provide a definitive history of the personal and professional relationship forged by Brian Mulroney and Ronald Reagan. Such an inquiry would far exceed the scope of this undertaking. Rather, this chapter reveals how their friendship created multiple opportunities to find common ground even when their political and policy agendas did not necessarily align. Information about how Mulroney and Reagan were able to balance competing domestic and foreign political interests with the desire to strengthen bilateral relations is coming into greater light with the release of documents previously closed to the public. Indeed, memos based on meetings, correspondence, and phone calls between the two leaders help shed light on this critical aspect of bilateral diplomacy.

There is little doubt that the rules of diplomacy, combined with an abundance of mutual respect, decency, and integrity helped create a unique and enduring bond between Mulroney and Reagan. Many current and recent world leaders have a propensity to take to X/Twitter and other social media to express their support or condemnation of others who occupy high office; by contrast, Mulroney and Reagan placed a premium on maintaining an open and candid dialogue. Instead of trying to embarrass or humiliate each other by leaking sensitive information that might create an unfavourable impression, they had each other's back. And if it was not possible to support the other's political priorities because of competing national interests, they went out of their way to explain why they had to maintain their position. Put simply, both leaders recognized that together they could accomplish great things, and they rarely wavered from this commitment. Politics mattered, but in many ways, their friendship mattered more. Well after they left office and were no longer required to weigh in on various policy matters, Mulroney and Reagan remained close. What the two leaders accomplished in office will be recounted by historians and political scientists for decades, but it was their friendship that helped shape and solidify their legacy.

Much can be learned about Canada–US bilateral cooperation and international diplomacy by highlighting some of the critical interactions between Mulroney and Reagan. By examining how they sought to cooperate, we can learn even more about how leaders should govern themselves, especially when, due to circumstances and political differences beyond their control, there is a temptation to sacrifice friendship for more immediate political gains. This was not a path that either Mulroney or Reagan felt the need to take because they recognized that it was both possible and indeed necessary to rely on their friendship to achieve desirable political outcomes. This chapter lays the foundation for a discussion about their backgrounds and personalities, what drew them together, and what ultimately allowed them to form a special bond. In the process, it offers important lessons about how leaders who have a strong foundation of friendship can influence the course of world history.

In the first section of the chapter, I provide an overview of the respective backgrounds of Brian Mulroney and Ronald Reagan. This is done to identify how the core values and lived experiences of both leaders contributed to their rise to power and, ultimately, to the relationship they established. Although Mulroney and Reagan came of age decades apart, they shared much in common, from their working-class roots and Irish ancestry to their ambition to reach great heights. They arrived at their destinations by pursuing different careers, but in many ways, it is not surprising that they became close friends and allies. In the second section, attention will shift to the key issues that shaped the bilateral agenda when Mulroney and Reagan were in office and what steps they were prepared to take to ensure significant progress on the Canada–US file. Finally, some consideration will be given to the lengths Reagan was prepared to go to help his friend hold on to political power, even as he was preparing to leave the White House. Among his many motivations for helping Mulroney win a second election was to ensure that his successor, George H.W. Bush, could continue to manage the Canada–US relationship with a prime minister whom Reagan greatly respected and admired.

The Journey and the Destination: Mulroney, Reagan, and the Path to Power

Most leaders who reach the apex of political power do not follow a preordained path, nor is their journey necessarily linear. It often happens that various factors and circumstances converge to propel them to public office. Such was the case with Brian Mulroney and Ronald Reagan, who together transformed the bilateral relationship between their two countries (Blake 2007; Clarkson 1982; Savoie 1994) and also, by virtue of their special and enduring friendship and mutual respect, were able to leave an indelible mark on world affairs.

Mulroney and Reagan came to appreciate the art and practice of politics and the importance of effective leadership. Both were born into in working-class families and embraced a strong work ethic. Moreover, both were shaped by the towns in which they were raised; both attended small liberal arts universities; and both turned to politics only after first exploring other avenues: Mulroney as a lawyer with one of the most prestigious law firms in North America, a member of a high-profile commission investigating corruption in the Quebec construction industry, and president of Iron Ore Canada; Reagan as a Hollywood actor and president of the Screen Actors Guild, positions that afforded him great notoriety before he served two terms as governor of California.

THE BOY FROM BAIE-COMEAU

Martin Brian Mulroney was born on 20 March 1939 to Mary Irene O'Shea and Benedict Martin Mulroney. Raised Irish Catholic in the predominantly French-speaking community of Baie-Comeau (founded in 1936 by Colonel Robert R. McCormick, owner and publisher of the *Chicago Tribune*), Brian Mulroney and his five siblings grew up in what the future prime minister regarded as an "idyllic" town (Mulroney 2007, 3). The year he was born, Baie-Comeau had a population of around 1,500; by 1942, it had grown to around 2,000. Mulroney's father worked as an electrician in a paper mill owned by the Quebec North Shore Paper Company, established in 1938 by McCormick to supply newsprint for his newspaper. Benedict Mulroney would take on other jobs in his spare time to supplement the family's income. Mulroney's mother would contribute in significant ways as well, often accepting boarders in their modest home. Like most Irish Catholics in Quebec at the time, both of Mulroney's parents voted Liberal. However, when John Diefenbaker ran for the leadership of the Progressive Conservative Party in 1956, Benedict Mulroney changed his party allegiance; he would remain a loyal Conservative for the rest of his life.

From an early age, Brian Mulroney internalized the sacrifices his parents made to raise their children and felt a profound obligation to help his family. One Sunday evening after his father returned from work, Mulroney, sixteen at the time and a graduate of St Thomas High School (now St Thomas University) in Chatham, New Brunswick, discussed with him the possibility of entering an apprenticeship program at the mill. He noted in his memoirs that "I raised with my dad the thought that perhaps I would enter the excellent new apprentice program at the mill for a few years to assist the family financially. My father looked straight at me and said, 'I appreciate the offer, Brian, and we *do* need the help. But the only way out of a paper mill town is through a university door. That's what I want you to do' [italics in original]" (Mulroney 2007, 15).

This conversation, which the former prime minister has shared with many audiences over many years, transformed his life. He wanted to help his family financially, but his father, a man whom he greatly admired, loved, and respected, understood that for his son to have a better life, he had to take advantage of his keen intellect. It was because of his insistence that he pursue a higher education that, in September 1955, Brian Mulroney enrolled as a freshman at St Francis Xavier University (St FX).

Mulroney embraced his new life at St FX, which occupied a hilltop overlooking the picturesque town of Antigonish in northeastern Nova Scotia. The university, with its talented faculty and diverse student body, was an ideal environment for him to find his voice. While pursuing an honours degree in political science, which he would complete in 1959, he distinguished himself as a champion debater and gradually became immersed in the politics of the day. He followed and scrutinized the policies of Conservative Prime Minister John Diefenbaker, whom, while a student, he managed to reach by phone and eventually meet, and he paid close attention to the views of other leaders in provincial and federal politics. At St FX, he was also exposed to the teachings of Rev. Dr Moses Coady, founder of the Coady Institute, who stressed the importance of promoting social justice, a lesson that would resonate with Mulroney throughout his political career as he sought to address injustices committed in Canada and abroad (Hampson 2018).

Mulroney never regretted his decision to attend St FX, and his commitment to his alma mater has remained steadfast for more than sixty years. Most recently, he raised more than $105 million for the university to build Mulroney Hall, a state-of-the-art teaching and research complex housing the Brian Mulroney Institute of Government. When he was asked by senior administrators what quote he would like to adorn the Institute's Donors Wall, in Mulroney Hall's foyer, he said, without hesitation, "Use the quote from my Dad. That's how I ended up here" (Mulroney 2019).

In 1961, Mulroney took his thirst for politics to Laval University in Quebec City, where he studied law and closely followed debates in the province's National Assembly. Three years later, the young law school graduate, specializing in labour law, joined Howard, Cate, Ogilvy, et al., a prestigious Montreal law firm (which would later become Norton Rose Fulbright). It was at Norton Rose Fulbright, where Mulroney continues to practise, that he developed a reputation as a highly skilled labour negotiator representing major companies, including Iron Ore Canada and Power Corporation of Canada. As his profile in Montreal's legal circles grew, he caught the attention of Quebec Premier Robert Bourassa, who in 1974 established a Royal Commission – the Cliche Commission – to investigate corruption in the province's construction industry. Mulroney joined Robert Cliche, a former New Democratic Party leader and judge, and Guy Chevrette, leader of the province's teacher's union and a supporter of the Parti Québécois, in the three-member inquiry.

The exposure Mulroney generated in Quebec and across Canada as he and his colleagues probed corrupt practices in the province's construction industry helped showcase his vast talents. There was no doubt that he could ask difficult questions, and it was even clearer that he would not allow himself to be intimidated even in the face of death threats against himself and his family. Mulroney and his colleagues had been appointed to serve the public interest, and there was little anyone could do to distract them. With these kinds of leadership qualities on full display, it is not surprising that Mulroney, who had never run for public office, decided to throw his hat into the ring to become the next leader of the Progressive Conservative Party of Canada in 1976.

He finished third in the leadership race behind Joe Clark and Claude Wagner. Clark was elected prime minister in 1979, but less than a year later, he was defeated at the polls by Pierre Trudeau, who formed a majority Liberal government. This would not be Clark's only major defeat. In 1983, concerned that he was leading a divided party, Clark made the fateful decision to call a leadership convention in the hope of bolstering his support, which at the time stood at 66.9 per cent. Clark having opened the door for a leadership review, Mulroney, who had been president of Iron Ore Canada since 1977, walked through it. On 11 June 1983, Mulroney leapfrogged Clark on the fourth ballot at the PC convention, capturing 54.4 per cent of the vote. A little more than a year later, he was elected Canada's eighteenth prime minister, with a huge majority in the House of Commons.

EUREKA! THE RISE OF RONALD REAGAN

Reagan's path to the presidency, like that of so many of his predecessors, was filled with more twists and turns than the Pacific Coast Highway, a scenic drive he would one day travel regularly. Ronald Wilson Reagan took his first breath in a small apartment above the Pitney General Store in Tampico, Illinois, on 6 February 1911. His father, Jack, nicknamed him "Dutch" because of his Dutch Boy haircut and pudgy cheeks. Reagan's early years did not resemble a storybook life. His father was a salesman, mainly of shoes, and the family moved to several towns across Illinois before settling in Dixon in 1920. Jack was an alcoholic (Reagan 1990).

Raised Catholic in the Disciples of Christ Church by parents loyal to the Democratic Party, Reagan observed his mother Nelle's lifelong commitment to others. According to veteran journalist and Reagan biographer Lou Cannon (n.d.), Nelle's compassion was not lost on him, nor was her generosity. Like many small-town children, Reagan found plenty of ways to be mischievous, but he also showed a talent for sports, especially swimming, football, and basketball, that kept him busy during his high school and college years (Cannon n.d.). In high school, Reagan also became involved with the drama club and wrote for the school yearbook. These and other interests, including debating, would follow him to Eureka College, a small liberal arts university with less than 500 students where, in 1932, he graduated with a degree in economics.

Reagan's formal education ended at Eureka, but the skill set he acquired through acting and covering various sporting events at university served him well in the ensuing years. So too did his Hollywood good looks, which caught the attention of the Warner Bros. film studio in 1937 when Reagan travelled to California to report on the Chicago Cubs in spring training (Cannon n.d.). His timing could not have been better. Warner Bros. was looking for a fresh face to replace "a promising young star who had died in a car accident," and Reagan, standing six feet, one inch, "with wavy brown hair, blue eyes, and an inviting broadcaster's voice," fit the bill (Cannon n.d.). Following a screen test, the studio offered him a $200 per week contract, the equivalent of almost $4,000 today. Reagan would go on to appear in more than fifty films. As a second lieutenant in the Army Air Corps First Motion Picture Unit during the Second World War, he would serve his country narrating training films for young recruits (Cannon n.d.; see also Vaughan, 1994).

By 1954, Reagan's career as a Hollywood actor was coming to an end, but he managed to secure a contract with General Electric to narrate *General Electric Theater*, a new Sunday night television program that would soon top the ratings chart. Eight years later, he left that show over a contract dispute. Later, with the help of his older brother Neil, he hosted a popular western series.

As Reagan's profile in the entertainment industry began to fade, he devoted more of his time and attention to representing and advocating for working actors, first as a member and then as president of the Screen Actors Guild, a position he held from 1947 to 1954. During the 1950s, Reagan, a lifelong Democrat, began to shift his political allegiance to the Republican Party. Although not a fan of Richard Nixon, his growing distrust of John F. Kennedy and the Democratic Party convinced him to change his registration to Republican. He supported Nixon in his narrow defeat to Kennedy and again lent him his support as the former vice-president launched an unsuccessful bid to become governor of California in 1962.

Reagan's growing concerns over the management of the largest state in the union convinced him to take a run for the California governorship in 1966, and to the dismay and surprise of many, he defeated two-term incumbent Edmund G. ("Pat") Brown. Serving as governor from 1967 to 1975 (see Hayward 2009; Perlstein 2015; Spitz 2018) took Reagan's national profile to new heights. His positions on a range of state and national issues shaped his conservative persona, and he often generated controversy in his dealings with major California institutions, including the University of California, Berkeley. After leaving office, he wrote a regular column that appeared in 175 newspapers, provided on-air commentaries to more than 200 radio stations, and became a regular on the speech circuit (Cannon n.d.). Reagan, who as early as 1968 was widely considered a strong contender for the Republican presidential nomination, had an important decision to make: should he try to unseat President Gerald Ford in the 1976 Republican presidential primaries? He decided to do so, and ran a strong campaign, but still finished second to Ford. Even so, his political career was far from over. Four years later, he would become the fortieth president of the United States, defeating Jimmy Carter with almost 51 per cent of the popular vote and all but forty-nine electoral votes. His margin of victory in 1984 was even more impressive: he defeated the Democrat Walter Mondale with close to 59 per cent of the popular vote and over 97 per cent of the electoral vote.

Mulroney, Reagan, and the Birth of a Historic Friendship

Ronald Reagan and Brian Mulroney both came of age during momentous periods in world history: Reagan during the Great Depression and Mulroney during the Cold War. Yet despite growing up decades apart, and under very different circumstances, the two had much in common. Both had grown up in small towns and attended small liberal arts universities where they pursued the social sciences, and both were drawn to politics and debating at an early age. They also supported the tenets of liberalism well before they identified as conservatives. As noted, Reagan was a registered Democrat before embracing the Republican Party, and Mulroney entered St FX "as a liberal and left as a conservative" (Mulroney 2017). Interestingly, they also suffered significant political setbacks in 1976, only to rebound soon after with back-to-back victories.

In some ways, Mulroney and Reagan had similar personalities. They were incredibly effective communicators, had great empathy, were charismatic, exuded confidence, and had the capacity and willingness to build and mend fences. They could, and often did, reveal their displeasure with political foes, yet their first instinct was not to raise the ire of adversaries but to facilitate political cooperation. If this proved impossible, both had the capacity and inclination to rely on hard and soft power strategies to achieve desirable political outcomes.

It became abundantly clear to those who watched them interact that it would not take long for the two to form a lasting friendship, one that would transcend politics. Relations between Canada and the US are generally friendly, but prime ministers and presidents do necessarily become friends (CBC Archives 2019; Gray 2017). When that does happen, as it did with Mulroney and Reagan (and George H.W. Bush), their respective countries can benefit tremendously.

In his oft-quoted address to the Canadian Parliament on 17 May 1961, President Kennedy declared: "Geography has made us neighbors. History has made us friends. Economics has made us partners. And necessity has made us allies. Those whom nature hath so joined together, let no man put asunder. What unites us is far greater than what divides us" (in Abelson and Lajeunesse 2020, 3). The hypocrisy of Kennedy's remarks was not lost on those close to the president and to Prime Minister Diefenbaker, who knew full well that the two leaders despised each other. Diefenbaker once described Kennedy as a "hothead" and a "fool – too young, too brash, too inexperienced, and a boastful son of a bitch!" (in Abelson and Lajeunesse 2020, 3). Lester B. Pearson's relationship with Lyndon B. Johnson was not always cordial. In 1965, Pearson met with Johnson at Camp David after delivering an unwelcome speech about the Vietnam War. The president reportedly startled Pearson by shouting, "You pissed on my rug!" (in Abelson and Lajeunesse 2020, 3). Richard Nixon and Pierre Trudeau were even more hostile. On his private tapes, Nixon was overheard calling Trudeau "an asshole," "a son of a bitch," and a "pompous egghead." When the tapes became public, Trudeau's response was simply, "I've been called worse things by better people" (in Abelson and Lajeunesse 2020, 3). More recently, Justin Trudeau, Pierre Trudeau's son, found himself on the receiving end of insults hurled at him by Donald Trump in the wake of various bilateral and international meetings. This may help explain why he welcomed a victory by Joe Biden, despite some of the latter's policies, which have not been helpful to Canada. Given the tensions that have surfaced between Canadian prime ministers and US presidents in the twentieth century, it is worth remembering that Mulroney and Reagan were able to make the Canada–US relationship the envy of other leaders around the globe. It is now important to reflect on how they became friends.

It is hardly a secret that Reagan often found his interactions with Pierre Trudeau challenging. In his autobiography, *Ronald Reagan: An American Life* (1990), Reagan barely mentions Trudeau, and when he does, it is not flattering. Indeed, the president castigates Trudeau for being rude on various occasions to Margaret Thatcher, which created a toxic environment for high-level policy discussions (Reagan 1990, 353). However, in his diaries edited by historian Douglas Brinkley (2007), Reagan's meetings with Trudeau take on a more positive tone. In his first official visit to Ottawa on 7 March 1981, Reagan wrote: "Off to Canada … It was a warm welcome with Canadians lining the streets cheering & clapping … Went to Parliament (h)ill to meet P.M. Trudeau. Discovered I liked him. Our meetings were very successful. We have some problems to be worked out having to do with fishing, energy [and] environment but I believe we've convinced them we really want to find answers" (Brinkley 2007, 7). Later entries, however, make clear that his patience for the prime minister wore thin over time.

Trudeau's *Memoirs*, released in 1993, three years after Reagan's autobiography, suggest why the president would have had reservations about the prime minister. Trudeau noted, "Later, in my final term, I even got along well with Ronald Reagan, even though we were about as far apart in outlook and personality as two people could be" (Trudeau 1993, 220). He added, "President Reagan was not a man for thoughtful policy discussions, but he was pleasant and congenial and my children found him entertaining" (Trudeau 1993, 301). As if this praise was not faint enough, Trudeau further observed, "President Reagan was a great storyteller and a very sociable man. But his outlook was dominated by a deep faith in the free market system and by what I can only call an obsession with communism. His view of the world was largely anecdotal" (Trudeau 1993, 329).

When Brian Mulroney was preparing to assume office in the fall of 1984, Pierre Trudeau offered this advice about working with the US: "Be friends with the United States – the Canadian people like the Americans – but don't be subservient to the American government, because Canadians are very proud people" (Trudeau 1993, 358). It is unlikely that Mulroney required advice on how best to strengthen Canada–US relations, especially from someone who was perceived by the US president as condescending. He understood that Canadians thought highly of Americans, findings consistent with several years of polling conducted by Environics Research. He also understood that the Canadian government did not have to be subservient to the US to make its policy positions clear. After all, for Mulroney, Canada's relationship with the US was the most important one it had in the world, and it had to be carefully managed, monitored, and nurtured. But unlike Trudeau, Mulroney appreciated the value of establishing and maintaining strong ties to the US president, a relationship that could bolster Canada's stature internationally. As Mulroney stated recently, "If it is widely known that you are on friendly terms with the president of the United States, and you have ready access to the Oval Office, this opens many doors elsewhere around the world. And the reverse is also true" (MacDonald 2021, 2).

Mulroney genuinely liked and admired Ronald Reagan, so embracing him as a friend and confidant required little effort. In reflecting on his first impressions of President Reagan, based on his initial meeting with him in June 1984, Mulroney (2021) stated,

> What impressed me most was his good nature, good humour, and sense of serenity sitting in the Oval Office and surrounded by all the problems in the world. He was enthusiastic about meeting me. I don't know why. I felt the beginnings of a genuine friendship. Perhaps it was the Irish thing, and we were both conservative. He also had to deal with Pierre Trudeau and none of the G-7 leaders liked him … But most of all I was impressed with his capacity to articulate his positions and listen to me and my concerns about acid rain, tariffs on Canadian steel, fish and lumber and he paid a lot of attention to it and said Brian when you are prime minister I think we can do something about this. (See also Mulroney 2007)

President Reagan was equally effusive in recalling the many times he spent with Prime Minister Mulroney and his family. In his autobiography, he noted: "Nancy and I travelled to many countries when I was president and among our most enjoyable trips were the short ones across our nation's northern border. Prime Minister Brian Mulroney of Canada was a valued ally and we became good friends with him and his lovely wife, Mila" (Reagan 1990, 388).

The president's entry on 18 March 1985 during the Shamrock Summit in Quebec City was even more revealing. He wrote: "A morning of meetings and then a lunch where I made a speech on American-Canadian relationship – well received. On to the Citadel for the signing of several agreements, treaties, etc [and] to the airport & home. I have to believe U.S.–Canadian relations have never been better & certainly not at the leader level. Brian Mulroney & I have really established a warm personal friendship. He will be a welcome newcomer to the Bonn Summit" (Brinkley 2007, 309).

President Reagan's fondness for, and friendship with, Prime Minister Mulroney would in many ways prove invaluable to Canada during the remainder of his term in office. Although the US and Canada would at times disagree on the importance and substance of several high-profile policy files, including strategic defence, free trade, and acid rain, the friendship that had been established and nurtured between Mulroney and Reagan would pave the way for bilateral cooperation on multiple fronts. How the relationship between the two leaders played out when vital national interests were at stake will be the focus of the next section.

Friendship, Politics, and Canada–US Relations

When asked recently about the importance of his friendship with President Reagan in facilitating bilateral cooperation and managing policy disagreements with the US, Prime Minister Mulroney said simply, "It was indispensable" (Mulroney 2021). Mulroney recalled that in the lead-up to the 1986 G7 Summit in Tokyo, he was informed that Japan, along with the US, the Federal Republic of Germany, Britain, and France, had established a separate G5 meeting to discuss international monetary policy and that Canada and Italy had been excluded. Trudeau was aware that this group had been created, but according to Mulroney, he did little to express Canada's opposition (Mulroney 2021). Unlike Trudeau, Mulroney was not prepared to remain silent. At the G7 summit, he went to great lengths to condemn Canada's exclusion from this body. Feeling dispirited by the lack of support he received from the European powers, Mulroney recounted, President Reagan stood up, slammed his leather notebook shut and said, "If this is a club that won't have Brian as a member, I don't want to be part of it either. That's how Canada got into the G5." Mulroney added, "Reagan felt great loyalty to Canada and loyalty and friendship to me" (Mulroney 2021).

This was not the last time Reagan stood up for Mulroney, and no one appreciated his support more than the prime minister: "If you are a close friend of the President of the United States, everyone knows it.

It gives you extra prestige and advantages around the world. Access to the president, his time, is the most precious thing you can have, and I could walk into the Oval Office anytime I wanted" (Mulroney 2021). As friends and partners in one of the world's most important bilateral relationships, both Reagan and Mulroney acknowledged that it was unlikely they would agree on the content and management of every policy initiative. After all, they represented sovereign powers and had been elected to advance the core interests of their respective countries. They also knew that however strong their personal connections, the goals of their two countries would not always align. Fortunately, because of the goodwill – and political will – they had created, strong stands against policies with which they disagreed could be accommodated. Without this foundation in place, many of the policy initiatives outlined below could have easily derailed.

BEING STRATEGIC ABOUT THE STRATEGIC DEFENSE INITIATIVE

Despite growing protests across Canada about the testing of unarmed cruise missiles over Cold Lake, Alberta, the Canadian government agreed to a five-year agreement with the US on 16 July 1983. This announcement came close to four months after President Reagan unveiled SDI, dubbed "Star Wars," in a nationally televised address in which he called upon the scientific community to render nuclear weapons impotent and obsolete. The goal of SDI, as outlined at the time, was to deploy a ground- and space-based system that would permit the US to track, intercept, and destroy incoming ballistic missiles. Reagan believed that SDI, if successful, could provide the US with an alternative to the nuclear doctrine of mutual assured destruction by affording the country both first- and second-strike capability. Looking for support from their allies, Caspar Weinberger, then US Secretary of Defense, reached out to Canada to participate in SDI research. When Prime Minister Mulroney was sworn into office, it did not take long for SDI to make its way onto the bilateral agenda.

Mulroney was committed to establishing a strong relationship with the Reagan administration, but he was also concerned that Canada's endorsement of this initiative could trigger another costly arms race besides generating considerable political fallout at home. Thus, he "found the thought of the weaponization of space extremely disconcerting"

(2007, 349). After proposing the creation of a parliamentary committee to assess the response of parliamentarians to Canada's potential involvement in SDI research, and after extensive consultations with several high-level advisers, including the late Allan Gotlieb, then Canadian ambassador to the US (Gotlieb 2006), Mulroney made a decision. In a phone call to President Reagan on 7 September 1985, Mulroney stated that, although he felt that SDI was consistent with the terms of the Anti-Ballistic Missile Treaty (a treaty the US would terminate during the administration of George W. Bush), and although it was "a prudent action on the part of the US in view of Soviet initiatives of a similar kind, there would be no participation on a government-to-government basis in SDI research, but that private industry and universities were free to participate as they wished" (Mulroney 2007, 352).

Reagan wrote in his diary that he was satisfied with Mulroney's response: "Late in the day had a call from P.M. of Canada Brian Mulroney. Brian wanted me to know that the Canadian government was voting not to join us in SDI research but that he was voicing his approval of our doing it & that any private researchers, businesses & institutions in Canada were free to join us. All in all I think there is no problem" (Brinkley 2007, 351).

Mulroney's skillful handling of what turned out to be a very delicate political issue, combined with Reagan's faith in a close friend and ally, enabled both leaders to manage an important issue at home while moving the bilateral relationship forward. Had this issue found its way into the hands of other prime ministers and presidents, the result could, and likely would, have been very different. History is filled with examples, as already noted, of US presidents and Canadian prime ministers exchanging insults over how each approached various regional conflicts, including the Cuban Missile Crisis, the Vietnam War, and the Iraq War.

As their relationship grew stronger, Prime Minister Mulroney did not hesitate to reach out to President Reagan when the US was considering implementing programs or initiatives that could have harmed Canadian interests. For example, on 1 August 1986, Mulroney contacted Reagan from Harrington Lake, the country residence of Canadian prime ministers, while the president was staying at Camp David. In their fifteen-minute phone conversation, Mulroney spoke to Reagan about how the US Export Enhancement Program would impact Canadian wheat exports. Mulroney told him: "The Soviet Union and China take over one half of all Canadian wheat exports and these proposals could reduce our markets by as much as 30 per cent or result in revenue losses of over $500 million. I know the pressures you're under with the protectionists in the Congress and the delicate situation you sometimes find yourself. I would appreciate anything you can do to find an alternative and less damaging way of alleviating problems faced by your own farmers" (LAC, MG 26, P18-4, vol. 19#45; see also Martin 1986).

Reagan's response was swift and direct: "Let me assure you that the US will not increase its market share as a result of this. We will allow grain sales at current market prices" (LAC, MG 26, P18-4, vol. 19#45). Despite the president's assurances, and Mulroney's ongoing protests, the Export Enhancement Program was signed into law. But once again, this exchange revealed the willingness of the two leaders to engage constructively on important matters, even when political interests in their respective countries made it all but impossible to reach an agreement. In fact, the successful negotiation and passage of the Canada–US Free Trade Agreement can be credited to their willingness to go the extra mile to assuage each other's concerns.

FREE TRADE AND THE 1988 CANADIAN FEDERAL ELECTION

In the lead-up to the Shamrock Summit, held in Quebec City on St Patrick's Day, 17 March 1985, Mulroney penned a letter to Reagan. On 19 December 1984, he wrote: "The site of Quebec City represents an historical antecedent of interest. In 1943 and 1944, our respective predecessors, President Roosevelt and Prime Minister King, met there with Prime Minister Churchill to plan the course of war and the peace they were working together to restore. My hope is that our Governments can accomplish together something of lasting significance" (LAC, MG 26, P8, vol. 26#19).

Before Mulroney, Reagan, and their wives, Mila and Nancy, joined Canadian opera singer Maureen Forrester in a rendition of "When Irish Eyes Are Smiling" during a gala evening celebrating the historic summit, the two leaders had much to talk about, including acid rain, US foreign policy in Central America, relations with Soviet leader Gorbachev, and the importance of reducing and perhaps even eliminating barriers to trade. While progress was made in the ensuing months on a number of these fronts, the issue that Mulroney believed was of "lasting importance," and the one that would come to dominate bilateral relations, was free trade.

On 6 April 1985, in his personal journal, Mulroney recorded his thoughts about the importance of the Shamrock Summit: "We talked about trade, our upcoming agenda, and I received a commitment from Reagan that he would 'go to bat for Canada,' guaranteeing us secure access to the American market. This is absolutely vital as far as we're concerned. Unless I am totally wrong I think we're going to need it, because the American Congress will soon be working itself into a giant lather about Japan, and I don't want us to get hurt in the process" (Mulroney 2007, 229).

In Mulroney's view, Canada's future prosperity would depend heavily on greater access to US markets. Previous Canadian prime ministers had sought paths to reduce Canadian dependency on its southern neighbour, whereas for him, Canada's best option was to negotiate a trade agreement that would benefit Canadian consumers and manufacturers. Negotiating a free trade agreement with the US would require considerable tenacity and sensitivity, as well as an acute understanding of how a range of concerns in both countries could be addressed. It was just the fight for which Mulroney was built. With the business acumen of a seasoned executive, the experience and confidence of a skilled negotiator, and the insight of a visionary statesman capable of navigating the political waters on both sides of the border, Mulroney was well-positioned – and equipped – to transform the bilateral policy landscape.

The academic literature on the benefits and pitfalls of the Canada–US Free Trade Agreement is extensive and need not be summarized here (see Gotlieb 2006; Hart, Dymond, and Robertson 1994). Suffice it to say that while many Canadians grasped that a free trade agreement could benefit the country, others feared that if implemented, thousands of jobs would be lost, the manufacturing sector would be decimated, and our sovereignty would be further eroded. There was no shortage of anger, vitriol, and contempt directed at Mulroney and his government as they sought to negotiate this historic agreement. Undeterred by those who shouted, "Free Canada, Trade Mulroney," Mulroney remained committed to finalizing the terms of the treaty.

Following months of negotiations, the issue that would make or break the agreement boiled down to Mulroney's insistence that the treaty include a binding dispute settlement mechanism to ensure that there would be ample safeguards in place that would allow Canada – a much smaller power in an asymmetrical relationship – to initiate and respond to perceived violations of the free trade agreement. Canada faced considerable resistance from US negotiators regarding this demand, but Mulroney didn't flinch. In fact, as members of Reagan's team remained unwilling to make this concession in the final hours leading to the conclusion of the negotiations, Mulroney persisted: no binding dispute settlement mechanism, no agreement. In the end, it was Mulroney's friendship with Reagan that ultimately led to a deal (Gotlieb 2006; Hart, Dymond, and Robertson 1994). As Mulroney observed (2007), when he met with Reagan at the G7 Summit in Venice in June 1987 to discuss the progress of the free trade negotiations, he "didn't waste time with opening pleasantries" (501).

Mulroney later wrote: "I had told Ron many times that a binding dispute settlement resolution system was key to Canada's demands. In repeating this in Venice, I bluntly warned him that Canada needed to know if he couldn't deliver, as we'd then prepare to leave the negotiating table. 'If you can't deal with your largest trading partner and best friend, who can you negotiate with?' I asked" (Mulroney 2007, 501).

There is no doubt that it was Mulroney's friendship with, and access to, Reagan that led to a successful negotiation of the Canada–US Free Trade Agreement, which the two leaders signed on 3 January 1988 (Hart, Dymond, and Robertson 1994). However, it was not until a year later, after the implementing legislation was approved by both governments, that the agreement was enacted into law. In the interim, Mulroney had to return to the campaign trail to secure a second term in office. While there were several other issues at hand in the 1988 Canadian federal election, the main one was whether free trade with the US would be good for Canada.

In the last two weeks before the 21 November election, a Gallup poll reported that "43 per cent of decided voters favoured the Liberals, 31 per cent chose the Conservatives and 22 per cent supported the New Democratic Party" (Janigan 1988). News of the poll made its way to the White House. On 10 November, President Reagan noted: "Canada's presenting a problem. P.M.'s opponent Turner looks like he's going to be the winner" (Brinkley 2007, 665). Margaret Thatcher shared Reagan's concerns and appreciated what was at stake if Mulroney's successor decided to nullify the Canada–US Free Trade Agreement. In a phone call following the election, Thatcher told Mulroney: "If ever a Canadian prime minister repudiates an international treaty, it would be the end of any influence for Canadians in the international sphere" (Mulroney 2007, 634).

Allan Gregg was president of Toronto-based Decima Research Inc. and a Conservative pollster. When the Gallup poll was released, Gregg "personally reassured Prime Minister Mulroney that [Decima's] soundings were far more favourable" than Gallup's (Janigan 1988). Gregg was correct about that. Canadians' confidence in Mulroney's leadership resulted in a second majority government. With 43 per cent of the popular vote, Mulroney had the mandate he required to pursue his agenda – one that included the ratification of the Canada–US Free Trade Agreement, which was brought into force on 1 January 1989.

DON'T RAIN ON ME! THE ACID RAIN AGREEMENT

Reagan's concerns about Mulroney's re-election prospects were not new. As early as March 1987, he recognized that his friend was facing challenges and that his administration had to do something to help. During a meeting of the National Security Council on 3 March 1987, while he was preparing for his summit in Canada with Mulroney, Reagan wrote in his diary: "He's [Mulroney] in big political trouble & part of it is based on political attacks that's he's beholden to me and the U.S. We're trying to find some things to bolster him. One possibility (if we can do it) some pick up in the acid rain situation" (Brinkley 2007, 480).

President Reagan's willingness to help Mulroney is notable, and that generosity was not lost on the prime minister. Mulroney was acutely aware that his efforts to fortify Canada's ties with the US would be welcomed by some Canadians and repudiated by others. Indeed, despite years of polling that confirmed Canadians' positive opinion of the US, a strong current of anti-Americanism continued to flow through Canada, and Mulroney's desire to strengthen ties to the US made him an obvious target. One way that Mulroney tried to keep rising anti-American sentiments at bay was to strike an agreement with the US to combat acid rain, a serious issue on both sides of the border that would require a coordinated policy response.

From the time Mulroney and Reagan first met, the prime minister remained steadfast in his commitment to significantly curtail and eventually eliminate emissions of sulfur dioxide and nitrogen oxides into the air by factories on both sides of the border. When these compounds are released, they can cause a chemical reaction known as acid rain that kills trees and poisons rivers, estuaries, and lakes. Reagan was sensitive to Mulroney's concerns but for a time was under the impression that Canada, not the US, was largely responsible for this problem. That claim that was quickly disputed; evidence soon revealed that 50 to 70 per cent of acid rain came from the US and as little as 2 to 10 per cent from Canada.

In principle, drafting an agreement that would combat acid rain and the damage it was causing in both Canada and the US made perfect sense. It would certainly have gone a long way toward addressing the concerns of environmentalists. But politics isn't necessarily about what makes sense; it is often more about what is expedient. Reagan's willingness to listen to Mulroney's concerns and to engage him on this matter helped raise the profile of this important issue, but relative to other domestic and foreign policy challenges the president was confronting at the time, including the Iran-Contra Affair, nuclear arms negotiations with the Soviets, and building a stronger US economy, this file was often relegated to the sidelines. Mulroney would have liked nothing more than to sign an agreement on acid rain with Reagan, the political stars did not align while the president was in office. Mulroney would have to wait until Reagan's successor, George H.W. Bush, assumed the presidency before an agreement on acid rain could be reached. Canada ratified the Canada–US Air Quality Agreement on 13 March 1991. This achievement, along with several other initiatives Mulroney undertook to protect the environment, explains why, in April 2006, he was recognized by a panel of experts as Canada's greenest prime minister.

Conclusion

POLITICS MATTER, BUT FRIENDSHIP MATTERS MORE

In reflecting on his nine years in office, Prime Minister Mulroney has often said that, in the heat of political battles, it is important not to lose sight of the many friendships, forged with people of all political stripes, that were formed along the way. As this chapter has shown, Mulroney and Reagan did not necessarily agree on how best to move certain policy files forward. Theirs was a special relationship, one that would generate critical opportunities to both promote cooperation and manage dissent. They had a chemistry that, unlike acid rain, was anything but toxic. Representing sovereign countries with distinct national interests and identities, and deeply embedded in an asymmetrical power relationship, they found creative and innovative ways to find common ground, even when politics at home could easily have driven a wedge between them.

Mulroney and Reagan did not achieve everything they hoped to, and at times there was obvious friction. There is no doubt that Mulroney would have liked the president to take a stronger stand against apartheid and to embrace a more comprehensive approach to managing relations with Gorbachev. Mulroney's insistence on having a dispute settlement mechanism in place before a free trade agreement could move forward and his decision not to provide a formal endorsement from the Canadian government for SDI likely created some tense moments in the Reagan White House. But despite some policy differences, in the history of Canada–US relations, rarely have a Canadian prime minister and a US president demonstrated more effective and competent leadership.

A more exhaustive analysis of the Mulroney–Reagan years, including a gender-based perspective, would reveal far more than has been discussed in this chapter. However, at the very least, this study has shown how two leaders who are willing to become more than allies can change the course of history. The relationship established and nurtured by Mulroney and Reagan unfolded over hundreds of hours and many years, not through dozens of tweets. In an age when leaders are more consumed by what is said on social media than on what they accomplish in their personal interactions with their colleagues, they would be well-served to reflect on what two small-town Irish kids from modest backgrounds were able to accomplish.

Brian Mulroney and Ronald Reagan remained close friends well after the president left office. As Alzheimer's robbed the president of his memory, Mulroney never lost sight of what this special man meant to him and to Canada. When President Reagan passed away in June 2004, Brian Mulroney was among a small group of people asked to eulogize him. He was the first Canadian prime minister in US history to speak at a president's funeral. Mulroney would later eulogize First Lady Nancy Reagan in March 2016 and President George H.W. Bush in December 2018.

The close and enduring bond between Brian Mulroney and Ronald Reagan offers more than a snapshot in history. It showcases how leaders should lead, how policy differences can be resolved through perseverance and mutual respect, and how the interests of nations can be advanced when there is an abundance of political will. It reminds us of what can be achieved when leaders are prepared to exchange more handshakes than insults.

Note

A version of this chapter was published by Truth North, Robert C. and Janice S. McNair Center for Advancement of Free Enterprise and Entrepreneurship, Northwood University, Midland, Michigan, 26 April 2022.

References

Abelson, Donald E., and Adam Lajeunesse. 2020. "Introduction: Canada–US Relations in the Age of Trump." *American Review of Canadian Studies* [special issue] 50, no. 1: 1–9.

Blake, Raymond B., ed. 2007. *Transforming the Nation: Canada and Brian Mulroney*. Montreal and Kingston: McGill-Queen's University Press.

Bothwell, Robert. 2015. *Your Country, My Country: A Unified History of the United States and Canada*. New York: Oxford University Press.

Brinkley, Douglas, ed. 2007. *The Reagan Diaries*. New York: HarperCollins.

Cannon, Lou. n.d. "Ronald Reagan: Life before the Presidency." Miller Center. https://millercenter.org/president/reagan/life-before-the-presidency.

CBC Archives. 2019. "From the 1960s to Today: Awkward Moments between Canadian and US Leaders." 6 December. https://www.cbc.ca/archives/from-the-1960s-to-today-awkward-moments-between-canadian-u-s-leaders-1.5385414.

Clarkson, Stephen. 1982. *Canada and the Reagan Challenge: Crisis in the Canadian-American Relationship*. Toronto: Lorimer.

Ginsberg, Gary. 2021. *First Friends: The Powerful, Unsung (And Unelected) People Who Shaped Our Presidents*. New York: Twelve Books.

Gotlieb, Allan. 2016. *The Washington Diaries 1981–1989*. Toronto: McClelland and Stewart.

Gray, John. 2017. "Friends or Frenemies: When Prime Ministers and Presidents Clash." *Business News Network*, 19 January. https://www.bnnbloomberg.ca/friends-or-frenemies-when-prime-ministers-and-presidents-clash-1.653736.

Hale, Geoffrey. 2013. *So Near Yet So Far: The Public and Hidden Worlds of Canada–US Relations.* Vancouver: UBC Press.

Hampson, Fen Osler. 2018. *Master of Persuasion: Brian Mulroney's Global Legacy.* Toronto: McClelland and Stewart.

Hart, Michael, Bill Dymond, and Colin Robertson. 1994. *Decision at Midnight: Inside the Canada–US Free Trade Negotiations.* Vancouver: UBC Press.

Hayward, Stephen F. 2009. *The Age of Reagan.* New York: Crown Forum.

Janigan, Mary. 1988. "The Numbers Game." *Maclean's*, 28 November.

Larkin, Janet. 2004. "Reagan, Mulroney Enjoyed a Rare Personal Bond." *Buffalo News*, 20 July. https://buffalonews.com/news/reagan-mulroney-enjoyed-a-rare-personal-bond/article_3957749b-0616-5390-bdc8-95ce392024cd.html.

Library and Archives Canada (LAC). MG 26 P8, vol. 26, no. 19.

– MG 26, P18-4, vol.19, no. 45.

Litt, Paul. 2011. *Elusive Destiny: The Political Vocation of John Napier Turner.* Vancouver: UBC Press.

MacDonald, L. Ian. 1984. *Mulroney: The Making of the Prime Minister.* Toronto: McClelland and Stewart.

– 2021. "The Relationship." *Policy Magazine,* 27 August, 1–7.

Martin, Douglas. 1986. "Canada's Dismay over Wheat Exports." *New York Times,* 4 August.

Mulroney, Brian. 2007. *Memoirs, 1939–1993.* Toronto: McClelland and Stewart.

– 2017. Remarks made at Groundbreaking for Mulroney Hall. St Francis Xavier University, Antigonish, Nova Scotia, 20 September.

– 2019. Remarks made during a visit to Mulroney Hall. St Francis Xavier University, Antigonish, Nova Scotia, March.

– 2021. Interview by Donald E. Abelson by phone. 28 September.

Murphy, Rae, Nik Auf der Maur, and Robert Chodos. 1984. *Brian Mulroney: The Boy from Baie-Comeau.* Toronto: James Lorimer.

Perlstein, Rick. 2015. *The Invisible Bridge: The Fall of Nixon and the Rise of Reagan.* New York: Simon and Schuster.

Policy Magazine. 2021. Special issue on Canada–US relations, 9, no. 5 (September–October).

Reagan, Ronald. 1990. *Ronald Reagan: An American Life.* New York: Simon and Schuster.

Savoie, Donald. 1994. *Thatcher, Reagan, and Mulroney: In Search of a New Bureaucracy.* Toronto: University of Toronto Press.

Sawatsky, John. 1991. *Mulroney: The Politics of Ambition.* Toronto: Macfarlane, Walter and Ross.

Spitz, Bob. 2018. *Reagan: An American Journey.* New York: Penguin.
Stewart, John. 2017. *Strangers with Memories: The United States and Canada from Free Trade to Baghdad.* Montreal and Kingston: McGill-Queen's University Press.
Trudeau, Pierre Elliott. 1993. *Memoirs.* Toronto: McClelland and Stewart.
Vaughan, Stephen. 1994. *Ronald Reagan in Hollywood: Movies and Politics.* Cambridge: Cambridge University Press.

7

Canadian Nationalism and the Canada–US Special Relationship

STEPHEN BROOKS

Canadian nationalists have always been uneasy with the idea of maintaining a special relationship with the US. Wary of any and all forms of American influence that might seriously limit or compromise Canadian decision-making, thereby undermining Canadian sovereignty, nationalists have been suspicious of a relationship that, at its core, suggests an exceptional and perhaps unbreakable intimacy. The familiar adage, "Close, but not too close," has long been a fair description of most Canadians' preference when it comes to the Canada–US relationship. "It's way too close, and that's bad for Canada and Canadians," more accurately describes how nationalists have viewed this bilateral relationship.

The roots of Canadian nationalism reach back as far as the American Revolutionary War (Lipset 1990; Wise and Brown 1967). This chapter focuses on the nationalism that arose in English Canada in the post–Second World War era, particularly in the 1960s and 1970s, and whose influence on the Canadian political conversation, although much attenuated, continues to this day. This wave of Canadian nationalism was often referred to as the "New Nationalism," characterized by a more aggressive tone and a more ambitious agenda of distancing Canada from the US than previous forms of Canadian nationalism (see Preston 1975; Rotstein 1976). While its focus was on such matters as trade dependence, direct investment, American cultural domination, and what were believed to be threats to Canada's political sovereignty, it also implicitly rejected the notion that a special relationship with the US was in Canada's interests.

At the height of its political influence, the New Nationalism was unable to eclipse the belief that Canada's destiny and prosperity were bound to the special relationship. Canadians and many of their leaders were and remain largely ambivalent about their country's relationship with the US. Indeed, they are not convinced that these relations can or should be viewed as fundamentally different from those with other important partners. In recent years, however, the belief that the US may be in decline globally and suffering from major political dysfunction has raised concerns over whether the special relationship continues to be in Canada's interests. These concerns are quite aside from questions about whether, beyond ritualistic expressions of goodwill, American policy-makers see the idea of a Canada–US special relationship as anything more than a sort of atavistic relic of times past.

The "New" Canadian Nationalism

In the years following the Second World War, more and more Canadians, and certainly their opinion leaders, came to believe that their country's relationship with the US was a subject worthy of public concern and policy action. Between 1949 and 1972, no fewer than four royal commissions as well as a federal task force and a special senate committee produced major and much discussed reports about various aspects of American cultural and economic influence on Canada (Government of Canada 1951, 1955, 1957a–b, 1960, 1972; Senate of Canada 1970). These influences were regularly examined in the Canadian media, often in near apocalyptic terms.

"It's the U.S. or us!," declared Hugh MacLennan, one of English Canada's most celebrated post-war writers. "The Americanization of Canada – by which I mean the swamping of our national purpose by that of the United States and of our habits by a state of mind totally American – has been such a subconscious process on our part, and such an unmalicious one on theirs, that no reasonable man could call it a conquest." It was, rather, a sort of seduction, he argued, in which Canadians were entirely complicit (MacLennan 1960). MacLennan's contemporary, Farley Mowat, went further. "Let's get roaring mad," he wrote in a rallying call to Canadian nationalists:

> There is no need for me to list the formidable array of incontrovertible facts which prove conclusively that we are rapidly

> being engulfed by the United States. Despite the best efforts of the professional apologists and propagandists of radio, newspapers and magazines, these facts are undeniable. Even the most brotherly amongst us is uncomfortably aware of them. But there is a need for me to attempt the restoration of some honor to my caste, by speaking out against *this monstrous cult whose symbol is the benevolent image of our good neighbor to the south.* (Mowat 1958; emphasis added)

Magazine articles, newspaper op-eds, and television and radio interviews purveying the new Canadian nationalism were common during this era.[1] Anti-Americanism had long been the bedrock on which English Canada's identity was built. What was new about the post-war nationalism was its strident and often aggressive tone, as represented by the fulminations of MacLennan and Mowat, as well as the insistence on the need for policy measures guaranteed to place serious strain on the Canada–US relationship (Hutchison 1959; Lower 1958; Newman 1956).

There was some pushback from figures such as novelist Morley Callaghan (Callaghan 1958), journalist Robert Fulford, and prominent radio and television broadcaster Gordon Sinclair. Indeed, Sinclair's 1973 radio editorial, "The Americans," would become iconic in the US and was even mentioned gratefully by President Ronald Reagan during his 1981 visit to Canada. Even so, defences of the US ran very much against the tide of the times; indeed, that is what made them noteworthy. The prevailing spirit of the age was that American influence had become too great and that, on the whole, its effects were negative. That had been the essential plank in the proto-Canadian nationalism that emerged during the colonial era, embraced by much of the English-speaking elites although not nearly as enthusiastically by the general population. The new Canadian nationalism of the 1950s and 1960s was premised instead on the conviction that the US represented a comprehensive and existential threat to Canadian values and institutions and even to Canadian political sovereignty.

This new turn in Canadian nationalism found its most prominent voice in the writings of the philosopher and descendant of Loyalists George Grant. His book, *Lament for a Nation: The Defeat of Canadian Nationalism* (1965), argued that an independent Canada that is not dominated in all important respects by the agents of American power, including American corporations, cultural industries, and US government policies, had become impossible. The book became a must-read for Canadian nationalists across the ideological spectrum, and among Canadian opinion leaders, Grant became synonymous with resistance to what he described as the "technological bulldozer of the American empire." Canada would not be its only victim.

Lament for a Nation was not specifically about US influence in the world, although it was situated within an interpretation of that influence that by this point was highly critical and not particularly original. In *Technology and Empire*, published a few years later, Grant elaborated on the argument already made in his lament for what he deemed to be the end of the possibility of genuine Canadian independence from the US. America was, he argued, merely the chief embodiment and the principal motor of "a universally-administered, technology-driven, homogenous society … This future society would necessarily be a tyranny [although it would wear a mask], one that would unhinge peoples the world over from all national customs and traditions, their character and lives instead would be determined by the needs of unbridled change and technological advance" (Bickerton 2006, 37) Corporate power wedded to an American notion of progress would ensure this bleak outcome.

Sixty years after the publication of *Lament for a Nation*, the scope and duration of its influence may be gleaned from the fact that it remains the single most recognizable title, by far, from an era that generated a profusion of nationalist books. They included such evocative titles as *Silent Surrender*, *Close the 49th Parallel*, *Independence: The Canadian Challenge*, *The New Romans: Candid Canadian Opinions of the United States*, and *(Canada) Ltd.: The Political Economy of Dependency*. These years also saw the creation of the Committee for an Independent Canada (1971), headed by the nationalist icon and former Liberal finance minister Walter Gordon. Grant was the philosopher of the new Canadian nationalism, but Gordon, with his roots in the Toronto business world and deep ties to the Liberal Party, more than anyone ensured that the New Nationalism would enter the mainstream of Canadian politics. There it would remain until the 1980s (Azzi 1999).

As was true of the tide of anti-Americanism that gained strength throughout Western democracies in the 1960s and 1970s, the new Canadian nationalism was strongly influenced by the global role the US had assumed during and after the Second World War. Opposition to US involvement in Vietnam fuelled increasing doubts about American global leadership among many Western populations during the Cold War (Isernia 2007). The idea that the US was part of the problem of global instability and conflict, rather than a necessary part of its solution – an idea that in the two decades immediately after the Second World War was mainly limited to the fringes of the intellectual and political left in Western societies – became standard fare among those on the left. In some societies, such as France, this view of America was widely accepted across the ideological spectrum.

Vietnam was only part of the story behind what might be described as the declining standing of the US in the eyes of many of its allies. As the politics of assassination, violent racial conflict, and political corruption plagued the domestic scene, many observers came to view the American empire as rotten, malevolent, and predatory. "The new anti-Americanism," declared Canadian journalist Robert Fulford (1970) in 1970, "begins with the proposition that the United States is a colossal empire and a corrupt one, and that its imperial designs are forcing its corrupt nature on us" (12). This was certainly the view among English Canada's left nationalists, who came to dominate political science, sociology, media studies, and history departments in Canadian universities (Brooks and Gagnon 1989, ch. 5). It was also expressed through the country's New Democratic Party (NDP) and embraced by many in the left-leaning, more nationalist wing of the Liberal Party. The image of the US as a militaristic bully with no serious claim to the moral high ground over the Soviet Union, its Cold War rival, was embraced by many if not most members of Canada's cultural elites and resonated with a significant share of the general public (Granatstein 1996). Indeed, the Liberal prime minister of Canada for most of this period, Pierre Trudeau, was himself more than dubious about the role of US in the world, and at one point he appeared to favour Canadian withdrawal from the North Atlantic Treaty Organization (Kelly 2017). There is no evidence in his published memoirs that Trudeau ever saw the US as less of a threat to world peace and stability than the Soviet Union.

Thus, an important and distinguishing aspect of the new Canadian nationalism in the 1960s and 1970s was a growing tendency among Canadian elites – albeit weaker in the general population – to be critical of America's impact on the world stage (Sigler and Goresky 1974). This disposition was further strengthened by Canada's insecure identity in the shadow of its rather overwhelming neighbour. "When we look at Americans," said Canada's ambassador to the US, Allan Gotlieb (1987), "we often do so to seek reassurance about our image of ourselves." Canadian characterizations of their country as a "peacekeeper," "honest broker," "middle power," and "moral superpower" – this latter self-description was regularly used by some Canadian government officials in the 1990s – were formulated in tandem with a much less flattering image of the US role in the world.

The new Canadian nationalism arose at the same time that the idea that Canada had a "special relationship" with the US was gaining traction. By the 1960s, in response to the Canadian government's successful request for exemptions from US trade laws intended to deal with that country's balance of payments deficits, it had become a familiar part of the Canadian conversation about the country's relationship with the US. "Special," in this case, had a precise meaning. It signified that Canada would receive different and favourable or preferential treatment that was not likely to be extended to the US's other economic partners. Since then and to the present day, the term has served as a sort of benchmark and, for some, a gold standard when it comes to assessing the state of this bilateral relationship. Other Canadians disagree and view the idea of the special relationship as indicative of a sort of vassalage that their country should reject. This certainly was the view championed by the new Canadian nationalism.

The End of an Independent Canada?

It would be an exaggeration to say that the special relationship was central to the nationalist conversation regarding the prospects for Canadian independence and what needed to be done to ensure it. US investment in Canada, trade dependence on the US, and Canadians' overwhelming preference for the products of US cultural industries were the principal concerns of Canadian nationalists. On all these counts, it was argued, Canada depended too heavily on the US in ways that limited its ability to make decisions – political, economic, and cultural – that contravened US interests. While the special relationship, according to its defenders, held the promise that Canadian points of view and interests would receive a more immediate and sympathetic hearing in Washington, nationalists gave this little credence. They pointed to the asymmetry of economic and military power in the Canada–US relationship, receiving perhaps unexpected support in President Richard Nixon's 1972 declaration to the Canadian Parliament that "no self-respecting nation can or should accept the proposition that it should always be economically dependent upon any other nation."

Pierre Trudeau's years as prime minister were the high times for policies whose ostensible aim was to free Canada from what nationalists believed to be excessive dependence on the US. Those policies led to the Canada Development Corporation (1971), the Third Option foreign policy (1972), the Foreign Investment Review Agency (1973), state-owned Petro-Canada (1975), and the National Energy Program (1980). Not since the creation of the Canadian Radio Broadcasting Commission (1932), Trans-Canada Airlines (1937), the National Film Board (1939), and the Canada Council (1957) had such a raft of nationalist measures been enacted, all of which were intended in various ways to limit US influence in Canada.

Notwithstanding these policies, nationalist anxieties about Canadian independence persisted; they would reach a climax in the late 1980s. The issue would be free trade with the US, an idea that had its origins in the Liberal Party under Wilfrid Laurier. Free trade agreements inevitably raise issues of political sovereignty and economic independence. In Canada, the issue of free trade has always been influenced by an undercurrent of fear that it is a step toward annexation by the US and the end of an independent Canada.

US desires to annex Canada, be they real or imagined, have occupied an important place in the Canadian *imaginaire* since the early nineteenth century. They first surfaced during the War of 1812, then again in the lead-up to the Canadian–American Reciprocity Treaty of 1854, still again at the time that treaty was abrogated by the US in 1866, during and after the American Civil War, and yet again in the Canadian elections of 1891 and 1911 (Brooks 2024, chs. 2, 3) With the emergence of the new Canadian nationalism in the 1960s and 1970s, such beliefs experienced a resurgence not seen since the 1911 Canadian election, when a barrage of dire predictions of annexation were made by the Conservative Party, Canadian manufacturing interests in Ontario and Quebec, and their allies in a cultural elite that was still very British in its leanings and therefore wary, to say the least, of anything that appeared to hold the promise of greater American influence in Canada and on Canadians.

These perceived dangers were reflected in a genre of Canadian fiction that might be described as *possession fantasies.* It can be seen in Margaret Atwood's early novel *Surfacing* (1972), in which the Americans in their powerboats tear apart the peace and harmony of Canadian nature. In *Surfacing*, it is money that enables Americans to possess, in a figurative way, their northern neighbour. But invasion and possession are more literal in a clutch of Canadian novels from the 1960s and 1970s that include Ray Smith's *Cape Breton Is the Thought Control Center of Canada*, Ian Adam's *The Trudeau Papers*, and Richard Rohmer's bestselling books, *Annexation* and *Exoneration.* As the titles of Rohmer's books suggest, Canada is first taken over militarily by the US, then manages a heroic liberation from the American invader. Valerie Broege's (1986) assessment of the possession fantasy embodied in Rohmer's books seems apt: "The popularity of Rohmer's [books] has much to do with tapping the resentment many Canadians feel in regard to America's greater power and aggressiveness. The novel[s] reflect the Canadian desire to see Uncle Sam get his comeuppance for going too far and assuming too much" (34).

What might be described as a soft version of the possession fantasy is found in the 1985 Canadian-made film *My American Cousin* (Wilson 1985). Although only Canadians of a certain age and education are likely to have seen it – Canadian-made feature films seldom achieve wide commercial distribution – *My American Cousin* remains the classic Canadian portrayal of America and of the relationship between these countries and their respective peoples.

The film captures beautifully the ambivalence that many Canadians have often felt toward the US: a place where exciting things happen, where fortunes can be made, and whose culture and style are envied and avidly consumed. But the rather overwhelming neighbour is also portrayed as shallowly materialistic, rapacious in its approach to nature, and morally inferior to Canada. Sandy, a young Canadian girl who longs for something different from the quiet, rather stifling routine of her life, admires her American cousin and thinks she wants nothing more than to return with him to America. But she has doubts about his parents – "Those are your parents?" – doubts that even golden boy Butch – "Yeah, don't rub it in" – seems to share. Torn between desire for something that life in Canada seems unable to deliver and her inability to leave, it seems that Sandy may have to resign herself to the sensible if uneventful life of her mother.

The idea that the US wishes to possess Canada, not through military means but through the fascination its model holds and its apparent ability to buy all it wants, is expressed in a widely cited 1984 article by Margaret Atwood. So too is the conviction that there is virtue in resisting the seductions of the American suitor:

> [We share] the longest undefended backyard fence in the world. The Canadians are the folks in the neat little bungalow, with the tidy little garden and the duck pond. The Americans are the other folks, the ones in the sprawly mansion with the bad-taste statues on the lawn. There's a perpetual party; or something, going on there – loud music, raucous laughter, smoke billowing from the barbecue. Beer bottles and Coke cans land among the peonies … Sometimes [Canadians] drop by next door, and find it exciting but scary. Sometimes the Americans drop by their house and find it clean. This worries the Canadians. They worry a lot. Maybe those Americans want to buy up their duck pond, with all the money they seem to have, and turn it into a cesspool or a water-skiing emporium. (Atwood 1984)

Over the next several years Atwood would be one of the best-known voices in a phalanx of English-speaking Canada's foremost writers, artists, and broadcasters opposed to the free trade treaty signed in 1988 between Canada and the US. The Council of Canadians, created in 1985, spearheaded this opposition. Besides making alarmist predictions that free trade would accelerate the economic takeover of Canada by US capital, undermine political sovereignty, and lead inevitably to the emaciation of Canada's more generous social programs, the council's spokespersons predicted that Canada's cultural autonomy and distinctiveness would be jeopardized. The country's 1988 federal election was fought mainly on the issue of free trade with the US.

The impetus for a free trade deal with the US, as the 1984 report of the Royal Commission on the Economic Union and Development Prospects for Canada made clear and as the historical record shows, had much to do with the sense that the special relationship could no longer be counted on to protect Canada from protectionist measures enacted by the US government. It did not imply the abandonment of the special relationship concept as a pillar of the bilateral relationship. Rather, it proposed a treaty and institutional framework to avoid exclusive reliance on amical and intimate relations between policy-makers to resolve differences in matters of trade and investment.

It is not necessary to try to judge whether the claims made in opposition to or in support of free trade were more plausible at that time, let alone whether history has vindicated one side or the other. What is relevant to the current analysis is that the anti–free trade arguments drew heavily from a deep well of Canadian nationalist fears of US annexation. This was graphically and dramatically illustrated in one of the most remembered of the many prominent political cartoons from the 1988 election, which showed the erasing of the border between Canada and the US. Prominent Canadians and organizations that supported free trade, including Conservative Prime Minister Brian Mulroney, were portrayed as willingly and even enthusiastically complicit in the final step in the process that George Grant had lamented two decades earlier (Cameron and Watkins 1993; Clarkson 2002). Given that among the three national parties that polled any significant number of votes in the 1988 election, the two anti–free trade parties – the Liberals and the NDP – outpolled the victorious pro–free trade Conservative Party by 52 per cent to 43 per cent, one might be inclined to conclude that the Canadian electorate agreed. But as prominent as the free trade issue was in this election, as it was back in 1891 and 1911, this was not a referendum. It would, therefore, be baseless to conclude that all voters cast their ballots according to their views on this issue.

What is clear is that the Canadian electorate was divided on this issue. A significant share of the public, even if they did not accept the annexation narrative that was heard so often leading up to and during the 1988 election campaign, did not support greater integration between Canada and the US. But a significant share did (Janigan 1988). Canadians' historical ambivalence toward the US and their relationship with it was once again on full display.

The notion of a special relationship was framed by nationalists as, at best, acquiescence to Canadian dependence on the US, or, at worst, acceptance of a sort of servility that was blind to the dangers of closer integration between the two countries. This latter view was expressed by Stephen Clarkson, for decades a prominent voice in Canadian nationalism, who claimed that "many Canadians had found embarrassing and even demeaning" Brian Mulroney's close personal relationships and general ideological agreement with presidents Ronald Reagan and George H.W. Bush (Clarkson and Lachappelle 2005, 66). Clarkson's claim that some Canadians felt this way is certainly correct. But there were also many who welcomed what appeared to be evidence of close personal connections between Canadian and US heads of government, as opposed to the rather distant relations between Pierre Trudeau and Ronald Reagan that preceded the Mulroney years.[2]

The Special Relationship and Canadian Nationalism in the Era of Free Trade

The years after the 1989 ratification of the Canada–US Free Trade Agreement (CUSFTA) and particularly following the 1994 ratification of the North American Free Trade Agreement (NAFTA) witnessed a steady decline in the political relevance of the nationalist message. Support for the national NDP, an important advocate of the nationalist message, was dismal in the three elections between 1993 and 2000. At the same time, however, the nationalist measures implemented during the Trudeau years, particularly restrictions on foreign ownership of the Canadian economy, continued to set hearts racing at the Council of Canadians and in some academic circles. Nationalist publisher and writer Mel Hurtig's *The Betrayal of Canada* was quite possibly the most discussed book in Canada in 1991. Moreover, the Liberal Party returned to power in 1993 with a promise that it would renegotiate several provisions of NAFTA that had just been agreed by Canada, the US, and Mexico, and claimed that abrogation of free trade was an option if "satisfactory changes cannot be negotiated" (Liberal Party of Canada 1993, 23–4). Nothing came of this Liberal election promise, and while closer ties with the US continued to be criticized by nationalists, their movement and its policy demands seemed distinctly out of fashion in the years after the 1993 election.

On the face of it, this might seem puzzling. Surveys indicated that a large proportion of the Canadian population remained leery of Canada's ties with the US. Indeed, a 1992 Gallup poll found that 67 per cent of respondents agreed that the US had too much influence on the Canadian way of life. This was up from 58 per cent in 1985, the highest level recorded since the question was first asked in 1956. That same 1992 survey found that 37 per cent of Canadians believed that Canada would be part of the US within fifty years (Canadian Press 1992).[3]

It might appear, then, that the new nationalism's fears about American influence, to say nothing of long-standing Canadian anxieties about eventual annexation, continued to resonate widely among Canadians. But these sentiments had far less political traction than during previous decades. "Close, but not too close," continued to characterize Canadian opinion when it came to relations with the US. But if the results of elections and the policies of Canadian governments are any guide, there was now very little popular support for steps to distance Canada from its obvious and continuing dependence on the US.

In fact, only a decade after the 1988 free trade election an Ipsos poll found that seven in ten Canadians supported NAFTA, with 40 per cent agreeing that it had benefited Canada compared to 27 per cent who said the treaty had hurt the country (Ipsos 1998). By 2007, almost six in ten Canadians agreed that the country would be worse off without free trade (CTV News 2007). As Wolfe (2018) observes, support among Canadians for free trade has, with short downward blips, remained quite high since the 1990s.

At the same time, however, and consistent with their long-standing ambivalence when it comes to their country's relationship with the US, Canadians have continued to worry that foreign ownership threatens national sovereignty. The waters are muddied by the fact that questions about foreign ownership used to evoke concerns about US influence, whereas over the past two decades, many Canadians are as likely to bring China to mind when asked such questions. Regularly, majorities now say they are somewhat or very concerned about "US and foreign ownership of Canadian companies" and that they somewhat or strongly oppose "the purchase of Canadian businesses by foreign-owned companies." The fact that such concerns are greater when respondents are asked about state-owned foreign companies strongly suggests that Chinese investment is seen as a greater threat than US or other foreign investment (Graves 2016).

While suggestive, none of these survey measures are convincing proxies for Canadians' thoughts about the special relationship. No survey – as far as this author has been able to determine – has ever asked Canadians in a direct manner whether they have heard this term applied to Canada–US relations, whether they think that such a relationship exists, or whether they think it should exist.[4] It is evident, however, that most of those who report to Canadians on the bilateral relationship, and interpret it for them, have continued to believe that the concept of the special relationship should be a touchstone for assessing this relationship.

Media commentary on the special relationship is almost exclusively restricted to those moments when there is a meeting of the heads of government or when a major disagreement roils the waters of the Canada–US relationship. Much of the coverage tends to be superficial, focusing on such things as the golfing friendship between Prime Minister Chrétien and President Clinton, the lack of positive chemistry in the Chrétien–George W. Bush and Harper–Obama relationships, or the "bromance" between Justin Trudeau and Obama. It is not that these personal relationships at the top do not matter. But they have never provided the foundation for an enduring special relationship as that concept is generally understood in international relations.

Moments of elevated stress have generated spikes in media commentary on the state of the special relationship. Such moments provide greater insight into the relationship between Canadian nationalism and the Canada–US bilateral relationship. Reflecting on the obvious and building tensions between the Bush administration and the Chrétien government during the period 2001–3, Roussel (2003) writes,

> If the degradation in Canada–US relations is merely due to personality conflicts between the heads of the executive branches, differences in style, or again manoeuvering by a group dissatisfied with the political clientele of the leaders in power, then these are merely random events that might be forgotten in a changing of the guard in Ottawa and/or Washington. On the other hand, *if the tension is due to structural transformations, then the situation would, in large measure, lie beyond the control and will of the political leaders, and could be more difficult to manage.* (573; emphasis added)

This latter possibility that Roussel mentions obviously poses a greater threat to the special relationship, understood as a Canada–US relationship characterized by an exceptional degree of consultation as well as responsiveness to the other's interests. Those who believe that the special relationship is important for Canadian economic and security interests, insofar as these are linked to the actions of the US government, worry that the structural transformations Roussel alludes to have arrived and may be irreversible. This fear is not shared by Canadian nationalists.

American Decline, the Rise of Trumpism, and Canadians' Image of America

The last decade, and particularly the years since the 2016 election of Donald Trump as president, have seen a proliferation of articles in Canada with such titles as "Searching for the American Dream? Go to Canada" (Khanna 2021), "The American Dream Has Moved to Canada" (Gilmore 2017), "The 'Canadian Dream': Has It Overtaken the American Dream?," and "It's Official, Canadians Now Make More Money Than Americans" (Howse 2019). Very similar analyses have proliferated in the US as well. But Americans' contributions to this story of role reversal take the form of laments over what has been lost and concerns about how Americans can recover the promise of the American Dream, whereas those from Canada tend to celebrate Canada's achievements and what is seen as proof that the Canadian model is superior to that of the US. By the end of the Trump presidency, the self-congratulatory mood of many Canadians when they looked south was joined by something rather new: pity. They were not alone in experiencing this unfamiliar sentiment (Earle 2020).

To be clear, the belief among many Canadians and their opinion leaders that the US is in decline and that Canada offers the world a better path toward the ideals that were once associated most closely with the US is not something that began with the election of Donald Trump. A 1986 editorial in Toronto's *Globe and Mail* expressed a widespread sentiment: "We do not turn to the United States as a model of social justice or even intelligent self-interest when it comes to domestic policy. Far from it … America is not the ideal … in many of the civilized aspects of life, though the dynamism of the US economy is impressive and attractive. America pays too little attention to the community" (*Globe and Mail* 1986). Canadians have long been avid consumers of news from the US, and their views about what many of them have long seen as the multiple crises of American society – including racial conflict, a gun-related homicide rate without equal among democracies, growing economic inequality, and political polarization – have been reinforced by events over the past several decades. Many if not most Canadians also believe, as is true in most Western democracies, including the US, that America's global influence is in decline and that this is not likely to be reversed, regardless of which party controls the White House.[5]

There is no "Canadian view" as to whether declining US influence abroad and increasing trouble at home matter for Canada, and if so, how. Long before the Trump presidency, polls had indicated that most Canadians believe that America is in decline, albeit a significant minority do not. Nevertheless, there is not much doubt that among Canadian opinion leaders as well as the general public, the recent anxiety about the consequences of US domestic politics for Canada has been widespread.

That anxiety was on full display during the Trump presidency, reaching its highest levels after the Capitol Hill riots of 6 January 2021, a historic event in which Trump's complicity was plain to see. It certainly has not abated since it has become apparent that the re-election of Donald Trump in 2024 is by no means out of the question. Media stories with such titles as "Canada Should Be Preparing for the End of American Democracy" (Danisch 2022), "The American Polity Is Cracked and Might Collapse" (Homer-Dixon 2022), "Is the US on the Verge of Civil War?" (Paikin 2022), and "Angst of the Americas: Four-in-Five Canadians Worry about the Domestic Impacts of Continued US Political Turmoil" (Angus Reid 2022) were not uncommon after Trump's reluctant departure from the White House.

In an op-ed published in the *Globe and Mail* two weeks before the assault on Capitol Hill, the prominent Canadian political scientist Thomas Homer-Dixon wrote that "by 2025, American democracy could collapse, causing extreme domestic political instability, including widespread civil violence … By 2030, if not sooner the country could be governed by a right-wing dictatorship" (Homer-Dixon 2022). David Frum, a prominent Canadian writer and political commentator who is best known as an analyst of the US political scene and a former speech writer for President George W. Bush, had made similarly dire predictions in his 2018 book, *Trumpocracy: The Corruption of the American Republic*. Among Canadian left nationalists, the past several years have simply deepened their long-standing conviction that Canada needs to create far more distance between itself and the US. This view was expressed in a 2021 article in *Canadian Dimension*:

> In the current circumstances, deeper integration with the United States is profoundly contrary to Canada's long-term interests. Our interests would best be served by reducing our reliance on the American economy and ending our deference to the United States government. We can do this both by pursuing an independent and non-aligned foreign policy, enhancing our trade relations with other stable, functioning democracies and, most importantly, by investing massively in our capacity to produce domestically the goods and services upon which the well-being of Canadians depends. (Lascaris 2021)

The Trump presidency amplified concerns that many Canadians and some of their leaders already had about US decline on the global stage. Recent years, though, have seen the emergence across much of the West of a widely held view that Trump is a symptom of something deeper and that the structural issues Roussel referred to in his analysis of stresses in the Canada–US relationship two decades ago are at the root of whatever ails the special relationship (Krastev and Leonard 2021). The reasoning goes roughly like this: If American influence in the world, particularly economic and political influence, is declining, while that of other countries and regions, including China, the Asia-Pacific region more generally, India, and the European Union (this thesis has also included the BRICS – Brazil, Russian, India, China, and South Africa – at various points over the past couple of decades), is increasing, then Canada should reduce its dependence on the US and develop more robust ties to these newer centres of world power. A special relationship with a fading superpower is not in the interests of Canadians. Writing in 2016 as he was assuming his new role as a foreign policy adviser to Prime Minister Justin Trudeau, Roland Paris (2016) wrote: "No longer can the United States be relied upon either to drive Canadian economic growth or to single-handedly underwrite the global trading system and international security" (1).

The need to take such steps is given added urgency by mounting evidence of what most Canadians believe to be undemocratic tendencies within American society and domestic polarization that renders the US a problematic and less reliable partner. An Angus Reid poll taken in February 2022 found that roughly eight in ten Canadians agreed with this statement: "I'm worried America's democratic conflict will affect Canada's economy and security." Indeed, almost one-third of respondents said they strongly agreed. Fears about how conditions in the US might affect Canada were high in all regions of the country and among supporters of all political parties. Close to half the respondents agreed that the US is on the way to becoming an authoritarian state. While agreement was highest among voters on the left, it was not lower than about four in ten respondents among supporters of any of the four main parties (Angus Reid 2022).

At the same time, and consistent with the ambivalence that has always characterized Canadians' perceptions of their southern neighbour, any evidence that Canada appears to be losing influence with the US government, and that the "special relationship" that many Canadians and their opinion leaders had come to think was a given could no longer be taken for granted, continues to be greeted with dismay by much of the political commentariat. This dismay reached depths not seen since the famously strained relationship between Kennedy and Diefenbaker in the early 1960s when it became clear that Canada would not receive an exemption from the protectionist policies that were a pillar of Trump's "Make America Great Again" agenda. It is fair to say that most Canadians, including those who were never convinced that the closeness implicit in the idea of the special relationship was in Canada's interests, were shocked at the disdain the Trump administration frequently showed toward their country. They were in for another surprise when, after Joe Biden was elected in 2020 and the Democrats regained control of Congress, protectionist sentiments in the White House and on Capitol Hill did not vanish. The insults were gone, and the bonhomie had largely returned, but there were few tangible signs that Washington decision-makers viewed Canada as a partner deserving of special treatment. Halfway through the Biden administration, this had not changed.

Conclusion

Worries that the Canada–US special relationship may no longer be quite so special have never been shared by Canadian nationalists. On the contrary, they have viewed the notion of the special relationship, whether conceived of as an exceptional degree of integration and intimacy in the economic, cultural, and intergovernmental relations between Canada and the US, or in the more specific sense of Canada having and warranting unique treatment by the US government when it comes consultation, as indicative of an unfortunate dependency relationship that is not in Canada's best interests. The measures championed by the New Nationalism in the 1960s and 1970s contributed to stress in the Canada–US relationship and to the sense that the special relationship that had emerged in the post-war years was no longer relevant. The passage of the CUSFTA and then NAFTA and the dismantling of nationalist policies enacted during the Trudeau years were unequivocal signs that the influence of Canadian nationalism on Canada's most important bilateral relationship had declined rather dramatically. What persisted, however, was Canadians' long-standing ambivalence about their country's relationship with the US. Indications that Washington was not duly sensitive to Canadian interests – on issues ranging from those of undeniable consequence, such as trade protectionism and border security, to whether Canada received the first visit from a newly elected president or the first telephone call after his inauguration – have continued to spark a flurry of media hand-wringing about the special relationship. At the same time, polls have continued to show that many Canadians are dubious about the scale of American influence on their economy and on their society more generally.

Former Liberal cabinet minister Allan Rock has described the special relationship as "mystical" (as quoted in Porter 2021). He is right, in the sense that for Canadians the concept evokes long-held, complicated, and contradictory ideas and sentiments about their country's relationship with its much larger and sometimes overwhelming neighbour. Experts disagree on whether the special relationship still exists in a meaningful form. But in the minds of Canadians and their opinion leaders, it continues to frame their expectations for and assessments of Canada–US relations.

Notes

1 For the most part, French Canadian opinion leaders did not share this concern with the Americanization of Canada. They were far more worried about another relationship of dominance and dependency, that between English and French Canada.

2 John Turner's time as prime minister was so brief, from 30 June 1984 to 17 September 1984, that it is not reasonable to speak of whatever relationship he may have had with President Reagan.

3 Those who expressed this belief were not asked whether they thought this would be a good or a bad thing.

4 In a 2021 poll, Britons and Americans were asked whether they believed that a special relationship existed between their countries. Interestingly, Americans were twice as likely as British respondents to believe that such a relationship exists. See https://policyexchange.org.uk/news/new-poll-america-believes-in-special-relationship-more-than-britain.

5 In 2008, 35 per cent of Canadians named the US as the world's leading economic power, compared to 37 per cent who said it was China. By 2020, 36 per cent said the US and 47 per cent named China. The margins identifying China over the US as the world's leading economic power are even larger in some European countries (Krastev 2021; Pew n.d.).

References

Angus Reid Institute. 2022. "Angst of the Americas: Four-in-Five Canadians Worry about the Domestic Impacts of Continued US Political Turmoil." 9 February. https://angusreid.org/wp-content/uploads/2022/02/2022.02.09_US_Can_Democracy.pdf.

Atwood, Margaret. 1984. "Through the One-Way Mirror." *The Nation*, 22 March.

Azzi, Stephen. 1999. *Walter Gordon and the Rise of Canadian Nationalism*. Montreal and Kingston: McGill-Queen's University Press.

Bickerton, James. 2006. "Lament: The Anguished Conservatism of George Grant." In *Freedom, Equality, Community: The Political Philosophy of Six Influential Canadians*, edited by James Bickerton, Stephen Brooks, and Alain-G. Gagnon, 35–54. Montreal and Kingston: McGill-Queen's University Press.

Broege, Valerie. 1986. "War with the United States in Canadian Literature and Visual Arts." *Journal of American Culture* 9, no. 1: 31–6.

Brooks, Stephen. 2024. *Imagining Each Other: Mutual Perceptions and United States–Canada Relations*. Edinburgh: Edinburgh University Press.

Brooks, Stephen, and Alain-G. Gagnon. 1988. *Social Scientists and Politics in Canada: Between Clerisy and Vanguard*. Montreal and Kingston: McGill-Queen's University Press.

Callaghan, Morley. 1958. "Go Easy." *Maclean's*, 7 June. https://archive.macleans.ca/article/1958/06/07/go-easy.

Cameron, Duncan, and Mel Watkins, eds. 1993. *Canada under Free Trade.* Toronto: James Lorimer.

Canadian Press. 1992. "US Has Too Much Influence in Canadian Life: Poll." 9 January.

Clarkson, Stephen. 2002. *Uncle Sam and Us: Globalization, Neoconservatism, and the Canadian State.* Toronto: University of Toronto Press.

Clarkson, Stephen, and Erick Lachappelle. 2005. "Jean Chrétien's Legacy in Managing Canadian–American Relations." *Canadian Foreign Policy Journal* 12, no. 2: 65–82.

CTV News. 2007. "Poll Says Most North Americans Support Free Trade." 30 September. https://www.ctvnews.ca/poll-says-most-north-americans-support-free-trade-1.258314?cache=dvgujsbn.

Danisch, Robert. 2022. "Canada Should Be Preparing for the End of American Democracy." *The Conversation*, 13 February. https://theconversation.com/canada-should-be-preparing-for-the-end-of-american-democracy-176930.

Earle, Renee M. 2020. "International Opinion of the US Slides from Respect to Pity." *American Diplomacy*, August. https://americandiplomacy.web.unc.edu/2020/08/international-opinion-of-the-u-s-slides-from-respect-to-pity.

Frum, David. 2018. *Trumpocracy: The Corruption of the American Republic.* New York: Harper.

Fulford, Robert. 1970. "The New Anti-Americanism." *Saturday Night*, March. Reprinted in Hugh Innis, ed., *Americanization*, 18–20. Toronto: McGraw-Hill Ryerson.

Gilmore, Scott. 2017. "The American Dream Has Moved to Canada." *Maclean's*, 28 February. https://www.theglobeandmail.com/opinion/article-searching-for-the-american-dream-go-to-canada.

Globe and Mail. 1986. "That American Model." *Globe and Mail*, 7 February.

Gotlieb, Allan. 1987. "Some Canadian Myths about the United States." Address delivered at the Empire Club, 9 April, Toronto.

Government of Canada. 1951. *Final Report of the Royal Commission on National Development in the Arts, Letters, and Sciences.* Ottawa.

– 1955. *Final Report of the Royal Commission on Canada's Economic Prospects.* Ottawa.

– 1957a. *Final Report of the Royal Commission on Broadcasting.* Ottawa.

– 1957b. *Final Report of the Royal Commission on Canada's Economic Prospects.* Ottawa.

– 1960. *Final Report of the Royal Commission on Publications.* Ottawa.

– 1972. *Final Report of the Task Force on Foreign Ownership.* Ottawa.

Granatstein, J.L. 1996. *Yankee Go Home? Canadians and Anti-Americanism.* Toronto: HarperCollins.

Grant, George. 1970. *Lament for a Nation: The Defeat of Canadian Nationalism*. Toronto: McClelland and Stewart.

Graves, Frank. 2016. "Understanding the New Public Outlook on the Economy and Middle-Class Decline: How FDI Attitudes Are Caught in Tentative Closing of the Canadian Mind." *SPP Research Papers* 9, no. 6. School of Public Policy, University of Calgary. https://journalhosting.ucalgary.ca/index.php/sppp/article/view/42569/30451.

Homer-Dixon, Thomas. 2022. "The American Polity Is Cracked, and Might Collapse: Canada Must Prepare." *Globe and Mail*, 1 January. https://www.theglobeandmail.com/opinion/article-the-american-polity-is-cracked-and-might-collapse-canada-must-prepare.

Howse, Allysha. 2019. "It's Official, Canadians Now Make More Money Than Americans." *Narcity*, 30 August. https://www.narcity.com/canadians-now-make-more-money-than-americans-new-study-shows.

Hurtig, Mel. 1991. *The Betrayal of Canada*. Toronto: Stoddart.

Hutchison, Bruce. 1959. "Will the Whole Continent Go Hollywood?" *Maclean's*, 6 June. https://archive.macleans.ca/article/1959/6/6/will-the-whole-continent-go-hollywood.

Ipsos. 1998. "Canadians' Views on NAFTA." 19 January. https://www.ipsos.com/en-ca/news-polls/canadians-views-nafta.

Isernia, Pierangelo. 2007. "Anti-Americanism in Europe During the Cold War." In *Anti-Americanisms in World Politics*, edited by Robert O. Keohane and Peter J. Katzenstein, 57–92. Ithaca: Cornell University Press.

Janigan, Mary, et al. 1988. "The Numbers Game." *Maclean's*, 28 November.

Kelly, Brendan. 2017. "The Politician and the Civil Servant: Pierre Trudeau, Marcel Cadieux, and the Department of External Affairs, 1968–1970." *International Journal* 72, no. 1: 5–27. doi:10.1177/0020702017694212.

Khanna, Parag. 2021. "Searching for the American Dream? Go to Canada." *Globe and Mail*, 15 October. https://www.theglobeandmail.com/opinion/article-searching-for-the-american-dream-go-to-canada.

Krastev, Ivan, and Mark Leonard. 2021. "The Crisis of American Power: How Europeans See Biden's America." European Council on Foreign Relations Policy Brief. 19 January. https://ecfr.eu/publication/the-crisis-of-american-power-how-europeans-see-bidens-america.

Lascaris, Dimitri. 2021. "Canada Must Prepare for America's Rapid Decline: It's High Time That Canada Reclaimed Its Sovereignty, Diversified Its Trade Relationships and Strengthened Its Self-sufficiency." *Canadian Dimension*, 12 December. https://canadiandimension.com/articles/view/canada-must-prepare-for-americas-rapid-decline.

Liberal Party of Canada. 1993. *Creating Opportunity: The Liberal Plan for Canada*. Ottawa.

Lipset, Seymour Martin. 1990. *Continental Divide: The Values of the United States and Canada*. New York: Routledge.

Lower, A.R.M. 1958. "The Gods Canadians Worship." *Maclean's*, 25 October. https://archive.macleans.ca/article/1958/10/25/the-gods-canadians-worship.

MacLennan, Hugh. 1960. "It's the U.S. or Us!" *Maclean's*, 5 November. https://archive.macleans.ca/article/1960/11/05/its-the-us-or-us.

Mowat, Farley. 1958. "Get Tough." *Maclean's*, 7 June. https://archive.macleans.ca/article/1958/06/07/get-tough.

Newman, Peter C. 1956. "Who Really Owns Canada?" *Maclean's*, 9 June. https://archive.macleans.ca/article/1956/6/9/who-really-owns-canada.

Paikin, Steve. 2022. "Is the U.S. on the Verge of Civil War?" *The Agenda*, 10 January. YouTube video, 45:31. https://www.youtube.com/watch?v=cagQGM2abec.

Paris, Roland. 2016. *The World Won't Wait: Why Canada Needs to Rethink Its International Policies*. Toronto: University of Toronto Press.

Pew Research Center. n.d. "U.S. Global Image." Global Attitudes Project. https://www.pewresearch.org/topic/international-affairs/global-image-of-countries.

Porter, Catherine. 2021. "Justin Trudeau Gets Call From Biden as Canada and U.S. Mend Relations." *New York Times*, 22 January. https://www.nytimes.com/2021/01/22/world/canada/biden-canada.html.

Preston, Robert. 1975. "The New Nationalism Viewed from across the Border: Chauvinism or Survival? A Background Study." *American Review of Canadian Studies* 5, no. 2: 48–65.

Rotstein, Abraham. 1976. "Canada: The New Nationalism." *Foreign Affairs* 55, no. 1: 97–118.

Roussel, Stéphane. 2003. "'Honey, Are You Still Mad at Me? I've Changed, You Know…': Canada–US Relations in a Post-Saddam/Post-Chrétien Era." *International Journal* 58, no. 4: 571–90.

Senate of Canada. 1970. *Report of the Special Senate Committee on Mass Media*. Ottawa: Government of Canada.

Sigler, John H., and Dennis Goresky. 1974. "Public Opinion on United States–Canadian Relations." *International Organization* 28, no. 4: 661–5.

Wilson, Sandy. 1985. *My American Cousin*. https://canfilmday.ca/film/my-american-cousin.

Wise, S.F., and Robert Craig Brown. 1967. *Canada Views the United States: Nineteenth-Century Political Attitudes*. Seattle: University of Washington Press.

Wolfe, Robert. 2018. "Where Does the Public Sit on NAFTA?" *Policy Options*, 19 April. https://policyoptions.irpp.org/magazines/april-2018/public-sit-nafta.

8

Quebec's Relations with the US under Jean Charest

Building a Special Relationship

STÉPHANE PAQUIN

Quebec's relationship with the US is of vital importance. Louis Balthazar (2006), the researcher who has most analyzed the relationship between the US and Quebec, argues that Quebec's southern neighbour has been, "for better or for worse, an essential partner in Quebec's development" (115; author's translation). There is clearly no "special relationship" between Quebec and the US like the one between Canada and the US (Blanchard 1998; Paquin 2014a, 2016).

Still, if historically it was the France–Quebec relationship that favoured the construction of an international policy on the part of the Quebec government from the Quiet Revolution of the 1960s onwards, the US has gradually become a central object of concern. Today, the budgets Quebec allocates to Quebec–US relations have grown to exceed those for France–Quebec relations. This has been the case since the early 2000s, around the time Jean Charest became premier of Quebec (2003–12).[1]

Prior to the 1960s, the Quebec government had little interest in what was happening south of the border. Quebec's "mini-embassy" in New York City, which was established during the Second World War mainly to attract tourism and investment, was virtually powerless until the early 1960s. It was under a Union Nationale government in the late 1960s that Quebec expanded its network of delegations to the US. Under Robert Bourassa, at the beginning of the 1970s, the importance of economic and financial issues compelled the Quebec government to restructure its policy toward the US. However, it was during the first term of the Parti Québécois (PQ), which had promised to hold a referendum on sovereignty-association, that the Quebec government grasped the importance of implementing a sustained and coherent US policy. The election in 1976 of a sovereigntist government that had a program advocating for neutrality in international relations and that wished to withdraw a sovereign Quebec from the North Atlantic Treaty Organization (NATO) and the North American Aerospace Defense Command (NORAD) had the potential to worry the US government in the context of the Cold War. In addition, the big banks in New York had been lending heavily to the Quebec government for hydropower projects since the 1960s. Here too, the concern was palpable. Free trade negotiations with the US in the late 1980s and the second referendum of 1995 made economic and trade issues still more important; the 9/11 terrorist attacks in New York and Washington, DC, and climate change then added security, energy, and environmental issues to the mix.

Oddly enough, Quebec's international policy toward the US took a major step backward after the 1995 referendum and the austerity policy implemented by the PQ government of Lucien Bouchard (1996–2001) (Paquin 2006). It became clear, however, in a context where Quebec's economic growth increasingly depended on its exports south of the border, that this strategy was ill-advised. After its re-election in 1998, the PQ decided to revive its international relations in general and its international initiatives toward the US in particular. The renewal of Quebec's presence in the US began gradually in the late 1990s after Lucien Bouchard began trade promotion missions there. Jean Charest then built on this momentum, raising the relationship between Quebec and the US to an unprecedented level.

What explains the Quebec government's international activism under Premier Jean Charest, and specifically toward the US? This chapter hypothesizes that the premier's exceptional leadership on international policy issues, more than any other factor, was key to this development. In this chapter, I attempt to explain why Quebec was so active under Charest's leadership; I base my findings on the results of anonymous semi-structured interviews with four senior Quebec government officials, a former Quebec delegate, two former political advisers to Charest, a senior official from the European Commission, and Charest himself. I then explore in more detail Quebec's US policy – the building of a special relationship – under Charest.

The International Activism of the Charest Government

During Charest's time as premier, the Quebec government's international policy was the most dynamic it had ever been. None of his predecessors had participated in as many activities abroad as Charest (Richer 2011). In this regard, he even rivalled the heads of state of the G7 countries. Charest's legacy is indeed significant: he was instrumental in launching trade negotiations between Canada and the European Union (EU) (the Comprehensive Economic and Trade Agreement [CETA]), the Entente Québec–France sur la reconnaissance mutuelle des qualifications professionnelles (Agreement between Quebec and France on the Mutual Recognition of Professional Qualifications),[2] and an ambitious new international policy toward the US. The Charest government also left its mark on the international environmental scene, as evidenced by Quebec's participation with California in what was, at the time, the second largest carbon market in the world, the Western Climate Initiative.

Charest has been praised for his international actions even by his political rivals, despite the controversies that surrounded his government, notably around allegations of corruption that led to a public inquiry. According to Gérard Deltell, a former Coalition Avenir Québec MLA, and now a Conservative MP, "our current premier [Jean Charest], in international affairs, acts with stature, dignity, and talent" ("50 ans de Présence" 2011; author's translation). Jean-François Lisée, Quebec's former Minister of International Relations and Parti Québécois leader, went so far as to award Charest the "Most Outstanding Parliamentarian Outside Quebec Award." Lisée, whom one would hardly expect to be generous toward a federalist former premier, wrote that "once he crosses the border, Jean-Charest-the-partisan becomes Jean-Charest-the-great-ambassador. The members of Quebec's small but dynamic diplomatic corps (and foreign diplomats) tell you privately: he is perfect" (Lisée 2009; author's translation). Bernard Landry, former premier and Charest's rival in the 2003 election campaign, strongly supported Charest's initiative on the free trade agreement with Europe (Robitaille 2008). Sylvain Simard, Quebec's Minister of International Relations under the PQ in the 1990s, commented thus on France–Quebec relations: "I believe that the Premier of Quebec has followed in the footsteps of all the great premiers of Quebec in his relationship with France, he has deepened this relationship, and I think that we can be proud of this" (Robitaille 2008). For his actions on the environment, the former premier won the South Australia International Climate Change Leadership Award; he was also praised by Al Gore, the climate activist and one-time US vice-president (Journet 2010; Chaloux, Séguin, and Paquin 2015).

None of Charest's predecessors as Quebec premier had travelled so much abroad. Between 2003 and 2011, he undertook sixty-two international missions – an average of eight trips per year. He thus crossed Quebec's borders almost twice as often as his two predecessors,[3] Lucien Bouchard and Bernard Landry, combined (thirty-two trips in seven years) (Richer 2011). Premier Charest travelled twice as often on official missions to France as Lucien Bouchard and Bernard Landry, both of whom are known to be Francophiles. French President Jacques Chirac, on vacation in Quebec in 2003, even went to the premier's residence for a private dinner, an unprecedented event in Quebec history. Premier Charest attended the World Economic Forum in Davos more often (six times) than Lucien Bouchard and Bernard Landry combined (five times), and it was because of his personal interest in climate change issues that he attended the United Nations Conference of Parties on Climate Change twice (Chaloux, Séguin, and Paquin 2015). Charest travelled far more often than the premiers of Alberta (Ralph Klein and Ed Stelmach), even though Alberta is the richest province in Canada on a per capita basis. Between 2003 and 2011, Klein and Stelmach went on twenty-two missions abroad, visiting fifteen countries and thirty-six cities. Charest completed almost three times as many missions, visiting sixteen countries and fifty-one cities (Richer 2011).

Charest's international travels put him on a par with several Canadian prime ministers and heads of state of G7 countries. According to data obtained from the Privy Council Office of Canada under the Access to Information Act, Canadian prime ministers Jean Chrétien (1993–2003), Paul Martin (2004–05), and Stephen Harper (2008–14) travelled an average of nine, eleven, and ten times per year, respectively, during their terms in office. In France, former French prime ministers Jean-Pierre Raffarin (2002–05) and Dominique de Villepin (2005–07) travelled outside of France only six times per year during their respective terms (Jeudy 2008). Even former US president Barack Obama left his country an average of only seven times per year between 2008 and 2014 (Department of State 2022).

Charest was also the most quoted Quebec personality outside Quebec. A study commissioned by the Ministère des relations internationales et de la Francophonie (MRIF) in 2012, of which I have obtained a copy, shows that toward the end of Charest's government, between 2010 and 2011 (i.e., before the 2012 student strike), the premier was the most quoted Quebec personality in the major newspapers of twelve selected states (US, Mexico, France, the UK, Spain, Belgium, Germany, Italy, India, China, Japan, and Brazil).[4] Indeed, Charest accounted for 44 per cent of all mentions, well ahead of the usual traditional ambassadors, such as the Cirque du Soleil (6 per cent) and the Montreal Canadiens players (5 per cent) (Influence Communication 2012).

This is paradoxical, because one would expect a federalist provincial government to accept the primacy of the Canadian government on international issues, or to seek to limit the possibility of conflict with the federal government in order to demonstrate that federalism works. One might also expect a federalist provincial party to be less aggressive on international issues than a sovereigntist party, whose fundamental objective is to make Quebec a sovereign country (Fry 2000; Noda 2001).

Yet the facts show otherwise. Under the Charest government, Quebec's international agenda expanded considerably – especially compared to the PQ under Lucien Bouchard and Bernard Landry (Paquin 2006), and to Robert Bourassa's government from the mid-1980s onwards; indeed, on many occasions the Quebec government under Charest set itself in opposition to the Canadian government's own position on important international policies, such as climate change and carbon pricing. And on many issues, the Quebec government has exerted great influence on the Canadian government, for example, on the question of Quebec's place in UNESCO or in trade negotiations with the EU. Regarding relations with the US, the Quebec government has greatly expanded its actions south of the border.

How can the Charest government's international activism be explained? Since that government was more active than any previous government – indeed, more active than any of its successors – in comparable international contexts, one must rule out systemic factors such as globalization or internationalization as an explanation. The sovereigntist/federalist factor can also both be ruled out, given that Charest's government was more active on the international scene than the PQ governments of Pauline Marois (2012–14), Lucien Bouchard (1996–2001), and Bernard Landry (2001–3), as well as René Léves-que (1976–84), despite its unconditional support for Canadian federalism.

The factor that explains Quebec's activism on the international scene was more related to the personality of the premier and his interest in international issues. For Charest, it was not incompatible for Quebec to have its own international policy and to defend the province's interests within the framework of Canadian federalism. This was stated by several sources. According to one political adviser, "he saw it as a way for Quebec to stand out, to develop, to show an openness to the world … It is really a priority for him" (anonymous interview; author's translation). Another source said,

> Every Monday morning, Mr. Charest would arrive with 12, 15, 20, sometimes 30 articles cut out, annotated with questions, a request for an opinion, a follow-up or a request for a recommendation. These articles came from the *New York Times*, *The Economist*, *L'Express*, and so on. One wondered if he had done anything else on the weekend besides read the news. Mr. Charest would underline the important parts of the article and in the margin, he would indicate his questions and ask for a follow-up. (Anonymous interview)

According to several sources, the premier was strongly aware of international political and diplomatic trends. He knew the facts and was constantly on the lookout. He regularly sent letters to foreign heads of state (or sub-state), corresponded with them, and proposed international projects. A great many initiatives with an international scope came directly from him. The labour mobility agreement between France and Quebec that he presented to Nicolas Sarkozy is one example. According to a top senior public servant, those present in Paris at the bilateral meeting were surprised to learn of such a project at a joint press conference between Jean Charest and Nicolas Sarkozy, the French president. John Parisella, the former Quebec delegate general in New York and former chief of staff to Robert Bourassa when he was premier, maintains that Charest was behind various international environmental initiatives; for example, his connection with Arnold Schwarzenegger led to the Western Climate Initiative (Parisella 2016).

According to one senior official, the premier personally and often, if not weekly, followed up on high-priority international issues. One senior official testified that in his nearly thirty-year career as a civil servant, he had never known a premier to be so directly involved in international issues. Whereas in the past in Quebec, premiers gave a great deal of leeway to ministers to manage international policies, Charest personally set the direction of the government.

Charest also had a strong network of contacts abroad. During his time in Rio de Janeiro as chair of the Canadian delegation to the Earth Summit, he befriended an Indian minister, Kamal Nath. When he became premier of Quebec, he used this personal relationship to undertake trade missions in 2006 and 2010 to India. He also established ties with US governors, notably the governor of Vermont, and also with high-level politicians in France and in the French-speaking world, including former presidents (Jacques Chirac and Nicolas Sarkozy), former prime ministers (Jean-Pierre Raffarin and Alain Juppé), and the head of la Francophonie, Abdou Diouf (Richer 2011).

According to several sources, the premier's leadership was decisive for Quebec's activism on the world stage. From the moment he took office, he expressed international ambitions for Quebec. His interest in this subject stemmed from his experience as a minister on the federal scene, notably during the Jeux de la Francophonie, and then as federal minister of the environment during the 1992 Rio Earth Summit. MPs in Ottawa are more aware of the importance of international issues than are MLAs in Quebec City. He was also very interested in the US while in the Canadian government. When he was elected premier of Quebec, he brought his interest in international issues to the Quebec government.

In terms of vision, Premier Charest arrived on the provincial scene without any "complexes" regarding Quebec's international relations. He never hesitated to assert Quebec's international character and to push the Gérin-Lajoie doctrine of 1965. As Charest himself stated,

> I have no inhibitions in my relationship, in my desire to do international relations. There is nothing holding me back in my own mind. Whereas my predecessors, consciously or unconsciously, saw themselves as the head of a provincial government and not of a country, and did not see themselves playing a role on the international level. I saw things quite differently. In our federal system, the provinces have very

> important jurisdictions, and when Quebec's jurisdictions were exclusive, the government also had to have a full dimension at the international level, they had to be expressed outside Quebec. Gérin-Lajoie's speech resonated for me, and I fully assumed it in a relaxed manner. Going abroad and asking for a meeting with a head of state or government was normal for me and I was not inhibited. And I found out in the trial that when a premier of Quebec asks for a meeting, most of the time the answer is yes. Foreign leaders meet with you … If you are a true federalist and understand how things work in the federal structure [you will know that provinces are] not the federal government's sub-government. We are equals in our respective areas of jurisdiction. So you have to approach it like that. (Interview with Jean Charest, quoted in Jeyabalaratnam and Paquin 2016; author's translation)

In his approach to international relations, Premier Charest went beyond the Gérin-Lajoie doctrine, dealing with issues such as trade negotiations between Canada and the EU that went well beyond Quebec's jurisdiction. The Gérin-Lajoie doctrine had been based on Quebec's constitutional jurisdiction; the "Charest Doctrine" went beyond that and was based on Quebec's interests.

According to several sources, even though Quebec's international policy created friction with the Canadian government on various issues (especially environment), Charest felt that the federal government and its institutions (embassies, consulates) had to work in support of the Quebec government's actions. Thus, it was very common for Quebec to ask for support from federal public servants and the Canadian diplomatic corps. The premier also did not hesitate to call upon the private sector, notably the powerful Desmarais family, which had close ties with Nicholas Sarkozy, when it was useful to his government. The transformations in the relationship between Quebec and France are also due to Charest. He believed that the issue of sovereignty made it more difficult to create projects between France and Quebec and that the Quebec Liberal Party had given up and left the field to the PQ. Even in opposition, Charest wished to "remove the constraint on this issue in the relationship between Quebec and France, which in a way cast a shadow on the types of projects we could do together" (interview 2015; author's translation).

Quebec–US Relations under Charest

In its *2001–2004 Strategic Plan*, adopted under Lucien Bouchard, the Quebec government made its relationship with the US the priority of its international relations (Government of Quebec 2001, 37). After that, Quebec redeployed its network in six US cities, following the closure of thirteen Quebec offices abroad between 1996 and 1997. Offices were opened or reopened in Boston, Chicago, and Los Angeles, and a small office was opened in Miami (in 2006, the Miami representation was closed, but one was reopened in Atlanta). The Quebec government also created research chairs focused on the US within Quebec universities.

The Charest government, then, accelerated the development of a Quebec policy toward the US. It has left an important legacy in international policy and specifically policy toward the US. Unlike France–Quebec relations, relations between Quebec and the US Executive Branch have always been considered difficult, if not practically non-existent.

Relations between Quebec and the US under Charest do not follow the same logic as the France–Quebec relationship, as several French presidents and prime ministers have maintained direct and privileged relations with Quebec premiers (Bernier 1996; Paquin 2022a). John Ciaccia, former minister of international affairs under the Bourassa government (1989–94), even maintained that if Quebec wants to go to Washington, it must go with the Canadian government. According to Balthazar and Hero (1999), for the US government, Canada's federal government is the sole Canadian interlocutor.

There are of course a few exceptions. Jean Charest had a one-on-one meeting with US Secretary of State Colin Powell soon after he took office. In 2005, during another trip to Washington and Virginia, he met with three senior members of the Bush administration: Secretary of Homeland Security Michael Chertoff, Secretary of Commerce Carlos Gutierrez, and Secretary of Energy Samuel W. Bodman (Paquin 2016). Charest is notably responsible for the creation of a true Quebec political office in Washington, DC (rather than a simple tourist office), something that no Quebec government, even under a PQ government, had been able to do because of Ottawa's obstruction (Paquin 2014a).

Still, relations between Quebec and the US are less about developing bilateral relations between the premier and the president or members of the Executive Branch than they are about developing relations with the governors of US states. It is also about building connections with US civil society and with the business community. Since Quebec has very little access to the federal government, the dominant strategy under Charest was to insert Quebec into networks of important federal states and to maintain bilateral relations with key US states.

Under Charest's leadership, the Government of Quebec published two key documents with regard to Quebec's policy toward the US. The first was *La politique internationale du Québec: la force de l'action concertée* (Quebec's International Policy: The Strength of Concerted Action; 2006); the second was *Stratégie du Gouvernement du Québec à l'égard des États-Unis* (The Quebec Government's Strategy towards the United States; 2010).

The first document, for which Charest wrote the preface, laid out the most comprehensive international relations policy ever produced to that point. It was accompanied by an action plan (a first). The themes addressed included strengthening the state's capacity for action and influence (concerted action); the economy and investment; security, identity, and culture; and international solidarity. No prior international policy Quebec had crafted had gone so far in terms of analyzing and integrating government actions. However, it should be noted that several themes were not treated separately: education, the environment, and immigration, unlike the previous themes, were not given individual chapters. This is surprising given the importance of environmental issues, especially the carbon market with California, for the Charest government. In precision and consistency, this document surpassed the international policies adopted in the past (Criekemans 2010). The previous international policies, published in 1985 and 1991 by Minister of International Relations Bernard Landry and Minister of International Affairs John Ciaccia, were more narrowly economic in orientation, and in 1999, the PQ government did not adopt an international policy statement, only strategic plans (MRIF 1985, 1991, 2001).

The Quebec government's policy toward the US has become much more professionalized and goes beyond trade promotion, as evidenced by the second document, published in 2010 (MRIF 2010). That document explained why the US is an important strategic partner and confirmed that, in addition to long-standing policies for export promotion and investment attraction, new themes in the relationship with the US are emerging, such as Quebec's leadership in energy and the environment, and its contribution to the security of the North American continent (Leblond 2011; MRIF 2010, 21–30).

Quebec's 2010–13 action plan regarding the US proposed five broad objectives and thirty-eight concrete measures aimed at promoting economic exchanges, ensuring Quebec's leadership in energy and environmental matters, contributing to the security of the continent, promoting Quebec's culture and identity, increasing Quebec's capacity for action, and supporting the development of expertise (Bernier, Blouin, and Faucher 2011).

In these documents, the Quebec government argued that the increasing interweaving of the Quebec economy with the US economy ensured that Quebec's economic destiny would be tied as closely to the northeastern US as is was to central Canada. Quebec would therefore set out to forge closer ties with the US states, be it bilaterally or in the context of multilateral forums of federated states (Chaloux 2014).

Under Charest, the Government of Quebec increased its participation in more than a dozen multilateral cross-border groupings, such as the Conference of New England Governors and Eastern Canadian Premiers and the Eastern Regional Conference of the Council of State Governments. It also maintained important bilateral relationships with several states, such as New York and Vermont (Paquin and Chaloux 2011).

According to the MRIF, since 2003, "members of the Quebec government have undertaken several missions to the United States. The Premier has been there more than 20 times and the Minister of International Relations more than 10 times. Some 20 other members of the Cabinet have made at least one mission to the United States" (MRIF 2015).

Under the Charest government, Quebec co-founded, with Georgia, an alliance of the southeastern US states and Canadian provinces. This alliance is an economic forum that promotes trade and investment and strengthens technological and scientific exchanges among members. It was launched in Montreal in 2007 with the signing of a joint declaration (SEUS-CP 2007). The association brings together six southeastern US states (Georgia, South Carolina, North Carolina, Tennessee, Mississippi, and Alabama) and seven Canadian provinces (Quebec, Ontario, Manitoba, New Brunswick, Nova Scotia, Prince Edward Island, and Newfoundland and Labrador). This association hosts an annual meeting, alternating between a Canadian province and a US state. The last meeting was in Savannah, Georgia, in May 2022 (SEUS-CP 2022).

In 2007, Quebec also joined the North American Strategy for Competitiveness, a coalition of government, business, and education representatives working together on energy, trade, and transportation issues in the three NAFTA states. Premier Charest participated in several meetings and hosted the annual conference in June 2009.

With Charest in power, Quebec was more prominent than any other government in Quebec on environmental issues. While the Government of Canada under Stephen Harper was accumulating Fossil Awards at the Paris Conference of the UN Framework Convention on Climate Change (a "lemon" award given by the Climate Action Network, which brings together 400 NGOs), Charest was praised by Al Gore and was presented with the South Australia International Climate Change Leadership Award. A portion of forest land on the outskirts of Adelaide, Australia, was even renamed in his honour (Journet 2010).

Quebec has also been very active in the fight against climate change. Under Charest, Quebec was active in several institutions such as the Climate Group, the Network of Regional Governments for Sustainable Developments, the International Carbon Action Partnership, and the International Emissions Trading Association, as well as many other institutions, notably in relation to the Organisation internationale de la Francophonie.

In North America, Quebec is an observer in the Regional Greenhouse Gas Initiative, which brings together several states in the US northeast and aims to cap and trade greenhouse gas emissions. It has also participated in the Climate Registry since 2007. The goal of this not-for-profit entity is to create a voluntary registry to record and validate greenhouse gas emissions and carbon credits. This member-driven registry can be used in the event that regional carbon markets are organized. All Canadian provinces, no less than thirty-nine US states, and six Mexican states are official members (Paquin 2016, 280).

The Charest government was also a founding partner in the Western Climate Initiative with California, starting in 2008. The Government of Quebec has linked its cap-and-trade system to California's. This carbon market is the largest North American carbon market and, at the time of its creation in January 2014, the second largest in the world after the EU (Chaloux 2014). The association, created in 2007, eventually brought together several Canadian provinces, Mexican states, and US states; however, several of the latter (Arizona, Oregon, Washington, New Mexico) quickly withdrew, using the economic crisis of 2008 as an excuse. In Canada, British Columbia, Manitoba, Ontario, and Nova Scotia also joined the initiative at first. However, the election of Doug Ford would end Ontario's participation. Conservative Brian Pallister's Manitoba also withdrew from the organization, in 2016. British Columbia no longer sends a representative to the board and does not participate in emissions trading. Nova Scotia, meanwhile, joined the organization in 2018 and has been participating in the carbon market since 1 January 2019.

Conclusion

Charest's international policy was clearly exceptional in terms of Quebec's international relations. This raises a question: How did the Canadian government respond to this strong activism? Charest saw three Canadian prime ministers during his tenure: Jean Chrétien (for a few months), Paul Martin (2003–06), and Stephen Harper (2006–15). Relations between Quebec and Ottawa on the issue of Quebec's international relations improved significantly compared to the previous period when the Parti Québécois was in power. Thus, after the strongly conflicted relations between Quebec and Ottawa on issues of Quebec's international relations in the referendum and post-referendum years, the situation between Quebec and Ottawa changed dramatically with the arrival of Charest, an unquestionably federalist premier, despite the strained personal relations between Charest and Harper (Paquin 2006, 2014b). The relationship between Quebec and Ottawa can even be considered exceptional during the negotiation of the free trade agreement between Canada and the EU, and Charest's role in that effort is recognized by all parties that have come to power in Ottawa (Paquin 2022b).

Paul Martin showed himself open to the idea of giving the provinces a role in international negotiations, after a formal request by the Quebec government under Charest. This change of direction by the Liberal prime minister was noteworthy, given that the Chrétien government had refused in October 2002 to allow Quebec's minister of international relations, Louise Beaudoin, to speak for Quebec at UNESCO. Paul Martin's position marked a historic break with his party's policies, given that the Liberals since the 1960s had been against the idea of giving the provinces a role in international relations (Paquin 2022a).

Harper, for his part, broke with his predecessors regarding the provinces' role in international negotiations by granting Quebec a place on the Canadian delegation to UNESCO. This gesture set a precedent, even if it only formalized what by then was a standard practice. It was, indeed, very common for Quebec and the Canadian provinces in general to participate in Canada's activities at UNESCO, since this international organization touches on the provinces' fields of competence. The most significant precedent was the collaboration between Louise Beaudoin, then minister of international relations, and Lisa Frulla, minister of Canadian heritage, to adopt the Convention on the Protection and Promotion of the Diversity of Cultural Expressions in 2005. Even so, Harper's move was courageous, considering the state of public opinion and the hostile editorials in the Canadian press on the issue (Paquin 2014b, 2022c). The historical significance of this Quebec–Ottawa agreement should nevertheless be qualified. From the outset, what Harper proposed was more a continuity with the Mulroney years, rather than in rupture. Mulroney had expressed openness regarding France–Quebec relations and Quebec's place in la Francophonie (Paquin 2022a). Moreover, Harper's actions were quite limited. The prime minister did not wish to negotiate an agreement for the participation of the provinces in all international negotiations that affected their areas of jurisdiction; his decision applied only to a rather peripheral international organization (Paquin 2014a, 2022c).

Moreover, the Harper government went against well-established precedents that favoured the presence of Quebec representatives in Canada's international climate negotiations. In the case of trade negotiations, it was only because it is a requirement of the EU that the provinces participate as part of the Canadian delegation in Canada–Europe negotiations that this role for Quebec and other provinces was conceded by Ottawa (Paquin 2022b).

Overall, Charest's international policy was without equal in the history of Quebec. Since his departure, no premier has been as active as Charest was during his years in office. The minority PQ government of Pauline Marois did not have time to leave its mark on Quebec's international relations with the US; the Liberal government of Philippe Couillard (2014–18) later set Quebec's international relations back. Couillard made the same mistake as Lucien Bouchard in 1996–97, namely, he implemented an austerity policy that significantly weakened Quebec's international policy. However, after two years of severe austerity, the Couillard government, like the Bouchard government, revived Quebec's international relations, albeit too little too late, for that government earned only one mandate. The election of Donald J. Trump to the US presidency and his demand that NAFTA be renegotiated confirmed, as if it were necessary, not only the importance of a separate international relations policy for Quebec but also the need to place the US at the forefront of those relations (Paquin 2022b).

After the October 2018 Quebec provincial elections, the Coalition Avenir Québec, led by François Legault, succeeded Philippe Couillard's Liberals. In 2019, the MRIF minister Nadine Girault released a revision of Quebec's international policy document (previously published by the Couillard government) so as to focus it more on the economy. This revision was released under the title *Vision Internationale du Québec (VIQ) – Le Québec: Fier et en affaires partout dans le monde* (Quebec: Proud and in Business around the World). This reorientation of Quebec's international activities was conveyed through a triptych promoting the province's economic development beyond its borders. This new version differs from its predecessor in that it strengthens economic activity at the international level, relies more on networks as economic levers, and modernizes international action.

The strategy toward the US promulgated by Legault's government identifies priority sectors to be exploited, namely trade and investment; energy, environment, and climate change; and cross-border issues. Moreover, market diversification is a primary objective of the strategy developed by the Quebec government. In terms of energy, Quebec is promoting the export of its hydroelectricity through projects such as the New England Clean Energy Connect in the states of Maine and Massachusetts and the Champlain Hudson Power Express in New York State. Moreover, the Legault government is calling for a renewed focus on trade and investment issues and energy exports in order to make Quebec the "green battery" of the US northeast.

Because of COVID-19, the dynamism of the relationship between Quebec and the US waned considerably relative to the Charest years. Since Charest, no premier has shown as much interest in international issues. During the 2022 election campaign, four of the five parties in the race had nothing to propose in terms of international relations. François Legault's party proposed continuing to implement economic diplomacy; the Quebec Liberal Party made a brief mention of its past actions (referring to the Charest years but without mentioning him); and the Conservative Party made no mention of the subject at all.

Even one of the two sovereigntist parties, Québec solidaire, has little to say on the subject. Québec solidaire wants to withdraw from trade agreements, such as the US–Mexico–Canada Agreement and CETA, as well as from military agreements (such as NATO and NORAD) if Quebec becomes sovereign, which seems unlikely. Only the Parti Québécois wants to see Quebec be more active in the world. To do so, it plans to double the number of Quebec delegations and offices abroad.

Decidedly, the Charest years are over.

Notes

1 Some of the data in this article comes from Jeyabalaratnam and Paquin (2016) and Paquin (2014a).

2 *Entente Québec-France sur la reconnaissance mutuelle des qualifications professionnelles*, Quebec and France, 17 October 2008.

3 Figures for the Bourassa government are not available.

4 The majority of the quotes were related to the Plan Nord, a vast development plan for Northern Quebec launched in 2011 at the initiative of Jean Charest.

References

"50 ans de Présence Québécoise en France. L'Opposition en Profite pour Encenser Jean Charest ... Oui, Oui, Vraiment." 2011. *Le Courrier Parlementaire*, 29 September. http://www.courrierparlementaire.com/article/loppositionenprofitepourencenserjeancharestouiouivraiment.

Balthazar, Louis. 2006. "Québec-États-Unis: une Relation Primordiale." In *Les Relations Internationales du Québec depuis la Doctrine Gérin-Lajoie (1965–2005)*, 115–24, edited by Stéphane Paquin. Quebec: Presses de l'Université Laval.

Balthazar, Louis, and Alfred O. Hero, Jr. 1999. *Le Québec dans L'espace Américain*. Montreal: Québec Amérique.

Bernier, Luc. 1996. *De Paris à Washington. La politique internationale du Québec*. Montreal: Les Presses de l'Université du Québec.

Bernier, Luc, Geneviève Blouin, and Mathieu Faucher. 2011. "La Nouvelle Politique Internationale du Québec. In *Le Destin Américain du Québec: Américanité, Américanisation, et Anti-Américanisme,* edited by Guy Lachapelle, 265–91. Quebec: Presses de l'Université Laval.

Blanchard, James. 1998. *Behind the Embassy Door: Canada, Clinton, and Québec*. Toronto: McClelland and Stewart.

Chaloux, Annie. 2014. "Paradiplomatie environnementale: Analyse de la mise en œuvre de trois engagements internationaux du Québec dans l'espace Nord-Américain." PhD diss., École nationale d'administration publique, Quebec.

Chaloux, Annie, Hugo Séguin, and Stéphane Paquin. 2015. "Federalism and Climate Change Negotiations: The Role of Québec." *International Negotiations* 20, no. 2: 39–58.

Criekemans, David. 2010. "Regional Sub-State Diplomacy from a Comparative Perspective: Quebec, Scotland, Bavaria, Catalonia, Wallonia, and Flanders." *Hague Journal of Diplomacy* 5, no. 1–2: 37–64.

Department of State. 2022. "Presidential and Secretaries Travels Abroad: Barack Obama." Office of the Historian. https://history.state.gov/departmenthistory/travels/president/obama-barack.

Fry, Earl H. 2000. "Québec Confronts Globalization: A Model for the Future?" *Québec Studies* no. 30: 57–69.

Gouvernement du Québec. 2001. *Le Québec dans un ensemble international en mutation. Plan stratégique 2001–2004*. Quebec, ministère des Relations internationales.

Influence Communication. 2012. "Analyse de la Personnalité Médiatique du Québec dans la Presse Internationale (12 pays) en 2010 et en 2011." 24 February.

Jeudy, Bruno. 2008. "François Fillon, premier ministre globe-trotteur." *Le Figaro*, 28 March. http://www.lefigaro.fr/politique/2008/04/30/01002-20080430ARTFIG00018-francois-fillon-premier-ministre-globe-trotteur.php.

Jeyalalaratnam, Gopinath, and Stéphane Paquin. 2016. "La politique internationale du Québec sous Jean Charest: L'influence d'un premier ministre." Special issue. *Revue Québécoise de droit international*, June 2016, 165–83.

Journet, Paul. 2010. "Une forêt nommée Charest." *La Presse*, 8 December. http://www.lapresse.ca/environnement/dossiers/changements-climatiques/201012/07/01-4350059-une-foret-nommee-charest.php.

Leblond, Patrick. 2011. "Le partenariat Nord-Américain pour la prospérité et la sécurité: Quel rôle pour le Québec?" In *Le destin Américain du Québec: Américanité, Américanisation, et Anti-Américanisme*, edited by Guy Lachapelle, 83–200. Quebec: Presses de l'Université Laval.

Lisée, Jean-François. 2009. "Jean Charest: Prix du parlementaire s'étant le plus illustré hors Québec." *L'Actualité*, 10 December. http://www.lactualite.com/politique/blogue-de-jean-francois-lisee/jean-charest-prix-du-parlementaire-setant-le-plus-illustre-hors-quebec.

Ministère des relations internationales et de la Francophonie (MRIF). 1985. *Le Québec dans le monde: Le défi de l'indépendance*. Quebec.

– 1991. *Le Québec et l'interdépendance: Le monde pour horizon. Éléments d'une politique d'affaires internationales*. Quebec.

– 2001. *Le Québec dans un ensemble international en mutation. Plan stratégique 2001–2004*. Quebec.

– 2006. *La politique internationale du Québec: La force de L'action concertée*. Quebec.

– 2010. *Stratégie du gouvernement du Québec à l'égard des États-Unis*. Quebec.

– 2015. *La reconnaissance mutuelle des Qualifications professionnelles: Entente Québec-France*. Quebec.

Noda, Shiro. 2001. *Entre l'indépendance et le fé*déralisme. La *décennie marquante des relations internationales du Québec,1970–1980*. Quebec: Les Presses de l'Université Laval.

Paquin, Stéphane, Ed. 2006. *Histoire des relations internationales du Québec*. Montreal: VLB.

– 2014a. "La politique internationale du Québec envers les États-Unis: un essai de périodisation." *Études Internationales* 45, no. 2: 261–84.

– 2014b. "Le fédéralisme d'ouverture et la place du Québec (et des autres provinces) dans les négociations internationales: rupture dans la continuité?" *Canadian Foreign Policy Journal* 20, no. 1: 28–37.

– 2016. "Quebec–US Relations: The Big Picture." *American Journal of Canadian Studies* 46, no. 2: 149–61.

– 2022a. "Le Québec et la France depuis 1960: Une relation d'exception." Special issue of *Bulletin d'histoire du Québec* 30, no. 1.

– 2022b. "Means of Influence, the Joint-Decision Trap, and Multilevel Trade Negotiations: Ontario and Quebec and the Renegotiation of NAFTA Compared." *Journal of World Trade* 56, no. 5: 853–78.

– 2022c. "La réforme inachevée: le fédéralisme canadien et le rôle des provinces dans les négociations internationals." *Revue québécoise de droit international* (special issue), January: 73–111.

Paquin, Stéphane, and Annie Chaloux. 2011. "Paradiplomatie Multilatérale du Québec aux États-Unis." In *Le Destin Américain du Québec: Américanité, Américanisation, et Anti-Américanisme*, edited by Guy Lachapelle, 293–311. Quebec: Presses de l'Université Laval.

Parisella, John. 2016. *La politique dans la peau*. Montreal: La Presse.

Richer, Jocelyne. 2011. "Les tours du monde de Jean Charest." *L'Actualité*, 4 July. http://www.lactualite.com/politique/les-tours-du-monde-de-jean-charest.

Robitaille, Antoine. 2008. "Le libre-échange Canada-Europe – Charest l'Européen." *Le Devoir*, 23 February. http://www.ledevoir.com/international/europe/177489/le-libre-echange-canada-europe-charest-l-europeen.

SEUS-CP. 2007. Déclaration conjointe visant la conclusion de l'Alliance des États du Sud-Est des États-Unis et des provinces canadiennes. https://www.gov.mb.ca/asset_library/en/premier/seus_joint_declaration.fr.pdf.

– 2022. Conference June 19–21. https://www.georgia.org/seus-cp-2022.

PART THREE

Cooperation and Conflict on the Canada–US Bilateral Agenda

9

The Specialness of the Canada–US Environmental Relationship

From Environmental Interdependence to Earth Systems Crisis

DEBORA L. VANNIJNATTEN AND ANDREA OLIVE

Amid all the public hand-wringing about whether US president Joseph R. Biden is actually a true friend of Canada or merely an ambivalent albeit more genial partner, compared to former president Donald J. Trump, the Canada–US environmental relationship continues to hum along. The two countries released the *2022 Progress Report of the Parties* (IJC 2022a) and the *State of the Great Lakes 2022 Report* (IJC 2022b), both in July 2022, highlighting achievements and continuing challenges in terms of implementing shared commitments made under the 2012 Great Lakes Water Quality Agreement. In addition, Canada and the US have coordinated a ban on oil and gas activities in the Beaufort and Chukchi seas to better consider the impacts of resource development in the fragile Arctic (see, for example, *Canada Gazette* 2021), and they have been working closely in international forums such as the Arctic Council, the Climate and Clean Air Coalition, and the Global Methane Partnership.

And when Canadian Prime Minister Justin Trudeau and President Joe Biden met on the sidelines at the Summit of the Americas in June 2022, they expressed their continuing commitment to "deepening the Canada–US partnership on a wide range of bilateral, regional, and global challenges" (Prime Minister of Canada 2022). Concerns about sustainability and climate change were threaded throughout the meeting, as the two leaders explored how they could cooperate on green technologies and develop the critical minerals needed for those technologies. Not long after this meeting, in July, the US Congress passed the Inflation Reduction Act, which is seen as providing enhanced opportunities for Canada to cooperate with its southern neighbour on electric vehicle manufacturing, battery production, and green public procurement requirements (Zacharias 2022).

In this vein, the editors of this volume have tasked us with determining whether the concept of a "special relationship" describes accurately both the features and the associated consequences of the Canada–US environmental partnership. In responding to this charge, our chapter has three sections. First, we argue that if there is any evidence of a "special" relationship, we will find it in the environmental policy arena, given that the two countries share ecosystems along the longest shared border in the world, which itself fulfills the conditions for "exemptionalism" set out by the editors of this volume (see the introduction). Next, we lay out and apply indicators of "specialness," drawn not only from our editors' introductory discussion and the Canada–US relations literature but also from the unique features of the environmental policy field itself. We use examples from climate change policy, biodiversity policy, and water management to show the depth and extent of the Canada–US environmental relationship. Finally, in our concluding remarks, we make the case that, due to the earth systems crisis in which we find ourselves, along with the global geopolitical situation, the close relationship between the two countries on environmental policy is likely to bleed more directly into other areas of the relationship, including economics, trade, and Arctic relations.

Why Expect a "Special" Relationship?

If we are to see evidence of a "special" or "distinct" or "unique" relationship between Canada and the US, such that their relations with each other are more intense and multifaceted than the relations either partner has with any other country, it is very likely to be found in the environmental policy arena. The reasons for this are based, first and foremost, on geographic realities and the environmental crises that now face us.

Most obviously, the two countries must manage a wide variety of ecosystems along the world's longest border and within the Arctic region; they are environmentally interdependent. As we have argued elsewhere with respect to Canada and the US (Olive and VanNijnatten 2023), "one of the most compelling explanations of similarity in agendas and goals, of course, derives from the reality of sharing a

6416-kilometre (3,987 miles) border from the Atlantic Ocean to the Pacific that comprises multiple ecosystems." Pollution in the Great Lakes, the world's largest body of fresh water, cannot be managed without the coordination of national goals, policy instruments, and public resourcing among all the jurisdictions around the basin. In fact, all thirteen transboundary water bodies that lay across the 49th parallel require joint management. Moreover, land and wildlife conservation cannot move forward without active cross-border collaboration among states, provinces, non-governmental organizations (NGOs), and Indigenous partners, given that migratory routes and broad ecoregions straddle the 49th parallel (i.e., from the Marine West Coast and Northwestern Forested Mountains, through the Great Plains and the Northern Forests, to the Eastern Temperate Forests). Coordination on recovery plans for species at risk, communications between parks, and the extensive networks sustaining the cross-border movement of agricultural (including animal) products are all evidence of an interdependent environment jointly and cooperatively managed.

Beyond a shared geography, there is also a shared set of challenges. Climate change and biodiversity loss are the two most important environmental issues confronting humanity today. These crises are unfolding similarly across Canada and the US (droughts, forest fires, hurricanes, loss of species, etc.). Moreover, the response is also unfolding similarly in the form of regulations on vehicle and industry emissions, green energy investments, species-at-risk recovery planning, marine and land protected areas, and so on (Olive and VanNijnatten 2023). In this respect, we should expect to see a special relationship between the two countries, including both their governments and their citizens, that is more intense and multifaceted than other cross-border relationships. As others have argued about the Canada–US relationship, the enduring fact that "we share common problems binds North American actors together and dictates that we work to resolve these problems through shared institutions" (Lovecraft 2007, 222).

Indeed, this reality in the bilateral relationship is not (and cannot be) replicated in any other relationship that either Canada or the US has with any other country. This volume's editors point to the numerous works that argue that a US–UK special relationship exists, but they also note that any "specialness," real or perceived, in that relationship pertains primarily to issues of security and the international order. In the environmental policy arena, neither Canada nor the US can treat the other as "just another country," given the unique biophysical conditions that underlie the relationship. Here, Canadian officials can reasonably expect special treatment that is not likely to be extended to the US's other partners. Furthermore, this environmental interdependence is compounded by the growing recognition that, given the way earth's systems are interrelated, a crisis in one system has impacts on other systems. Thus, actions taken to address climate change have an impact on the growing biodiversity crisis (and vice versa), requiring even more integrated and multifaceted cooperation across the border. We return to this discussion at the end of the chapter.

Our readers might reasonably argue that the US–Mexico southern bilateral relationship is also special due to the reality of shared ecosystems – especially the North American Desert – along a similarly long border. US and Mexican governments at all levels, NGOs, border communities, and average citizens do indeed encounter each other within cross-border networks that support often dense political, economic, and sociocultural ties. However, we argue in this chapter that the US–Canada relationship is distinct given its history, depth, immediacy, and intensity.

Indicators of "Specialness"

In this section, we assess the Canada–US environmental relationship based on five indicators:

1. The *durability and effectiveness of the institutional architecture* that supports cooperation on environmental matters.
2. The *strength of non-governmental ties.*
3. The degree to which the relationship can *withstand changes in the personal relations* among leaders.
4. The extent of *similarity in political values and attitudes* toward the environment on the part of citizens in each country.
5. The growing *priority on involving Indigenous peoples* in environmental management.

For each indicator, we discuss the ways in which these various facets of environmental policy draw the two countries together into a uniquely close relationship, using examples from climate change policy, biodiversity policy, and water management to illustrate our points.

1. DURABILITY AND EFFECTIVENESS OF THE INSTITUTIONAL ARCHITECTURE

The Canada–US relationship is built on a legacy of strong and durable institutional pillars, which serve to anchor and stabilize political interactions. This architecture rests on several key bilateral treaties – including the 1909 Boundary Waters Treaty, the 1961 Columbia River Treaty, the Pacific Salmon Treaty, and the 1916 Convention Between the United States and Great Britain for the Protection of Migratory Birds (known as the Migratory Bird Treaty) in the US and Canada – as well as a series of executive agreements, including the 2012 Great Lakes Water Quality Agreement, the 1991 Canada–United States Air Quality Agreement, and the 1987 Agreement Between the Government of Canada and the Government of the United States on the Conservation of the Porcupine Caribou Herd. These more formal agreements, whose commitments are recognized in domestic law on both sides of the border, are complemented by hundreds (perhaps thousands) of memorandums of understanding (MOUs) that lay out cooperative actions to be taken regarding such matters as protecting polar bear populations, monitoring transboundary air pollutants, experimenting with more sustainable agricultural practices, and developing the critical minerals needed for green technologies.

While these treaties, agreements, and MOUs provide a relatively strong spine for environmental cooperation, setting out objectives to be met over particular timelines, the real essence of cooperation comes from the transgovernmental networks that develop and continue to expand as agency officials (e.g., from environment, natural resources, energy, and fisheries departments) in the two countries coordinate their efforts to meet such commitments. Our editors, in the introduction, argue that the Boundary Waters Treaty is "an exemplary model of shared sovereignty and consensus decision-making and an early pillar of the special relationship," and we could include the Great Lakes Water Quality Agreement in that assessment as well. However, in the Great Lakes alone we find a huge number and variety of basin-, lake-, and subregional-level committees, joint task groups, scientific linkages, public/private initiatives, and community group projects in the region that have grown out of or alongside the bilateral commitments in these agreements. These institutions encourage regular meetings, information exchange, consensus-building on how to move forward, and close personal ties, as the two countries undertake scientific research and monitoring, progress reporting, and project implementation (VanNijnatten and Johns 2020). The result is an extraordinarily dense and by and large mutually sympathetic network of contacts at the agency level of each country.

Indeed, ties are just as dense (sometimes more so) at the subnational and even international or multilateral scales. Since the 1990s, Canada and the US have both gone through a process of general devolution whereby many responsibilities for environmental issues have been passed from the federal purview down to "states, provinces, and municipalities, and have increased collaborative decision making through stakeholder groups, private[/]public partnerships, and flexibility in enforcement" (Lovecraft 2007, 218). We can easily point to several forums and agreements that bring states and provinces/territories together to work on shared environmental issues within cross-border regional networks (VanNijnatten 2009). Examples include the Great Lakes and St Lawrence Governors and Premiers, the New England Governors and Eastern Canadian Premiers, and the Pacific NorthWest Economic Region – all forums that pursue environmental and climate cooperation.

Certainly, transgovernmental networks, those that act independently of their central government, are better developed with respect to some environmental issues than they are to others. One could argue that the two countries are most well developed and strongly entrenched with regard to water, especially in the Great Lakes (discussed earlier). Yet there is also considerable coordination and collaboration on transboundary species at risk and connectivity conservation (Beazley et al. 2021; Thornton et al. 2017). NGOs, academics, and government scientists often participate across borders in developing domestic recovery strategies of shared species. However, these relationships are loose networks, and one could argue that for biodiversity and species at risk, there are fewer long-standing transgovernmental networks, committees, or partnerships compared to what is found in water management. The obvious exceptions are the "dawn of conservation diplomacy" (Dorsey 2010) at the turn of the twentieth century that resulted in coordination to protect parks and wildlife and, of course, the 1916 Canada–US Migratory Birds Treaty, which has withstood the test of time. Otherwise, the "dense thickets" of networks that exist for species at risk and conservation are more recent (Boardman 2006, 180). Examples include the Canada–US Transboundary Resource Steering Committee in the Gulf of Maine and Georges Bank, which dates back to 1995, and the trilateral (with Mexico) North American Marine Protected Areas Network, created in 1999.

Interactions on climate change and reducing greenhouse gas emissions are even more recent and not yet mature. At international and domestic forums, Canada and the US have both committed themselves to ambitious reductions in greenhouse gas emissions. Through the Canada–US High-Level Ministerial Dialogue on Climate Ambition, launched in February 2021, the two countries are working on cooperative actions to achieve their common objective of net-zero emissions by 2050, aligning policy solutions and regulatory approaches as well as building resilience to climate impacts. The dialogue meets semi-annually, with working group meetings held more frequently. Several MOUs have recently been put in place to guide cooperation (e.g., on energy development and critical minerals).

Scholars and practitioners also point to the "slow, steady diplomacy of relationship building" that happens through bilateral, trilateral, and international forums (Dawson and Speer 2016, 9). In 1988, Canada and the US signed a free trade agreement that eventually was joined by Mexico – the North American Free Trade Agreement (NAFTA). A critically important side treaty of NAFTA is the 1994 North American Agreement on Environmental Cooperation (NAAEC), which also established the trilateral Commission for Environmental Cooperation. This commission has numerous working groups, such as the biodiversity group mentioned earlier, that bring Canada and the US into close collaborative contact at the national and subnational levels. Trump came into office in 2017 with a strong desire to dismantle and replace NAFTA, and after protracted and difficult negotiations, in 2020 the Canada–US–Mexico Agreement (CUSMA) came into force; it includes an environmental working group to develop, oversee, and/or implement the agreement. While CUSMA replaces NAFTA, it does not replace or impact the NAAEC or any trilateral environmental committees.

Moreover, Canada and the US work closely in multilateral forums, such as the G7 and G20, North Atlantic Treaty Organization (NATO), the Organisation for Economic Co-operation and Development, the Arctic Council, the World Trade Organization, and the UN, all of which address environmental issues. Some are obviously more environment-focused than others; in one example, through the Arctic Council, Canada and the US are together confronting climate change impacts, toxic chemical deposition, biodiversity loss, and water pollution. In addition, privileged and close consultation occurs between the two countries in such international forums as the Global Methane Partnership and the Climate and Clean Air Coalition, as well as before and during negotiations under the UN Framework Conference on Climate Change, and even before President Biden's Climate Summit in April 2021. The US is not a signatory to the UN Convention on Biological Diversity (UN CBD), although it "remains actively engaged in the work" and "strongly supports the objectives of the convention" (US Mission to UN 2021). Like Canada, the US is committed to conserving 30 per cent of its land and water; this is part of a global goal and is a cornerstone of the Post-2020 Global Biodiversity Framework agreed upon at the 15th Conference of the Parties to the UN CBD, held in Montreal from 5 to 17 December 2022.

What we have straddling the Canada–US border, then, is a complex and dense architecture built around a slim but strong spine of treaties and agreements, largely media-specific (water, air, species protection), at the bilateral level. From this foundation there are many overlapping institutions, networks, and ad hoc working arrangements that pull a wide variety of public, private and non-governmental interests into interactions with one another across the border. There is no question, though, that institutionalization differs across sectoral issues, with more formal and intense working relations on water, a much lighter and more informal institutional imprint for climate change policy, and working arrangements for species protection and biodiversity somewhere in between. Still, outside of the EU, which functions as a single political unit on many aspects of environmental protection, it is difficult to imagine another two countries that are so closely bound together via concrete and active environmental policy linkages.

2. CLOSE NON-GOVERNMENTAL TIES

NGOs, from charities to citizens' groups to GoFundMe campaigns, have also expanded across the borders, tying citizens together on environmental campaigns. This is perhaps not surprising given the "simultaneous rise of environmental activism" in the two countries (Stoett and Le Prestre 2006, 7). Second-wave environmentalism swept

Americans and Canadians into action during the 1960s and 1970s as chemical and air pollution as well as nuclear energy inspired average citizens to work together for change. It was during this era that many environmental groups, such as Pollution Probe (1969) and Greenpeace (1969), were founded, bringing together Americans and Canadians concerned about transboundary environmental issues like air and water pollution. These linkages have continued to grow as more networks expand across the border. But at the same time, the US and Canadian governments have heightened their surveillance of social movement activists, including environmental groups, as a result of national security concerns (Monaghan and Walby 2017). It is not uncommon for protesters – against pipelines and other infrastructure projects, for example – to be viewed as possible domestic or foreign terrorists, and Greenpeace is often assessed as "potentially violent" in security assessments (Leahy 2013). But by and large, cross-border environmentalism does not involve violent protest and instead focuses on education and joint lobbying.

A recent emblematic example of close non-governmental ties between the US and Canada is the Yellowstone to Yukon (Y2Y) organization. The region on which it focuses stretches 3,400 kilometres through the traditional lands of seventy-five Indigenous groups, five US states, two Canadian provinces, and one Canadian territory. Dating to 1993, Y2Y is a registered Canadian charity with more than 450 partner groups on both sides of the border, including small grassroots groups like Albertans for a Coal Free Southwest, cross-border tribal groups like the Blackfoot Confederacy Tribal Council, and large NGOs like Greenpeace and the World Wildlife Fund. Over the past thirty years, this transborder network has expanded protected areas in the region by 80 per cent, reduced invasive species, helped to decommission roads (to restore habitat and reduce wildlife fatalities), planted thousands of trees, and restored rivers and streams (Y2Y n.d.). Most importantly, Y2Y has created a shared vision around connectivity for a region that crosses numerous political borders, including, of course, the international boundary. The organization and its partnerships are illustrative of what is possible for Canada–US transboundary environmental collaboration.

Another good example of how environmental concerns draw citizens and groups along the border together has been the concerted, multi-year, cross-border campaigns against pipeline development, particularly the

Keystone XL Pipeline. This involved organizing Indigenous climate action workshops for Indigenous activists in Canada and the US (Honderich 2021); also, training workshops were developed by 350.org to equip local groups to organize more effectively against the pipeline. Meanwhile, a wide range of both grassroots and national organizations pushed their respective governments to stop the pipeline. These lobbying efforts represented democratic opposition to capitalism and natural resource-based economies, but that opposition was non-violent and was meant to highlight the impacts of colonialism, climate change, and resource extraction.

Y2Y and pipeline protests are just two examples of the deep coalition-building that happens across political borders. There are thousands of other examples, such as the Pact for a Green New Deal relationships, the Algonquin to Adirondacks Collaborative (A2A), the Coast Salish Gathering, the Salish Sea Marine Survival Project, and the Great Lakes Network. These tight non-governmental ties are also rooted in "societal awareness" as well as "information technologies" that have brought people in Canada and the US into "closer contact than at any other time in history" (Lovecraft 2007, 220). From Facebook and Twitter to TikTok and Instagram, social media and instant communication technologies are enabling citizens to post images and share stories of environmental destruction that speak to like-minded citizens across political borders. Similarly, communication platforms like Zoom and Google Hangout have enabled NGOs to meet regularly to discuss environmental issues with members and/or other NGOs across borders. This was possible even during COVID border lockdowns.

Certainly, close ties between neighbours are partly a result of regionalism. Indeed, geography looms so large in North America that Americans and Canadians living on a borderland may feel "more in common with their neighbors on the other side of the line than with their respective countrymen who many live hundreds, or even thousands, of miles away" (Morris 1999, 469). For example, regions can have so much in common that the bridge across the border is shorter and more secure than the bridges to the respective national capitals. This is unique to the Canada–US relationship. Americans feel closer to Canadians than they possibly could to the citizens of any other country. For example, rural Montanans likely feel closer to rural Albertans, just across the border, than either do to urban New Yorkers, Torontonians, or Vancouverites. The urban–rural split is very real throughout North America and reinforces this sort of connectedness.

3. WITHSTANDING CHANGE IN LEADERSHIP AT THE TOP

Because of the well-developed and productive institutional framework that supports and fosters Canada–US environmental cooperation, as well as close NGO ties, the relationship can weather personal differences at the top. The editors argue in the introduction to this volume that "the special relationship has never depended on personal relationships at the top" although "they have made an important difference in Canada–US relations at various moments in our shared history." This argument certainly applies to bilateral environmental relations. It would be difficult to ignore, for example, the role that the close personal relationship between former Prime Minister Brian Mulroney and former President George H.W. Bush played in securing the 1991 Canada–US Air Quality Agreement. On the other hand, the lack of any ambitious climate change policy initiatives under President Barack Obama and Prime Minister Stephen Harper may have been at least partly explained by the lack of affinity between the two men, who possessed very different perspectives on the immediacy of the climate crisis and the role of national governments in addressing it.

Justin Trudeau has been prime minister of Canada since November 2015, and his tenure has so far overlapped with those of Presidents Obama (three months), Trump (four years), and Biden (more than two years, at the time of writing). Much was made of the Trudeau–Obama "bromance" and the meeting of policy minds with respect to environmental protection and climate change. Both leaders often referred to their personal rapport, which swiftly produced a US–Canada Joint Statement on Climate, Energy and Arctic Leadership. The Joint Statement committed the two countries to playing a leadership role in international and continental efforts to promote a green economy and mitigate greenhouse gas emissions, especially methane.

After the election of Donald Trump to the White House in November 2016, however, Canada–US relations took a decided turn for the worse. According to Greaves (2020, 2), bilateral relations under Trump were "rocked by diplomatic disputes across a range of issues, including a multilateral trade war, contentious free trade renegotiations, US–China competition, numerous policy disagreements, personal attacks by the president against Prime Minister Justin Trudeau, candid 'hot mic' comments by Trudeau about President Trump, and the ineffective American response to the COVID-19 pandemic." During this time, however, bilateral environmental cooperation managed to continue;

this is a good example of the complex but well-entrenched web of transnational public and non-governmental networks rooting policy- and project-level interactions. Stephen Brooks argued in 2020, in fact, that "the environmental policy conflicts between Canada and the United States are fewer and less fractious than many anticipated."

As Dawson and Speer argue, "warm personal relationships are not a sufficient condition for effective bilateral engagement" – but they certainly help. Trudeau compared a conversation with Biden to a "dam breaking" after four years of the Trump administration (Delacourt 2021). Yet, although the Democratic president and the Liberal prime minister may share a commitment to ambitious climate policy and a Green and Just Transition, the relationship between them has been challenged by domestic pressures – for Trudeau, the need to push new pipelines as a compromise to Western provincial interests and, for Biden, the need to pursue green policies that favour US workers and business interests only and that can be sold to more conservative (and protectionist) voters and states.

To observe the interaction between personal rapport at the top and legacy working relations, we need look no further than shared management of the Great Lakes. Since 2015, the two countries, US states, Canadian provinces, and cities all around the Great Lakes basin have continued to implement their bilateral agreements, scientists have continued to collaborate, environmental groups and Indigenous peoples have continued to monitor government actions and press for new commitments, and public resources have continued to be devoted to this precious continental resource. In fact, successive attempts by the Trump administration to cut the federal budget for the Great Lakes Restoration Initiative (an Obama-initiated program) were roundly criticized and successfully rebuffed by a coalition of agency officials, state governments, environmental groups, and their congressional and Canadian allies, which have been working hard for decades to address pollution problems in the Great Lakes.

4. SIMILARITY IN POLITICAL VALUES AND ATTITUDES

There is no denying that Canada and the US are "grappling with a complex series of shared problems related to climate change, economic globalization, pollution, and internal conflicts over the use of natural resources" (Lovecraft 2007, 218). But there is also no denying that the two countries approach these problems against a backdrop of broadly similar values and attitudes, especially when comparisons are made on an international scale. We make here several observations when comparing Canadian and US political and environmental attitudes and note some implications for policy-making on the continent.

Comparable public opinion questions administered in each country show that in 2021, 72 per cent of Americans and 69 per cent of Canadians believed that global warming is happening (Abacus Data 2021; Yale Climate Opinion 2021), and these percentages have been fairly stable in recent years. Of those who believe warming is occurring, 57 per cent of Americans and 75 per cent of Canadians think it is a result of human activities. However, Americans express less faith in climate science – which is a difference worth noting. Yet there are similar levels of support for government and industry investment in green technologies among citizens in both countries, especially developments in nuclear energy, green hydrogen, and carbon capture and storage (Pew 2022).

Global surveys of environment- and climate-related attitudes indicate that Americans and Canadians are more similar to each other than they are to citizens of other countries. A thirty-one-country public opinion survey conducted by IPSOS Global Advisor in April 2022 probed attitudes toward climate policy, in particular how concerned people are about climate change, how willing individuals are to change their behaviour to address their own emissions, and who they believe should be responsible for mitigating emissions. The results show that Canadians and Americans cluster together on almost all questions, often showing less concern (than respondents in other countries) about the impacts of climate change on their own country as well as on other parts of the world. They are also less convinced that their governments, corporations, or individual citizens must act *now* to address emissions, and they show less optimism that their own or other governments will get their collective acts together to address climate change (IPSOS Global Advisor 2022). Interestingly, Mexican attitudes on the same questions tend to cluster together with those in other Latin American countries.

A spring 2021 Pew Research Center survey of global attitudes highlights similarly small spreads between age groups in Canada and the US in terms of concerns about the climate and willingness to make lifestyle changes, as compared with other countries (i.e., our youth are less concerned); comparably low levels of concern that climate change will impact respondents during their lifetime; and similar feelings about whether the international community will be able to address climate impacts effectively (a fairly even split in both countries) (Pew 2021). Note, however, that breaking the data out according to ideology within each country (i.e., the spread between those professing left versus right ideological leanings) shows quite different situations in Canada and US; Americans are considerably more polarized than are Canadians on questions about whether the government is handling the issue effectively and whether individuals bear some responsibility or should change their behaviour.

Overall, the public opinion data lend support to the "special relationship" argument, although there are some differences between the two countries stemming from the political/ideological context. As Charles Doran has argued in his study of the Canada–US relationship, the psychological-cultural dimension of Canada–US relations may be the most important determinant, but it is also the most complex one (Doran 1984, 85). In this respect, the similarities of outlook we have observed across the Canadian and American publics are not necessarily favourable for pushing the environmental and climate policy agenda in North America.

5. THE GROWING ROLE OF INDIGENOUS PEOPLES IN ENVIRONMENT AND CLIMATE POLICY

Canada and the US share a violent colonial history, but in their present-day relationships with Indigenous people, they are quite different from each other. In a short chapter (written by settler-scholars), we cannot adequately cover Indigenous history and the resulting consequences for environmental relations. However, it is crucial to acknowledge that Turtle Island is home to many Indigenous peoples who have practised stewardship over their lands for centuries. The shared colonial histories of Canada and the US, and the attempts being made to address these histories, must be considered as we track developments in domestic environmental policy approaches and in the bilateral relationship.

First, it is important to realize that the "Indigenous people" are distinct *groups of peoples*. Canada has Inuit peoples in the Northern region, at least 650 First Nation bands, many from different linguistic and cultural groups spanning the country, and Métis peoples living coast to coast to coast. Similarly, in the US, there are 574 federally recognized tribes, half of which have reservation lands, across the contiguous US and in Alaska. Other Indigenous people in the US include Native Hawaiians, Chamorros, and Samoans.

Across the two countries, then, it is difficult to make general statements about "Indigenous peoples" and environmental management. However, there are similarities in the broad approach that federal and subnational governments have taken to Indigenous environmental issues and natural resource management that should be noted. Both Canada and the US have approached natural resource development and parks and protected areas with a colonial mindset rooted in state "ownership" over those lands and natural resources, which have been acquired through settlement and the establishment of control over Indigenous peoples in these areas.

It is also important to note that both Canada and the US were reluctant to sign the UN Declaration on the Rights of Indigenous Peoples, which sets out the collective and individual rights of Indigenous peoples; in particular, Article 26 states that "Indigenous peoples have the right to the lands, territories and resources which they have traditionally owned, occupied or otherwise used or acquired," and it directs states to give legal recognition to these territories. In fact, Canada and the US were among only four countries that voted against the declaration in 2007 – 143 states voted in favour. Canada has only recently signed, in 2021, after decades of advocacy by Indigenous peoples.

However, changes are under way in terms of the role of Indigenous peoples in environmental management, at various scales. First, Indigenous representation in national politics is increasing, and this in turn is raising the profile of Indigenous approaches to politics and policy. In Canada, the first Indigenous governor general was appointed in 2021. Mary Simon is Inuk from Kangiqsualujjuaq, Quebec, and had previously served as a lead negotiator in the creation of the Arctic Council. Also in 2021, the country elected eleven Indigenous people to Parliament – a record high. This mirrored what happened in the 2020 federal election in the US, when six Native Americans were elected to Congress. Moreover, Deb Haaland was selected by President Biden to serve as secretary of the interior, which makes her the first Native American to serve as a cabinet secretary.

In tandem with this enhanced political representation, the two countries are reassessing their relations with Indigenous peoples more broadly. The US initiated this process earlier and in very concrete ways with respect to environmental management. During the 1970s and 1980s, the US federal government began to act on the recognition that "states generally lack regulatory authority over Indian activities on Indian lands unless clearly authorized by Congress" and initiated the handover of implementation of federal environmental programming to tribal authorities (US EPA 2022). The Environmental Protection Agency's (EPA) 1984 Indian Policy declared tribes to be the appropriate entities to set standards, make environmental policy decisions, and manage programs for reservations, in accordance with broader federal support of tribal self-government and government–government relations. Over the ensuing decades, tribal roles in water management, toxics prevention, air pollution, and land management were built out, alongside a growing institutional architecture within EPA to support tribal capacity-building and involvement within the agency (US EPA 2022).

Canada, for its part, is undertaking what might be regarded as a more thoroughgoing, national public conversation about how settler and Indigenous communities can address past harms and move forward to create stronger and more sustainable societies. The Government of Canada has engaged in a reconciliation process with Indigenous peoples in Canada, working cooperatively to establish and maintain a mutually respectful framework for living together based on nation-to-nation relations (Crown-Indigenous Relations and Northern Affairs Canada 2022). Reconciliation is a broader lens that is intended to frame *all* public policy and decision-making, including environmental and natural resource management. We can see its impacts in policy initiatives such as Indigenous Protected and Conserved Areas (where Indigenous authorities have the primary role in protecting ecosystems through Indigenous laws, governance, and knowledge systems); the involvement of Keepers of the Waters, an organization representing First Nations, Métis, and Inuit peoples in the creation of a new Canada Water Agency and the development of a new legislative framework for water governance; and the implementation of the Indigenous Knowledge Policy Framework for Proposed Project Reviews and Regulatory Decisions (Government of Canada 2021), among others.

And there is considerable activity at the grassroots level by Indigenous groups that is changing environmental and natural resource practices along the border and is underpinned by a more holistic perspective on nature (Hessami et al. 2021). One example is the Buffalo Treaty, which brings together First Nations and Native American tribes in the West to support bison reintroduction across North America. In 2014, at the Blackfeet Reservation in Montana, eight nations,[1] with about 6.3 million acres of grassland habitat, signed the treaty. As of 2022, more than forty tribes and nations across the western states and provinces have signed. The stated objective of the Buffalo Treaty is to "welcome buffalo" back onto the landscape as "wild free-ranging" animals and to "nurture" the cultural and spiritual relationship between human and wild buffalo. This is to be achieved "on both sides of the United States and Canadian border" (Buffalo Treaty 2014). Collectively, the signatories are working to increase wild bison on tribal lands and public lands. They are also engaged in education and awareness campaigns in both countries.

And there are other examples. Through the Arctic Council, Inuit and Native Alaskan communities work collaboratively on climate change, biodiversity loss, water pollution, and other environmental issues. Furthermore, US tribes and Canadian First Nations are taking part in cross-border management in the Great Lakes through the International Joint Commission and its task forces.

These parallel efforts to recognize and engage Indigenous peoples on either side of the border as partners in meeting environmental challenges are viewed on both sides of the border with understanding and shared purpose, and have reached an intensity and level of institutionalization that is not matched along the southern US–Mexico border.

Conclusion

Given the durable and well-articulated architecture for cooperation on environmental matters that spans governance scales and the public/private realms, as well as the legacy of shared values and tentative moves toward reconciliation with Indigenous peoples, the Canada–US environmental relationship is multifaceted, dense, and productive. Certainly, we would not expect the environmental relationship to be equal, given demographic and economic differences, combined with pollution potential (with the huge US economy having a larger impact on watersheds and airsheds), policy capacity, and public resources. However, as Greg Anderson (2018) has argued, Canada benefits from the overall relationship more often than one might expect, and this also applies to the environmental relationship.

Charles Doran argued in his 1984 book *Forgotten Partnership* that the special relationship operated on two rails, one structural and the other involving politics and policy. At the structural level, he observed that "the Canadian-American relationship continues to appear unique or special, because no other pair of countries can demonstrate the combination of close governmental interaction, institutional ties and buffers, pacific conflict resolution, and extensiveness of cross-border bureaucratic and private sector activity" (Doran 1984, 83). We suggest here that this holds true some forty years later. At the policy level, however, Doran observed a different picture. He noted that "the factors that have made the relationship special in the past – consultation, preferential economic treatment for Canada, and a secure, hospitable atmosphere for U.S. investment – have all begun to erode" (Doran 1984, 83). Similarly, Greaves (2020), writing at the end of the Trump presidency, cautions that "despite its history, there is no guarantee that the Canada–US relationship will remain rooted in shared identity, mutual trust and a commitment to democracy" (17). This is certainly the challenge facing President Biden and Prime Minister Trudeau as they face domestic polarization and new instabilities in the global context.

However, we would argue that, due to the global earth systems crisis in which we find ourselves, along with an unstable geopolitical situation, the close relationship between the two countries on environmental policy is likely to bleed more directly into other areas of the relationship, including emergency management, industrial and technological development, trade, and Arctic relations, to name just a few. As heat domes such the one that descended on the west coast of North America in the summer of 2021 become more frequent, as hurricanes endanger our shared coastal areas, and as extreme precipitation events change the course of waterways and flood border towns and cities, Canada–US cooperation will need to dig more deeply into shared climate-proof infrastructure, emergency planning, and energy networking to ensure that the lights stay on. As species and ecosystems rapidly degrade and we face the likely extinction of shared wild species like caribou, whales, polar bears, and native pollinators (to name just a few), transboundary networks will need to work harder than ever to protect habitat, decrease pollution, strategize on harvesting, and prevent massive irreversible impacts on ecosystem services and food security. Furthermore, as an increasingly thirsty southwest looks to the water-abundant north for new water sources, Canada and the US will need to manage their shared water resources in more intense and protective ways. And as the Arctic region warms at three times the rate of the rest of the world on average, the two countries will face new land and water management challenges, as well as new geopolitical threats from both Russia and China, both of which have extensive plans for natural resource development in the Polar North.

Indeed, the global situation is evolving rapidly, on the security and economic fronts. Even as the global economy transitions – in fits and starts – away from hydrocarbons, Canada and the US will need to ensure for themselves a place in a highly competitive green technology marketplace, where a race to commercialize, establish, and export new technologies is taking place. They are already lagging behind countries such as China and South Korea, as well as the EU. Critically, many of the new technologies that are becoming dominant – for example, electric vehicles – will need to be embedded in continental supply chains and integrated manufacturing networks, necessitating coordinated Canada–US action. Other technologies, such as carbon capture and storage, will need to be positioned to take advantage of shared geology suitable for underground CO_2 storage. The US has made it clear that its own green technology aspirations will be difficult to realize without a ready supply of Canada's critical minerals. Green economic opportunities lie ahead for North America, but reaping the benefits will require close cooperation and joint efforts between the two countries.

Furthermore, conserving 30 per cent of the land in Canada and the US, respectively, is no small task. While Biden and Trudeau have made ambitious promises, the federal governments of each country must rely on subnational jurisdictions and private landowners to help meet international targets. And both must meaningfully include Indigenous partners and their knowledge in moving the continent toward a more sustainable and biodiverse future. As provinces like Ontario have signalled that endemic species within provincial borders should be the main priority (Bethlenfalvy and Olive 2021), NGOs and the federal government will have to continue to build relationships that extend through and across shared ecosystems. Moreover, all levels of government will need to think more broadly about sustainability and work toward mainstreaming biodiversity into different policy and economic sectors (Whitehorn et al. 2019). North American trade policy, especially food policy, is going to be challenged by biodiversity loss as urbanization, climate change, and pollution press ecosystems to their breaking points.

Given the magnitude of the impending crisis of climate change and biodiversity loss, then, all policy – domestic, bilateral, and international – will be environmental policy in the coming decades. This is likely to force Canada and the US into deeper policy conversations and perhaps even confrontation in the coming decades. With a strong legacy of institutional, citizen and political ties, the two countries have the tools they need to meet the moment but will need to utilize them to their fullest potential.

Note

1 The original signatories to the Buffalo Treaty include the Blackfeet Nation, Kainai/Blood Tribe, Siksika Nation, Piikani Nation, the Assiniboine and Gros Ventre Tribes of Fort Belknap Indian Reservation, the Assiniboine and Sioux Tribes of Fort Peck Indian Reservation, the Salish and Kootenai Tribes of the Confederated Salish and Kootenai Indian Reservation, and the Tsuut'ina Nation.

References

Abacus Data. 2021. "What Do Canadians Think about Climate Change and Climate Action?" https://abacusdata.ca/climate-change-cop26-canada.

Anderson, Greg. 2018. "David and Goliath in Canada–US Relations: Who's Really Who?" *Canadian Foreign Policy Journal* 25, no. 2: 115–36. doi: 10.1080/11926422.2018.1542604.

Beazley, Karen F., Gabriel Oppler, Leanna R. Heffner, Jessica Levine, Aaron Poe, and Gary Tabor. 2021. "Emerging Policy Opportunities for United States–Canada Transboundary Connectivity Conservation." *Parks Stewardship Forum* 37, no. 3. doi: http://dx.doi.org/10.5070/P537354732.

Bethlenfalvy, Allegra, and Andrea Olive. 2021. "Recent Amendments to the Endangered Species Act and an Uncertain Future for Species at Risk: A Cast Study of Niagara's Region." *FACETS* 6, no. 1: 1168–83.

Boardman, Robert. 2006. "Multi-Level Environmental Governance in North America: Migratory Birds and Biodiversity Conservation." In *Bilateral EcoPolitics: Continuity and Change in Canadian–American Environmental Relations*, edited by Phippe Le Prestre and Peter Stoett, 179–96. London: Routledge Press.

Brooks, Stephen. 2020. "Canada–United States Environmental Relations during the Trudeau-Trump Years: A Story of Divergence and Resilience." *American Review of Canadian Studies* 50, no. 1: 48–65. doi: 10.1080/02722011.2020.1742998.

Buffalo Treaty. 2014. https://www.buffalotreaty.com/treaty.

Canada Gazette. 2021. *Order Amending the Order Prohibiting Certain Activities in Arctic Offshore Waters: SOR/2021-272*. https://canadagazette.gc.ca/rp-pr/p2/2022/2022-01-05/html/sor-dors272-eng.html.

Crown–Indigenous Relations and Northern Affairs Canada. 2022. "The Reconciliation Journey." https://www.rcaanc-cirnac.gc.ca/eng/1651868378940/1651868435684.

Dawson, Laura, and Sean Speer. 2016. "Commentary: Managing the Canada–US Relationship from the Honeymoon to the Long-Term." From a Mandate for Change to a Plan to Govern Series, no. 12. MacDonald-Laurier Institute. https://www.macdonaldlaurier.ca/files/pdf/MLISpeerDawsonCanadaUS-03-16-webready.pdf.

Delacourt, Susan. 2021. "Justin Trudeau Talks about the Challenge of Trump, His Relationship with Biden, and the Canadian Idea the New President Might Steal." *Toronto Star*, 31 January. https://www.thestar.com/politics/political-opinion/2021/01/31/justin-trudeau-talks-about-the-challenge-of-trump-his-relationship-with-biden-and-the-canadian-idea-the-new-president-might-steal.html.

Doran, Charles F. 1984. *Forgotten Partnership: US–Canadian Relations Today*. Baltimore: Johns Hopkins University Press.

Dorsey, Kurkpatrick. 2010. *The Dawn of Conservation Diplomacy. US–Canadian Wildlife Protection Treaties in the Progressive Era*. Seattle: University of Washington Press.

Government of Canada. 2021. "Indigenous Knowledge Policy Framework for Proposed Project Reviews and Regulatory Decisions." https://www.canada.ca/en/services/environment/conservation/assessments/environmental-reviews/environmental-assessment-processes/discussion-paper-development-indigenous-knowledge-policy-framework.html.

Greaves, Wilfred. 2020. "Democracy, Donald Trump and the Canada–US Security Community." *Canadian Journal of Political Science* 53, no. 4: 800–20.

Hessami, Mateen A., Ella Bowles, Jesse N. Popp, and Adam T. Ford. 2021. "Indigenizing the North American Model of Wildlife Conservation."

FACETS 6, August 5. https://www.facetsjournal.com/doi/10.1139/facets-2020-0088.

Honderich, Holly. 2021. "Keystone XL: Why I Fought For – or Against – the Pipeline." *BBC News*, 27 January. https://www.bbc.com/news/world-us-canada-55816229.

International Joint Commission (IJC). 2022a. *2022 Progress Report of the Parties*, 29 July. https://binational.net/2022/07/29/2022-prp-rep.

– 2022b. State of the Great Lakes 2022 Report, 29 July. https://binational.net/2022/07/29/sogl-edgl-2022.

IPSOS Global Advisor. 2022. *Earth Day 2022: Public Opinion on Climate Change*. https://www.ipsos.com/sites/default/files/ct/news/documents/2022-04/ipsos-earth-day-2022-global-advisor-survey-report.pdf.

Leahy, Stephen. 2013. "Canada's Environmental Activists Seen as Threat to National Security." *The Guardian*, 14 February. https://www.theguardian.com/environment/2013/feb/14/canada-environmental-activism-threat.

Lovecraft, Amy Lauren. 2007. "Transnational Environmental Management: US–Canadian Institutions at the Interlocal Scale." *American Review of Canadian Studies* 37, no. 2: 218–45.

Monaghan, Jeffrey, and Kevin Walby. 2017. "Surveillance of Environmental Movements in Canada: Critical Infrastructure Protection and the Petro-Security Apparatus." *Contemporary Justice Review* 20, no. 1: 51–70. doi: 10.1080/10282580.2016.1262770.

Morris, P.S. 1999. "Regional Ideas and the Montana–Alberta Borderlands." *Geographical Review* 89, no. 4: 469–90.

Olive, Andrea, and Debora L. VanNijnatten. 2023. "Twin Crises – Twin Ambitions – Twin Vulnerabilities: Confronting Climate Change and Biodiversity Loss in Canada and the United States." In *Differences That Count*, edited by David Thomas and Christopher Sands, 5th ed. Toronto: University of Toronto Press.

Pew Research Center. 2021. *Spring 2021 Global Attitudes Survey*. https://www.pewresearch.org/global/2021/09/14/in-response-to-climate-change-citizens-in-advanced-economies-are-willing-to-alter-how-they-live-and-work.

Prime Minister of Canada. 2022. "Prime Minister Justin Trudeau Meets With the President of the United States, Joe Biden," 9 June. Los Angeles. https://pm.gc.ca/en/news/readouts/2022/06/09/prime-minister-justin-trudeau-meets-president-united-states-america-joe Accessed 08/23/22.

Stoett, Peter, and Philippe Le Prestre. 2006. "Introduction: From Neglect to Concern: The Study of Canadian–American Ecopolitics." In *Bilateral EcoPolitics: Continuity and Change in Canadian–American Environmental Relations*, edited by Philippe Le Prestre and Peter Stoett, 1–17. London: Routledge.

Thornton, Daniel H., Aaron J. Wirsing, Carlos Lopez-Gonzalez, John R. Squires, Scott Fisher, Karl W. Larsen, Alan Peatt, Matt A. Scrafford, Ron A. Moen, Arthur E. Scully, Travis W. King, and Dennis L. Murray. 2018. "Asymmetric Cross-Border Protection of Peripheral Transboundary Species." *Conservation Letters* 11, no. 3: e12430. doi: https://doi.org/10.1111/conl.12430.

US Environmental Protection Agency (US EPA). 2022. "Tribes and EPA: 50 Years of Environmental Partnership." https://www.epa.gov/tribal/tribes-and-epa-50-years-environmental-partnership.

US Mission to the UN. 2021. Explanation of Position for the Adoption of the Implementation of the Convention on Biological Diversity and Its Contribution to Sustainable Development Resolution. https://usun.usmission.gov/explanation-of-position-for-the-adoption-of-the-implementation-of-the-convention-on-biological-diversity-and-its-contribution-to-sustainable.

VanNijnatten, Debora L. 2009. "Environmental Cross-Border Regions and the Canada–US Relationship: Building from the Bottom Up in the Second Century." In *Transborder Environmental Governance in Canada and the United States*, edited by Barry G. Rabe and Stephen Brooks, 115–32. Washington: Woodrow Wilson Center for International Scholars.

VanNijnatten, Debora L., and Carolyn Johns. 2020. "The IJC and the Evolution of Environmental and Water Governance in the Great Lakes–St Lawrence Basin: Accountability, Progress Reporting, and Measuring Performance under the Great Lakes Water Quality Agreement." In *The First Century of the International Joint Commission*, edited by Murray Clamen and Daniel Macfarlane, 395–432. Calgary: University of Calgary Press.

Whitehorn, Penelope R., Laetitia M. Navarro, Matthias Schroter, Miguel Fernandez, Xavier Rotllan-Puig, and Alexandra Marques. 2019. "Mainstreaming Biodiversity: A Review of National Strategies." *Biological Conservation* 235: 157–63.

Yale Climate Opinion Maps 2021. 2022. https://climatecommunication.yale.edu/visualizations-data/ycom-us.

Yellowstone to Yukon (Y2Y). n.d. "Y2Y's Impact." https://y2y.net/work/our-impact.

Zacharias, Mark. 2022. "Opinion: America's Inflation Reduction Act Just Gave Canada's Economy a Shot in the Arm." Clean Energy Canada, 22 August. https://cleanenergycanada.org/americas-inflation-reduction-act-just-gave-canadas-economy-a-shot-in-the-arm.

10

When Irish Eyes Are Smiling

Arctic Sovereignty and the Impact of Personal Diplomacy

ADAM LAJEUNESSE

On 1 August 1985, the US Coast Guard (USCG) cutter *Polar Sea* departed Thule, Greenland, heading west for Canadian waters. Little more than a week later, the heavy icebreaker emerged from its week-long journey through the Northwest Passage into the Beaufort Sea. While the voyage itself was uneventful, it quickly took on an uncomfortable political significance. The details of the voyage had been organized in advance by the US and Canadian Coast Guards; however, there had been no formal request for permission by the US government. The spectre of a US challenge to Canada's Arctic sovereignty soon worked its way into public discourse, and what had begun as a repositioning voyage quickly evolved into a litmus test for Canada–US relations and, by extension, the Mulroney government's emphasis on cooperation and friendly relations.

The dispute over the Northwest Passage was nothing new. In the 1950s, attempts to resolve the issue met with no success, and later Canadian and US governments chose to ignore it, sidestepping awkward legal disagreements when they threatened to intrude upon vital joint defence operations. The disagreement first burst into public consciousness in 1969 when the US company Humble Oil sent its massive icebreaking tanker *Manhattan* through the passage. As was the case with the *Polar Sea*, extensive Canadian cooperation was then seen by many in the media and opposition as no substitute for formal diplomatic clearance (Kirton and Munton 1987). Were the waters of the Northwest Passage entirely Canadian or were the Arctic islands bisected by an international strait? The matter had never been resolved, which meant that in 1985, the new Progressive Conservative government of Brian

Mulroney inherited a legal and political dilemma that had vexed the governments of Louis St Laurent, John Diefenbaker, Lester Pearson, and Pierre Trudeau.

Arctic sovereignty has long been and still is a highly emotional issue in Canada, transcending simple debates over maritime delineation or transit rights. In a report to cabinet, External Affairs noted that the region – and Canada's sovereignty there – carried "a certain mystique in the Canadian mind." Wording from that report ultimately fed into the 1985 External Affairs Green Paper, *Competitiveness and Security*, which declared the Arctic "a special region and ourselves as special because of it" (Report to Cabinet 1985). That emotional connection had always complicated negotiations and limited space for compromise.

In many respects, the Mulroney government's handling of this disagreement echoed previous Canadian efforts to bring the Americans around to its interpretation of Arctic sovereignty. Indeed, the dispute had not changed much in its essentials. However, the *Polar Sea* crisis arose at a time in Canadian–American relations particularly suited to compromise. In 1986, quite unlike in the past, the US administration was genuinely interested in finding a solution, largely driven by President Ronald Reagan's personal relationship with Prime Minister Mulroney. The two leaders, who famously crooned a duet of "When Irish Eyes Are Smiling," were well placed to manage the crisis differently than previous governments. In Donald E. Abelson's words, the two leaders "had each other's back," and this created the kind of trust that smoothed political differences and facilitated genuine cooperation and compromise (Abelson 2022).

This relationship led Reagan to push the US security establishment and legal bureaucracy out of their comfort zones, creating a new space for discussion. The Arctic negotiations highlighted not only the importance of national leadership in cutting through institutional positions but also the value of trust at the highest levels. Leonard Legault, one of Canada's lead negotiators, put it well when he said that "the President understood a political problem when he saw one, and he knew that his friend Brian had a problem" (Kirkey 1996, 452). Approaching that problem as one to be solved rather than as an adversarial contest to be fought made all the difference. The result was not a complete victory for either side but rather a friendly and functional agreement that satisfied both states' vital requirements and that continues to frame Canadian–American Arctic cooperation to this day.

Sovereignty on Ice: Canada's Track Record

The origins of Canada's Arctic sovereignty dispute with the US can be traced back to the early nineteenth century, when the North-West Mounted Police were sent north to police American whaling vessels operating in Hudson Bay and the Beaufort Sea. At the time, Canadian governments assumed certain "privileges" (King 1905) and jurisdiction in those waters, although the nature of that sovereignty was never fully defined in official policy. The dispute crystallized in the late 1940s, when the developing Cold War brought significant US shipping into the Canadian Arctic for the purpose of building and maintaining joint defence facilities.[1] In 1946, Lester Pearson – then Canada's ambassador to the US – published an article in *Foreign Affairs* in which he claimed that Canada's sovereignty extended to "the frozen sea north of the mainland between the meridians of [Canada's] east and west boundaries extending to the North Pole" (Pearson 1946, 638). That same month, US undersecretary of state Dean Acheson was warned by his department that if either Canada or the Soviet Union attempted such a claim, "additional and serious problems would arise" and the US would have no option but to "vigorously resist" (Memorandum from Dean Acheson 1946). In a formal policy statement in 1951, the US State Department declared in no uncertain terms its rejection of any such claims to the Arctic waters beyond the three-mile territorial sea (US Department of State 1951, 1724).

Concerns within External Affairs over the US reaction to any forceful assertion of Canadian sovereignty ensured that the matter remained low-key.[2] Throughout the 1940s and 1950s, Canadian and US officials recognized the difference of opinion on the legal status of the waters but did their best to ignore it. This arrangement was described as a "modus vivendi" by the Advisory Committee on Northern Development: a way of allowing "each country [to maintain] its position while refraining from asserting it in such a manner as to embarrass the other publicly" (Memorandum for Cabinet 1969).

This framework for northern relations served its purpose. It facilitated joint operations and defence cooperation, but it was always something of a stopgap. Still, it survived, largely because efforts to negotiate US recognition of Canada's position consistently failed. In 1963, the government of Prime Minister Lester Pearson tied the Arctic into a broader set of negotiations on maritime jurisdiction with the US. Looking back at the process in 1985, Ambassador Allan Gotlieb described the effort as "an unqualified fiasco." "The Americans rejected each and every claim" and threatened to send ships and aircraft to challenge that sovereignty, Gotlieb (1985) wrote. Then secretary of state for external affairs Howard Green warned of economic repercussions, such as US import restrictions on Canadian oil and lumber. US negotiators also told the Canadians that the drawing of straight baselines to enclose the Arctic would result in an immediate referral to the International Court of Justice (ICJ) (Minutes of Cabinet Meeting 1963) The Americans may have been serious about this; State Department records do contain a draft note, ready to be delivered to the Canadian embassy, formally notifying Canada that the matter was being referred to the ICJ (Draft Contingency Note 1963).

Six years later, the supertanker *Manhattan* reignited the sovereignty debate, and the relationship was, again, acrimonious. Canadian suggestions that the US request transit permission for its icebreaker escort (not the *Manhattan* itself) were quickly rebuffed, and, again, US officials informed the Canadians that any formal Canadian claim to the Northwest Passage would be referred immediately to the ICJ (Kirton and Munton 1987).

The Trudeau government also feared economic retaliation. In 1969, Canada announced new pollution prevention regulations that would expand its jurisdiction in the Arctic. This was a useful step in its own right but also a political compromise for a government unwilling to push a more overt declaration of sovereignty. Still, the *proposed* legislation brought retaliation in the form of a 20 per cent reduction in US imports of Canadian oil. A week later, President Richard Nixon telephoned Trudeau to warn of even more severe cuts if Canada went ahead with its proposed legislation (Kirton and Munton 1987, 93). Talking to the Soviets in 1971, Prime Minister Pierre Trudeau's special foreign policy assistant, Ivan Head, remarked that Canada had no choice but to refrain from any overt declaration of sovereignty. In Head's words, "it would be better to be silent than to speak out and be knocked down" (Record of Meetings Held in the Department of External Affairs 1971).

The failure of the Canadian and US governments to reach an agreement on the status of the Arctic waters, or even to establish a formal framework for cooperation, stemmed from several overlapping factors. In the 1960s and 1970s, the international law of the sea was continuously evolving, with obvious implications for Canadian jurisdiction in the Arctic. This process took place in tandem with developments in the global maritime security dynamic and the expansion of coastal state claims around the world. Many different factors, therefore, informed the US position on the Arctic, although at its heart was always the zero-sum assessment that any sovereignty "ceded" to Canada would result in a loss of global freedom of navigation for the US, not only in the Arctic but also around the world as other states latched on to the "precedent" set by Canada.[3]

This adversarial framework for addressing the Arctic dispute was consistently unproductive. Political scientist Christopher J. Kirkey (1996, 425) pointed to this distributive bargaining, in which a victory for one party must represent a defeat for the other, as one of the principal hurdles to any political resolution. There were logical reasons for this adversarial framework. The principle of the freedom of the seas was (and remains) inviolate to the US government, while the Canadian understanding of Arctic sovereignty brooked no compromise. Pushing past these impediments therefore required both political will and space to compromise. This was not always the case in the 1960s, a time when relationships at the highest levels were often frosty.

The Pearson government's maritime negotiations with the Americans in the early 1960s were not helped by the prime minster's chilly relationship with President Lyndon Johnson. President Nixon and Prime Minister Trudeau were even more hostile. Trudeau reported that their relationship was "not one of intimacy and great fellowship" (CBC News 2019). On his private tapes, Nixon went further, calling Trudeau "an asshole," "a son of a bitch," and a "pompous egghead." When these tapes were made public, Trudeau's response was simply: "I've been called worse things by better people" (Goodman 2008).

When the Progressive Conservative government of Brian Mulroney took office in 1984, Canada's Arctic policy remained in a state of limbo: "the heir to a long history of ambitious, vague, and ineffectively implemented claims," as Allan Gottlieb described it to one of Mulroney's advisers (Gotlieb to Doucet 1985). The transit of USCGS *Polar Sea* once again highlighted this ambiguity and forced the issue of Arctic sovereignty back to the top of the government's agenda.

The Crisis

That the *Polar Sea's* voyage would become a political crisis was far from preordained. Indeed, that voyage was launched as a collaborative and friendly operational deployment. The decision to send the ship through the Northwest Passage was made in April 1985, and discussions began with the Canadian Coast Guard that same month (Huebert 1993, 211). Then commandant of the US Coast Guard Admiral James S. Gracey described the initially casual process of clearing the voyage in his memoirs. In the spring of 1985, he phoned the commissioner of the Canadian Coast Guard, Ranald Quayle, whom he had worked with previously on Great Lakes pilotage and had come to like and trust. "So I called Quayle," Gracey recalls, "and I said, we've got this situation, and we're supposed to meet your guys off of Barrow. How about if we just go across the top and meet you there? Would that be okay?' He said, 'I think so. I'll check.' He called back and said yes. I didn't think to ask whom he might have talked to or whatever. And I can't remember whom I talked to. Of course, we had 'requested permission' but not at the right level" (Gracey 2004, 709). The initial work was done by Canadian Coast Guard official J.Y. Clarke, who travelled to Washington to work out a plan to cover the transit, which was to include the use of Canadian helicopters as well as assistance from the Canadian weather and ice forecasting services. The order was written with relative ease and was signed by both coast guards shortly thereafter (Huebert 1993, 211).

While the US Coast Guard anticipated some Canadian sensitivity, a public outcry was considered unlikely. *Polar Sea* was a government icebreaker after all, not a supertanker like *Manhattan*. More attuned to the Canadian public's sensitivities, the Mulroney government placed a greater political emphasis on the voyage and began to engage with the matter in July. That month, External Affairs Minister Joe Clark met with Secretary of State George Shultz at the Association of Southeast Asian Nations Ministerial Meeting in Kuala Lumpur and raised the issue of Arctic sovereignty; he was surprised to see that his counterpart had no idea what the *Polar Sea* was planning to do. In a description of the matter to the Canadian embassy in Washington, External Affairs expressed some frustration that Canada's higher-level attention was not being matched in the US, where the matter was delegated in its entirety to Coast Guard officials and lawyers (Telegram from EXTOTT 1985).

Hoping to move the voyage forward without controversy, Ottawa sought to facilitate the voyage and exercise some control through existing legal frameworks. Initially, that meant a request that the US seek an exemption from the Canadian pollution control regulations.[4] In the first signs of trouble, the Americans countered that no request for exemption was required, because the Northwest Passage was an international strait through which it enjoyed the right of transit passage. This disagreement was pushed aside, however, and the two governments agreed to continue to disagree on that legal question. The Canadian Coast Guard, meanwhile, provided the US with updated charts and promised more support on weather forecasting (Lajeunesse and Huebert 2017). Crucially, both sides agreed that the trip was being made without prejudice to the legal position of either country (Government of Canada 1985).

Both governments would have preferred to set aside the thorny question of sovereignty, but public reaction was soon enough to scupper that hope. About three weeks before the voyage commenced, the Canadian press began to publicize it. As public indignation rose, the Mulroney government came under attack for apparently doing nothing to protect Canada's sovereignty, and even its honour. The *Montreal Gazette*, for instance, called the Conservatives' cooperation "a major flop by a spineless government" (Young 1985) and a "servile wimpy response … enough to enrage even a lukewarm Canadian nationalist" (Braid 1986). Franklyn Griffiths, a political scientist at the University of Toronto, captured a great deal of attention with a *Globe and Mail* op-ed warning that the transit imperilled Canadian sovereignty. Griffiths even implied that the transit was a purposeful attempt on the part of the US government to undermine that sovereignty, writing that "we appear to be faced with a carefully calibrated move, not with an attempt to undo the Canadian position in a single act" (Griffiths 1985). This interpretation was echoed by other commentators (Morrison in Ted McDorman 1987, 1421); while it was baseless, it made for good headlines. Political scientist Robert Huebert has even made a convincing case that much of this attention was attributable to the voyage taking place during an abnormally slow news season (Huebert 1993, 255). In the words of famed Canadian icebreaker captain Thomas Pullen, the Canadian public was "more agitated than informed" (Elliot-Meisel 1998, 148).

In the House of Commons this agitation was manifest. Jean Chrétien described the voyage as "part of the cronyism between Brian

Mulroney and the Americans." "He goes on his knees all the time," Chrétien declared, clearly in reference to some sort of religious devotion (148). The New Democratic Party offered its own criticism; in one of the House's more preposterous statements, MP Jim Fulton likened the voyage to "psychological rape" (House of Commons 1985, 6467). More concerning, the Inuit Tapirisat of Canada voiced its displeasure, labelling the voyage "a challenge not only to Canadian sovereignty and jurisdiction, but also to Canadian responsibilities towards Inuit who made possible that sovereignty in the Arctic in the first place" (External Affairs 1985).

Placed in the awkward position of having to defend a sovereignty claim that no previous government had ever been able to formalize – or even delineate – the Mulroney government determined that the politics of ambiguity were no longer appropriate or tenable (External Affairs 1985). On 10 September 1985, Joe Clark announced the immediate adoption of an Order in Council establishing straight baselines around the Arctic Archipelago, defining those internal waters and formalizing Canada's sovereignty claim (External Affairs 1985). Since the Arctic waters were considered historic, the baselines did not constitute a claim per se but rather the delineation of what the country had long considered its historic waters.[5]

This was a significant milestone, which Canadian governments had long avoided placing for fear of the US reaction. *Polar Sea*'s voyage was the immediate catalyst; however, that claim also represented a long-held vision of a more active Arctic, one where uncertainty over Canadian jurisdiction would cause serious political and legal problems. An External Affairs report to cabinet in August 1985 put it well, stating that "the Canadian public ... would undoubtedly be no longer satisfied with buying time or with lesser substitutes for sovereignty. Delay will only diminish Canada's credibility at home and abroad" (Report to Cabinet by the SSEA 1985).

Declaring and delineating sovereignty was the easiest part of the process. External Affairs now moved immediately to negotiate with the US, with an eye toward securing US recognition of the Canadian position or at least forestalling an American challenge. Similar negotiations had failed in the past, and the outlook was still poor. Surveying the scene, Ambassador Gotlieb pointed to "implacable U.S. opposition" derived from the Americans' strategic need for freedom of the seas, a "fundamental and unalterable principle of U.S. military strategy" (letter from Gotlieb 1985). And while it was these broader principles that were most important for the Americans, Canadian sovereignty over the Northwest Passage itself was also problematic. The US Navy operated submarines along the strait (Lajeunesse 2013), and, according to Gotlieb, while no US government would ever admit it, the possibility of "an unfriendly or even hostile government in Canada" denying access was always a concern (letter from Gotlieb 1985). Success in shifting the Americans off this position was therefore never assured.

The Negotiations

While the US position on the Arctic had not changed in its fundamentals since the 1960s, the environment in which these negotiations took place had improved somewhat. The UN Law of the Sea Conference had resolved many of the unsettled principles of international law in 1982, clarifying the legal environment and reducing (although hardly eliminating) US concerns over negative global precedents. More importantly, the tenor of the bilateral relationship had improved considerably. This had been one of the Mulroney government's core foreign policy objectives and was well summed up by Clark in an address to Dalhousie University: "We recognized the importance of the United States to so many aspects of our national life, and set out deliberately to restore our national life, and set out deliberately to restore goodwill and a sense of partnership between the two countries in order that problems could be resolved in a spirit of cooperation and the Canadian interest served" (statement by the Right Honourable Joe Clark 1985).

From the beginning, the Canadian strategy was to leverage its improved relationship with Washington and to highlight the centrality of the Arctic to continued good relations. Avoiding the transactional, zero-sum negotiations that had failed in the past, External Affairs and Canada's senior negotiators pushed the Arctic as one part of a broader effort to improve bilateral cooperation on the environment, defence, trade, and foreign relations. External Affairs made sure the Americans knew that their actions, "however innocently or operationally motivated," had "weakened [the] hand of those [in Canada] who have argued that overt friendliness to USA can pay off for Canada, and strengthened case of those who believe USA approach will always be quote me first unquote" (Telegram from EXTOTT 1985). Foreign policy adviser Robert Fowler put it well in a note to Mulroney: "Reagan must be made to understand that, to paraphrase your own words at the beginning of your mandate, you put yourself at the end of a rather slim limb and it makes little sense to have him handing out saws" (memorandum for the PM from Robert R. Fowler 1985).

In fact, that cooperative spirit paid immediate dividends. While the US government was unwilling to accept the straight baselines that Clark had just announced in the House, it was anxious to do what it could to limit the damage caused by the disagreement. Canadian diplomats had long feared the legal and political ramifications of an explicit US rejection of Canadian sovereignty. Even more concerning was the prospect of US action to emphasize that rejection, be it in the form of economic sanctions or what today would be called a "freedom of navigation voyage." These worst-case scenarios were avoided, however, and US and Canadian diplomats managed to work out a compromise that kept the US from issuing a formal protest. Instead of launching an immediate protest for the record, the State Department was convinced to issue a simple reservation of their position. This was a creative way of postponing, perhaps even avoiding, the protest that Canadian governments had long feared. For Canada, this US flexibility bought a few months of negotiating time; it also held off protests from other quarters, as most of the world's shipping states waited to see what action the US would take.[6]

The US was also extremely cooperative in supporting Canada's communication efforts, which were essential to the Mulroney government's efforts to dampen concerns at home. Recognizing the political position the Canadians were in, the US Coast Guard and diplomatic staff went so far as to coordinate interviews and press releases with External Affairs. One US Coast Guard captain, who made the mistake of telling journalists that Canadian observers on the *Polar Sea* had no "operational authority," was taken to task by State Department representatives. The captain, described in communication with Ottawa as "an expert in ice and naïve on journalists," was instructed not to answer any more calls (Washington UNGR16072 to EXTOTT 1985). Even as the icebreaker was still in Canadian waters, US ambassador Paul Robinson received a telegram ordering "more effective USA performance with CDN media on Polar Sea" after some officials were tracked responding to Canadian media on their own. Robinson promised "complete cooperation" and to "spell out in no uncertain terms" the "need for USA to keep lid on its dealings with press" (Telegram: EXTORR to Washington Embassy 1985).

It was a promising beginning, and formal negotiations began in September 1985. In the beginning, the principal negotiators were Leonard Legault and Barry Mawhinney of External Affairs and David Colson and Richard Smith of the State Department. The initial talks were informal and dedicated as much to discovery as to serious negotiations. They also provided some encouraging signs for the Canadians. The External Affairs representatives hoped the US could be brought around to recognizing Canadian sovereignty in exchange for transit rights for American icebreakers, warships, and other public vessels. Leonard Legault even suggested a system similar to the one governing the St Lawrence Seaway (Telegram: EXTORR to Washington Embassy 1985).

Initially this approach seemed to win some acceptance, and Canadian diplomats reported back tentative support from certain State Department officials, who believed it might be possible for the US to recognize the Canadian Arctic as an exceptional and unique case without damaging America's global position. Brian Hoyle, the State Department's director of Ocean Law and Policy, said over lunch with the Canadians that he thought there was a growing consensus on the US side that a solution could be found that both countries would be happy with (Washington DC to External Affairs). Hoyle suggested that if Canada's claims could somehow be separated from the principle of straight baselines and worked into some kind of "Lex Arctici" (Law of the Arctic), then the US could probably live with it, since the precedent would not apply outside of the Arctic (Washington DC to External Affairs). Reporting back to Ottawa, Leonard Legault wrote that "never before have we had such a clear sign of flexibility from the United States on the question of Arctic navigation" (memorandum for the Secretary of State for External Affairs).

Despite the interest in finding an accommodation, the prospect of Canadian baselines gaining acceptance continued to raise concerns, particularly within the US defence establishment. Ideas went back and forth, but what a Canadian exception might look like couldn't be pinned down. In an interview after the fact, David Colson recounted: "There was no chance that this was going to be a recognition situation … We wanted to work it out in political terms … We might be quite happy to give Canada their position, but we couldn't do that because that's not the way the world works, and we couldn't be seen doing something for our good friend and neighbor that we would not be prepared to do elsewhere in the world" (as quoted in Kirkey 1996).

With a clear-cut recognition of sovereignty seemingly off the table, the Americans pushed for a functional agreement that would not prejudice either state's position (Colson quoted in Kirkey 1996). While not ideal, such an agreement would still be a victory for Canada. If the negotiators could come to a compromise that accepted Canadian authority over shipping and commercial aviation, it would represent a major achievement. If it looked like the US was accepting de facto Canadian sovereignty, and did not make a distinct separation between sovereignty and jurisdiction, and if the US and others would be prevented from protesting Canada's Arctic baselines, then it would certainly be something that Canada could live with (Kirkey 1996). Giving shape to the idea proved difficult, however.

With talks reaching an impasse, the second phase began in March 1986 with a direct appeal from the prime minister to the president. That opportunity came in March 1986 at a summit meeting in Washington. There, Mulroney conveyed to Reagan the importance of the Arctic to Canadians generally and to his political fortunes in particular. For Canadians, Mulroney insisted, this issue went beyond questions of Arctic navigation. It was an emotional matter powerful enough to derail the ongoing free trade negotiations and damage the bilateral relationship that the two leaders had worked so hard to improve. It had to be resolved quickly. In Reagan, Mulroney found a sympathetic ear, and the president made what the Canadians felt to be a groundbreaking promise. Reagan said it would be best if the two nations simply let the sovereignty issue "lie where it is" and that "anything we do in [Canadian Arctic waters] will be with your permission" (Mulroney 2007, 431). The previous day the president had also promised that the US would not "challenge" Canadian sovereignty. Taken together, it seemed as though Reagan had come just short of explicitly accepting Canadian sovereignty. This was a far cry from the adversarial approach taken by Nixon sixteen years earlier.

These heartening signs injected new life into the negotiations, and it was agreed that both nations would appoint special negotiators to expedite the process. Undersecretary of Science and Technology Edward

Derwinski was given this post for the US, and Derek Burney, Mulroney's chief of staff, for Canada. Derwinski recalled that his instructions from Reagan were simple and straightforward; the president had called and said: "Ed, I understand you're going to handle this and I wish you well … get this nailed down" (interview with Derwinski in Kirkey 1996, 411).

Burney and Derwinski had worked together in the past and, like their bosses, had developed a good working relationship. They immediately began meeting informally in an attempt to break away from the adversarial approach that had characterized so many past negotiations on the subject. Some progress was made, but a crucial sticking point remained: the question of recognizing Canadian sovereignty or any phrasing that seemed to imply it. Over the following year the negotiators worked on a constructive way around this legal impasse. Regardless of what Reagan might have implied, any hope of winning outright US recognition had long since disappeared. In March 1987, the president wrote to Mulroney to convey his frustration with the process: "Brian this vexing issue has proven to be more difficult for us to resolve than I thought when we discussed it … I have to say in all candor that we cannot agree to an agreement that obliges us to seek permission for our vessels to navigate through the Northwest Passage. To do so would adversely affect our legitimate rights to freely transit other important areas globally" (Mulroney 2007, 431).

With the process once again deadlocked, the prime minister pushed Reagan directly, and personally. During a presidential visit to Ottawa, Mulroney showed Reagan a nineteenth-century globe, depicting the Northwest Passage in its natural ice-covered state. Derek Burney explained the exceptional nature of the passage and described how the ice had been used by the Inuit for centuries for transportation, hunting, and fishing. Mulroney said frankly to the president, "Ron that's ours. We own it lock, stock, and icebergs" (Mulroney 2007, 497).

It seems that this appeal shifted the president's view even further toward the Canadian position. Burney said afterwards that, upon seeing the globe, Reagan commented that it "looks a little different than the maps they showed me on the plane coming into Ottawa" (Kirkey 1996, 412). Afterwards, the president reportedly became increasingly annoyed with his advisers seeking to hold off the Canadians. That afternoon, Reagan told national security advisor Frank Carlucci: "I think we should do something for Brian." Carlucci replied, "Mr. President, we're doing well holding our positions on acid rain, the free trade agreement, and the Northwest Passage." To that, Reagan lost his temper somewhat and countered "No, no, no, we ought to do something." Carlucci went right from the meeting to find Derek Burney and asked him to reiterate Canada's positions on acid rain, trade, and the Arctic. When Burney asked why, Carlucci responded "because they're our positions now" (Mulroney 2007, 498).

This may have been something of an exaggeration, but, in addressing the House of Commons that day, Reagan did announce that he had "had a full discussion of the Arctic waters issue, and he and I [Reagan and Mulroney] agreed to inject new impetus to the discussions already underway. We are determined to find a solution based on mutual respect for sovereignty and our common security and other interests" (US Department of State 1987, 7). A month later, when the president was asked at a press conference about the US position on Arctic sovereignty, he noted that the choke points were a concern but that the Arctic was "different" because of the ice. When the reporter commented, "You seem to be saying that Canada had some legitimate claim to sovereignty for that," Reagan replied, "Yes, I think that is a difficult situation there. And I am hopeful that … we can find an answer" (Huebert 1993, 161–2).

The Agreement

The president was on record describing the Arctic waters as an exceptional case because of the ice cover and had promised the Canadian prime minister that the US would show respect for Canadian sovereignty. Reagan overcame a great deal of internal opposition to deliver this vital political support. It relaxed the overall US position and kept the negotiations moving. After the summit, the negotiating teams went back to work and began to revise their approach. The lengthy multi-article agreements they had been working on were found to be too complex. Something simpler was needed.

Reagan had said that the US would only operate in the Arctic with Canadian consent, and this was what the Canadian negotiators had been pushing for. Yet for many in the US government, consent went too far towards implying recognition of sovereignty. The solution was reached by David Colson, who came upon the ingenious idea of linking the question of consent to scientific research. The UN Convention on the Law of the Seas (Article 245) states clearly that in the territorial sea and on the Continental Shelf, maritime research "shall be conducted only with the express consent of and under the conditions set forth by the coastal state" (UNCLOS 1982). Both Huebert and Kirkey have already noted the vital importance of this particular passage (Huebert 1993, 483–4; Kirkey 1996, 421). If the US requested consent to transit *while conducting scientific research*, then both nations could secure that which was most important to them. Canada had its political victory, since Mulroney could legitimately claim that the Americans were now requesting Canadian permission to transit. Meanwhile, the Americans could say that such permission did not represent recognition of Canadian sovereignty, since conducting research along the way necessitated such a request under accepted international law. The two countries were free to interpret as they saw fit.

For Canada this was not a complete victory, but it was still a significant achievement. For decades, External Affairs had recognized that full US recognition of Canada's Arctic sovereignty was probably out of reach, and during multiple rounds of negotiations in the 1960s, Canada had pinned some hope on the US offering only token resistance. This was that sought-after token resistance. In a 1987 memorandum, the agreement was thus framed as "a specific but a limited achievement" that did not secure sovereignty but did ensure that the US would not challenge the Canadian position in such a way as to damage it legally or politically (Memorandum to Cabinet 1987).

In a practical sense, the deal was also seen as supportive of Canada's long-term position. Cabinet was told that requiring Canadian "consent" for icebreakers owned or operated by the US government "would probably strengthen and certainly not weaken Canada's position … if the matter were subsequently referred to the court, which of course, is always an option open to the two countries" (Memorandum to Cabinet 1987). The deal, therefore, presented Canada with a far more attractive framework for controlling its own Arctic than what External Affairs had foreseen only a few years earlier, when concerns over the lack of US recognition and growing shipping activity in the North led to serious concerns that a new "right of passage" might soon emerge (Memorandum to Cabinet 1987).

This was a true compromise, and, as with any real compromise, it was tenuous. Many within the US defence establishment remained wary about any use of the word consent and were unhappy with how far the US government had gone. US negotiator Ty Cobb warned that the "submarine people" in particular – by which he meant US opponents of Canada's then active nuclear submarine acquisition program – were asking a lot of questions about the link between these boats and the Arctic agreement with "evident purpose of causing trouble" (Telegram: Washington Embassy to EXTOTT 1987). From the Canadian perspective, the fact that there was no explicit US recognition of Canada's sovereignty left the agreement open to criticism. A November 1987 memorandum to cabinet estimated that Canadian support for the agreement would probably be 60 per cent for and 40 per cent against (Memorandum to Cabinet 1987). Uncertainty therefore prevailed to the end. At one point, a delay in the signing left Cobb venting to Gotlieb: "I spent half my [expletive deleted] time ramming that treaty through [the interagency process]" (Telegram: Washington Embassy to EXTOTT 1987).

The deal, which came to be called the Agreement on Arctic Cooperation, won the support of cabinet and was introduced in a speech to the House of Commons in January 1988 by Joe Clark. Clark told Canadians that "as a result of that agreement, the United States now acknowledges and has a legal obligation to seek Canada's permission before there is a transit through the Northwest Passage" (House of Commons 1988). Clark did not say that the Americans had an obligation to request permission *before conducting research*, only before transiting. The interpretation was still a bit of a balancing act. The US government viewed that "permission" differently, and External Affairs warned the government that it must not "oversell the agreement," since that might invite a backlash from US officials and politicians, many of whom still saw this as too great of a concession (Memorandum to Cabinet 1987).

The deal was signed by Joe Clark and Secretary of State George Shultz on 11 January 1988. The key provision reads as follows: "The government of the United States pledges that all navigation by US icebreakers within waters claimed by Canada to be internal will be undertaken with the consent of the government of Canada" (Agreement Between the Government of Canada and the Government of the United States of America on Arctic Cooperation 1988). In practice, it worked very well. The first request to transit was made by the icebreaker *Polar Star* in 1988, and, in keeping with its promise, the US sent the Canadian government a note requesting consent, which Ottawa naturally granted.

In the years that followed, the US Coast Guard made a number of voyages through the Northwest Passage, all of which were arranged within this framework, and all of which proceeded smoothly and without incident. The Canadian government hailed it as a triumph; while Ottawa had not won US acceptance of its claims, it had taken a significant step forward. Responding to criticism that the Conservatives had not won sufficient concessions from the US, Joe Clark reasoned that "we would have preferred naturally, to have the Americans accept the legal concept of sovereignty. What we are trying to do here, is assert a step that will close another hole in the claims of Canada to control of our North" (Hunter 1987). And it did close a significant and potentially troublesome gap, one that no previous government had managed to address.

Conclusion

The Agreement on Arctic Cooperation did not resolve the legal dispute over Arctic sovereignty; however, it reframed the issue in a way that was politically and legally beneficial to Canada, while also ensuring that no other sovereignty crises emerged. From a strictly transactional perspective, the US had little reason to concede so much to Canada. It gained no new right of passage and had allowed the word "consent" to be enshrined into the bilateral agreement. That consent was still framed by the technicality of research activity, and the agreement itself was explicitly without prejudice to the legal positions of either state (Hunter 1987); even so, the idea of requesting consent to transit a strait was anathema to US national policy.

Securing that compromise from the US was a considerable achievement. For generations, State Department lawyers and Coast Guard and Navy officials had pushed back against such a concession. In his memoirs, Gotlieb recounts a meeting in Washington, which he expected to be an informal "one-on-one" with Derwinski. "Never will I forget the enormous crowd of officials in the room," he recounted, "some two dozen or so – most of them agitating for a hard line against the Canadian claim" (Gotlieb 1991, 113). In many respects, Reagan's greatest challenge was pushing his own officials toward agreement.

The president's partnership with Mulroney was a crucial motivator in getting this done. He recognized the political importance of this issue and took it to heart when the prime minister told him it would impact his own electoral fortunes in Canada (Kirkey 1996, 424). The result was enough of a push to move the US negotiators toward Canada's position to seal the deal. "You couldn't get this kind of an agreement from an [American] administration that wasn't inclined fundamentally to try to do something" recounted Derek Burney. "Ed Derwinski and I with all the will in the world couldn't have done this if we didn't know that the guy in charge on both sides wanted this thing to be resolved in a way that didn't make it a problem for them" (Kirkey 1996, 424–5). The result was a constructive step forward in the long-standing Arctic sovereignty dispute and the establishment of a new framework for bilateral cooperation that remains in place more than three decades later.

Notes

1 For the best work on this early activity, see Heidt and Lackenbauer (2022).

2 For an in-depth overview, see Lajeunesse (2016, Chs. 2–5) and Lackenbauer and Kikkert (2011).

3 The issue of global precedent was raised by the US continuously in conversations with Canada. See, for instance, Statement of the Deputy Undersecretary of State (1963); Memorandum for the Deputy Prime Minister (1983); and an interview with David Colson, quoted in Kirkey (1995, 409–10).

4 In accordance with Section 12 of the act, the governor in council can issue an exemption to foreign public vessels if s/he believes they are in substantial compliance with the act.

5 The position of the Government of Canada is that these have been internal Canadian waters since 1880. See statement by Gaillard (2001).

6 These powers being primarily Japan, the United Kingdom, and France. Memorandum for the Secretary of State for External Affairs (1986).

References

Abelson, Donald E. 2022. *Brian Mulroney, Ronald Reagan, and the Politics of Friendship*. Mulroney Papers in Public Policy and Governance, no. 8. May, https://www.mulroneyinstitute.ca/sites/mulroney/files/2022-05/MPPG%20No%208%20Abelson_web.pdf.

Address by the Right Honourable Joe Clark at Dalhousie University. 1985. 14 September.

Agreement between the Government of Canada and the Government of the United States of America on Arctic Cooperation. 1988. *Canada Treaty Series*, no. 29, 11 January. LAC, MG 26, P16-2, vol. 10.

Braid, Don. 1986. "Polar Sea a Turning Point for Mulroney." *Montreal Gazette*, 14 August.

Canada. External Affairs. 1985. "Policy on Canadian Sovereignty." *Statements and Speeches*, no. 85/7.

Canada, House of Commons. 1985. *Debates*. 10 September.

– *Debates*. 1988. 18 January. 33rd Parliament, 2nd session, 1999.

Canada. Minutes of Cabinet Meeting. 1963. 4 March. RG 2- A-5-a vol. 6253.

Canada and United States. 1988. "Agreement between the Government of Canada and the Government of the United States of America on Arctic Cooperation, 11 January. *Canada Treaty Series*, no. 29.

Carey, Elaine. 1985. "Trip by US Ship Called Threat to Arctic Sovereignty." *Toronto Star*, 23 July.

CBC News. 2019. "From the 1960s to Today: Awkward Moments between Canadian and US Leaders." 6 December.

Chronology of Decision Making and Clearances for the 1985 Transit of the Northwest Passage by the US Coast Guard Icebreaker POLAR SEA. 1985. 11 October.

Draft Contingency Note. 1966. 9 August. NARA, RG 59, Central Foreign Policy Files, 1964–1966, box 1999.

Elliot-Meisel, Elizabeth B. 1998. *Arctic Diplomacy*. New York: Peter Lang.

Gaillard, M. 2001. Legal Affairs Bureau, Department of Foreign Affairs and International Trade. "Canada's Sovereignty in Changing Arctic Waters." 19 March.

Goodman, Lee-Anne. 2008. "Nixon Tapes Include Testy Trudeau Chat." *The Star*, 8 December.

Gotlieb, Allan. 1991. *I'll Be with You in a Minute Mr Ambassador: The Education of a Canadian Diplomat in Washington*. Toronto: University of Toronto Press.

Gotlieb, Allan. Ambassador (Washington) J.A. Doucet, Sr Adviser to the PM, 7 August 1985, LAC, MG 26 P16-2, vol. 10.

Government of Canada. 1985. Voyage of *The Polar Sea*. News release. 31 July.

Gracey, James S. 2004. "The Reminiscences of Admiral James S. Gracey U.S. Coast Guard (Retired)." Interviewed by Paul Stillwell. Annapolis: US Naval Institute.

Griffiths, Franklyn. 1985. "Arctic Authority at Stake." *Globe and Mail*, 13 June.

Heidt, Daniel, and P. Whitney Lackenbauer. 2022. *The Joint Arctic Weather Stations: Science and Sovereignty in the High Arctic, 1946–1972*. Calgary: University of Calgary Press.

Huebert, Rob. 1993. "Steel, Ice, and Decision-Making: The Voyage of the *Polar Sea* and Its Aftermath: The Making of Canadian Northern Foreign Policy." PhD diss., Dalhousie University.

Hunter, Iain. 1987. "Arctic Claims Not at Risk, Government Says." *Ottawa Citizen*, 7 December.

Inuit Tapirisat of Canada. 1985. "Inuit Call on Federal Government to Take Stand on Canadian Arctic Sovereignty." News Release. 2 July.

King, W.F. 1905. *Report on the Title of Canada to the Islands North of the Mainland of Canada*. Ottawa.

Kirkey, Christopher J. 1995. "Smoothing Troubled Waters: The 1988 Canada–United States Arctic Co-operation Agreement." *International Journal* 50, no. 2: 401–26.

– 1996. "The Arctic Waters Pollution Prevention Initiatives: Canada's Response to an American Challenge." *International Journal of Canadian Studies* 13: 41–59.

Kirton, John, and Don Munton. 1987. "The *Manhattan* Voyages and Their Aftermath." In *Politics of the Northwest Passage*, edited by Franklyn Griffiths, 67–97. Kingston and Montreal: McGill-Queen's University Press.

Lackenbauer, P. Whitney, and Peter Kikkert. 2011. "Sovereignty and Security: The Department of External Affairs, the United States, and Arctic Sovereignty, 1945–68." In *Serving the National Interest: Canada's Department of Foreign Affairs and International Trade, 1909–2009*, edited by Greg Donaghy and Michael Carroll, 101–20. Calgary: University of Calgary Press.

Lajeunesse, Adam. 2013. "A Very Practical Requirement: Under-Ice Operations in the Canadian Arctic, 1960–1986." *Cold War History* 13, no. 4: 507–24.

– 2016. *Lock, Stock, and Icebergs: The Evolution of Canada's Arctic Maritime Sovereignty*. Vancouver: UBC Press.

Lajeunesse, Adam, and Rob Huebert. 2017. *From Polar Sea to Straight Baselines*. Documents on Canadian Arctic Sovereignty and Security no. 11. Arctic Institute of North America and the Center for Military, Security, and Strategic Studies.

McDorman, Ted. 2009. *Salt Water Neighbors: International Ocean Law Relations between the United States and Canada*. New York: Oxford University Press.

Memorandum attached to letter from Dean Acheson to William L. Clayton, 15 July 1946, NARA, RG 165, entry 421, box 598.

Memorandum for Cabinet. 1969. 20 March. LAC, RG 12, vol. 5561, file 8100-15-4-2, pt. 1.

Memorandum for Cabinet, "Arctic Sovereignty," 10 November, 1987 LAC, MG 26

Memorandum for the Deputy Prime Minister. 1983. 3 November. LAC, RG 25, LAC, RG 12, vol. 5561, file 8100-15-4-2(s), pt. 4.
Memorandum for the PM from Robert R. Fowler. 1985. "Arctic Sovereignty and the Canada–US Bilateral Relationship. Lessons Learned and Future Options, a Personal Perspective." 20 August. LAC, MG 26.
Memorandum for the Secretary of State for External Affairs. 1985. 6 September. LAC, MG 26, vol. 5561, file 8100-15-4-2(s), pt. 4.
– 1986. 22 January. LAC, RG 12, vol. 5561, file 8100-15-4-2(s), pt. 4.
Mulroney, Brian. 2007. *Memoirs 1939–1993*. Toronto: McClelland and Stewart.
Outline of a report to cabinet by the SSEA on Canadian sovereignty in Arctic waters, 14 August 1985, LAC, MG 26.
Pearson, Lester. 1946. "Canada Looks Down North." *Foreign Affairs* 24, no. 4 (July): 638–47.
Record of Meetings Held in the Department of External Affairs to Discuss the Proposed Multilateral Conference on Safety of Navigation and Prevention of Pollution in Arctic Waters. 1971. 11–12 February. LAC, RG 25, vol. 15732, file 25-5-5-CDA-5.
Statement by the Right Honourable Joe Clark in House of Commons, Ottawa, 10 September 1985.
Statement of the Deputy Undersecretary of State to a Meeting with Canadian External Affairs Representatives. 1963. 4 December. NARA, RG 59, Central Foreign Policy Files 1957–1966, POL 33-8 CAN-US
Telegram: EXTORR to Washington Embassy. 1985. 2 August. LAC, MG 26, P16-9, vol. 25.
Telegram: Washington Embassy to EXTOTT. 1987. 16 December. LAC, MG 26, P5, vol. 10.
Telegram from EXTOTT to Washington Embassy. 1985. 8 August. LAC, MG 26, P16-2, vol. 10.
Telegram from Washington DC to External Affairs. 1985. 29 September. LAC, vol. 5561, file 8100-15-4-2(s), pt. 4.
United Nations. Convention on the Law of the Sea (UNCLOS). 1982. Signed 10 December at Montego Bay, Jamaica. Came into effect 16 November 1994, Part XIII, Section 3, Article 245.
United States. Department of State. 1951. *Foreign Relations of the United States*. "Department of State Policy Statement." *Polar Regions* 1. 1 July.
– 1987. "President's Visit to Canada." *Bulletin*, June 1.
Washington UNGR16072 to EXTOTT JCT JCD Flash. 1985. "Subject Polar Sea Approach to the USA Press; captain WUBOLD." 1 August.
Young, Christopher. 1985. "We've Flopped on *Polar Sea*." *Montreal Gazette*, 14 August.

11

Mirror, Mirror, on the Wall

AUKUS and the Question of a "Special" Canada–US Defence Relationship

DAVID G. HAGLUND AND WESLEY NICOL

Is Canada the Fairest Ally of Them All?

In words almost always misquoted (deliberately so by us in this chapter's title), the Evil Queen in a 1937 Disney film classic seeks reassurance about her looks from the slave residing in her wall mirror. The kind of reassurance sought would have a familiar ring to many analysts of Canada–US defence and security relations in our own time, for what the queen was endeavouring to have ratified was her number one status in a beauty contest that, in her own mind at least, pitted her against a lowly and unworthy challenger who had the added demerit of keeping company with a squadron of diminutive coal miners, from whom the movie took its name, *Snow White and the Seven Dwarfs*. The Evil Queen's question, "Magic mirror on the wall, who is the fairest one of all?," seems particularly apt when thoughts turn from Hollywood to the current state and future prospects of Canada–US defence cooperation, as well as to the Canada–US relationship in the variety of other dimensions explored in this volume.

Much attention has been accorded over the years to the idea that one of the US's security and defence partners surely *must* be the fairest of them all, in the sense of being the most "special" partner of Washington. For many, should Canada *not* be deemed to hold this status, it becomes a matter calling for some lamentation and much remediation. Others, however, take a less alarmist attitude, holding the possible loss of perceived status associated with not being in a special relationship with the US to be a matter of indifference, possibly even – to a few – a cause for celebration, signifying in their minds Canada's autonomy in security and defence policy.

In this chapter, we use the recent debate that has swirled around an entity called AUKUS (Australia, United Kingdom [UK], and the US) to contextualize and update the question of Canada–US defence relations. The acronym relates not to some exotic ornithological species but to a trilateral defence accord announced in September 2021 between the three countries. Significantly (perhaps), Canada was not included in this arrangement, an omission that has rekindled in some minds the kind of soul-searching that intermittently takes place in scholarly and policy-making circles in this country, so well reflected in the editors' introductory chapter in this volume. In what follows, we use the AUKUS accord as a vehicle for elaborating upon what we take to be the essential features of Canada–US defence and security cooperation. We will argue, in the chapter's next section, that in some non-trivial empirical sense, the Canadian–US relationship really *does* deserve to be considered a behaviourally "special" one. Following this conceptual and theoretical section come two further sections, respectively, a discussion of the details of the September 2021 arrangement and a conclusion that queries what, if anything, AUKUS tells us about the status of Canada–US defence cooperation.

"Special Relationships" in Theoretical and Comparative Context

Ever since Britain's once and future prime minister Winston Churchill baptized the Anglo-American relationship a "special" one in a March 1946 speech in Fulton, Missouri, there has been an endless outpouring of scholarly writing on the generic topic, to say nothing of the particular variants of this genre of interstate relationship, said to be unusual because of its presumption that states, like people, can be "friends." Churchill's speech is mostly remembered for his insertion of a powerful metaphor into debates about the post–Second World War security environment. He evoked that metaphor, the "Iron Curtain," to draw attention to the urgency of Western countries' adopting a robust response to what was looking very much like an attempt by the recent Soviet ally to reserve for itself as much of Central and Eastern Europe as it was capable of bringing into its political and military orbit. Although we invariably recall Churchill as the originator of this figure of speech, others had in fact used it before him (Ryan 1979, 897–8).

No less significant, but definitely more original, was a second figure of speech employed in that same 1946 address: the "special relationship." Although usually interpreted as calling for a particularly close security and defence partnership between the US and *the UK*, Churchill's vision was not simply a bilateral one. He advocated a "fraternal association of the English-speaking peoples. This means a special relationship between the British Commonwealth and Empire and the United States" (Reynolds 1989, 94). This time, no one appears to have beaten Churchill to the semantic punch, for unlike the Iron Curtain, this second metaphor truly was "a Churchillian invention" (Edelman 2010, 29). More than that, it expressed, as we know, a vision geographically commodious enough to embrace Canada. Its origins can be traced to late 1945, when Churchill, now a member of the Opposition, saw fit to instruct his Downing Street successor, Clement Attlee, about to make a trip to the US, that "we should fortify in every way our special and friendly connections with the United States," and that "we should not abandon our special relationship with the United States *and Canada* about the atomic bomb" (Rasmussen and McCormick 1993, 516).

"Special relationship" may have been a Churchillian term of wartime provenance, but the idea intended to be advanced by its invocation had a considerably longer pedigree than that. Visions of "special" security relations between the two leading English-speaking powers had been dancing in the heads of quite a few intellectuals and policy elites on both sides of the Atlantic since the late nineteenth century. These visions were grandiose ones, aimed at preparing the ground for nothing less than the establishment of a "universal peace" predicated on close political and military bonds between the "Anglo-Saxon" peoples (Anderson 1981; Bell 2014; Vucetic 2017). Over time, those bonds would materialize in the form of an Anglo-American special relationship (AASR), regularly taken to represent the platinum standard for close bilateral ties between sovereign states on matters appertaining to defence and security. True, not all analysts buy into this assertion, rejecting outright claims about the relevance (some hold, even the existence!) of the AASR.[1] The critics to the contrary notwithstanding, however, we believe this platinum standard to be of heuristic value; with it as a template, we assess, in this section, the quality of the Canada–US defence and security relationship, which we think clearly constitutes a special relationship.

Before we proceed to that demonstration, we need to define "special," for if we fail to specify what we take this adjective to imply, we will not get terribly far in our bid to determine the impact (if any) of AUKUS upon the Canada–US defence and security relationship. International relations (IR) scholars have long tended to give a wide berth to the supposition that states might actually be, or become, "friends,"[2] and since it is friendship that many take routinely to be the most relevant marker of "specialness," it follows that there is a natural basis for the skepticism expressed by many, in Canada and elsewhere, as to the utility of the term special relationship. We find this skepticism about the term's utility to be misguided, for while it may indeed be the case that friendship is a somewhat anomalous category in world politics, it hardly follows that for a relationship to be deemed a special one it must also be a regularly amicable one. While countries can certainly have cordial relations with any number of other countries – and might even be considered "friends" with some of these – amicability in and of itself does *not* a special relationship make. Something else is involved in this business of identifying and analyzing special relationships.

The place to begin looking for that "something else" is with the meaning of specialness, which, as used in IR, is a concept whose definition is anything but self-evident. Notwithstanding all the scholarly attention lavished, understandably so, upon the US–UK tandem, this is far from representing the sole instance of the US's being connected with another country in a manner so noteworthy as to merit employment of the adjective *special*. Not too many years ago, President George H.W. Bush was proclaiming Germany to be the US's emergent "partner in leadership."[3] But the mood changed so radically with the passage of time that during the tumultuous Trump years, few would have wished to wager their life savings on Berlin–Washington replacing London–Washington as the *ne plus ultra*[4] of special partnerships!

Besides the UK and Germany, in recent decades various other countries have been nominated as special security and defence partners of the US. This list, hardly an exhaustive one, could include Canada, Australia, New Zealand, the Netherlands, and Israel (Dumbrell and Schäfer 2009). But before we can figure out what, if anything, such a qualitatively distinctive partnership must entail, we need to return to this chore of definition. Standard dictionary renderings of the adjective tend to treat it in one of two ways, as either an affective concept or a behavioural one. In the case of the first usage, special conveys a *normative* judgment, usually a positive such judgment (as in the assertion that people or states can be each other's "best" friend). In the case of the latter usage, special can be understood as referring to a particular quality that sets whatever is being assessed apart descriptively from other cases, especially from those that can, at first glance, be taken to be so comparable as to be virtually identical. The emphasis here gets placed upon observable *behavioural* differences among comparable cases. In the words of a leading British expert on this kind of relationship, "'special' is an obvious marker of something beyond the ordinary; the mundane is elevated discursively to a higher significance" (Marsh 2020, 38).

It is the behavioural, or empirical, sense of special that guides our analysis in this chapter, although we do not deny or intend to minimize the idea that "history" might have made Canada and the US the kind of friends that President John F. Kennedy's words quoted in this volume's title suggest they have become.[5] Still, Canada and the US have their own rosters of other friends, with these days Germany looming more and more, in some minds, as Canada's very own partner in leadership.[6] So to heed the implied injunction of Steve Marsh, we need to specify what it is about the quality of Canada–US security and defence cooperation that warrants it being regarded as special because it bespeaks, in his words, "something beyond the ordinary." We think that there are, objectively, three things that do set Canada–US defence and security relations apart from other otherwise comparable relations either state has with any other ally.

The first of these is the nature of the North American "security community." By security community we mean an order in which the use of force as a means of conflict resolution between members of the group has simply become inconceivable, so that they neither go to war against one another nor even consider doing so. Whatever problems arise between them, they undertake to resolve peacefully. With neither organized armed conflict nor the threat of such conflict playing a part in the resolution of intra-group problems, policy-makers and other policy elites are able to entertain "dependable expectations" that peaceful change will be the only kind of change that occurs (Adler and Barnett 1957).

There are, of course, any number of security communities in existence, but the Canada–US dyad can be taken to be special in two senses. It is remarkably stable, with few if any sentient observers prepared to risk their reputation (or sanity) worrying out loud about a war erupting between the two countries (Adler and Barnett 1998; Deutsch 1957).[7] Even more singular is the longevity of the Canada–US security community, thought by many to be special because it is often held to be the first pluralistic security community ever to have come into existence between neighbours *anywhere* in the world. Admittedly, some scholars accord the honour of being first to another region, Scandinavia, where following Norway's 1905 separation from Sweden a long period of peaceful conflict resolution came to characterize their bilateral relationship.[8] Indeed, if we were to date the definitive arrival of the Canada–US tandem into the "zone of peace" from the two states' abandonment of war plans against each other, then it would seem the Scandinavians did beat the North Americans off the mark, since it was not until the second half of the 1930s that Washington ceased wasting taxpayers' dollars paying military officers to plan the use of force against their neighbour – something Ottawa had ceased doing early in the 1920s.

By contrast, the Scandinavians stopped this wasteful and pointless activity a few years ahead of the North Americans, the 1920s being the years in which both Oslo and Stockholm abandoned planning for military contingencies against each other (Ericson 2000). However, they could not manage to sustain their security community unbroken over the years, for the Nazi conquest of Norway in April 1940 suspended, for a time, the latter's sovereign status, effectively placing into suspension as well the Scandinavian security community. So even if, as some scholars maintain, the two regional security communities came into existence more or less at the same time and independently of each other,[9] there can be no question that only one of those, the Canada–US security community, has enjoyed an unbroken existence since its origins. This has to be considered impressive, all the more so in light of recent developments in Europe and elsewhere that highlight how being a country's neighbour is no guarantee that "neighbourliness" invariably corresponds with peacefulness. It might even, if Russia is to be our guide, be regarded as an invitation to military aggression.

The second way in which Canada and the US can be said to be behaviourally special relates to their alliance, both its longevity and its multidimensional nature. Unlike with the Canada–US security community, the starting date of which remains a matter of legitimate debate, it is easy to specify when the Canada–US alliance came into existence and to say what makes it so special empirically. It dates from an agreement struck by President Franklin D. Roosevelt and Prime Minister William Lyon Mackenzie King in the upstate New York town of Ogdensburg on 18 August 1940 (Gibson and Rossie 1993). Significantly, it remains to this day the US's oldest unbroken alliance, notwithstanding the mistaken view of so many that the accolade really belongs to the 1778 alliance the US struck with France – an alliance that so many tend to forget expired in 1800.

In time, the first institutional embodiment of that August 1940 alliance, the Permanent Joint Board on Defence (PJBD) (Conliffe 1989), would be supplemented with, and to an extent eclipsed by, newer institutional means of strengthening North American defence cooperation, among the most important of these being the Military Cooperation Committee (MCC) of 1946 and the North American Air (now Aerospace) Defense Command (NORAD) of 1958. To these must be added a thick network of other accords, committees, and arrangements pertaining to North American defence, whose numbers are no easy matter to keep count of, which testifies to the "complex interdependence" of Canada–US security and defence relations. Thus, in a manner different from most of the US's transatlantic relations, the US and Canada were solidly allied (if not always in total agreement when it came to perceiving and responding to threats) nine years before the formation of the North Atlantic Treaty Organization (NATO) and would almost certainly still be allied had the latter organization never come into existence.

The third and final distinctive behavioural aspect of Canada–US defence and security cooperation concerns "homeland security," broadly construed as continental defence. This third aspect, call it the "Kingston Dispensation" (Haglund 2023), is the most noteworthy of all. It sets the Canada–US defence relationship so behaviourally apart from either state's other bilateral relationships as to warrant, even in the absence of the two other attributes discussed above, Canada–US relations being deemed special. It is not to be equated with either security community or alliance, although it clearly relates to both. Instead, this "dispensation" establishes the relationship between the two North American countries on a distinctly different plane from any of the defence and security linkages either has with allies elsewhere. It does so because it sets out the boundary conditions for the two countries' participation in continental security: neither is permitted, nor permits itself, the luxury of believing that defending North America can be its exclusive responsibility.

The norm dates from the August 1938 Sudetenland crisis, which presaged the imminent outbreak of another European war. During this crisis atmosphere, President Roosevelt told an audience at Queen's University in Kingston, Ontario, that America would "not stand idly by" were the physical security of Canada threatened by a European adversary as a consequence of the country's participation in a European war. This was the first time ever that an American leader extended a commitment to safeguard Canadian physical security against a foreign aggressor (not named, but clearly Germany). For his part, Prime Minister Mackenzie King, speaking a few days later in Woodbridge, Ontario, made a reciprocal commitment: he pledged that Canada would ensure that nothing it did would jeopardize the physical security of the US. Taken together, the two leaders' remarks reflected a new dispensation that would constitute the unalterable normative core of North American security: henceforth, each country understood that it had a "neighbourly" obligation to the other not only to refrain from any activities that might imperil the security of the other but also to demonstrate nearly as much solicitude for the other's physical security needs as for its own (MacCormac 1940).

For more than eight decades, the Kingston Dispensation has represented the most important constitutive norm in the realm of Canada–US defence and security cooperation. It, along with the two other features of Canada–US security and defence cooperation we have discussed in this section, provides the empirical (behavioural) baseline for assessing what it means when we refer to the bilateral relationship as a special one. Indeed, in light of the evidence mustered in this section, it would be difficult to avoid concluding that if the Canada–US defence and security relationship is not a "special" one, then no such relationship, not even the AASR, can be said to exist.

Against this empirical backdrop, in the next section we assess the challenge that some argue AUKUS presents to the Canada–US special relationship.

The AUKUS "Challenge"

In mid-September 2021, President Joseph R. Biden Jr was joined by British Prime Minister Boris Johnson and Australian Prime Minister Scott Morrison in a virtual unveiling of a new trilateral security arrangement, AUKUS (White House 2022). This quickly dominated the headlines, for several reasons. First and foremost was the news that the US had agreed to share its nuclear submarine technology with Australia so that it could possess and operate nuclear-powered attack submarines for the Royal Australian Navy (RAN). Nuclear-powered attack submarines, or SSNs in American military classification, constitute a formidable military platform, even though they are not intended to carry nuclear weaponry (and thus should never be confused with a related acronym, SSBN, standing for nuclear-propelled ballistic missile submarine).

What distinguishes SSNs from conventionally powered submarines is that the latter are propelled by a more finite energy supply (diesel), which limits their operational capabilities and ranges. SSNs, by contrast, are powered by nuclear reactors that do not require refuelling for years (possibly as many as twenty-five), which allows them to stay on station for a greater length of time (US Environmental Protection Agency 2018). Furthermore, SSNs are far stealthier than diesel-electric submarines, whose combustion engines generate more noise because they make significant demands on air intake, associated with their frequent need to recharge batteries. SSNs are also faster than diesel-electric submarines. This means that SSNs contribute to deterrence even though they do not deploy weapons of mass destruction, by dint of their ability greatly to complicate the decisions and calculations of a foe. And should deterrence fail and fighting break out, they can attack enemy targets at sea and even, in some cases, on shore (if equipped with cruise missiles) (Szondy 2017).

Granting Australia access to this military technology is politically significant, for two important reasons. The first is that the US has only shared this type of technology with one other country. That country is the UK, starting in 1958, when Washington amended the Atomic Energy Act and gave Britain, in the words of two scholars, "what had been refused almost a decade earlier: a free exchange of nuclear information" (Dawson and Rosecrance 1966, 49–50). For this reason alone, AUKUS represents a highly exclusive club – one whose membership doubled overnight, with two American allies now being deemed worthy of such cooperation and technology sharing.

Second, prior to the announcement of AUKUS, Australia had agreed to buy from France some AUS$66 billion worth of conventionally powered submarines, in what would have been France's largest-ever sale of military equipment. The sudden and abrupt cancellation of the deal angered France so deeply that it recalled for consultation its ambassadors to both Australia and the US. And while ties between the latter country and France had known far greater strains in recent years – including and especially tensions occasioned by the 2003 invasion of Iraq[10] – relations between Paris and Canberra plummeted to their lowest point ever. For France, the loss of this submarine deal represented more than the cancellation of a lucrative contract; it also struck at the very heart of national pride by calling into question its status as a global power with important political, military, and territorial interests of its own in the Indo-Pacific. France considers itself, and in many ways is, a resident power in the Indo-Pacific due its territorial holdings (especially New Caledonia) and naval bases in the region. Accordingly, it had been fashioning its own Indo-Pacific strategy within which Australia was envisioned as a key pillar of France's enduring presence. By cutting France out of its submarine deal, Washington and its two partners were partly cutting France off from Indo-Pacific affairs. As well, they were certainly annoying their important ally (Kauffmann 2021).

AUKUS is not simply about SSNs, as important as those submarines are. The second major feature of the September 2021 announcement was its commitment to trilateral cooperation across a broader range of domains including cyber security, artificial intelligence, quantum computing, hypersonic missile technology, and unmanned underwater vehicles. While some observers, including Canada's prime minister, Justin Trudeau, initially branded AUKUS a mere submarine purchasing deal for Australia (Connolly 2022), it is actually much more than that.

This gets us to the third notable feature of the announcement of AUKUS: it is less about what should be done than it is about whom it should be done *against*. While press releases from the White House did not list any specific adversary AUKUS is intended to counter, one does not need to be a soothsayer to realize that the other areas of cooperation included in the pact bespeak a desire by the US and its partners to parry Chinese efforts to attain dominance over the "commanding heights" of global technology, with all the implications that such dominance would have for the future of an international system in which the currency of military capability is technological capability.

The two dimensions of AUKUS – military with the SSNs and technological with the other elements of the package – converge on the question of Taiwan's future, which very much has to be considered the Banquo's ghost lurking in the background of this pact. The White House's affirmation, in April 2022, of AUKUS as reflecting a commitment to a "free and open Indo-Pacific, and more broadly to an international system that respects human rights, the rule of law, and the peaceful resolution of disputes free from coercion," may not have singled out Taiwan, but one would have had to have been extremely obtuse to miss the affirmation's meaning (White House 2022). Yet, it was not just Taiwan that AUKUS was intended to safeguard. The agreement is aimed at strengthening an American bulwark against Chinese military power more generally in the Indo-Pacific; as such, it marks a major step in the "pivot to Asia" strategy first introduced during the administration of Barack Obama.[11] While China, to no one's surprise, condemned the announcement of AUKUS in its customary bombastic manner (Girard 2021), other countries in the Indo-Pacific region, including some American allies, had concerns of their own.

Those concerns tended to be focused on two possibilities. The first is the prospect that AUKUS might trigger a regional arms race. The second, related to the first, adds *nuclear* weaponry to the mix, the argument being that somehow Australia's acquisition of SSNs will encourage nuclear proliferation. According to those who fret about this second possibility, it is unrealistic to imagine that Australia will long remain the only country in the world to operate SSNs without at the same time possessing nuclear weapons of its own. Those entertaining this fear think it will only be a matter of time before the highly enriched uranium (HEU) needed by the RAN to fuel its boats is slightly further enriched so as to enable the development of nuclear weapons.

Of course, for Australia to make the transition from reactor-grade uranium to weapons-grade HEU, it would need to possess its own enrichment facilities rather than simply purchase the fuel from allies with those facilities, France possibly among them. Australia is the world's third-leading exporter of natural uranium, but it does not enrich the metal, nor does it have any plans to do so. But, say the worriers, even if Australia never enters the enrichment business, its acquisition of SSNs will set a precedent for other countries to pursue SSN development by breaking norms surrounding arms control and encouraging other US allies to lobby for access to the technology (Kapetas 2021).

These concerns are largely overblown and echo similar objections that had been registered a generation earlier, when Canada was thinking of acquiring SSNs, a desire that had been showcased with the publication of the 1987 white paper on defence (Government of Canada 1987, 52–5). In the end, Canada never did purchase the SSNs, which, in an ironic twist on the AUKUS imbroglio, would likely have been French boats of the *Améthyste/Rubis* class, because the US Navy (USN) did not at the time look with favour upon Canada's acquiring SSNs, thus it could veto, and likely would have vetoed, any British transfer of *Trafalgar*-class SSNs to Canada (Haglund 1989). Yet neither the USN nor the disarmament community managed to accomplish what budgetary realities, coupled with the fortuitous ending of the Cold War, were able to do, which was to convince Ottawa to scupper the project altogether.

Still, the AUKUS announcement is not without implications. We have already noted China's displeasure with the pact, as well as that of France. Each of these countries could not reasonably have been expected to be pleased with AUKUS. But what of those two allies who, along with the AUKUS trio, constitute the exclusive intelligence sharing club known as the Five Eyes? Presumably, they might feel a bit annoyed at having been cut out of the action? Those countries are New Zealand and Canada. Since it is only the latter that is of interest to us in this chapter, we will simply note apropos of the former that, from where we sit, there does not seem to have been any palpable wringing of hands and gnashing of teeth on the part of the Kiwis. Besides, Wellington has had a long-standing and well-publicized allergy to anyone's using nuclear technology for military purposes, so it cannot be imagined that policy-makers in the capital have lost too much sleep about the apparent "snub," if that is what it is (see McClure 2021).[12]

The case of Canada, however, is different. In theory, AUKUS's formation should concern Ottawa, not least because Canada is much more of a Pacific Rim country than the UK and shares with the latter an interest in salvaging as much as possible of what remains of the American-led liberal international order in our current era of "deglobalization" (see Ripsman 2021). Moreover, any great power war that arises in this region would almost certainly place Canada in a bind, even if it were not directly involved, because it is so closely aligned with the US. China's "wolf warrior" (and self-defeating) diplomacy of recent years has certainly not made a practice of sparing Canadian sensibilities, with the country being disparaged for being "America's lapdog" (Hopper 2019) as well as being castigated for a host of other failings.[13]

So, it might have been supposed that Justin Trudeau's government would have taken umbrage not just at Beijing for its insulting behaviour but also at Washington, London, and Canberra for not bringing Canada into an arrangement that, whatever Trudeau happens to believe, is about much more than nuclear-propelled submarines. This is all the more so given that some analysts believe, possibly correctly, that the formation of AUKUS constitutes the most significant American alliance development in the Indo-Pacific region since the Second World War (Mix and Vaughn 2022). Whether or not AUKUS is more significant than America's post–Second World War bilateral defence treaties with Japan, South Korea, the Philippines, and even (for a time) Taiwan – to say nothing of its trilateral alliance with Australia and New Zealand – there can be little question that Canada was taken as much by surprise as was France by the announcement of the pact (Fife and Chase 2021). But does it also follow that Canada's not being in AUKUS constitutes a reason for us to join the lengthening line of analysts who, approvingly or not, have been reading the last rites for the Canada–US special relationship for as long as anyone can remember? We think not, for reasons we explain in the next, concluding, section of our chapter.

Conclusion: Does Special Mean "Better"?

In this chapter we have advanced two major claims. The first is that there are important empirical differences that so set Canada's alliance with the US apart from America's other set of allies as to warrant its being regarded as a special relationship – one that might even be, with a nod to George Orwell's famous assessment of the status of the pigs on the revolutionary animal farm, regarded as "more special" than America's other special relationships (Orwell 1951).[14] But does it follow that special, or even "more special," must also mean better, or even best, when it comes to assessing the affective qualities of the bilateral relationship? This question goes to the heart of the current angst expressed in some quarters by Canada's not being part of AUKUS and does so irrespective of whether Canada was excluded from the pact, or simply chose not to take part in it.

Our argument in this chapter has been that AUKUS in and of itself does not constitute a basis for anyone claiming that Canadian non-involvement has put paid to the notion of a special Canada–US relationship in security and defence, at least when that category is measured in accordance with its empirically observable, behavioural attributes, as these have been made manifest in the two countries' security community, their alliance, and their embrace of the Kingston Dispensation.

But, in closing, we could well ask whether Canada's non-involvement in AUKUS suggests that the US has, in the *affective* sense, "better" relations with both the UK and Australia than it does with Canada. In particular, we might wonder whether Australia has somehow outdistanced Canada in the category of a "good" ally, and we could note that if so, AUKUS would be the proof of that pudding. This focus on Australia rather than on the UK would be all the more relevant given that Canada and Australia, being more or less "equally" sized countries, make a more useful comparative dyad than Canada and the UK, for obvious reasons. To cite a leading work on the topic of Canada–Australia relations in security and defence, the two countries are nothing less than "strategic cousins" (Blaxland 2006), having more in common with each other than either has with anyone else.

To those who measure Canada against Australia, and find that the comparison does not flatter Canada, the problem exemplified by AUKUS is that Canada's not being part of the arrangement testifies to two apparent realities. The first is that Australia takes security more seriously than Canada does, a criticism made recently in a hard-hitting report on Canadian national security produced by the University of Ottawa, whose authors worry that Canada is basically asleep at the wheel in the current darkening global security environment (Task Force on National Security 2022). The second apparent reality, and the one of greater relevance for the theme of this volume and our chapter, is that Canadian non-involvement in AUKUS puts the lie to claims about the solidity of Canada–US defence and security, held to be special no more – if indeed it ever *had* been!

We have already stated our views on the Canada–US special relationship. In closing, two observations require being made about Canada–Australia comparison(s). The first is simply that AUKUS is a regional-security undertaking, and while Canada certainly does have security interests in the Indo-Pacific, these are not as significant as its interests in other regions of more immediate concern to it, namely North America and Europe, nor can they hold a candle to Australia's own security interest in Asian regional security. Canada, yes, has some interests in the Asia-Pacific; Australia, by contrast, *lives* there. It makes a difference. Seen in this way, the surprise is not so much that Canada is outside of AUKUS as it is that anyone should have imagined it to have been an obvious candidate for inclusion. And while a case can be made that the non-SSN aspects of AUKUS suggest reasons for Canadian participation, the reality is that Ottawa is already involved with the US in a variety of those other spheres of defence technology identified above. Contemplated in this light, Canada's being "left out" of AUKUS turns out to be as unremarkable as Australia's being "left out" of NORAD or NATO.

And this gets us to our second, and last, comment. There is a reason why Australia does give the impression that it takes security more seriously than Canada. The very same conditions that we described above in discussing the Kingston Dispensation – conditions that ensure (indeed, oblige) tight bilateral cooperation in matters of homeland security – ironically grant Canada a certain freedom from alliance constraint beyond the North American continent. For the Kingston Dispensation testifies to the existence of what has been termed an American "involuntary" (sometimes "automatic") guarantee of Canada's own physical security. This guarantee can be perceived in a minatory way by some Canadians who ponder the cost – political but also economic – of securing for the country "defence against help" (Ørvik 1984).

Notwithstanding its alleged menacing aspects, to say nothing of the potential implications of such security (inter)dependence upon the national ego, the American guarantee does provide a temptation for Canadian leaders, no matter their political stripe, to seek to spend less on defence than would be the case in the absence of the guarantee. The temptation is a powerful one, and it proves all too easy for sentient policy-makers to succumb to it. Who can blame them, if political decisions are supposed to be a function of "rational" action, with rationality construed in terms of a sustainable match between the ends and means of policy? For if the end be that of defending Canada against attack by the US, no imaginable means could be conjured forth to attain it, should America decide to emulate Vladimir Putin and assault its neighbour. Conversely, if the US can be counted upon to safeguard Canada's physical security against anyone else (or *everyone* else, for that matter), then there exists an incentive to do no more than what is minimally required to satisfy the Americans that Canada is pulling its weight (national dignity, on the other hand, might demand more than this minimum, but that is a different matter).

Joel Sokolsky has cogently summarized the ongoing challenge faced by Canadian leaders pondering which level of commitment is sufficient to keep Washington minimally satisfied: "The current policy," he wrote at the start of the twenty-first century, "is very much in the Canadian tradition of asking *not* 'How much is enough?' but rather, 'How much is just enough?'" (Sokolsky 2000, 31). That amount is easier to determine when it concerns North American security, harder to assess when global security is in question, for the good reason that Canadians, unlike geographically distant US allies, do not have to ask themselves, in the way for instance that Australians do, whether support for a US overseas endeavour (for instance, the 2003 invasion of Iraq) might make sense as a means of purchasing insurance for some future contingency, when an American reciprocal gesture would come in more than handy.

Canada, like it or not, *has* that insurance policy, as an entitlement established by propinquity. Australia lacks such an entitlement. And that, it seems to us, is the deeper meaning of AUKUS. Whatever else that arrangement does, it does not negate the very special Canada–US relationship in matters appertaining to security and defence.

Notes

1 For some skeptical, not to say cynical, assessments of the AASR, see Lagadec (2012); Arnold (2014); Mumford (2017); and especially Ingram (1997).

2 For a thoughtful commentary on this tendency, see Berenskoetter (2007); and Oelsner and Vion (2011).

3 Bush made this claim in an early 1989 speech in Mainz and repeated it in Berlin late the following year; see Mensel (1992, 81–109).

4 To use the term employed by one scholar (Webb 2020, 296), who notes that, alone among special relationships, the Anglo-American one is regularly signified through employment of the definite article, signalling it is "*the* special relationship ne plus ultra [emphasis added]."

5 A competing, and oft-quoted, reference is the backhanded compliment to amicability uttered during the Diefenbaker era by Social Credit leader Robert Thomson that "the United States is our friend, whether we like it or not" (Thomson quoted in Azzi 2015, 162).

6 For one particularly hopeful expression of the potential gains from this partnership, see Kinsman and Rowswell (2022). The idea of a special Canada–Germany relationship is far from new. Contrasting perspectives on the validity of the trope are offered in Dolata-Kreutzkamp and Kitchen (2008); and Rempel (1996).

7 On the stability of the Canada–US security community, see Roussel (2004).

8 On that breakup, see Stolleis (2005).

9 As argued by Lebow (1994).

10 The best source on the impact of Iraq upon Franco-American relations is Bozo (2017). Also see, more broadly, Gordon and Shapiro (2004).

11 On the origins of that strategy, see Dian (2015).

12 For an overview of the strains introduced by New Zealand's anti-nuclear policy on its key alliance relations, see Janiewski (2009).

13 For two books chronicling the downward trajectory of Canada–China relations over the past decade, see Evans (2014); and Hampson and Blanchfield (2021).

14 The reference is to Orwell's critique of the perpetuation of oppression under communism, expressed in the slogan painted on Farmer Jones's barn by the revolutionary junta of pigs: "All the animals are equal, but some are more equal than others" (Orwell 1951, 114).

References

Adler, Emanuel, and Michael N. Barnett, eds. 1998. *Security Communities.* Cambridge: Cambridge University Press.

Anderson, Stuart. 1981. *Race and Rapprochement: Anglo-Saxonism and Anglo-American Relations, 1895–1904.* Rutherford: Fairleigh Dickinson University Press.

Arnold, Guy. 2014. *America and Britain: Was There Ever a Special Relationship?* London: Hurst.

Azzi, Stephen. 2015. *Reconcilable Differences: A History of Canada–US Relations.* Toronto: Oxford University Press.

Bell, Duncan. 2014. "Before the Democratic Peace: Racial Unionism, Empire, and the Abolition of War." *European Journal of International Relations* 20: 647–70. doi:https://doi.org/10.1177/1354066113497491.

Berenskoetter, Felix. 2007. "Friends, There Are No Friends? An Intimate Reframing of the International." *Millennium: Journal of International Studies* 35: 647–76. doi:https://doi.org/10.1177/03058298070350031501.

Blaxland, John C. 2006. *Strategic Cousins: Australian and Canadian Expeditionary Forces and the British and American Empires.* Montreal and Kingston: McGill-Queen's University Press.

Bozo, Frédéric. 2017. *A History of the Iraq Crisis: France, the United States, and Iraq, 1991–2003*. Translated by Susan Emanuel. Washington and New York: Woodrow Wilson Center Press and Columbia University Press.

Conliffe, Christopher. 1989. "The Permanent Joint Board on Defense, 1940–1988." In *The US–Canada Security Relationship: The Politics, Strategy, and Technology of Defense*, edited by David G. Haglund and Joel J. Sokolsky, 45–65. Boulder: Westview Press.

Connolly, Amanda. 2022. "Was Canada Invited to Join AUKUS? Officials Mum but Stress No Interest in Subs." *Global News*, 22 May. https://globalnews.ca/news/8196164/aukus-defence-deal-canada-china-relations.

Dawson, Raymond, and Richard Rosecrance. 1996. "Theory and Reality in the Anglo-American Alliance." *World Politics* 19: 21–51. doi: https://doi.org/10.2307/2009841.

Deutsch, Karl W. 1957. *Political Community and the North Atlantic Area: International Organization in the Light of Historical Experience*. Princeton: Princeton University Press.

Dian, Matteo. 2015. "The Pivot to Asia, Air-Sea Battle, and Contested Commons in the Asia Pacific Region." *Pacific Review* 28, no. 2: 237–57. doi:https://doi.org/10.1080/09512748.2014.995124.

Dolata-Kreutzkamp, Petra, and Veronica Kitchen. 2008. "Canada, Germany, Canada–Germany: Relations in the Third Dimension." *International Journal* 63, no. 3: 527–31. doi:https://doi.org/10.1177/002070200806300302.

Dumbrell, John, and Axel R. Schäfer, eds. 2009. *America's "Special Relationships": Foreign and Domestic Aspects of the Politics of Alliance*. London: Routledge.

Edelman, Eric. 2010. "A Special Relationship in Jeopardy." *The American Interest*, July, 25–34.

Ericson, Magnus. 2000. "A Realist Stable Peace: Power, Threat, and the Development of a Shared Norwegian–Swedish Democratic Security Identity, 1905–1940." PhD diss., Lund University, Sweden.

Evans, Paul. 2014. *Engaging China: Myth, Aspiration, and Strategy in Canadian Policy from Trudeau to Harper*. Toronto: University of Toronto Press.

Fife, Robert, and Steven Chase. 2021. "Canada Caught Off Guard by New Security Pact between U.S., Australia, and Britain." *Globe and Mail*, 17 September. https://www.theglobeandmail.com/politics/article-canadian-government-surprised-by-new-indo-pacific-security-pact.

Gibson, Frederick W., and Jonathan G. Rossie, eds. 1993. *The Road to Ogdensburg: The Queen's/St Lawrence Conferences on Canadian-American Affairs, 1935–1941*. East Lansing: Michigan State University Press.

Girard, Bonnie. 2021. "China's AUKUS Response Highlights Beijing's Bunker Mentality." *The Diplomat*, 30 September. https://thediplomat.com/2021/10/chinas-aukus-response-highlights-beijings-bunker-mentality.

Gordon, Philip H., and Jeremy Shapiro. 2004. *Allies at War: America, Europe, and the Crisis Over Iraq*. New York: McGraw-Hill.

Government of Canada, Department of National Defence. 1987. *Challenge and Commitment: A Defence Policy for Canada*. Ottawa: Minister of Supply and Services, 52–5.

Haglund, David G. 1989. "The SSNs and the Question of Nonproliferation." In *The US–Canada Security Relationship: The Politics, Strategy, and Technology of Defence*, edited by David G. Haglund and Joel Sokolsky, 239–66. Boulder: Westview Press.

– 2023. "The 'Kingston Dispensation' and the North American Stable Peace." In *The Legacy of 9/11: Views from North America*, edited by Andrea Charron, Alexander Moens, and Stéphane Roussel. Montreal and Kingston: McGill-Queen's University Press.

Hampson, Fen Osler, and Mike Blanchfield. 2021. *The Two Michaels: Innocent Canadian Captives and High Stakes Espionage in the US–China Cyber War*. Toronto: Sutherland House.

Hopper, Tristin. 2019. "'Canada Is a White Supremacist Foreign Enemy': A Sample of Chinese Media's Recent Canada Bashing." *National Post*, 25 January. https://nationalpost.com/news/canada/canada-is-a-naive-american-lapdog-what-chinese-media-has-been-saying-about-us.

Ingram, Edward. 1997. "The Wonderland of the Political Scientist." *International Security* 22: 53–63. doi:https://doi.org/10.2307/2539328.

Janiewski, Dolores E. 2009. "Yearning and Spurning: New Zealand's Special Relationships with Britain and the United States." In *America's "Special Relationships,"* edited by John Drumbell and Axel R. Schäfer, 93–114. London: Routledge.

Kapetas, Anastasia. 2021. "Limiting the Nuclear-Proliferation Blowback from the AUKUS Submarine Deal." *The ASPI Strategist*. 21 September. https://www.aspistrategist.org.au/limiting-the-nuclear-proliferation-blowback-from-the-aukus-submarine-deal.

Kauffmann, Sylvie. 2021. "No Wonder the French Are Angry." *New York Times*, 22 September. https://www.nytimes.com/2021/09/22/opinion/france-us-china-submarines.html.

Kinsman, Jeremy, and Ben Rowswell. 2022. "Opinion: Germany and Canada Can Work Together to Reinforce Democratic Values." *Globe and Mail*, 23 August. https://www.theglobeandmail.com/opinion/article-germany-and-canada-can-work-together-to-reinforce-democratic-values.

Lagadec, Erwan. 2012. *Transatlantic Relations in the 21st Century: Europe, America, and the Rise of the Rest*. London: Routledge.

Lebow, Richard N. 1994. "The Long Peace, the End of the Cold War, and the Failure of Realism." *International Organization* 48: 249–77. doi:https://doi.org/10.1017/S0020818300028186.

MacCormac, John. 1940. *Canada: America's Problem*. New York: Viking.

Marsh, Steve. 2020. "Beyond Essential: Britons and the Anglo-American Special Relationship." *Journal of Transatlantic Studies* 18: 382–404. doi:http://dx.doi.org/10.1057/s42738-020-00054-x.

McClure, Tess. 2021. "AUKUS Submarines Banned from New Zealand as Pact Exposes Divide with Western Allies." *The Guardian*, 16 September. https://www.theguardian.com/world/2021/sep/16/aukus-submarines-banned-as-pact-exposes-divide-between-new-zealand-and-western-allies.

Mensel, Klaus-Dieter. 1992. "The United States and the United Germany: Partners in Leadership?" In *Can America Remain Committed? US Security Horizons in the 1990s*, edited by David G. Haglund, 81–109. Boulder: Westview Press.

Mix, Derek E., and Bruce Vaughn. 2022. "AUKUS and Indo-Pacific Security." Congressional Research Service. 19 May. https://crsreports.congress.gov/product/pdf/IF/IF12113.

Mumford, Andrew. 2017. *Counterinsurgency Wars and the Anglo-American Alliance: The Special Relationship on the Rocks*. Washington, DC: Georgetown University Press.

Oelsner, Andrea, and Antoine Vion, Eds. 2011. "Special Issue: Friendship in International Relations." *International Politics* 48: 1–9.

Ørvik, Nils. 1984. "Canadian Security and 'Defence Against Help.'" *Survival* 42: 26–31. doi:https://doi.org/10.1080/00396338408442145.

Orwell, George. 1951. *Animal Farm: A Fairy Story*. Harmondsworth: Penguin Books.

Rasmussen, Jorgen, and James M. McCormick. 1993. "British Mass Perceptions of the Anglo–American Special Relationship," *Political Science Quarterly* 108: 515–41. doi:https://doi.org/10.2307/2151702.

Rempel, Roy. 1996. *Counterweights: The Failure of Canada's German and European Policy, 1955–1995*. Montreal and Kingston: McGill-Queen's University Press.

Reynolds, David. 1989. "Re-Thinking Anglo–American Relations." *International Affairs* 65: 89–111. doi: https://doi.org/10.2307/2620984.

Ripsman, Norrin M. 2021. "Globalization, Deglobalization, and Great Power Politics." *International Affairs* 97: 1317–33. doi:https://doi.org/10.1093/ia/iiab091.

Roussel, Stéphane. 2004. *The North American Democratic Peace: Absence of War and Security Institution-Building in Canada–US Relations, 1867–1958*. Montreal and Kingston: McGill-Queen's University Press.

Ryan, Henry B. 1979. "A New Look at Churchill's 'Iron Curtain' Speech." *Historical Journal* 22: 895–920. doi:https://doi.org/10.1017/S0018246X00017179.

Sokolsky, Joel J. 2000. "Over There with Uncle Sam: Peacekeeping, the 'Trans-European Bargain,' and the Canadian Forces." In *What NATO for Canada?*, edited by David G. Haglund, *Martello Papers* 23, 15–36. Kingston: Queen's University Centre for International Relations.

Stolleis, Michael. 2005. "The Dissolution of the Union between Norway and Sweden in 1905: A Century Later." In *Rett, nasjon, union – Den svensk-norske unionens rettslige historie 1814–1905*, edited by Ola Mestad and Dag Michalsen, 35–48. Oslo: Universitetsforlaget.

Szondy, David. 2017. "Rising Tide: Submarines and the Future of Undersea Warfare." *New Atlas*, 5 July. https://newatlas.com/future-submarines-modern-warfare/49896.

Task Force on National Security. 2022. *A National Security Strategy for the 2020s*. Ottawa: Graduate School of Public and International Affairs, University of Ottawa.

"The United States, Australia, and the United Kingdom Announce 'AUKUS' Alliance Focused on Indo-Pacific Security." 2022. *American Journal of International Law* 116, no. 1: 164–70. doi:10.1017/ajil.2021.69.

US Environmental Protection Agency. 2018. "Nuclear Submarines and Aircraft Carriers." Overviews and Factsheets. 30 November. https://www.epa.gov/radtown/nuclear-submarines-and-aircraft-carriers.

Vucetic, Srdjan. 2017. "'Anglo-Saxon World Domination': The Fulton Address as Racial Discourse." In *Churchill and the Anglo-American Special Relationship*, edited by Alan Dobson and Steve Marsh, 96–115. London: Routledge.

Webb, Clive. 2020. "Observing America: What Mass-Observation Reveals about British Views of the USA." *Journal of Transatlantic Studies* 18: 296–313. doi:https://doi.org/10.1057/s42738-020-00050-1.

White House. 2022. "FACT SHEET: Implementation of the Australia – United Kingdom – United States Partnership (AUKUS)." 5 April. https://www.whitehouse.gov/briefing-room/statements-releases/2022/04/05/fact-sheet-implementation-of-the-australia-united-kingdom-united-states-partnership-aukus.

12

The 49th Parallel

Balancing Cooperation with Sovereignty

SARA K. MCGUIRE

> I see a long, straight line athwart a continent. No chain of forts, or deep flowing river, or mountain range, but a line drawn by men upon a map, nearly a century ago, accepted with a handshake, and kept ever since. A boundary which divides two nations, yet marks their friendly meeting ground. The 49th parallel: the only undefended frontier in the world.
>
> Prologue to *49th Parallel* (Powell 1941)

Introduction

The Canada–US border is often touted as the longest undefended border in the world. Stretching more than 8,891 kilometres, the land border between these two states touches seven provinces and thirteen states. With 119 legal land border crossings facilitating transport, nearly 400,000 individuals crossed the border between the US and Canada on a daily basis (prior to the COVID-19 pandemic) (Government of Canada 2022). While the neighbouring states view each other as allies and participate in numerous bilateral initiatives and international alliances, there is an inherent power imbalance that characterizes Canada–US relations. Indeed, Daniel Drache (2004) once compared the Canada–US border to a giant connector plug, noting that "when this plug misfires or isn't working as it should, it creates a bad connection between Canada and the U.S. … Canadians feel the effects of this distortion" (xii). While the two states have historically sought to work together to manage their shared interests pertaining to the 49th parallel, the power imbalance in the Canada–US relationship is evident in the ways in which policies are drafted and implemented. Distinct phases in cooperation are noticeable when border policies are examined. The "Smart Border" phase ushered in by the 9/11 attacks has given way to a perimeter approach to border relations in more recent years. Canada has addressed border policies in a manner that favours collaboration with the US on shared issues pertaining to immigration, security, and trade while, at the same time, protecting Canadian sovereignty.

The Canada–US Border in Historical Perspective

The Canada–US border is the longest contiguous land border in the world. When it was established, the boundary between the two states ran through swathes of undeveloped wilderness. Today, it passes through numerous highly developed cosmopolitan centres. The history of the "special relationship" begins with boundary demarcation. From 1794 to 1903, sections of the land border between the two states were addressed by mixed commissions and through arbitration ("Settlement of International Disputes" 2011). Shaped by the powerful forces of "trade, migration, family connection, cooperation, and community across the border," the division between the US and Canada involved state and non-state actors in the US, Mexico, and the United Kingdom (UK) (Konrad and Nicol 2008, 61). Ultimately, following a convention that originated with the Treaty of Ghent in 1814, the 49th parallel was identified as the divide between the US and British North America. The process of delineating the boundary was gradual, involving official interstate negotiations as well as informal lower-level agreements (Sutcliffe and Anderson 2019).

While the relationship between Canada and the US has generally been peaceful, the demarcation of the dividing line between the countries has not been without conflict. The permanent location of the border was confirmed in the aftermath of the War of 1812; however, later conflicts demonstrate Canada's concern about losing ground to US interests. After the Klondike Gold Rush in 1897–98, which swelled the local population, the Alaska Boundary Dispute, which was inherited by British North America following protracted disagreement between the UK and US, sought to determine the territorial boundary between the Alaska Panhandle and present-day Yukon and British Columbia (BC) (Sutcliffe and Anderson 2019, 49). The issue was referred to an international tribunal comprised of three Americans, two Canadians, and a representative of the British government; the latter ultimately sided with the Americans, who concurred that the BC Panhandle was not quite cut off from the rest of that province (Keenleyside and Brown 1952). The settlement of this dispute foreshadowed the apprehension with which Canada would view future issues involving the 49th parallel and its neighbour to the south.

The role of Indigenous peoples in the Canada–US border relationship cannot be overlooked. The border between the two states runs through reserve lands, and Indigenous groups have helped shape this geopolitical boundary. It should be noted that Indigenous groups "predated the colonial powers' presence in North America and were a factor in the conflicts that led to the establishment of the border" (McDougall 2006, 47). The 1794 Jay Treaty, signed by the US and Britain, contained provisions relating to Indigenous lands and led to the creation of the Mohawk Reservation. These lands are situated in both Ontario and New York; the 49th parallel bisects reserve lands on Cornwall Island in the St Lawrence River (Office of the Historian). In 2009, Indigenous activists precipitated the temporary closure of the Cornwall, Ontario, border crossing as part of their opposition to a plan to arm Canadian border agents (Mann 2009).

The special relationship between Canada and the US is such that issues arising in one country are likely to reverberate in the other. As the US established itself as the most powerful country in the world, Canada came to feel the effects of US domestic events more strongly. Canadians have always been keenly aware of international entanglements involving the US. There has also been recurring sentiment about the "threat" posed by Canada's geopolitical position. Richard Gwyn (1985) noted that throughout the nineteenth century, many Canadians feared US military conquest, and that because of that fear, Canadian railways were constructed using a different gauge than was used in the US; the intent was to thwart potential US military advances into Canada. Indeed, Canadian defence strategies were being devised to address a possible conflict with our southern neighbour as late as 1922 (Sutcliffe and Anderson 2019). In 1951, Minister of External Affairs (and future prime minister) Lester B. Pearson remarked that "the United States is now the dominating world power on the side of freedom. Our pre-occupation is no longer whether the United States will discharge her international responsibilities, but how she will do it and whether the rest of us will be involved" (quoted in Mahant and Mount 1989, 191). Since the US has established itself as a global hegemon, US policy directives have had a significant impact on Canadian policy outcomes. Indeed, as Hale has noted, Canadians "fixate" on their relationship with the US, a consequence of the asymmetry between the two states (Hale 2012). This means that the bilateral relationship is of greater importance to Canadians than to Americans.

The Establishment of the Special Relationship

As discussed throughout this volume, the special relationship between Canada and the US was predicated on a shared understanding of the need for mutual support. However, this desire for collective security has always been underpinned by a competing Canadian need to exert national sovereignty in the face of its more powerful neighbour. After Canada gained control of its foreign and military relations from the UK in the interwar years, there was growing recognition of the need to coordinate national security policies with the US. The Kingston Dispensation of 1938 was the first articulation of the need for Canada–US cooperation. Speaking at Queen's University, President Franklin Delano Roosevelt declared that the US would not stand "idly by" should Canada face peril from a great power adversary of Britain (Fortmann and Haglund 2002, 17). The Ogdensburg Agreement, precipitated by an 18 August 1940 meeting between Prime Minister William Lyon Mackenzie King and President Roosevelt in Ogdensburg, New York, further established the basis for defence cooperation between the two states. Fearing a Nazi attack, the two leaders inaugurated closer military cooperation.

Despite the enhanced cooperation between Canada and the US following their mutual declarations of support, there was still concern among the Canadian public over the perceived transfer of sovereignty. Critics at the time argued that the Mackenzie King government had effectively transferred Canadian sovereignty to the US by shifting effective operational control of Canadian forces to their US counterparts (Grashoff 2012). Canadians' fear of giving up control to their more powerful neighbour has permeated present-day bilateral cooperation on a number of border policies.

The Ogdensburg Agreement served as a framework for closer continental security cooperation and led to the establishment of the Permanent Joint Board on Defence (PJBD). This body ultimately became the senior advisory board on continental security. While the PJBD still exists, its relevance has significantly diminished as other bilateral agreements and institutions have evolved to address current cross-border challenges such as counterterrorism, immigration, and global health crises.

In the context of the Canada–US border regime, an important aspect of the so-called special relationship is Canada's desire to be viewed differently than the US's southern neighbour, Mexico. Canadian policy-makers have sought to prevent what Andreas has termed the "Mexicanization" of the Canada–US border. Before the 9/11 attacks, Canada enjoyed a relatively close relationship with the US, with the movement of people and goods across the shared border taking place with minimal inspection. This was not the case with the US's shared border with Mexico, where US concerns over the illegal movement of drugs and people resulted in careful inspections of all vehicles crossing into the US. Andreas (2005, 449) explains that "what began as U.S. drug and immigration control anxieties, mostly focused southward, have now been extended northward, as U.S. border security worries have shifted in the post-9/11 era to focus on the potential entry of terrorists and weapons of mass destruction." Canada's response to border issues has sought to differentiate the Canada–US border from the US–Mexico border.

The border relationship between the US and Mexico can be described as contentious at best. US concerns about Mexican drug trafficking and illegal immigration led to the militarization of the US–Mexico border. Stemming from a perceived "crisis" of illegal immigration from Mexico, the US launched Operation Gatekeeper south of San Diego and Operation Hold-the-Line in El Paso. These initiatives, implemented in 1994, were part of a larger effort to prevent illegal immigrants from crossing the border into the US. To that end, the number of US border guards posted to San Diego and El Paso was drastically increased and a fourteen-mile wall was constructed with one foot in the Pacific Ocean (Stacey 2001). In addition to this, the US called on the military to "play an interdiction support role" in preventing illegal drugs from crossing the border (Hutchison 1966, 33). The growing trade relationship between the US and Mexico resulting from the North American Free Trade Agreement did not prevent the US from enacting strict militaristic policies aimed at preventing the irregular movement of people and goods across its southern border. The hard line taken by the US in dealing with its shared border with Mexico has been something that Canadian policy-makers have sought to avoid.

Managing the Border Relationship: From the 49th Parallel to Perimeter Security

Prior to the 9/11 terrorist attacks in the US, the Canada–US border was recognized as one facet of the special relationship shared by these neighbouring states. In his 1966 text "The Long Border," Bruce Hutchison articulated the friendly nature of cross-border relations:

> The border between the United States and Canada … is the most friendly and least visible line of international power in the world. It is crossed daily by thousands of travelers who hardly notice it in their passage. It is washed by a Niagara of congenial oratory and illuminated, or sometimes obscured, by a perpetual diplomatic dialogue. On both sides the border is taken as a fact of nature, almost an act of God, which no man thinks of changing. (Cited in Clarkson 2008, 370)

Indeed, throughout the nineteenth century, the governments' presence along the 49th parallel was generally restricted to the collection of customs duties. Even within the heightened security context of the Second World War and the Cold War, the US remained unconcerned about its northern border, remaining much more apprehensive about illegal immigration and drugs entering from Mexico.

North American border relations have typically oscillated between two different security models. The first views the border as two "land lines" separating the US from Mexico and Canada at two separate frontiers, each requiring levels of autonomous policing commensurate with the policy priorities and security issues of the time (Andreas and Biersteker 2003). The second border security model is the perimeter approach, which relocates the border to the continent's perimeter, within which the three national spaces must be defended against common external threats and which require some level of joint monitoring. Following the Second World War and the onset of the Cold War, the US remained unworried about its border with Canada and focused instead on building a military perimeter around itself and Canada as protection against possible German, Japanese, and, ultimately, Soviet attack. Since 9/11, however, the perimeter approach to border security has emerged as the dominant paradigm in the US. Always cognizant of its more powerful neighbour, Canadian policies have sought to respond to US national security concerns.

Following the 9/11 attacks, the "borderless world" of the 1990s was replaced by an instinctually territorial and autarchic response as Washington was confronted by the reality of global terrorism. The border regime that has emerged since 9/11 is premised on the objective of managing a border relationship where the risks have increased and the positions of the countries involved have diverged: 9/11 exposed the US's vulnerability and immediately precipitated a change in the way it approached the border. Following the attacks, a homeland-security-first approach was adopted that emphasized the possibility that threats to the US could originate at ports of entry. Border security was an element of the homeland security strategy, and securing the US approaches against future attacks became especially important. For this reason, US policy toward the Canada–US border shifted away from promoting bilateral agreements aimed at maintaining the two states' trade relations in favour of restrictive border security policies. This unprecedented shift in US border policies has had serious implications for Canada, which has sought to protect its own state interests while at the same time responding to US national security concerns.

After 9/11, US border inspectors were placed on Alert Level One, defined as a "sustained, intensive, antiterrorism operation" (Alden 2008, 42). By 11 a.m. on the morning of 11 September, all airports, seaports, and land border crossings in the US were placed on this alert level. At the time, this was the highest threat level short of a complete closure of the US border. Alden explained the significance of this alert status, noting that "if the passenger information system that helped to identify the hijackers is the equivalent of a sieve, allowing most people to pass through unhindered and leaving behind only a few to be examined, a level one alert is like a sponge that traps everyone and everything" (Alden 2008, 42). The implementation of Alert Level One required that US Customs and Immigration and Naturalization Services (INS) officers carry out intensive examinations of all people and transport cargoes approaching the US border.

The implementation of Alert Level One at all points of entry into the US was the first indication that Canada would have to be cognizant of US efforts to prioritize homeland security efforts over other border objectives. Alert Level One often entailed completely unloading cargo from transport trailers and searching the contents before reloading the trucks and allowing the drivers to continue. All drivers were required to hand over a valid driver's licence and then subjected to intensive questioning from border patrol guards. This increased scrutiny created massive line-ups at the border. Capling and Nossal (2009, 156) noted that in the days immediately after 9/11, the "line-ups of trucks stretched for more than thirty kilometers down highways leading into the U.S., with reported cross border waits of up to ten to twelve hours." These inspections dramatically slowed the pace of cross-border traffic. Andreas and Biersteker (2003, 10) found that in the days after the attacks, "delays for trucks hauling cargo across the border increased from one to two minutes to ten to fifteen hours, stranding parts, shipments, and perishable goods." The increased scrutiny of traffic entering the US from Canada, and the resulting slowdown in cross-border traffic, had an adverse effect on the Canadian economy by rendering the "just-in-time" trade model ineffective.

The declaration of Alert Level One at all US ports of entry illustrated how suddenly the previous US model of border security, which emphasized collaboration and cooperation with Canada, had shifted toward a model whereby other states were expected to adopt US security standards that prioritized homeland security. Robert Bonner (2004), then commissioner of US Customs and Border Protection, noted that "after 9/11 our priority mission … changed from the interdiction of illegal drugs and the regulation of trade to a security prevention mission: preventing terrorists and terrorist weapons from entering the United States."

On 12 December 2001, then foreign minister John Manley and US homeland security director Tom Ridge signed the Canada–United States Smart Border Declaration and Associated 30-Point Action Plan to Enhance the Security of Our Shared Border While Facilitating the Legitimate Flow of People and Goods (White House 2002). A general framework initiated at the federal level in both countries, the declaration underlay "a shared commitment to develop a border that securely facilitates the free flow of people and commerce, and that reflects the largest trading relationship in the world" (Foreign Affairs 2003). The objective of the Smart Border Declaration was to address national security concerns while facilitating legitimate trade and travel. The focus on "smart" borders represented by this agreement has since given way to a strategy that seeks to push the regulation of border activities away from the 49th parallel by means of a perimeter approach to border security.

The thirty-point action plan included with the Smart Border Declaration set out procedures for "identifying and addressing security risks while expediting the legitimate flow of people and goods across the border" (Smart Border Declaration 2001). The agreement states that the two countries will cooperate in identifying high-risk goods and, at the same time, ease the shipment of consumer products across the border. According to Canada's Department of Foreign Affairs and International Trade, the Smart Border Declaration was intended to develop a border that "securely facilitates the free flow of people and commerce, and that reflects the largest trading relationship in the world" (Foreign Affairs 2003). Smart Border initiatives include the expansion of the Free and Secure Trade Program and the NEXUS program, as well as the expansion of joint teams of customs officials to target marine containers. According to a Government of Canada website, "the 2008 federal budget has allocated $174 million over the next two years to ensure Canada has the best equipment, infrastructure, regulations, and cooperative framework in place to maximize the security and efficiency of the Canada–U.S. border" (Government of Canada 2008). Canada's participation in the Smart Border Declaration can be viewed as a strategic speech act on Canada's behalf, aimed at reassuring the US that it will live up to its "good neighbour" promises.

The Smart Border Declaration was followed in 2011 by the adoption of a perimeter approach to North American border security. On 4 February 2011, President Barack Obama and Prime Minister Stephen Harper announced this new bilateral initiative, Beyond the Border: A Shared Vision for Perimeter Security and Economic Competitiveness (Department of Homeland Security 2017). This declaration represents a paradigm shift in border security and has instituted a perimeter approach to governing the flow of people and goods across the 49th parallel. With this agreement, both states have sought to focus on cooperation away from ports of entry in order to "address the layered threats not only to our citizens and our cross border trade and travel, but also to our physical and cyber infrastructure" (Department of Homeland Security 2017). Many of the important developments initiated by this agreement have involved Canada's adoption of new border security protocols, including the 2016 Canadian Electronic Travel Authorization system, the 2016 Canadian deployment of Transportation Security Administration–certified Explosive Detection Systems, and the 2016 implementation by the Canadian Air Transport Screening Authority of its Security in Advance initiative (Department of Homeland Security 2019). The perimeter approach to border security has allowed Canada to collaborate with the US; it is no longer compelled to respond to US-initiated security policies and protocols.

Canada and the US renewed their commitment to perimeter security in 2019 with the announcement of the implementation of Phase III of the Entry/Exit Information System, a commitment made under Beyond the Border Action Plan. Phase I of this system initiated the exchange of information on "third country nationals and permanent legal residents at four land border ports along the U.S.–Canada border" (Government of Canada 2013). In June 2013, Phase II of the program expanded this exchange of information to all common land border ports.

In 2013, the bilateral Canada/U.S. Information Sharing Treaty facilitated further sharing of systemic immigration information. This treaty has automated the sharing of immigration and visa information between Canada and the US in order to better identify those individuals who might pose a threat to North American security (Government of Canada 2013). Phase III expanded this program further still to include US and Canadian citizens while continuing to facilitate the sharing of data on legal permanent residents and third-country nationals.

Immigration

Canada and the US have sought some measure of coordination regarding issues pertaining to asylum. Their differing approaches to immigration have led to surface-level collaboration. The two states have sought to demonstrate a coordinated commitment to facilitating the flow of people and goods across the shared border. However, the bilateral initiatives launched to facilitate this objective point to a power struggle between the two states and Canada's long-held preoccupation with maintaining state sovereignty. Canada and the US have different objectives related to immigration and asylum. These policy variances reflect cultural differences. US citizens take pride in their country's position as a world power with international influence, whereas Canadians recognize that they belong to a more modest power that represents "fair and equal treatment of all groups" and has a robust social security system (Esses et al. 2021). The two states continue to coordinate on immigration and asylum policies, but their policy objectives reflect different priorities pertaining to the balance between security and personal rights.

While both Canada and the US are long-established liberal democracies, their immigration policies reflect subtle cultural differences. Canada has historically focused on attracting highly skilled economic migrants. By contrast, the US has a higher share of family-based immigration (Boucher 2019, 3). Canada's point system was created in 1967 in order to facilitate a race-blind, non-discriminating process for selecting immigrants (de Eyre 2011). This system awards points based on youth, education, language skills, occupation, and experience (Iyer and Rathod 2011). The US immigration system, while providing avenues for skilled workers, focuses more strongly on family reunification.

The two decades following the 9/11 attacks have seen a shift in US immigration law and policy. In recent years, the US government has linked immigration screening and enforcement to national security. Immigration policies have been operationalized as part of the national security strategy. Immediately after 9/11, President George W. Bush instituted a special registration program, called the National Security Entry-Exit Registration System (NSEERS). This program was applicable largely to non-citizens from Middle Eastern countries. NSEERS established a national registry for temporary foreign visitors arriving from specific countries who met a combination of intelligence-based criteria and were identified as presenting an "elevated" threat to national security (Wadhia 2017). This program was suspended on 1 December 2003. Although the US Patriot Act is not an immigration act, it has had a profound impact on immigrants to the US in the post-9/11 period. That act authorizes the INS to detain any alien (non-American) certified by the attorney general as a "suspected terrorist." The law provides only a broad definition of "suspected terrorist." The clearance program avoids the spectre of deporting individuals and at the same time allows for prolonged preventive and investigative detention (Konrad and Nicol 2004).

Blame Canada? Asylum and Refugee Policies

While Canada and the US have sought to collaborate on refugee and asylum policies through the Safe Third Country Agreement, the strong connection between national security objectives and immigration policies in the US has led to distrust of Canadian asylum policies. A rhetorical sense of risk has been constructed, one that has externalized the threat to US national security by designating a scapegoat (Clarkson 2003, 76). Policy-makers and the media have focused on Canada as the "weak link" that has compromised the security of the US border. This "blame Canada" narrative, which incorporates complaints that Canadian asylum policies are too lax, reflects the differing approaches the two states have taken to asylum policy.

In the so-called terrorist era, US policy-makers have repeatedly sought to "blame Canada" for the terrorist attacks by referencing Canadian asylum policies and insinuating that the nineteen hijackers entered the US from Canada. Richard Holbrooke's pre-9/11 statement that Canada was "a Club Med for terrorists" was repeated over and over again in the media (CBC News 2000). Congressman Lamar Smith of Texas reiterated Holbrooke's statement (Hussain, Pattnayak, and Hira 2008). A number of US politicians have claimed erroneously that the nineteen individuals who hijacked the planes that crashed into the World Trade Center, the Pentagon, and a farmer's field in Pennsylvania were able to enter the US by crossing the Canadian border. Senator Byron Dorgan asserted that "it's a big porous border and it's very difficult to secure," holding up a pylon for the media as an example of Canada's lax stance on border security (Centner 2012, 494). Even Senator Hillary Clinton stated that the terrorists had come to the US through Canada. These comments reinforced the American public's view of Canada as a threat to US security.

Canada and the US have divergent approaches to adjudicating and assessing asylum applications. The US focuses on the national security threat posed by asylum seekers and detains those seeking refugee status, whereas Canada allows asylum claimants to move about freely in advance of their status hearings (Gallagher 2003). While the two countries have comparable acceptance rates for refugee claimants, Canadian policies lack the national security focus espoused by the US asylum system. Thus, some US officials have argued that asylum claimants posing a potential national security threat are able to destroy their identification papers, claim refugee status in Canada, and then disappear prior to their hearings (Uniting and Strengthening … Act 2001).

Several US policy documents have implied that Canada's refugee policies pose a threat to the US. Title IV of the US Patriot Act, titled Protecting the Border, portrays the Canada–US border as a permeable line that requires additional US attention to prevent would-be terrorists from crossing unchecked (Berry et al. 2003). Similarly, a 2003 report drafted by the US Federal Research Division declared Canada to be a nation "hospitable to organized crime and terrorism" (Hudnall 2004, 191–2). The report further alleged that "Canada has played a significant role as a base for both transnational criminal activity and terrorist activity" (191–2).

In the post-9/11 period, two examples were frequently employed by both policy-makers and the media in support of the argument that inadequate Canadian border security measures are hazardous to US security. These examples are the 1997 case of Gazi Ibrahim Abu Mezer and the 1999 case of Ahmed Ressam, two would-be "terrorists" who came to Canada before entering the US.

Gazi Ibrahim Abu Mezer was a Palestinian who entered the US through Canada using a false Jordanian passport. He met up with Lafi Khalil, another Palestinian national, who was in the US on a visa overstay. The two men rented rooms in a boarding house in Brooklyn, where they plotted to blow up the Atlantic Avenue subway in New York City (Hudnall 2004). Mezer and Khalil travelled together to North Carolina to build the bomb they would use. When they returned to Brooklyn to detonate the bomb in the subway system, an Egyptian man living in their boarding house reported their plot to the police. On 31 July 1997, police and members of the FBI arrived at the boarding house. Upon their arrival, Mezer and Khalil detonated the suicide vests they were wearing and were shot by police. Neither was killed, and both were subsequently charged and convicted for possession of pipe bombs, which they had intended to detonate in the subway and in other public places in New York City (Hudnall 2004).

This incident was rehashed by the US security apparatus and the media following the 9/11 attacks to demonstrate the threat Canada apparently posed to the US. Mezer, the Palestinian bombmaker, had arrived in Canada, claimed political asylum based on alleged persecution by Israelis, then skipped his hearing and entered the US in 1996.

He returned to Canada and re-entered the US in 1997 (Hoffmann and McGinley 2010, 90). The US was quick to label the Mezer incident a Canadian security failure; however, Mezer had used a false Jordanian passport both times he entered the US without it being detected by US border officials. Khalil, Mezer's associate, had entered the US directly from Palestine, bypassing Canada entirely. In the post-9/11 period, the US media often cited this case as an example of how Canada was a "weak link" in the homeland security chain. This narrative was quickly accepted by the US media, which disregarded the seemingly obvious US security failures pertaining to this case.

Another case that has been cited to demonstrate Canada's "failure" to secure the border is that of Ahmed Ressam, the would-be "Millennium Bomber." Ressam left Algeria for France in 1992 using a forged French passport and claimed asylum from political persecution. Avoiding detection in France, he fled to Corsica when his visa expired; there, he obtained another fake French passport (Hoffman and McGinley 2010). In February 1994, Ressam boarded a plane to Canada. Canadian authorities in Montreal detected his fraudulent passport, and he was arrested. To avoid being deported, Ressam applied for political asylum in Canada. After failing to show up at various court dates, he was ordered deported and fled to an Al-Qaeda training camp in Afghanistan. In 1996, Ressam entered the US through Afghanistan and then returned to Canada. Security personnel at the Los Angeles International Airport (LAX) stopped him, but after questioning him, he was allowed to return to Canada (Warner 2010, 201).

On 14 December 1999, Ressam, who was then in Vancouver, Canada, boarded the MV *Coho* ferry in Victoria, BC, in an attempt to enter the US at Port Angeles, Washington. The RCMP had notified US Customs that Ressam posed a potential bomb threat, yet he was pre-cleared by US immigration officers in Victoria. Upon arrival in Port Angeles, he attempted to flee further inspection when Diana Dean, a US border agent, decided to search his car. In it she found explosives that he intended to use to blow up LAX. Ressam was tried in the US and sentenced to twenty-two years in federal prison plus five years' supervision after release. Sentencing was delayed by the US State Department in order to secure Ressam's cooperation in providing investigators with information on Al-Qaeda sleeper cells in the US. Ressam remains in US federal custody following a third resentencing to thirty-seven years in prison (FBI 2012).

Ressam was dubbed the "Millennium Bomber" by the US media and was touted as the embodiment of the threat Canada posed to US security interests. The "blame Canada" narrative drowned out the fact that Ressam had returned to Canada from an Al-Qaeda training camp in Afghanistan through the US. The failure of French officials to detect Ressam's fraudulent passport in 1992 was also absent from reports. Nowhere was it mentioned that Ressam had initially received a somewhat lenient sentence in exchange for information regarding would-be terrorists already living in the US. Instead, politicians and the media alike seized on this event as an indication of Canada's lax immigration security practices – completely ignoring the fact that Ressam was cleared by US immigration officers twice before finally being arrested. The Ressam case reverberated strongly after the 9/11 attacks and was frequently employed as an example of how the hijackers had "likely entered the U.S. via Canada" (Struck 2005).

Asylum Policy Collaboration: The Safe Third Country Agreement

In recent years, there have been renewed efforts to enhance cross-border security focused on bilateral cooperation on asylum policies. The Safe Third Country Agreement, which took effect in 2004, requires asylum seekers to assert their claim to refugee status in their first country of arrival. This agreement, which is part of the bilateral Smart Border Action Plan, stipulates that those intending to seek asylum must seek protection in the "first safe country they arrive in," unless they meet the criteria for an exemption to the agreement (Heyman, Stack, and Guerra 2018, 761). The US remains the only country designated by Canada as a Safe Third Country under the terms of the Immigration and Refugee Protection Act.

This agreement has gained new significance in light of the influx of migrants to the US from the Northern Triangle region. As a result of ongoing violence in Guatemala, El Salvador, and Honduras, this region has become a significant source of both asylum seekers and economic migrants to the US. The arrival of these groups at the US southern border has placed renewed pressure on the country's border with Mexico. There is an unstated assumption among a faction of US policymakers that aspiring "illegal" migrants seeking entry into the US must be deterred; however, the current immigration system is not well equipped to address those with legitimate claim to asylum. Many Northern Triangle migrants make the journey to the US because of information distributed in their country of origin suggesting that asylum is a path to US citizenship (Keating 2018). The Safe Third Country Agreement must be updated in order to address loopholes that exist in the current asylum protocol. Canada should seek to participate in future discussions addressing the "well-founded fear of persecution" on which asylum claims are to be judged.

In November 2022, the Canadian government announced an ambitious plan to settle 500,000 immigrants per year in the country, with almost 1.5 million new arrivals to Canada over the next three years. The Canadian plan to increase immigration is meant to address a looming labour shortage in the country. The US, with almost ten times as many people as Canada, has not followed suit with a plan to increase immigration. This change in Canadian policy will once again alter the border relationship between the two states.

Continued Border Challenges

The advent of the perimeter approach to border security has not been without additional challenges to the Canada–US border relationship. Both countries have failed to account for the unique issues facing Indigenous people living on reserves that span the international border. In May 2009, members of the Mohawk Council of Akwesasne shut down the Seaway International Bridge that connects Cornwall, Ontario, with Massena, New York. This action was taken to protest the Canadian government's decision to arm border agents working on Mohawk territory. Akwesasne, which has been described as "the most geopolitically absurd place in North America," is a town with three different governing bodies: an elected council recognized by Canada, a council recognized by the US, and a tribal government affiliated with the Iroquois Confederacy (Forester 2021). This town, which is home to the Akwesasne Mohawk Casino Resort, draws thousands of visitors every day from both sides of the 49th parallel. Indigenous communities like Akwesasne that span the Canada–US border create unique challenges. Just last year, the Supreme Court of Canada ruled that Indigenous peoples whose territory straddles the Canada–US border can claim Aboriginal rights in Canada even if they do not hold Canadian citizenship (*R v Desautel* 2021). The Court's ruling in the case of *R v Desautel* means that Indigenous groups in the US can now be recognized as holding constitutionally protected Aboriginal rights in Canada (Government of Canada 2004). In the future, there is a need for better collaboration between the US and Canada in order to address the distinct issues faced by these communities while respecting Indigenous rights and land claims.

The NEXUS program, instituted in 2002 to facilitate the movement of legitimate people and goods across the Canada–US border in the post-9/11 period, has faced its own challenges in the past year. The NEXUS program's objective is to sustain the flow of people across the border. This program was instituted as part of the Smart Border Declaration. It recognizes the high volume of cross-border movement between the US and Canada. Sloan (2010, 62) describes NEXUS as "a clearance system that uses high-tech cards to allow frequent travelers between the two countries – especially business travelers – to cross the border more quickly." Transport Canada's website indicates that individuals approved to take part in the program will be issued a membership ID card to use when entering Canada or the US at a border crossing equipped to support the NEXUS program (Government of Canada 2023). NEXUS procedures differ between the two sides of the Canada–US border. When entering the US, NEXUS users display their pass cards as they approach a designated NEXUS lane. A computer chip embedded in the card sends a signal to the federal officer monitoring the lane with the participant's picture and personal information. Participants entering Canada enter a designated lane, where their licence plates are scanned. They then present their pass card to the inspector monitoring the lane to confirm their identity and membership in the program (Fife 2022). The NEXUS program allows low-risk individuals to avoid lengthy wait times at high-traffic border crossings and also allows officials from both Canada and the US to spend more time investigating individuals who might pose more of a security threat. This program recognizes that trade is contingent not simply on the free flow of goods across the border but also on the ability of people to cross the border in a timely and efficient manner.

Last year, Canada and the US came to dispute the continuation of NEXUS in the post-COVID-19 era. The US has taken issue with Canada's refusal to extend the same legal protections to US Custom and Border Protection (CBP) officers working in NEXUS offices as those afforded to preclearance officers operating at land crossings and airports. Canadian Public Safety Minister Marco Mendicino has stated that officers assigned to NEXUS offices will not be given the same legal protections as preclearance officers and that "there is an important principle of Canadian sovereignty around making sure the law applies to officials as it would to any other person" (cited in Fife 2022). This ongoing dispute has created dysfunction in the day-to-day workings of NEXUS. As a result of this disagreement, the US closed NEXUS offices in Canada that process applications for Canadian citizens seeking admittance to this program. The US has argued that CBP officers should receive immunity from prosecution, much like foreign diplomats, while Canada argues that extending such protections would constitute a violation of sovereignty. Speaking at a conference organized by the Future Borders Coalition, and hosted at the Canadian Embassy, Kirsten Hillman, Canadian ambassador to the US, stated, "I'm going to be super blunt and undiplomatic here because I think this is important for friends sometimes. The NEXUS program is being held hostage. It's disappointing and it's frustrating for us" (cited in Panetta 2022). Perhaps this dispute is indicative of future conflicts as Canada seeks to reassert its authority over border issues following the COVID-19 pandemic.

A COVID-19 Challenge to Perimeter Security? Looking Forward …

The COVID-19 pandemic has introduced new challenges to the Canada–US border relationship. On 21 March 2020, the Canada–US border was closed in response to the pandemic. This closure was extended monthly by the two countries, and for more than sixteen months, Canada and the US turned away tourists at entry points along the land border in order to contain the spread of the COVID-19 virus. The Canadian government has taken a much harder line than the US in terms of implementing and enforcing COVID-19 policies and protocols. Early in the pandemic, Canada put in place emergency border measures to "reduce the risk of the importation and transmission of COVID-19 and new variants of concern in Canada related to international travel" (Government of Canada 2022b). Canada's first COVID-19 Emergency

Order in Council (OIC) entered into force on 3 February 2020, one month before the border closure. In the months that followed, eighty OICs were made under the Canadian Quarantine Act. In April 2020, Canada introduced the ArriveCan app, which travellers – both Canadian citizens and international visitors – were required to use to enter the country. The app required everyone seeking entry to Canada to input travel and contact information, a quarantine plan, and a COVID-19 self-assessment prior to arrival at a port of entry. Those who failed to comply with this requirement were fined and could be subjected to enforcement action, including confinement in a COVID-19 quarantine centre. While the US required travellers to show proof of a negative COVID-19 test and, later, proof of vaccination, no app was required to enter the country. Adopting a hard-line stance in addressing the COVID-19 threat, Canada kept its pandemic border requirements in place until March 2022 (Stein 2022).

Canada's implementation of strict COVID-19–oriented border policies has provoked the ire of some US policy-makers. US politicians like Democratic congressman Brian Higgins from western New York State have decried Canada's COVID-19 border policies. Higgins, who represents both Buffalo and Niagara Falls, argued that

> for communities living on either side of the United States – Canada border, the days stretching between Canada Day and Independence Day typically represent one of the busiest for cross-border travel. It is a time to celebrate our shared bond, respect national traditions and simply enjoy time with our friends and families on the opposite side of the border during the height of the summer. Continued hurdles to the free flow of people across the Northern Border are fizzling the fireworks border communities customarily enjoy this time of year. What now amounts to two and a half years of border restrictions, are breaking the U.S.–Canada relationship and our economies. (Higgins 2022)

The lasting effects of the prolonged closure of the border remain to be seen.

Canada discontinued the forced use of its ArriveCan app in the fall of 2022; however, while travellers no longer needed to submit their information to the app, it remained a potentially notable tool for tracking the movement of people into Canada. Those entering the country were encouraged to use the optional app to enter an Advance Declaration before arriving at ports of entry. Officials have stated that this feature of ArriveCan will allow citizens and visitors to "save time at the airport" (Government of Canada 2022a). Has the implementation of pandemic-era border restrictions and policies posed a challenge to the perimeter approach to border security favoured by Canada and the US? While it probably has not, the two states' responses to COVID-19 have ushered in a new era in Canada–US border cooperation.

Conclusion

Policies regarding the Canada–US border have long been an important facet of the "special relationship" between the two countries. That relationship has seen periods of disagreement over various threats and external pressures. The collective defence approach to border security espoused during the war years gave way to a perimeter approach to security premised on the notion of a smart border. In recent years, the COVID-19 pandemic and diverging approaches to immigration have exposed the power imbalance between Canada and the US. The border relationship between Canada and the US is markedly different from the one between the US and Mexico. Ultimately, the special relationship between Canada and the US indicates a continuing desire and willingness by both states to cooperate when addressing shared border concerns.

References

"Agreement Between the Government of Canada and the Government of the United States of America for Cooperation in Science and Technology for Critical Infrastructure Protection and Border Security" [Smart Border Declaration]. E105000 (12 December 2001). https://www.treaty-accord.gc.ca/text-texte.aspx?id=105000.

Alden, Edward. 2008. *The Closing of the American Border: Terrorism, Immigration, and Security Since 9/11*. New York: Harper Perennial.

Andreas, Peter. 2003. "A Tale of Two Borders: The US–Mexico and US–Canada Lines after 9/11." Center for Comparative Immigration Studies, UC San Diego. 22 June.

– 2005. "The Mexicanization of the US–Canada Border." *International Journal* 60, no. 2: 449–62.
Andreas, Peter, and Thomas Biersteker. 2003. *The Rebordering of North America*. New York: Routledge.
Berry, LaVerle, Glenn E. Curtis, John N. Gibbs, Rex A. Hudson, Tara Karakan, Nina Kollars, and Ramaon Miro. 2003. *Nations Hospitable to Organized Crime and Terrorism*. A Report Prepared by the Federal Research Division, Library of Congress, under the Interagency Agreement with the US Government. October.
Bonner, Robert. 2004. Speaking in front of National Commission on Terrorist Attacks on the United States, Seventh Public Hearing. 26 January. http://www.9-11commission.gov/hearings/hearing7/witness_bonner.htm.
Boucher, Anna Katherine. 2019. "How 'Skill' Definition Affects the Diversity of Skilled Immigration Policies." *Journal of Ethnic and Migration Studies* 46, no. 12: 2533–50.
Capling, Ann, and Kim Richard Nossal. 2009. "The Contradictions of Regionalism in North America." In *Globalising the Regional, Regionalising the Global*, edited by Rick Fawn. Cambridge: Cambridge University Press.
CBC News. 2000. "US Committee Says Canada a Terrorist Haven."27 January. https://www.cbc.ca/news/world/u-s-committee-says-canada-a-terrorist-haven-1.218264.
Centre for Research and Information on Canada. "Security at Canada's US Borders: The Smart Border." http://www.cric.ca/en_html/guide/border/border.html#smart.
Centner, Adam. 2012. "Strengthening North America's Perimeter Security: An Analysis of United States and Canadian Immigration and Refugee Laws and the Collaboration Required to Harmonize Those Laws." *Canada-United States Law Journal* 37, no. 2: 493–516.
Clarkson, Stephen. 2003. "The View from the Arctic: Toward a Gated Continental Community?" In *The Rebordering of North America: Integration and Exclusion in a New Security Context*, edited by Peter Andreas and Thomas J. Biersteker. New York: Routledge.
– 2008. *Does North America Exist? Governing the Continent after* NAFTA *and 9/11*. Toronto: University of Toronto Press, 2008.
Cody, Howard. 2003. "US–Canada Trade, Defense, and Border Issues Since September 11: The View from Canada." *Canadian-American Public Policy* 54.
de Eyre, Steve. 2011. "The Prospects for a North American Security Perimeter: Coordination and Harmonization of the United States and Canadian Immigration and Refugee Laws." *Canada-United States Law Journal* 35, nos. 1–2.

Department of Homeland Security. 2012. "Considerations for United States–Canada Border Traffic Disruption Management." Washington, DC.

– 2017. *Beyond the Border. US Fact Sheet*. January. https://www.dhs.gov/sites/default/files/publications/2017%201%2019%20BTB%20Fact%20Sheet.pdf.

– 2019. "US and Canada Continue Commitment to Securing our Borders, Begin Phase III of the Entry/Exit Project under the Beyond the Border Initiative." 11 July. https://www.dhs.gov/news/2019/07/11/us-and-canada-continue-commitment-securing-our-borders-begin-phase-iii-entryexit.

– 2022. "Beyond the Border: A Shared Vision for Perimeter Security and Economic Competitiveness." 26 July. https://www.dhs.gov/beyond-border.

Drache, Daniel. 2004. *Borders Matter: Homeland Security and the Search for North America*. Halifax: Fernwood.

Esses, Victoria M., Alina Sutler, Joanie Bouchard, Kate H. Choi, and Patrick Denice. 2021. "North American Attitudes toward Immigration and Immigration in the Time of COVID-19: The Role of National Attachment and Threat." *Annals of the American Academy of Political and Social Science* 697, no. 1: 148–73.

Federal Bureau of Investigation (FBI). 2012. "Millenium Plot / Ahmed Ressam." https://www.fbi.gov/history/famous-cases/millennium-plot-ahmed-ressam.

Fife, Robert. 2022. "Canada–US Dispute over NEXUS Sparks Backlog of Applications." *Globe and Mail*, 4 October. https://www.theglobeandmail.com/politics/article-nexus-canada-us-backlog.

Foreign Affairs and International Trade Canada. 2003. "The Canada-U.S. Smart Border Declaration." http://www.international.gc.ca/anti-terrorism/declaration-en.asp.

Forester, Brett. 2021. "No Border for Indigenous Nations Straddling US, Canada." APTN *National News*, 23 April. https://indiancountrytoday.com/news/no-border-for-indigenous-nations-straddling-us-canada.

Fortmann, Michael, and David G. Haglund. 2002. "Canada and the Issue of Homeland Security: Does the 'Kingston Dispensation' Still Hold?" *Canadian Military Journal* 3, no. 1: 17–22.

Gallagher, Steven. 2003. "Canada's Dysfunctional Refugee Determination System." *Public Policy Sources*. Fraser Institute Occasional Paper no. 78.

Government of Canada. n.d. "Canada–US Safe Third Country Agreement." https://www.canada.ca/en/immigration-refugees-citizenship/corporate/mandate/policies-operational-instructions-agreements/agreements/safe-third-country-agreement.html.

– 2004. Transport Canada. "NEXUS Border Crossing Program. May 2004. http://www.tc.gc.ca/pol/en/tbwg/361.htm.

– 2008. “Responsible Leadership.” The Budget Plan. 26 February 2008. https://www.budget.canada.ca/2008/pdf/plan-eng.pdf
– 2013. “Canada/US Information Sharing Treaty Summary.” 7 May. https://www.canada.ca/en/immigration-refugees-citizenship/corporate/transparency/access-information-privacy/privacy-impact-assessment/us-canada-information-sharing-treaty.html.
– 2022a. “Canada–United States Relations.” October. https://www.international.gc.ca/country-pays/us-eu/relations.aspx?lang=eng.
– 2022b. “COVID-19 Border Measures.” September. https://www.canada.ca/en/public-health/news/2022/09/covid-19-border-measures.html.
– 2023. “How to Use NEXUS to Enter Canada.” 13 June. https://www.cbsa-asfc.gc.ca/services/travel-voyage/prog/nexus/how-utiliser-eng.html.
Grashoff, Matthew K. 2012. “Building Fences Together: The EU’s Lessons for the US–Canada Perimeter Security Plan.” *Canada–United States Law Journal* 37, no. 2: 517–50.
Gwyn, Richard. 1985. *The 49th Parallel: Canada in North America.* Toronto: McClelland and Stewart.
Hale, Geoffrey. 2012. *So Near Yet So Far: The Public and Hidden Worlds of Canada–US Relations.* Vancouver: UBC Press.
Heyman, Josiah, Jeremy Stack, and Emily Guerra. 2018. “Bordering a ‘Crisis’: Central American Asylum Seekers and the Reproduction of Dominant Border Enforcement Practices.” *Journal of the Southwest* 60, no. 4: 754–86.
Higgins, Brian. 2022. “Congressman Brian Higgins Says Continued Border Restrictions Are Breaking the US–Canada Relationship and Economies.” Press release. 30 June. https://higgins.house.gov/media-center/press-releases/congressman-brian-higgins-says-continued-border-restrictions-are.
Hoffman, Sandra K., and Tracy G. McGinley. 2010. *Identity Theft: A Reference Handbook.* Santa Barbara: ABC-CLIO, LLC.
Hudnall, Robert K. 2004. *No Safe Haven: Homeland Insecurity.* El Paso: Omega Press.
Hussain, A. Imitiaz, Satya R. Pattnayak, and Anil Hira. 2008. *North American Homeland Security: Back to Bilateralism?* Westport: Praeger Security International.
Hutchison, Bruce. 1966. *The Long Border.* Baltimore: School of Advanced International Studies, Johns Hopkins University.
Iyer, Deepa, and Jayesh M. Rathod. 2011. “9/11 and the Transformation of US Immigration Law and Policy.” *Human Rights* 38, no. 1: 10–12.
Keating, Joshua. 2018. “The Nation That Sits Astride the US–Canada Border.” *Politico Magazine*, 1 July. https://www.politico.com/magazine/story/2018/07/01/akwesasne-american-indian-community-218936.

Keenleyside, Hugh L.L., and Gerald S. Brown. 1952. *Canada and the United States: Some Aspects of Their Historical Relations*. New York: A.A. Knopf, 1952.

Konrad, Victor, and Heather Nicol. 2004. "Boundaries and Corridors: Rethinking the Canada–United States Borderlands in the Post-9/11 Era." *Canadian and American Public Policy* 60: 1–51.

– 2008. *Beyond Walls: Reinventing the Canada–United States Borderlands*. Aldershot: Ashgate.

Mahant, Edelgard E., and Graeme S. Mount. 1989. *An Introduction to Canadian-American Relations*, 2nd ed. Scarborough: Nelson Canada.

Mann, Brian. 2009. "Mohawk Protests Close US–Canada Border Crossing." *NPR*, 11 June. https://www.npr.org/templates/story/story.php?storyId=105210542.

McDougall, John. 2006. *Drifting Together: The Political Economy of Canada–US Integration*. Peterborough: Broadview Press.

Office of the Historian. "John Jay's Treaty, 1794–1795." https://history.state.gov/milestones/1784-1800/jay-treaty.

Panetta, Alexander. 2022. "Canada Says US Holding NEXUS Travel Program 'Hostage.'" *CBC News*, 13 October. https://www.cbc.ca/news/world/nexus-dispute-hostage-hillman-1.6615726.

Powell, Michael, dir. 1941. *49th Parallel*. Burbank: Columbia Pictures.

R v Desautel 2021-04-23. Supreme Court of Canada. https://decisions.scc-csc.ca/scc-csc/scc-csc/en/item/18836/index.do.

"Settlement of International Disputes between Canada and the USA." 2011. *Canada–United States Law Journal* 35, no. 1: 46.

Sheehan, Michael A. 2008. *Crush the Cell: How to Defeat Terrorism without Terrorizing Ourselves*. New York: Random House.

Sloan, Elinor. 2010. *Security and Defence in the Terrorist Era*, 2nd ed. Montreal and Kingston: McGill-Queen's University Press.

Smith, Tom W. 2006. "National Pride in Specific Domains." GSS Cross-National Report No. 27. May.

Stacey, Lee. 2001. *Mexico and the United States*. New York: Marshall Cavendish.

Stein, Emma. 2022. "Canada Lifts COVID-19 Travel, Border Restrictions: What It Means for Michiganders." *Detroit Free Press*, 26 September.

Struck, Doug. 2005. "Canada Fights Myth It was 9/11 Conduit." *Washington Post*, 9 April. https://www.washingtonpost.com/archive/politics/2005/04/09/canada-fights-myth-it-was-911-conduit/acffc429-8a59-430f-9d47-5e31cf74216a.

Sutcliffe, John B., and William P. Anderson. 2019. *The Canada–US Border in the 21st Century: Trade, Immigration, and Security in the Age of Trump*. Toronto: Routledge.

Uniting and Strengthening America by Providing Appropriate Tools to Intercept and Obstruct Terrorism (USA PATRIOT Act) Act of 2001. Public Law 107–56 (107th Congress). https://www.congress.gov/107/plaws/publ56/PLAW-107publ56.htm.

Wadhia, Shoba Sivaprasad. 2017. "Is Immigration Law National Security Law?" *Emory Law Journal* 66: 670–96.

White House. 2002. "Fact Sheet: U.S.-Canada Smart Border/ 30 Point Action Plan Update." 6 December. https://2001-2009.state.gov/p/wha/rls/fs/18128.htm.

Warner, Judith. 2010. *US Border Security: A Reference Handbook.* Santa Barbara: ABC-CLIO.

Contributors

DONALD E. ABELSON is academic director, Wilson College of Leadership and Civic Engagement, McMaster University. He has authored and co-authored many books, including *Do Think Tanks Matter? Assessing the Impact of Public Policy Institutes* (3rd ed., 2018) and *Understanding American Politics* (3rd ed., forthcoming). He has co-edited volumes including *Handbook on Think Tanks in Public Policy* (2021) and *Transatlantic Relations: Challenge and Resilience* (2022). Dr Abelson is also a regular commentator on national and international media outlets, discussing think tanks, current events in US politics, and Canada–US relations.

MICHAEL ADAMS is the co-founder of the Environics Research Group, one of Canada's leading marketing and public opinion research firms. He is currently the president of the non-profit Environics Institute for Survey Research, which he founded in 2006. The institute conducts survey research to help Canadians better understand themselves and their changing society. He is the author of a series of bestselling books on public opinion, attitudes, and social values, including *Fire and Ice: The United States, Canada, and the Myth of Converging Values* (2003), which won the Donner Prize as best book on public policy and was selected by the *Literary Review of Canada* as one of the hundred most important books ever published in the country. In 2016, he was awarded the Order of Canada for his work in helping Canadians understand who they are as a country and a people.

GREG ANDERSON is a professor of political science at the University of Alberta. His research and teaching interests are broadly situated within international political economy, particularly the political economy of North American integration. He has authored numerous pieces focused on Canada–US relations, the politics of international trade and investment policy, and US foreign economic policy. Dr Anderson's recent writing includes the co-edited volume *Navigating a Changing World: Canada's International Policies in an Era of Political and Economic Uncertainty* (2020).

STEPHEN BROOKS is professor of political science at the University of Windsor and director of the European Union Study Abroad Program, a collaboration of the University of Windsor and Western University. He has taught at various universities on both sides of the Atlantic, including the Katholieke Universiteit Leuven, Sciences Po Lille, the Université de Paris 3, and the University of Michigan. His most recent books focus on public and cultural diplomacy and US foreign policy.

SUSAN COLBOURN is associate director of the Program in American Grand Strategy at Duke University. She is the author of *Euromissiles: The Nuclear Weapons That Nearly Destroyed* NATO (2022).

DAVID G. HAGLUND is professor of political studies, Queen's University. His research focuses on transatlantic security and on Canadian and American international security policy. Among his books are *Latin America and the Transformation of US Strategic Thought, 1936–1940* (1984), *Alliance within the Alliance? Franco-German Military Cooperation and the European Pillar of Defense* (1991), *Ethnic Diasporas and the Canada–United States Security Community: From the Civil War to Today* (2015), *The US "Culture Wars" and the Anglo-American Special Relationship* (2019), and *Sister Republics: Security Relations between America and France* (2023). His current book project is titled *Rating "Canada's Presidents": A Comparative Assessment of the Impact upon Canadian Interests of America's Chief Executives, from Washington to Biden.*

MICHAEL K. HAWES is president and CEO of Fulbright Canada. A professor in the Department of Political Studies at Queen's University for more than twenty-five years, he has held visiting appointments at the University of California at Berkeley, the University of Southern California, Tsukuba University, and the International University of Japan. Recent books include *1968 in Canada: A Year and Its Legacies* (2021, co-edited with Andrew C. Holman and Christopher J. Kirkey), *Canadian Public Diplomacy* (2020, co-edited with Nicholas Cull), and *Canadian Foreign Policy in a Unipolar World* (2019, co-edited with Christopher J. Kirkey). He is guest editor of several special issues of refereed journals, including the *London Journal of Canadian Studies*, featuring scholarly works on inclusion and diversity, and the *American Review of Canadian Studies* on Canada, the United States, and Indigenous People, both in 2019.

CHRISTOPHER J. KIRKEY is director of the Center for the Study of Canada and Institute on Quebec Studies at State University of New York at Plattsburgh and previously served as president of the Association for Canadian Studies in the United States. His most recent work (with Richard Nimijean) is *The Construction of Canadian Identity from Abroad* (2022). Book volumes, chapters, and edited special journal issues and contributions include those published by Oxford University Press, Routledge, Ottawa University Press, University of Toronto Press, McGill-Queen's University Press, *Canadian Journal of Political Science, International Journal, Canadian Foreign Policy Journal, Armed Forces and Society, American Review of Canadian Studies, British Journal of Canadian Studies, Journal of Canadian Studies, International Journal of Canadian Studies, London Journal of Canadian Studies, Quebec Studies*, and *Journal of Eastern Townships Studies*.

ADAM LAJEUNESSE is associate professor of public policy at St Francis Xavier University in Antigonish, Nova Scotia. He is the author of *Lock, Stock, and Icebergs* (2016), an award-winning political history of the Northwest Passage; co-author of *China's Arctic Ambitions and What They Mean for Canada* (2017); and co-editor of *Canadian Arctic Operations, 1941–2015: Lessons Learned, Lost, and Relearned* (2017). Dr Lajeunesse works on questions of Arctic sovereignty and security policy and has written extensively on Armed Forces Arctic operations, maritime security, Canadian–American cooperation in the North, and Canadian Arctic history.

SARA K. MCGUIRE is assistant teaching professor in the Department of Politics at Drexel University. Previously, she held appointments in the International Relations Program at the University of Pennsylvania and in the National Security Studies Institute at the University of Texas at El Paso. She holds a PhD in international relations from McMaster University and an LLM in international public and comparative law from the University of Exeter. Dr McGuire completed her MA in war studies at the Royal Military College of Canada and her BA (Hons.) at Queen's University. Dr McGuire's research interests include American and Canadian foreign and defence policy, homeland security, and international law.

ASA MCKERCHER is assistant professor, Department of History, Royal Military College of Canada, and a senior fellow of the Bill Graham Centre for Contemporary International History. His books include *North of America: Canadians and the American Century* (2023), *Canada and the World since 1867* (2019), and *Camelot and Canada: Canadian-American Relations in the Kennedy Era* (2016).

WESLEY NICOL is a PhD student at the Norman Paterson School of International Affairs in Ottawa. His research focuses on Canada–China and Canada–US affairs, intelligence studies, and international peacekeeping operations. He also studies the Canadian Armed Forces and works for the Department of National Defence as an analyst at the Canadian Defence Academy. Mr Nicol is interested in AUKUS and the Five Eyes intelligence alliance, especially when it comes to matters pertaining to the People's Republic of China. His doctoral research has focused on foreign interference in Canada's electoral process and proposes to analyze Chinese Communist Party espionage tactics in comparison to other Five Eyes countries.

ROY NORTON is a former Canadian diplomat with four US postings, including minister (advocacy) at the embassy in Washington and consul general in each of Detroit and Chicago, in addition to serving as assistant deputy minister in the Government of Ontario (successively for trade and for international relations) and as chief of protocol of Canada. Since 2019, Roy has been adjunct assistant professor at the University of Waterloo. He is a fellow at the Balsillie School of International Affairs, the Canadian Global Affairs Institute, and the Canada Institute at the Wilson Center in Washington, DC. He holds master's degrees from Carleton University, Harvard, and the Johns Hopkins University School of Advanced International Studies (SAIS), and a PhD (SAIS). His most recent publication is a chapter, co-authored with Deanna Horton, in *Canada and the United States: Differences That Count* (5th ed., 2023).

ANDREA OLIVE is professor of political science and geography, geomatics, and environment, University of Toronto Mississauga. Her primary area of research and teaching interest is wildlife conservation policy in Canada and the United States. She is the author of two University of Toronto Press books: *Land, Stewardship, and Legitimacy* (2014) and *The Canadian Environment in Political Context* (2019). Her latest work is a monograph with the University of Regina Press, *Protecting the Prairies: Lorne Scott and the Politics of Conservation* (2023).

STÉPHANE PAQUIN holds the Jarislowsky Chair in Trust and Political Leadership (l'Université du Québec à Trois-Rivières–École nationale d'administration publique [UQTR-ENAP]) and is full professor at ENAP, where he is the director of the Centre interuniversitaire de recherche sur les relations internationales du Canada et du Québec (CIRRICQ). He has received numerous awards, including a Canada Research Chair in International and Comparative Political Economy and a Fulbright Distinguished Chair in Québec Studies, State University of New York at Plattsburgh. He has taught in many universities, including Northwestern University and Sciences Po. He has written, co-written, or edited thirty-five books and journals, including *Theories of International Political Economy* (2015), and many more books and articles about paradiplomacy and the international relations of non-central governments. He has also published in several journals, including *International Negotiation*, *The Hague Journal of Diplomacy*, *Canadian Journal of Political Science*, and *Revue canadienne d'administration publique.*

ANDREW PARKIN is the executive director of the Environics Institute for Survey Research, a not-for-profit agency created in 2006 to conduct in-depth public opinion and social research on the issues shaping Canada's future. Prior to joining the institute, he held leadership positions at several public policy organizations in Canada, including the Mowat Centre, the Council of Ministers of Education, Canada, and the Canada Millennium Scholarship Foundation. At the institute, Mr Parkin leads a series of comprehensive studies of Canadian public opinion, attitudes, and values, including the annual Confederation of Tomorrow and Focus Canada surveys, the Survey on Employment and Skills, tracking the impact of COVID-19 on the labour force, and the AmericasBarometer studies of support for the country's democratic institutions. Each year, he authors dozens of reports and articles on Canadian politics and society.

DEBORA L. VANNIJNATTEN is professor of political science, North American studies, and environmental studies, Wilfrid Laurier University, and is associate director (Laurier) of the Balsillie School of International Affairs. She is editor of the textbook *Canadian Environmental Politics and Policy* (5th ed., 2024) and has published more than fifty articles and book chapters, as well as two University of Toronto Press books on Canadian climate and green transition policy as well as transboundary environmental and water governance in North America.

Index